Game Birds
of North America

Game Birds
of North America

by *LEONARD LEE RUE III*

with Paintings by
DOUGLAS ALLEN, JR.

OUTDOOR LIFE

HARPER & ROW
NEW YORK, EVANSTON, SAN FRANCISCO, LONDON

Library of Congress Catalog Card Number: 73-80713
SBN: 0-06-013714-2

Designed by Jeff Fitschen

Manufactured in the United States of America

To

Lester Rowe
Jessie Markle
Bill Guthrie
Judy Rue

Contents

WATERFOWL

Preface

The entire concept of hunting has changed in recent years. For most people in our country, hunting is no longer a necessity to put food on the table. It does put food on the table, millions of dollars worth a year, but the food is a supplement, albeit a most welcome supplement. I know that I eat better and enjoy life more because of the food that I obtain from hunting.

Game is a crop that must be harvested. Today, federal, state and private agencies keep a close watch on the population and health of all of the game species so that the misuse of this natural resource is almost precluded. To aid these agencies, hunters are willing to pay self-imposed taxes on their firearms and ammunition, and pay license fees for the privilege of pursuing their favorite sport. The funds derived from these taxes and license fees pay for wildlife research, lands and for the enforcement of the laws governing wildlife. The lands that are purchased with these funds, the wildlife that is propagated and protected on these lands are utilized and enjoyed by everyone.

The hunter of today is interested as a conservationist in the game birds he seeks, not only as game but as the interesting, challenging, diverse creatures that such birds are. He is interested in the life history of the game birds. His interest in the food eaten by game birds is not only a key to where the birds can be found during the hunting season but is a key to what foods can be planted to help propagate more game birds. The hunter's understanding of the habitat requirements of various game birds allows him to help provide such habitat.

I have written this book to inform those hunters who may not be familiar with the habits of the birds they seek.

I do not want to represent all of the information in this book as the result of my own field observations, although my personal experiences are liberally sprinkled throughout. I could not have written the book without recourse to my vast reference library. I am indebteded to all of the authors, research and game departments whose tracts and texts I have consulted. I am also indebted to my many personal friends who have helped me over the years in many ways in gaining more knowledge of game birds.

I offer many thanks to William Sill, my personal friend and my editor at the Outdoor Life Book Division for being so patient with me over the slow progress of this book; to Henry Gross, managing editor, who is a pleasure to work with; to Jeff Fitschen, art director, for the fine work he did on the book's layout; and to my friend, Doug Allen, whose fine artwork greatly enhances this volume by portraying aspects of the birds that cannot be captured by a camera.

And my very special thanks to my sister, Evelyn Guthrie, who, despite leading a busy life as a wife and mother, somehow managed to read my handwritten manuscript and turn out the hundreds of neatly typed pages that became this book.

LEONARD LEE RUE III
Blairstown, New Jersey

Waterfowl

Order Anseriformes
Family Anatidae

Geese (Subfamily Anserinae)

Surface-feeding Ducks (Subfamily Anatinae)

Diving Ducks (Subfamily Aythyinae)

Sea Ducks (Subfamily Aythyinae)

Stiff-tailed Ducks (Subfamily Aythyinae)

Mergansers (Subfamily Merginae)

Introduction

The waterfowl of the world, the ducks and the geese, belong to the order Anseriformes and the family group Anatidae. There are one hundred and forty-five species found throughout the world, and thirty-eight of those found in North America will be discussed here.

The male and the female ducks are usually quite different in coloration. The male and female geese, except for size, are almost identical to each other in appearance. Some of these species have subdued coloration, others are very gaudy. The bills of all species are fairly long and flattened and fitted with strainers in most species but are narrow and toothed in the fish-eaters. The necks of these birds are medium long to long, their legs short and their feet webbed.

Most are excellent fliers, all become flightless during the summer molt, most of them migrate, and all are excellent swimmers. Some of the members of this family dive beneath the surface to feed, some dive only to escape from their enemies, some can spring into the air and fly off, others have to run along the surface of the water to gain momentum before flying. Most are gregarious and flock up except during the breeding season. They communicate by honking, quacking and cackling.

Their food consists mainly of vegetation but also includes some insects and animal life.

Most Anatidae nest on the ground, some in hollows in trees. The nests are usually well made and lined with the female's down. The female in most species does the incubating, occasionally helped by the male. Most of the male geese help care for the young, while most of the male ducks do not.

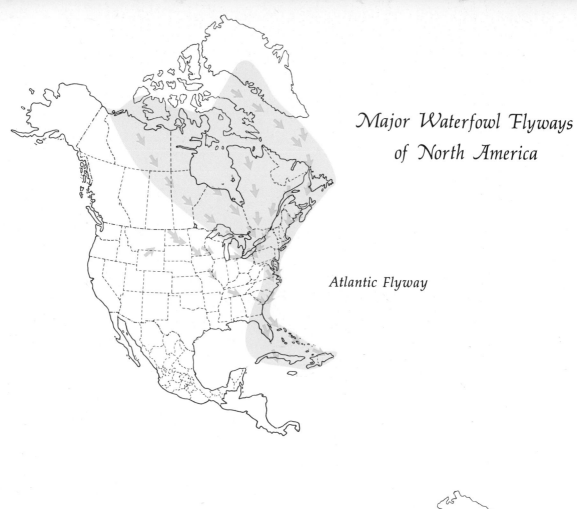

Major Waterfowl Flyways
of North America

Atlantic Flyway

Mississippi Flyway

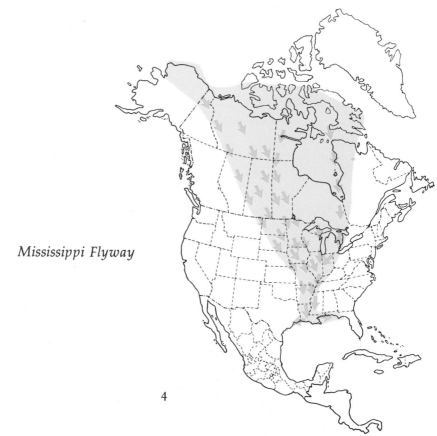

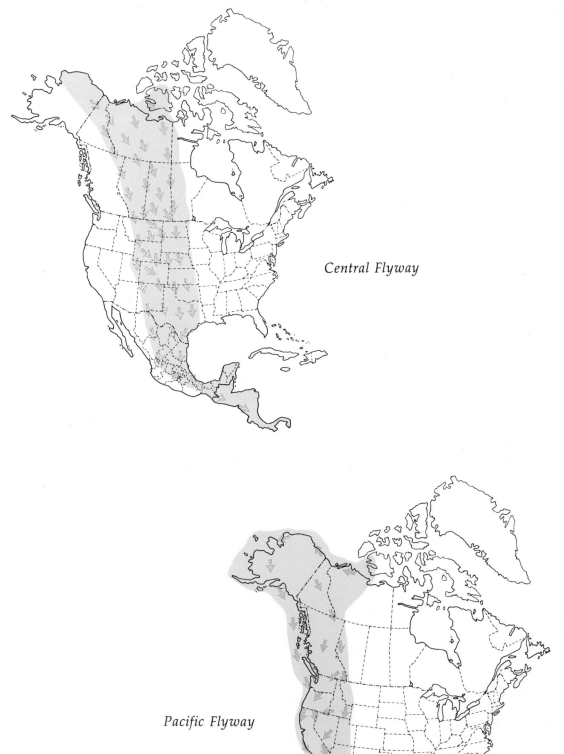

Central Flyway

Pacific Flyway

GEESE

(Subfamily Anserinae)

Common Canada Goose

Branta canadensis canadensis

Western Canada Goose   *Branta c. occidentalis*

Lesser Canada Goose   *Branta c. leucopareia*

Cackling Goose   *Branta c. minima*

Richardson's Goose   *Branta c. hutchinsi*

I'll never forget the morning, many years ago, that I stepped out of my Uncle Jim's kitchen and walked down to the edge of Lake Mattamuskeet in North Carolina. At first glance the lake appeared to be a horizon-filling mass of inundated brush. My binoculars showed, however, that the "debris" actually consisted of the necks of countless thousands of Canada geese. "That must be all the geese in the world," I thought.

At one time Lake Mattamuskeet had one of the largest concentrations of wintering waterfowl in the world, and there were an estimated 150,000 Canada geese on the lake when I was there. Fortunately, through some of the most successful game management policies on record, the Canada goose population has increased, so that numerous areas such as Chesapeake Bay, Maryland, and Horicon Marsh, Wisconsin, can now boast of equally large populations. This goose is now the most plentiful, most widespread, most hunted and best known goose in North America.

Canada Goose

DESCRIPTION: There are five subspecies of the Canada goose, four in addition to the common Canada goose. These four subspecies all have restricted ranges that are overlapped by that of the common Canada goose.

All five of the Canada goose subspecies look alike, the differences between them being in their sizes and color shadings. The common Canada goose is the largest of the five, with a length of 39 inches, a wingspan of 76 inches and a weight of up to 13 pounds. The western Canada goose has a length of 35 inches, a wingspan of 69 inches and weighs about 10 pounds. It used to be erroneously known as the white-cheeked goose, although its Latin name *occidentalis* means "western." Moreover the appellation "white-cheeked," or *leucopareia,* had already been given to the lesser Canada goose. This last goose is 30 inches in length, has a wingspan of 58 inches and weighs about 7 pounds. The Richardson's Canada goose is 28 inches in length, has a wingspan of 54 inches and weighs about 4½ pounds. When Sir John Richardson discovered this goose in 1831 near Hudson's Bay, he named it after a Mr. Hutchins, who was then a Hudson's Bay Company factor in that area. Over the years this little goose was forgotten. When it was rediscovered it was decided to give it the vernacular name of Richardson's goose, after the man who discovered it, and the Latin name *hutchinsi,* after the man whom Richardson had wanted to honor. The cackling Canada goose is the smallest of the lot, with a length of 27 inches, a wingspread of 52 inches and a weight of about 4 pounds.

The Canada goose is a large, brownish gray bird. The head and the long neck are jet black, except for a wide, white cheek and chin strap facial marking. The upper portions of the body are grayish brown, and each feather has a light edging, producing a barred effect. The flanks are similarly barred but are slightly lighter in color. The breast and belly are brownish gray with very faint barrings. The upper wing coverts are brown, the secondaries a darker brown and the primaries almost black. The underwing is grayish. The tail is black, and the tail coverts and under tail coverts are pure white. The bill, legs and feet are a dark blue-gray. The lesser Canada and Richardson's Canada geese have about the same color shadings, but the western Canada and cackling Canada geese are much darker. The bill size of all five subspecies is commensurate with the head size, so that the common and western Canadas' bills are about twice the size of those of the Richardson's and cackling Canada. The lesser Canada's bill falls about halfway between the two extremes.

*White chin strap facial marking and its
large size sets the Canada goose apart
from all other geese of the world.*

DISTRIBUTION: The range of the common Canada goose blankets
the United States and most of Canada, and the birds are constantly
extending their range. Some of the old range maps did not include
Wisconsin for either the breeding or wintering range of the Canada
goose. When the waters of Horicon Marsh were impounded, it was
to create areas for ducks; geese were seldom if ever seen. By the
fall of 1970 there were over 125,000 Canada geese in the marsh,
many of which had nested and would winter there. Even though
some of the geese were residents there, the area was packed with
the birds during migrations.

The wintering range of the common Canada goose embraces
just about all the forty-eight contiguous states. The main breeding
range extends from Kansas west to Nevada, north to British Columbia, northeast to the Northwest Territories, south to Minnesota,
and back to Kansas. Another breeding area runs from the west
coast of Hudson's Bay east to Labrador and Newfoundland. In
addition to these areas, almost every one of our states provides
breeding grounds for some of the common Canada geese. It always
seemed odd that in the seventeen summers that I spent guiding
wilderness canoe trips in the Quebec bush country of Canada, I
never saw a nesting or migrating Canada goose.

The western Canada goose winters along the coastal regions of
Washington, Oregon and northern California. It was along the coast
of Washington that I first saw these birds in 1967. The breeding

range for this subspecies is the coastal region of British Columbia, the Yukon and southeast Alaska.

The wintering area of the lesser Canada goose is divided into four sections. One group of birds winters in the inland valleys of Washington, Oregon, California and Nevada. Another group winters in southern California and Arizona, while a third stays in southern Arizona and New Mexico and northern Old Mexico. The fourth group winters along the coastal region of Texas and Old Mexico. The breeding grounds of this goose embrace almost all of Alaska, the Yukon and the Northwest Territories.

The wintering range of the Richardson's Canada goose is the coastal region of Florida's panhandle, Alabama, Mississippi and Texas. For some unaccountable reason, it does not include Louisiana. The breeding range of this subspecies covers the Franklin and Keewatin districts in northern Canada.

The cackling Canada goose has the most restricted range. It winters in the central valleys of California and breeds on the Bering Sea coast of Alaska.

COMMUNICATION: If any waterfowl call is well known, it is the honking of the Canada goose. Although the term "honker" immediately suggests all Canada geese, it is of course only the three larger species of the Canadas that honk; the two smaller geese make a cackling sound. In addition to honking, the large Canadas make a gabbling sound while feeding. Both sexes also hiss frequently. The two smaller Canadas have a high-pitched *luck, luck* call that sounds like the cackling of an old crone.

BREEDING AND NESTING: The Canada goose mates for life and, of all birds, leads the most exemplary mated life. The mated pair show great concern for one another, and frequently if one of the birds is killed, the other will be most reluctant to leave the area. However, it is not true that the survivor remains unmated. It may stay single for that particular season, but the following spring, it will seek out another mate.

The adult males that are seeking mate replacements and the younger males that have not mated as yet choose a mate and battle it out for her possession while they are all still on their wintering grounds. I have seen the males fight it out while the ground was still covered with snow at Harrison Park in northeastern New Jersey. The males approach each other with their necks lowered and outstretched, hissing very loudly. They peck at each other, and the jabbing of their long necks resembles the thrusts and counter-

Mated for life, a pair of Canada geese watch over their goslings.

thrusts of two swordsmen. When they succeed in getting hold of their opponent, they close ranks and flail out at each other with their powerful wings. Again the blows are met with counterblows that could break the bones of any lesser creature. There are no records, however, of ganders killing their rivals. When the inferior male finds that he is losing, he tries with all his might to disengage himself from combat and simply flees the scene. The victor pursues him for a short distance and is then content to tell the world of his prowess by loud, victorious honking.

Often, when a gander is enraged, he fluffs out his feathers and shakes his wing pinions until they make a rattling sound. His puffed-out feathers make him appear very large and *very* angry.

The long, sinuous neck of the goose is employed in the courtship. Both sexes rub their necks against each other and pass them all over the other's body, the male doing this more frequently than the female. The bird's neck is employed in so many ways that it almost seems to have a life of its own. The geese also go through the bill-dipping routine before copulation.

The nest of the Canada goose perhaps shows greater variation than that of any other species of bird. It is usually quite bulky, and no attempt appears to be made to hide it. It is built of whatever material happens to be near at hand, and usually contains copious amounts of down to soften, insulate and camouflage it.

The nest is often built on the top of a muskrat house and sometimes on the bank of a stream or on the edge of a slough or pothole. Such nests are made of reeds and rushes. I have seen two nests that were situated on the top of huge boulders, where they stuck out like sore thumbs. Another nest was on a small island, up against an old log. This was an extremely jerry-built affair and could not

13

have contained more than two handfuls of material. The three eggs were practically on the bare ground.

There are also many records of these geese building nests in trees on top of the abandoned nest of such birds as ospreys or eagles. The geese probably just take advantage of the existing mass of such nests without adding further material. They are also quick to take advantage of man-made platforms as a basis for their nests. In some game management areas, large galvanized washtubs are filled with hay or straw and put up on poles or in trees.

EGGS AND YOUNG: The Canada goose usually lays six or seven eggs, although some sets have as many as twelve. The eggs are a dull white when laid but are soon soiled with brown splotches. They are large, those of the common Canada goose averaging 85 millimeters in length by 58 millimeters in diameter. The eggs of the smaller Canadas are slightly less large, but the difference in egg size is not proportionate to that in body size. The eggs of the Richardson's Canada, for example, average 79 millimeters in length by 53 millimeters in diameter.

Incubation, which lasts twenty-eight to thirty days, is performed by the female. While she is brooding the eggs, the male is usually nearby. If she leaves the nest to eat or drink, he stays behind to guard the eggs. The male is able and willing to put up such a good fight that only the very largest of the predators will risk an encounter with him.

When the young hatch, they stay in the vicinity of the nest just long enough to allow their down to dry. Then, with the male leading, the goslings following and the female bringing up the rear, the entire family retires to the nearest body of water. While the young are on the water, the same convoy pattern is usually adhered to. The male keeps a good watch for the slightest sign of danger from any creature in the air, on the water or below the surface. Such vigilance is rewarded because geese are usually able to raise most of their young.

The young of the common, the lesser and the Richardson's Canada geese have black bills, legs and feet. They have a darkish cap and a streak going down the back of the neck. The back, wings, rump, tail and thighs are also darkish. The gosling's face is bright yellow, while the neck, breast and belly are whitish yellow.

The goslings of the western and cackling Canada geese have the same patterning, but the dark areas of the body are a much darker brown, and the yellow portions are more buff-colored. There is also a definite dark stripe running through the eye.

FLIGHT: There is a great time difference in the fledgling periods of the Canada geese. One would expect the larger races to take longer but, surprisingly enough, while the common and western Canada goslings take about eighty-five days to fly, the cackling and Richardson's Canada young can fly after about forty-two days. Many ducks are actually slower in learning to fly than the smaller Canadas.

Both male and female Canada geese go through a postnuptial molt during the month of August, so that both are flightless at the same time. The adults and the young of the larger subspecies are both able to fly at about the same time. The young of the smaller subspecies are capable of flight before the adults' primaries have been replaced.

The Canada goose appears slow and labored in flight owing to its sluggish wing beats and large size. Yet it is capable of flying at speeds of between 45 and 60 miles per hour and even faster with a favorable tail wind.

Canada geese usually fly quite high and exceptionally so in migration, sometimes appearing as mere specks in the sky. However, it is doubtful if they ever fly over a mile high, whereas some of the Asiatic geese fly at an altitude of over 5 miles because they cross the Himalayas in migration.

The V formation is the usual Canada flight pattern, although occasionally a single diagonal line formation is used. The flight is led by an old male. When he tires, he drops behind and takes his place at the tail end of one leg of the V. This formation is aerodynamically sound because each goose in the two lines encounters less air resistance because of the turbulence set up by the goose flying just ahead. This is why the leaders become more tired than the rest of the flock. They are the point that splits the air. While the geese fly, they keep up a constant honking.

As the geese approach a spot where they wish to land, they set their wings in a downward glide. They usually maintain their flight formation until they get within 100 feet or so of the water. They then break ranks, and it is usually each goose for itself as they land. They usually slide on their feet as they hit the water, their wings outstretched or cupped backwards, their tails depressed. With a splash, they settle into the water, where they usually cavort and bathe after their journey.

MIGRATION: Geese are not the harbingers of spring that they are often claimed to be. Most of their flights are delayed because they have to wait until the northern lakes are free of ice. April and the beginning of May see most of the flights passing north, but they may reverse their direction and come back south if an unexpected cold front has covered the northern regions with ice and snow.

The Canada geese fly direct routes to their ancestral breeding grounds, using all four of the major flyways. While some ducks and geese follow rivers or coastlines, the Canada geese lift off, gain altitude and fly over field, forest and city in their almost arrow-like flight north.

These geese may fly at night as well as during the daytime. They are so large that they have nothing to fear from aerial predators. They fly until they are tired, then land to feed and rest. They are often confused by dense fog and snowstorms. I once saw a flock of geese attempting to land on a rain-slicked tar road that they had mistaken for a small river.

HABITS: The Canada goose, like the bay ducks, has to run along the surface of the water for about six or eight paces before it gets enough lift to become airborne. However, unlike the bay ducks, the Canada does not feed by diving beneath the surface of the water. The only time I have seen it dive is in the springtime. I took this to be just an expression of exuberance, but it may have been part of the courtship display. One or more of the geese would dive underwater, only to reappear a few seconds later and just a few feet away. They then splashed along the surface with their wings slapping the water before diving again. This was all done to the accompaniment of loud honking.

Canada geese are extremely intelligent birds. They are smart enough to know or to learn what constitutes danger and how to avoid that danger. Nonetheless they can be called in and decoyed, although much less easily since live decoys were banned. They are shot from blinds and pits, by pass-shooting, and thousands upon thousands of them are successfully hunted every year.

As the hunting pressure mounts, the geese change their feeding patterns, coming in to feed at night and returning during the day to preserves and sanctuaries or to large bodies of water. They learn very rapidly where they are protected and are the quickest of all the geese to respond to such protection. Even though they become tame on the sanctuaries, they remain wary when they are away from such areas, and wherever they are they maintain sentinels or guards.

The Canada geese now nest in almost every state. In the olden days, they all migrated north and west, and the bulk of them still do. However, every year, ever increasing numbers of the geese stay behind and raise their families in city parks, lagoons, reservoirs and small farm ponds.

The populations of all of the Canada geese are constantly increasing.

FOOD: The Canada goose is by preference a grazing bird and feeds upon a tremendous variety of grasses. It is also capable of doing great damage to cultivated crops, particularly fall-planted wheat. It is one thing when the geese scavenge in a field for spilled grain, and quite another when they pull up the grain, roots and all, in a newly planted field. On a hard-rooted plant, they pluck off the foliage or grass blades, and in their feeding they can be as methodical and thorough as sheep. They usually feed early in the morning and again late in the afternoon.

When on the water, the Canadas feed on surface plants or by sticking their long necks underwater where it is shallow and by tipping up like the "puddle" ducks in deeper water. Among the wild grasses their favorites are cordgrass, widgeon grass, pondweed, spike rush, glasswort, bulrush, algae, sea lettuce, eelgrass and brome grass. They feed on wheat, oat, barley and corn plants in the spring and on the grains in the fall. Animal matter is not an important part of their diet, but they do eat insects, crustaceans, some mollusks and snails. I have seen them run down and capture grasshoppers and crickets.

LIFE SPAN: The Canada goose has a potential life span of from fifteen to twenty years. Many records have been kept on these geese, and in fact, more banding has probably been done of them than of all the other geese combined. The three top longevity records that I can find for the Canadas are twenty-five, twenty-nine and thirty-three years.

ENEMIES: The Canada goose has many enemies but is less subject to predation than any of the other waterfowl except swans. Its sagacity, size and courage are deterrents to all but the largest or most persistent of the predators. Some of the predators can feed only on the eggs, others can catch only the goslings, and a few can take the adults. Skunks, raccoons, foxes, coyotes, hawks, eagles, owls and turtles prey on the geese in one way or another, but only with limited success. Disease, parasites and accidents take their toll.

TABLE FARE: The Canada goose in late summer, fall or early winter, the period when hunting is allowed, is superb table fare.

American Brant

Branta bernicla

Black Brant   *Branta bernicla nigricans*

Nature has long shown that extreme specialization in a creature's habits can be its undoing. This was almost the case with the American brant. The brant's favorite winter food is eelgrass, a plant that grows in huge beds just off the seashore. In the early 1930s, a disease wiped out the eelgrass along the Atlantic coast and almost wiped out the American brant. The western eelgrass was not affected and so the black brant were not reduced in numbers. With their favorite food destroyed, the eastern brant starved to death by the tens of thousands. Fortunately some of the brant started to feed on sea lettuce and so survived. Today, the eelgrass is back and so is the brant population. It is not likely that such a catastrophe could happen again because now the brant are not only feeding again on eelgrass, but have continued to feed on sea lettuce and other plants. They have avoided becoming victims of specialization.

DESCRIPTION: The two brants will be treated together because even the experts cannot agree as to whether or not they are two separate species or subspecies. They have overlapping ranges and interbreed, but there are differences between them that will be duly pointed out. For the sake of comparison, we will call the Atlantic brant the American brant, while the Pacific brant is commonly known as the black brant.

As is true of all of the geese, the male and female are identical in appearance, although the female is slightly smaller in size. The brants are true maritime geese and are about the size of a mallard duck. Both the brants are about 24 inches in length, have a wing-span of 45 inches and weigh about 3 pounds.

The American brant, which is identical to the brant of northern Europe, has a black head, neck, breast and tail. There is a partial white ring with black markings on either side of the neck. The belly is a mottled white, while the under tail coverts and part of the upper tail coverts are pure white. The back and wings are dark

American Brant

Migrating southward, a flock of brant fly in irregular formation, each bird following the flight pattern of the one in front.

brown, the primary feathers having a lighter edge. The legs, feet and bill are black, and the eye is brown.

The black brant is identical in appearance to the American brant except that its belly is a dark blackish brown, and its flanks are ashy gray.

DISTRIBUTION: The American brant's wintering range extends along the coast of Massachusetts south to North Carolina. New Jersey usually has the largest winter concentration of these brant, but this year (1972), the winter has been exceptionally mild, and neither the brant nor the ducks are there in their regular numbers. The brant may also have had a poor nesting season. The latest census for New Jersey shows only 48,600 brant as compared with last year's figure of 129,400. The American brant's breeding range is among the Canadian islands of the Arctic Ocean and in Greenland.

The black brant's wintering range extends along the Pacific coast from the state of Washington south to Baja California. Its breeding range runs along Alaska's north coast from the Bering Sea to the Canadian Arctic islands. The black brant also breeds along the coast of eastern Siberia.

COMMUNICATION: Both the brants are voluble and can often be heard before they can be seen. Their most frequent call is a *kr-onk, kr-onk, kr-onk* sound. They also make a harsher growling *g-r-r-r-r* as well as a *ruck-ruck* or *wa-ruck* sound. As they fly, they keep up an almost constant chattering, gabbling call that often betrays their presence before they are visible. Whether they are resting on a sand bar or rafted up in huge flocks, the "conversation" goes on.

BREEDING AND NESTING: The brant arrive on their breeding grounds about the first of June. At this late date, they are already paired up when they arrive. There is good reason to believe that, like most of the other geese, they mate for life. For one thing, they engage in very little breeding display. The male puts on a threat display if other brant venture close. Tilting his body forward and holding his head and neck low and extended straight out, he advances upon his rival, hissing loudly.

Both the male and female engage in simultaneous head-dipping prior to copulation. In this display the neck is bent and the bills dipped into the water, but the head is not lifted as in the ritual drinking.

Another reason for the lack of display may be the late arrival of these geese on their breeding grounds, which simply does not allow time for a lengthy or leisurely courtship.

The brant's nesting grounds are usually the smaller islands and the coastline of the larger Arctic islands. Such islands are usually devoid of any vegetation except for some rank grasses. The nest is normally little more than a hollowed-out place among the stones with a scanty lining of seaweed and down. The more elaborate nests consist of small mounds made up of moss, seaweed and lichens and lined with down.

The brant are sociable birds and nest in colonies; their nests may be interspersed with those of the eider ducks.

EGGS AND YOUNG: The brant ordinarily lay a clutch of three to five eggs, although on occasion as many as eight eggs have been found. The eggs average 71 millimeters in length by 47 millimeters in diameter. Those of the American brant are creamy white, while the black brant's eggs tend to be buffy. The shell has a smooth, dull texture.

Although the male brant does not participate in the incubation, he stands guard at the nest during the twenty-eight days that his mate is confined with this task. His guard duty is not just for show because he actually drives off many of the predatory gulls that would destroy the eggs if possible.

The young brant's down is basically gray and brown. The top half of the head and face of the black brant is a sooty brown, while the back of the neck, breast, back, wings, tail and thighs are light brown. The cheeks and belly are ashy white and the flanks white. The young of the American brant lack the dark crown of the black brant, and the rest of their brown coloring is several shades lighter than the black brant's. The bills, legs and feet of both brants are black.

The young are strong and able swimmers from the very first and hurry after their mother down to the safety of the sea. Their fledgling period is about sixty days.

FLIGHT: The brant do not go into an eclipse plumage, but both the male and female shed their primary feathers during July and August. The males usually shed their flight feathers slightly before the females. With geese, the time lag between the sexes is not as long as it is among the ducks for the simple reason that both the male and female geese share the chore of caring for the young.

The brant have to run along the surface of the water before they can become airborne. They are strong fliers and have a short, rapid wing beat. They are capable of flying at speeds of 50 miles per hour and more. They do not fly in the regular V formation that is so common among the Canada geese. They are usually in long, straggly lines, although each brant follows almost exactly the same flight pattern as the bird directly in front of it. If not disturbed, the brant fly very low over the water, which they prefer to follow rather than fly overland, even if this means a more circuitous route. They seem to dislike flying over high ground. They will fly high only when they have been exposed to severe hunting pressure and when they are in migration.

MIGRATION: The birds start their northward migration in the month of February. This is a leisurely progress, as the southern-most flocks fly north a bit and then join the birds that have wintered at that particular rendezvous. Then the united flocks fly a bit farther north to join ever larger flocks. This leisurely journey is continued until the eastern birds have reached Massachusetts and the western birds have congregated around the state of Washington. The north-ward flight is deliberately slow to allow the ice to break up and move out, thereby freeing the brant's Arctic breeding islands. At last the flocks lift up, gain altitude, and the eastern flock takes off for the Hudson's Bay route to the Arctic. The black brant follow the Pacific coast until they reach the Yukon Territory, where they fan out east and west to seek their breeding grounds.

The southward migration is usually under way before mid-September and is much more rapid than the flight north. Many of the brant are back on their wintering grounds along the Jersey coast by October 15th.

HABITS: The brant's sociability is an important survival factor because there are always some birds in the flock that are on the alert. Almost all the brant's activities are performed as a group, and they actually seem to enjoy each other's company. Some creatures that constantly travel in groups do so for the protection but quarrel and fight among themselves. There never appears to be the slightest degree of animosity among the brant.

Usually birds that run along the surface of the water before taking off are diving birds, but the brant are not. They often tip up to secure food below the water's surface but almost never dive underwater. They swim very buoyantly and float high on the water. As they swim away, their white under tail coverts are very con-spicuous.

FOOD: The brant's favorite food, as has already been mentioned, is eelgrass, *Zostera marina*. This plant grows in the brackish water of bays and estuaries and along the ocean coasts. As the brant does not dive for its food, it must wait until the lowering tides expose the beds of eelgrass. It particularly favors the roots and white lower portion of this plant. Unless the water is shallow, it cannot get these choicest morsels, and when it first starts to feed, it just pulls loose the tops of the plants. These long green fronds are allowed to float loose and are eaten later by the brant when the incoming tide pre-vents it from feeding on the roots. When it is feeding on the long fronds of the eelgrass, it rolls them up into a little ball in its mouth before swallowing them.

The brant also feeds on sea lettuce and other types of algae, as well as widgeon grass, cordgrass and surfgrass. Its intake of animal matter is very low, although it does eat some insects, crustaceans, bivalves and gastropods.

LIFE SPAN: The brant have a potential life span of twelve to fifteen years. No individual longevity record is available for this species.

ENEMIES: The brant's habit of nesting on islands is an important defense against predators such as the Arctic fox. Polar bears rob the nests, but gulls, skuas, jaegers and ravens are the principal enemies. The Eskimos take many of the brant's eggs and also make concentrated drives to kill the adults during their flightless period.

TABLE FARE: The brant are rated as an epicurean delight. Their vegetarian diet produces flesh of the highest order, and many hunters claim that the brant rival, if they do not actually outclass, the canvasback duck as table fare.

Emperor Goose

Philacte canagica

I spent the summer of 1969 traveling along Alaska's west coast with a friend. We started out at Bristol Bay and ended up at Point Barrow, often camping in the vicinity of Eskimo villages. In Mekoryuk on Nunivak Island we met the head man of the village, George, who had just been out hunting. He had shot an emperor goose, even though the season on geese was closed. He told us that such hunting out of season angered some of the Federal men. In any other situation, I would have been on the side of the Federal men, but in this instance I could not resist George's logic. As he explained it, the white man studied the geese, counted them and made laws to determine when they could and could not be hunted. George said that the Eskimos had always hunted the geese, but only when they needed them to eat and never wastefully. They could not conform to the white man's law, but hunted according to a "belly" law.

DESCRIPTION: The emperor goose is thought by many to be our most beautifully marked goose. Small in size, it averages 27 inches in length, has a wingspan of 51 inches and weighs about 6 pounds.

As is the case with all geese, there is no difference in coloration between the sexes.

The head and back of the neck are white, the throat and front of the neck jet black. The back, breast and sides are blue-gray, each feather being edged in black with a white tip, which gives the bird a scaled appearance. The secondary feathers of the wings are also white-edged, but the primaries are not. The belly is ash-gray, and again the feathers are white-edged. The tail is all white and the bill pink. The feet are not dark like those of most geese, but bright orange. The emperor goose, like the snow goose and the Ross' goose, has a rusty stain on its face behind the bill.

DISTRIBUTION: The emperor goose's breeding range is on two continents. On the northeast coast of Siberia it breeds as far west as Koluitschin Bay. In North America, it breeds on St. Lawrence Island and from the mouth of the Kuskokwim River to the Seward Peninsula. In the winter it is found mainly in the Aleutian Islands and as far east as Bristol Bay and Cook's Inlet. It straggles south as far as British Columbia and occasionally down to California.

COMMUNICATION: The most commonly heard call note of the emperor goose is best described as *u-lugh, u-lugh*. This is a deep, resonant call. Another call heard when the birds are in flight is a strident *kla-ha, kla-ha, kla-ha*. When the birds are talking among themselves, they use a softer, more cackling note.

Female emperor goose, guarding her nest in marsh grass, stands a lonely vigil; her mate lends no assistance at this time.

BREEDING AND NESTING: The emperor geese are paired up by the time they reach their breeding grounds. Although they may arrive in a small flock, they split into pairs as soon as they land. The male is very belligerent and is quick to take offense at the presence of any other goose, even that of another species. It stretches out and lowers its head and neck in the standard threat position. Sometimes it fluffs out its wings to give an impression of greater size. The female is very attracted to her mate and seems to resent the intrusion of the rival male as much as her mate does. The emperors are very restless when they first arrive on their breeding grounds and are almost constantly on the move.

The delta areas that the emperors favor as a nesting site are usually exceptionally flat and very wet. The birds may nest in among the marsh grasses or right out on the sea beach above the tide level. Some of the nests are made up of vegetation, others are mere hollows scraped in the sandy soil and lined with down.

Unlike the males of most other geese, the male emperor does not mount guard at the nest and is usually absent at this time.

EGGS AND YOUNG: The emperor goose's average clutch consists of five to six eggs, which are usually a dull white color when first laid. As the female feeds most frequently on the mud flats, the eggs are soon mud-splattered and soiled, and therefore well camouflaged. They average 78 millimeters in length by 52 millimeters in diameter. Incubation, performed solely by the female, takes twenty-four days.

The male emperor goose does not entirely abandon his family because by the time the goslings hatch, he is back to assist the female in raising them. The young hatch about the first of July.

The chicks, when first hatched, have a pearl-gray down that is darker on the head and upper side of the body and lighter below. The legs and the bill are black.

By September the young emperors look like a darker, black-faced version of their parents as they still have the black head and feet, and their overall body coloration is darker. It is still several months before the young complete their winter molt, after which they look like the adults.

FLIGHT: The adults shed their flight feathers in August before the goslings are able to fly so that the entire family is flightless at this time. It was during this flightless period that the Eskimos used to gather together and make huge traps out of fish nets, into which the geese were driven and then killed by the thousands. By September the geese can fly again.

When traveling about or even in migration, the emperor geese do not flock up. Their flight is strong, but about 40 miles per hour is their average speed. They usually fly very low, in fact sometimes their wing tips dapple the water beneath them.

MIGRATION: The emperor goose has the shortest migration flight of any of our native geese. This, of course, is discounting the Canada goose which has taken up residence on many of the southern ponds and lakes where it formerly only wintered.

Since the birds winter in the Aleutians, they often have to travel only a few hundred miles to reach their breeding grounds. They usually arrive there about the first to the middle of May. The end of September finds them back on their wintering grounds.

HABITS: The emperor goose is especially wary and difficult to stalk. Many geese have guards on watch while the flock feeds, but the emperors usually have an exceptional number of such guards. The areas these geese frequent are usually so flat and bare that there is no cover for a hunter. The geese are most frequently shot by the hunter lying in wait along one of the flyways that the geese use in moving to and from the feeding flats. The emperors can be decoyed by a hunter imitating their call.

FOOD: The bulk of the emperor goose's food is animal matter. As soon as the tides recede, the geese are out dabbling about on the mud flats, where they feed upon all sorts of crustaceans and mollusks. They eat some grasses and berries.

LIFE SPAN: The emperor goose has a potential life span of about ten years.

ENEMIES: Gulls, jaegers, mink, owls, ravens and crows are all major enemies of the emperor goose. Exceptionally high tides or flooding of the river deltas are a constant threat during the nesting season. However, in former days the Eskimos were chiefly responsible for the decimation of the emperor population.

TABLE FARE: Most white hunters never get a chance to shoot at an emperor goose, and this is just as well because they would probably not eat the goose if they killed it. The food of the emperor, being mostly shellfish of some type, imparts a strong odor to the goose's flesh that most people find quite repulsive. It is said that if the goose is cleaned of its entrails and then hung up by the neck, still clothed in its feathers, and frozen, the fishy taste is removed.

White-fronted Goose

Anser albifrons

"Silly as a goose" is a false expression if ever there was one, for geese, far from being silly or stupid, are exceptionally alert and wary birds. No matter what their activity, they usually post sentinels, and domesticated geese often serve as watchdogs on farms.

It is white-fronted geese that are credited with having saved ancient Rome against an attack by the Gauls in 390 B.C. The Gauls, under cover of darkness, tried to infiltrate the capital. As they clambered up the hill in single file, they made no noise discernible to human ears, but they failed to reckon with the geese. The birds, upon being disturbed, set up such a racket that the Roman garrison was awakened and was able to repel the attack. In more recent history, during World War II, the geese around London would set up an excited cackling that foretold the approach of German airplanes long before any listening device could detect them.

DESCRIPTION: The adult male white-fronted goose is a large bird with a total length of about 29 inches, a wingspan of 58 to 60 inches and a weight of about 5½ pounds. It is basically gray-brown, and much grayer than the Canada goose. The head, neck, back, rump and wings are grayish brown. The tail is dark brown with a white edge, and the upper and under tail coverts are white. The breast and belly are gray-white with large blackish brown blotches, giving rise to this goose's common nickname of "speckle-belly." The feet and legs are yellow. The bill is pink, and a broad white streak extends behind the bill into the forehead. The female, as is the case with all geese, is smaller than the male but otherwise identical to him.

A rather rare subspecies of the white-fronted goose known as the tule goose, *Anser albifrons gamelli,* is slightly darker and about 30 percent larger.

DISTRIBUTION: The white-fronted goose is a western goose seldom, if ever, found east of the Mississippi River. It is a common goose on its range.

The breeding range of the white-fronted goose is the northern half of Alaska, the Yukon and the Northwest Territories of Canada and the south coast of Greenland.

Its wintering range is divided into three main areas. The western section encompasses the inland valleys, lakes and reservoirs of Washington, Oregon and California. The middle-western area of Old Mexico is its largest winter range. The third area is the coastal regions of Texas and Louisiana.

The tule goose breeds along the Perry River section of Canada's Northwest Territories and winters in the central valleys of northern California. Its breeding range was not discovered until 1941.

COMMUNICATION: Most geese are noisy birds, and the white-fronted goose is no exception. The Cree Indian word *wa-wa* means goose and is descriptive of the bird's loud, rollicking *wah, wah, wah, wah* call. This sound resembles wild laughing, so that this goose is sometimes referred to as the "laughing goose." The English version of the Indian word *wa-wa* is "wavey," hence yet another nickname. Another call can be described as *kow-yow-kow-yow.* When the geese are feeding, they make a constant, conversational gabbling.

BREEDING AND NESTING: The geese mate for life, so that pair formation is no problem. However, once they are on their breeding grounds, there are some threat displays made by the male to any male that comes too close to his mate. In the characteristic goose threat displays, the male draws himself up to his full height and points his bill skyward, or he extends his neck down and forward to its full length. This latter position is usually accompanied by much hissing. A version of the threat with neck lowered and extended is often done while the goose is swimming, in which case the neck is fully extended just above the surface of the water.

There is little evidence of actual courtship displaying by the male for the female, but both the sexes engage in bill-dipping just before copulation takes place. The geese, always noisy, now make the tundra regions ring with their calls and laughter.

The nest is a mere hollow scooped out in the earth by the female and lined with grasses, moss and some down. As the female lays an egg each day, she plucks a little more down from her breast. By the time her clutch of eggs is complete, the nest is well lined with the soft, insulating down.

Most of the nests are hidden among the grasses that edge the small pools and lakes. Dwarf willows and birches also provide shelter, although some of the nests are right out in the open.

EGGS AND YOUNG: The white-fronted goose usually lays about seven eggs to a set. The eggs average 79 millimeters in length by 52 millimeters in diameter and range in color from a light pinkish white to light buff. They are quickly soiled by the mud from the female's feet as she comes to the nest, so that it is soon exceedingly difficult to tell just what color the eggs originally were. Naturally those that are laid first become the most soiled and therefore the darkest.

Incubation is done entirely by the female, but the male does not desert her during her twenty-eight-day period of confinement. He stands guard near the nest and takes an active part in the defense of the nest and eggs. He also participates fully in the care of the young after they have hatched.

When danger threatens, the adult geese try to lead the young away by sneaking through the high grass. When they flatten themselves out in this sneaking position, it is amazing how little cover is actually needed to shield them effectively from sight.

The young white-fronted gosling has a bluish bill, feet and legs. Its face is a reddish buff color. A dark brown stripe goes from the bill through the eye to the similarly colored neck and crown. Its back is light brown, while its rump and thighs are dark brown. The wings are light brown with a white speculum. The gosling's throat, the forepart of its neck and its breast are light yellow, and its belly is a pale yellow-white.

FLIGHT: The young white-fronted goose is capable of flying after about two months of development. Both the male and female adults lose their primary flight feathers before the young can fly.

This goose has to run along the water's surface before it can gain the momentum needed to become airborne. Once in the air it can fly at speeds of between 45 and 50 miles per hour.

These geese usually fly in large flocks and at considerable heights. They are normally in a V formation, under the leadership of an old gander. Their wing beats are slow but strong and steady. The swiftness of their flight is not readily apparent because of their large size and slow wing beats. However, it is amazing how fast a flock passes from view after being first sighted. And after it has disappeared, its clangor still drifts back to earth as a reminder of its passage.

MIGRATION: In migration most of these birds use the Pacific flyway because California is probably their main winter home, but many of them also utilize the central flyway. It is during the fall migration that the white-fronted goose becomes such an important bird to the hunters of this flyway.

The birds often start north while the ponds are still covered with ice. The main flights arrive on their northern breeding grounds about the last of April and the first of May.

In the fall the birds linger on the breeding grounds until they are finally forced to head south by the icing over of all the open water. The end of September sees the birds under way, and the northern beaches do not hear their clamor and laughter again until the following spring.

HABITS: Geese are early risers and are usually feeding by sunrise. Within a couple of hours of daybreak, most of the geese have crammed their crops full, and the birds then seek the sanctuary of the open water of a large lake.

This goose, like most other geese, swans and ducks, forsakes the safety of the open water of the smaller lakes if it is disturbed and hides among the grasses and brush of the tundra. These birds never seem to realize that except in such cases as attack by an aerial predator, they would be safer out in the middle of even the smaller ponds.

Although this goose swims well and has to run across the water to be able to fly, it does not dive.

FOOD: The white-fronted goose feeds almost exclusively on vegetation. It sometimes causes destruction to cultivated grain crops. Its favorite foods are rice, grasses, sedges, barley, wheat, panic grass, wild millet, cattail, bulrush and sawgrass. On rare occasions, it will eat some forms of aquatic insects.

LIFE SPAN: The white-fronted goose has a potential life span of about twelve years. The oldest individual for which I can find a record lived to be eleven and a half years old.

ENEMIES: The white-fronted goose is exposed to hunting pressure for most of the year. The Eskimos hunt it in the summer and the Mexicans in the winter, with the United States' hunters blazing away at it in the fall. The natural predators such as skuas, jaegers, gulls, ravens, foxes and bears are a summer harassment. Disease, parasites and accidents claim other victims.

TABLE FARE: The white-fronted goose is considered the finest of all the geese for table consumption. It is apparently in good condition at all times of the year.

OVERLEAF ▶

Geese of North America

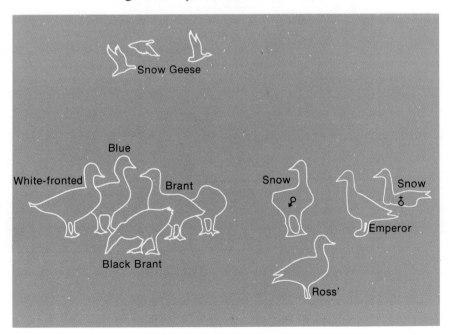

Blue Goose

Chen caerulescens

When I was a boy, one of the top names in citrus fruit was "Blue Goose." At that time, every orange came hand-wrapped in a small square of tissue paper. The Blue Goose paper was always orangy red with a picture of a blue goose inside a circle. I do not know if the blue goose thus depicted was just a figment of the fertile imagination of an adman or if it was actually copied from the wild blue goose. At that time, however, I did not even know that such a creature as a blue goose actually existed, and try as I may, I can't recall when or where I saw my first live blue goose.

DESCRIPTION: The blue goose is not a large goose. The male and female look alike, although the male is larger. An adult male has a length of about 27½ inches, a wingspan of 54 inches and weighs about 5½ pounds.

The head of the blue goose is very similar to that of the snow goose, to which it is related. It is generally accepted today that the blue goose is just a dark phase of the snow goose. The bill is pink with a very conspicuous dark "grinning" patch. The head, neck and throat are white. There is a rusty stain behind the bill, extending past the eye. The back feathers are dark brown with lighter tips.

Blue Goose

The breast, belly and sides are dark gray. The upper wing coverts are blue-gray, the primary and secondary feathers black with gray bases. The under tail coverts are white, and the legs are pinkish gray.

The immature blue goose is almost entirely sooty-brown from bill tip to tail tip. It has a small white spot under its chin.

DISTRIBUTION: The blue goose is a common enough bird within its range, but this range is so restricted that few people ever see a blue goose and thus consider it rare. Its winter range runs along the coast of Louisiana, Texas and Mexico. The goose follows the Mississippi flyway almost due north past Lake Winnipeg and Hudson Bay to Southampton Island, the Perry River in the Northwest Territories and the western region of Baffin Island. For many years the breeding grounds remained unknown, and it was not until 1929 that they were discovered by J. Dewey Soper.

COMMUNICATION: The blue goose is a noisy bird. When feeding, the flock keeps up a constant gabbling which sounds like the barking of a small terrier dog. From time to time, this goose gives vent to a really high-pitched, shrill call. A common sound is a very deep honking that is usually heard when the bird is in flight. It also makes a raucous quacking sound.

BREEDING AND NESTING: Like most geese, the blue goose probably mates for life, and if this is so, the geese are of course paired by the time they reach their breeding grounds. The blue goose often breeds with the snow goose, and the offspring of this hybridization are fertile.

Being paired for life does not excuse the male from going through the courtship procedure each spring. He runs off any rival male that approaches his mate. With lowered head and outstretched neck, he fluffs out his feathers and, hissing loudly, runs toward the intruder, who usually leaves the area.

To impress the female, the male raises his neck, points his bill toward the sky and calls. This favorite position is used both on the water and on land. Both male and female dip their heads toward the water before the act of copulation takes place.

The blue goose nests mainly in open tundra areas. It avoids the forested areas even in migration. Its breeding grounds are usually very flat and quite wet. The nest is situated on any spot that is high and dry enough to keep it and the eggs out of the water. It is quite bulky and is built up of whatever mosses and grasses are in the area. A heavy lining of down is used.

The blue goose nests in colonies. The male does not appear to help with the incubation, but he stands guard at the nest.

EGGS AND YOUNG: The blue goose lays three to five eggs to a clutch. They are basically white in color, although some have a slightly bluish cast. They average about 82 millimeters in length and about 55 millimeters in diameter.

If disturbed during the incubation period, some of the females sneak away from their nests while the danger is still a long way off. Most of them, however, stand their ground until the danger is imminent. Then, with loud protests, both male and female fly off 200 or 300 feet to continue their clamor from a safer distance. The female, if she has the time, always covers her eggs with down before she leaves the nest.

Incubation requires twenty-three to twenty-four days. The down of the young blue goose is smoky blue over the head and back. The breast and belly are a lighter, yellowish tone. The bill is dark blue with a white tip, and there is a white spot beneath the bill at the bird's throat. The feet and legs are a dark blue-gray.

Blue geese are gluttonous in their feeding habits, the young increasing their weight about twentyfold during their six- to seven-week fledgling period.

FLIGHT: Blue geese are strong fliers, although their flight seems labored because of their slow wing beats. They travel in large flocks and often fly at considerable heights. They have no trouble flying at 50 miles per hour and with favorable winds, can greatly increase that speed. Their flight lines do not follow the formalized V formation that is so typical of the Canada goose. Their irregular flight patterns may take the form of curves, bars or check marks. As they fly they keep up a constant gabbling.

MIGRATION: Blue geese fly one route in their spring migration and a different one in the fall. The spring migration is about 3,000 miles long and takes the geese about eleven weeks to complete. They usually leave their wintering grounds in Louisiana and Texas about the first of March.

The fall migration route is more easterly than the spring route and is about 600 miles shorter. The birds depart from the Arctic about the middle of September or even earlier, depending upon the icing conditions that force them out of their breeding range.

HABITS: The blue goose has the reputation of being a very wary bird. Its habit of feeding on pastures or grassland and of resting on mud flats provides it with good protection because in both cases there is no concealment for its enemies.

The birds can be decoyed, however, with both blocks and calls, but this is no proof of unwariness but merely of sociability.

The blue geese arrive on their feeding grounds before daylight and feed until 9 or 10 o'clock. They then retire to some expansive mud flat to rest, sleep and preen. About 2 p.m., they return and feed right up until dark. While the flock feeds some of the geese are always on guard, and the alarm call sends the entire flock thundering up and away.

FOOD: Having a voracious appetite, the blue goose feeds long, steadily and very destructively. The adults feed only upon vegetation. The geese favor the roots of plants as well as the tops and so dig out the entire plant, thus completely denuding any area that they feed upon. To extract the roots of the plants that they can't simply pluck out, the geese dig holes in the mud with their bills. They keep enlarging the holes, which keep filling up with water.

In a short time, not only is all the vegetation gone, but most of the area is pockmarked with water holes.

The favorite foods of the blue goose are the roots of the bulrush, cattail, cordgrass, salt grass, spike rush, horsetail and the entire plant of many different grasses. It sometimes invades cultivated fields, where it does widespread damage.

LIFE SPAN: The blue goose has a potential life span of ten to eleven years, and the longevity record goes to a bird that lived out its potential span to the age of ten and a half years.

ENEMIES: When the blue goose migrates north, it merely exchanges one set of predators for another. In the north gulls, jaegers, hawks, owls and the arctic fox are its principal enemies. In the south the adults are preyed upon by mink, otter, foxes, hawks, owls, eagles and snapping turtles. Disease, parasites and accidents take their toll.

TABLE FARE: The blue goose becomes very fat, and because it is almost entirely vegetarian, its flesh is highly esteemed.

Snow Goose

Chen hyperborea

A few minutes before, the bay had been in darkness. As the sun came up, so did the wind. In the darkness the bay had been quiet, almost oily-looking. Then a few initial ripples had grown to waves and these, pushed along by the wind, started to crash upon the shore, throwing flotsam higher and higher with each succeeding wave. Far out in the bay, raft upon raft of snow geese had been feeding throughout the night. Now, as the waves began to rise, so did the geese. Wave upon wave of them skittered into flight, banked around and came streaming overhead to seek the sanctuary of the impounded waters behind the snug dikes of the Brigantine National Wildlife Refuge. Borne by the wind, their high-pitched calls preceded the flight.

As they passed overhead their white bodies and wings had borrowed some of the dawn's pink. Approaching their destination, the geese set their wings, descended on a long glide and splashed down about 200 yards behind the dike onto the freshwater pond. As if to rinse the salt from their plumage, they dipped and splashed, waved their wings and flapped them about, setting up a loud and continuous clamor.

When the thousands of snow geese had at last flown in, the bay which they had forsaken was still white, but now with the angry white of the breaking waves and not with the beautiful animation of the snow geese.

DESCRIPTION: The male and female are similar in appearance. The snow goose has an average body length of about 30 inches and a wingspan of 60 inches. It weighs 5 to 6 pounds. The snow goose is all white except for its black primaries and wing tips. The bill and feet are pink. There is a brownish stain on the front of the face behind the bill that sometimes extends down over the chest. Young snow geese are a sooty white and have a gray bill and yellow feet. Both mature and immature snow geese have a very distinctive "grinning patch" on their bills.

In the West the snow goose may be confused with the smaller Ross' goose. In the East, however, there can be no mistaking it since there is no other white goose or duck in this area, and our three swans are pure white.

The above data applies to the lesser snow goose. The greater snow goose is identical except for its slightly larger size.

DISTRIBUTION: The snow goose winters along the Pacific coast, most of the Gulf of Mexico coast and along the Atlantic coast from Long Island south to Georgia. It may be seen across the continent during migration as it heads for its breeding grounds in northern Canada, Alaska and the Arctic islands.

The greater snow goose is strictly an eastern species, nesting around Baffin Bay in both Arctic Canada and Greenland and wintering along the Atlantic coast of Maryland, Virginia and North Carolina.

COMMUNICATION: The snow goose is very vociferous, and its high-pitched, shrill honking or gabbling travels a long distance.

BREEDING AND NESTING: The snow goose, like other geese, probably mates for life. Because it nests so far north, very little is actually known about its breeding and nesting habits. The information given here is based on the reports of Eskimos and on studies of snow geese kept in captivity.

Pairing up is probably done on the bird's winter range. If rivalry occurs on the breeding ground, the mated male confronts his adversary with the typical goose threat. In this position the gander tilts his body forward, lowers his neck to within a few inches of the

Snow Goose

ground and, hissing wildly, attempts to drive off the other male. If the geese are on the water, the mated gander assumes a threat position by tilting his neck forward.

The male displays for the female by stretching his neck full length, with his bill pointing toward the sky. The wings, although folded, are erected over the back. Before breeding, the male often dips his bill into the water repeatedly. Copulation takes place in the water, and when the male treads the female, her body is pressed under the water so that only her head remains above the surface.

The nest of the snow goose is usually just a slight depression in the ground, with little vegetation in its construction, but a copious lining of down. Most of the nests are found in or near wet situations for the simple reason that there is very little dry ground in the tundra regions.

43

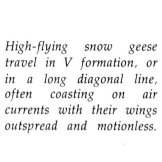

High-flying snow geese travel in V formation, or in a long diagonal line, often coasting on air currents with their wings outspread and motionless.

EGGS AND YOUNG: Seven or eight is a normal set of eggs, which average 76 millimeters in length by 52 millimeters in diameter. The color of the eggs varies from a creamy to a dull white. The slight gloss of the egg increases as incubation progresses. Incubation requires twenty-eight days and may be done by both sexes. If a male does not help with the actual incubation of the eggs, at least he remains in the immediate area and helps to provide a measure of protection for the female.

When the goslings hatch they are yellow, with a brownish or grayish overlay on the top of their heads, their backs, wings and sides. The feet are reddish gray, and the bill is dark with a white tip.

The young leave the nest shortly after hatching. At first they feed ravenously on the myriad insects and their larvae that apparently always abound in the Arctic regions. This rich protein diet allows them to grow very rapidly, but it is very soon abandoned for a vegetarian one.

The young geese retain their sooty juvenile plumage until they are a little more than a year old.

FLIGHT: The young geese can usually fly within about fifty days of hatching.

A strong flier, the snow goose can attain a speed of 50 miles per hour. A favorable wind, of course, can increase that speed. The geese fly very high, probably up to 5,000 feet, and in large flocks. They hold quite closely to V formation in flight or to a long diagonal line. Once they have worked up their flight speed, they give a perhaps deceptive impression of flying with shorter wing strokes than any other geese.

To become airborne, the snows must turn, face the wind and run along the surface of the water until they have sufficient speed to lift off. Their takeoffs are as laborious as their flight is effortless.

Snow geese often coast or sail along on outstretched, motionless wings. Of course, coming in from the heights at which they customarily fly, these geese can coast along just to use up the altitude they have gained.

MIGRATION: The extremely short summer season of the Arctic regions where the snow geese nest forces the birds to head south at an early date. By the middle of September most of them have left the breeding grounds and commenced their flight south. They travel at a leisurely rate because they seldom appear at Brigantine Refuge in New Jersey until the middle of October.

The departure of the snow geese in the spring creates a drastic change on the refuge. One day the water and sky are filled with the geese as they trade back and forth. The next day they take to the wing, and the landscape is barren, denuded, and the continued presence of thousands of other ducks and geese does not fill the void. The snow geese leave New Jersey about the end of March.

Each fall some of the snow geese leave Arctic Alaska, fly over to Siberia and follow the coast down to winter in Japan. The following spring they abandon Asia to nest again in North America.

HABITS: The thrilling sight of three, four or five thousand snow geese makes one long to have seen the flocks of tens of thousands that occured in this country during the mid-1800s.

During this period of great concentrations, the snow goose was a very trusting bird. Most of the geese had never seen a man or heard a gunshot and had no conception of what this sound denoted. The geese were startled into flight by the loud report, but they almost always settled down again immediately. Hunters would walk or ride through the flocks, killing the geese with clubs.

All this has changed. Yet although there is little likelihood today of the snow goose being exterminated, such persecution has made it much more wary than its ancestors.

FOOD: The bulk of the snow goose's diet is made up of vegetable matter as it is, like many of the geese, a grazing bird.

The snow goose's favorite winter foods are cordgrass, bulrush, cattail, and spike rush. It also feeds on cultivated grains such as wheat, barley and rice. Practically nothing is known about the snow goose's diet on its summer range.

LIFE SPAN: Geese have a much greater life span potential than ducks, many of them living to be over ten years old. No individual record for longevity appears to exist for the snow goose.

ENEMIES: In the far north the snow goose's most common enemies are gulls, jaegers, the arctic fox, ravens and, of course, man. The adults on the wintering grounds are vulnerable mainly to hunters, because few predators are large enough to take a full-grown goose. Diseases, parasites and accidents take their toll.

TABLE FARE: The snow goose is considered a "clean" feeder because it feeds mainly on vegetation. However, its flesh is not rated nearly as high as that of the Canada goose.

Ross' Goose

Chen rossii

In the late summer of 1970, during a brief stay in England, I visited Peter Scott's Waterfowl Trust on the west coast. I arrived there about 11 a.m., and for the rest of the day I was oblivious to the outside world.

The Waterfowl Trust has the largest collection of waterfowl in the world. There were thousands of ducks and geese representing over one hundred and fifty species. The grounds are divided into areas, each featuring the waterfowl of the different continents. I never got beyond the compound housing the waterfowl of North America. It was here that I saw my first Ross' goose, which is the smallest and the rarest of the geese found in North America.

DESCRIPTION: A smaller variation of the snow goose, the Ross' goose is slightly larger than a mallard drake. The male and female are identical. They average 24 inches in length, have a 50-inch wingspread and weigh about 2¾ pounds.

The adult Ross' goose's plumage consists of a white head, neck, belly, sides, back, tail and wings. The primaries, primary coverts and wing tips are black. There is usually a rust-colored stain on the goose's head behind the bill. The bill is pink on the tip but, unlike that of the snow goose, it has a greenish base. Moreover it lacks the dark "grin" mark of the snow goose's bill. At its base it has warty tubercles or protuberances. This goose's feet, like those of the snow goose, are a dark pinkish red.

The immature Ross' goose looks like its parents, but it has a sooty gray appearance instead of their sparkling white. Its bill also is gray. However, after about ten months, these gray feathers are molted, and the young bird attains the sparkling wash-day white of the adults. The feet of the immature snow goose are yellow, whereas the Ross' goose's feet are pink. Only after the young bird matures does it gain the warty protuberances on its bill.

Ross' Goose

DISTRIBUTION: The Ross' goose has a very limited range in North America. It winters in the San Joachim and Sacramento valleys in California. Its breeding range is the lower part of Canada's Arctic regions. It does not travel as far north as the snow goose.

In fact, the breeding range of the Ross' goose was long a mystery. When the birds lifted off their California wintering ranges and headed northeast over the Rocky Mountains, no one knew their destination. Then in 1938, Angus Gavin finally discovered their nesting sites on the Perry River on the boundary of the Mackenzie-Keewatin districts of Canada's northwest territories.

COMMUNICATION: The call notes of the Ross' goose are a very high, shrill, almost squeaky gabble.

BREEDING AND NESTING: The Ross' goose is usually very docile. During the breeding season, as might be expected, the male becomes more pugnacious. He lowers his head and extends his neck in the threat display, which is used against rival males and also to provide protection for the female during the incubation period. The male also displays for the female by extending his neck and bill skyward and calling. Both the male and female bob their heads up and down as part of their courtship ritual.

Being very sociable, the Ross' goose nests in colonies. The nest may be just a hollow in the ground filled with vegetation and down or it may be a considerable mound built up of moss and other vegetation.

EGGS AND YOUNG: Four or five eggs are an average sized clutch for the Ross' goose. The eggs average 74 millimeters in length by 47 millimeters in width. They are off-white in color. Incubation is performed by the female and requires a period of twenty-four days.

When the young geese hatch, their down is yellowish gray, darker on the upper side and lighter underneath. Their heads are bright canary yellow, their bills black, and their legs olive-green.

On their rich diet of insects the young geese grow rapidly, and by the time they are one month old, they are about the size of a domestic hen, and their down has been replaced, for the most part, by feathers. At six weeks of age, the flight feathers are completely developed, although the birds have not yet learned to fly. The legs and bill tip start to turn pink when the young geese are ten weeks old, by which time they are flying.

FLIGHT: The Ross' goose does not fly as high as the snow goose nor does it travel in as large a flock. It has a slower wing beat and a slower air speed, traveling at about 40 miles per hour.

MIGRATION: Although the Ross' goose may leave California as early as late March, it dawdles on its way north, spending quite a long time on Lake Athabasca in Alberta and Saskatchewan. It may not arrive on its breeding grounds until the end of May or the beginning of June.

The fall migration gets under way in late August or the first part of September. Again the geese seem to be in no great rush to get back to California, and it may take them until the middle of November to get there.

HABITS: Birds that breed in wilderness areas are either exceptionally wary or exceedingly tame. The Ross' goose has always been considered to be a very tame bird. It was at no time very common, and its unwariness made it an easy mark for huntsmen. No one really had an accurate idea of how many of these geese there were on the continent, but a few years ago the figure was thought to be about 2,000. The figure today is up to about 30,000. This increase in numbers results not only from more accurate identification and tabulation methods but from additional protection.

As mentioned before, this goose is very sociable and is commonly found mixed in with flocks of other geese, particularly snow geese. One of the main problems in censusing the Ross' goose was distinguishing it from the snows.

FOOD: Very little is known about the Ross' goose's diet, and in fact there appears to be no information on it at all for the summer months. In California, during the winter, the goose feeds on the wild oats that make up 83 percent of its total diet, in which barley is another important element.

LIFE SPAN: Since there are no records to go by, it must be assumed that the life span of the Ross' goose is about the same as that of the snow goose, an average of seven to ten years.

ENEMIES: The predators of the far north are gulls, jaegers, ravens, snowy owls and the arctic fox. Disease, parasites and accidents take their toll.

TABLE FARE: The Ross' goose's decline was in a large measure due to market hunting, which means that people were willing to buy this goose as food. However, it was less esteemed than the Canada goose as table fare.

Wings of North American Geese

Canada Goose

Brant

Emperor Goose

Black Brant

White-fronted Goose

Blue Goose

Ross' Goose

Snow Goose

SURFACE-FEEDING DUCKS

(Subfamily Anatinae)

Mallard

Anas platyrhynchos

The mallard duck is the world's most common, most numerous, and best known duck. As well as being a very sporting duck and a very tasty one, it is the common ancestor from which almost all our domesticated ducks have been derived. It can be one of the wildest and most wary of ducks and is also the most easily tamed. Every city park with a pond or lake has its resident mallards. Although most mallards migrate long distances, some stay in one area. Today, as more farm ponds are built, as shooting becomes more restricted in many areas, and more people take an interest in wildlife and provide food for them, more mallards are remaining as year-round residents in areas they only frequented before during the winter months.

DESCRIPTION: The mallard drake averages about 23½ inches in length, has a wingspan of 36 inches and weighs 2¾ pounds. The drake's bill is yellow, his feet bright orange. The iridescent green of the male's head has earned him the nickname of "greenhead," yet, in certain lights, the head may appear a dark, rich purple. A thin white ring encircles the neck. The chest and breast are brown-

Mallard

ish purple, the belly and underwing surfaces ashy white. The back and the top wing side are brown except for the blue-purple wing speculum, which is bordered in front and behind by white. The tail also is white-edged and, during the breeding season, the male sports a couple of feathers above the tail that curl up sharply, producing a very jaunty appearance.

The hen mallard is slightly smaller in size and weight. Hers is a demure coat of browns, and she has a dark streak running through the eye and an off-white chin and throat. Her bill is orange, spotted with dark green.

According to a count made, there are over 12,000 feathers on a mallard.

Albino mallards are occasionally found.

DISTRIBUTION: The mallard is found throughout the United States, although it breeds mostly in the northern third of the country and up into Canada and Alaska.

COMMUNICATION: The mallard is a noisy bird, especially the female. Her raucous quacking can be heard for an exceptionally long distance and is the sound most hunters try to imitate to attract not only mallards but other ducks as well. Her gabbling feed call is as enticing as a chuck-wagon cook's "Come and get it." The male duck has a very quiet quack, and in comparison his mate can only be called garrulous. The male also has a variety of whistled calls that are used mainly during the breeding season.

BREEDING AND NESTING: There is evidence of aggressive pairing activity among female mallards in the middle of October. A hen may not allow any other female anywhere near her mate. Although the mallards migrate north in large flocks in the spring, they are in most cases traveling as mated pairs. The peak of the pairing-up activity takes place in mid-November.

One of the female's aggressive actions is to turn her head back over her shoulder, bob her head up and down and swim at her rival. The drake uses aggression; he lowers his neck and body along the water and swims rapidly, trying to catch his rival. To increase his speed, he sometimes beats his wings against the water as if flying. If still more speed is needed, he flies after his rival and attempts to peck him. The peak period of the male's fighting occurs in the middle of March after the ducks are on the breeding ground.

It may seem strange that the mallards are already paired up before the main fighting takes place. The fights are in defense of the pair formation and because of this, the mated male almost always wins. It is a psychological fact that any creature fighting on its home ground, in this case the mated pair, will in almost every instance win out over its rivals.

Even though the female has been "going steady" with the male since the preceding October or November, she still expects to be courted in February and March. The mallard drake has quite a repertoire of display tactics, all of which he uses to impress the female. He faces her, raises his head up high and bends his body so that the tail is erected and brought forward. He bends his head around and preens behind his extended wing, displaying the beautiful blue colors of his speculum to the female. He often dips his bill into the water and then pulls his head back sharply, creating a little arc of water.

Much of the courtship takes place on the wing with the male, or males, flying after the female, who usually quacks loudly all the time.

When the male and female face each other on the water and begin to bob their heads up and down rapidly, the male's case seems to be won. When the female swims forward and touches his bill with hers, the pact between them is sealed.

Mallards are highly adaptable in their choice of a nesting site. Usually the nest is located near water in among the reeds, rushes or sedges. It is always well hidden, or at least this was the case with those I have discovered. I have found mallard nests under tree roots or large fallen logs, in a hollow log, in the middle of a brier patch, and this past spring I located one under an old brush heap. Some of the mallard nests I have found were at least two hundred yards from water, and other observers have located nests as much as a quarter of a mile away. There have been several reports of nests built on top of a muskrat house and in the crotch of a large tree like a hawk's nest. One nest was discovered constructed in a tree hollow like a wood duck's nest, while another was found built on a floating log.

The nest is about 14 inches in diameter and is composed of grass, leaves or any other available vegetation. There is always a good lining of down in the nest. This is used to keep the eggs warm and concealed, when the female leaves the nest to seek food and water.

EGGS AND YOUNG: The mallard's egg-laying reaches its peak about the first of April. Naturally, birds nesting in the far north lay their eggs later. A normal set of eggs numbers from eight to twelve, one egg being laid every day until the set is complete. In the southern part of the mallard's nesting range, for example in New Jersey, the hen renests if her original nest is destroyed. Usually the second set of eggs is smaller in number. This is not always so, however, and one mallard hen, whose nest was systematically robbed of eggs by a biologist, laid one hundred and forty-six eggs in one hundred and fifty-eight days. The eggs average 57 millimeters in length by 41 millimeters in diameter. They vary in color from off-white to buff or green. Buff-green appears to be the most common color.

The female does all the incubating. About the time that she begins to brood the eggs, the male goes off alone; his ties to the hen are over. Incubation takes twenty-six days. The mallard is a good mother and sits exceedingly tight; you almost have to step on her before she will flush from her nest.

The ducklings, when they hatch out and their down dries off, are basically brown on the top and yellow underneath. Their feet are yellow. They stay in the nest for a couple of hours after hatching to regain their strength.

The period between the time of hatching and reaching water is probably the most dangerous one of the ducks' lives. Danger is constant to all wild creatures in the out-of-doors, but for ducks it is concentrated in this phase. The hen is instinctively aware of the dangers and is anxious to get the venture under way. She moves away from the nest and calls softly to the little ones. However, until her image is imprinted upon them, they pay no attention to her.

Imprinting is the attachment formed between the young of waterfowl and whatever object moves continuously in their sight. Dr. Konrad Lorenz of Germany carried out many experiments where he became imprinted as the "mother" to greylag geese. Because he was the dominant moving object during this imprinting period, the geese accepted him as their mother, and he raised them in that fashion. Until the hen is imprinted upon the young mallards, they will not leave the nest.

The further the nest is from water, the longer the distance to be traveled, and the greater the risk to the young ducks. Many are eaten by predators, some fall into holes and are unable to get out, some become entangled in vegetation and are lost, and some become exhausted and fall behind. Solicitous as she is of all of her young, the mother mallard cannot sacrifice her entire brood to accommodate a single duckling, and so she presses on to water. Arrival at the water lessens the danger somewhat but does not eliminate it since usually land-based predators are replaced by water-based enemies.

The young ducks feed mainly on insects and perform a most useful function by concentrating on mosquito larvae. But anything that moves is considered food, and if it is small enough to be eaten, will be quickly snapped up. As the ducklings mature, they convert to a diet of seeds and vegetation.

Mallard ducklings have a fledgling period of about two months, during which they grow rapidly and lose their down. Both male and female acquire feathers of a somber brown, thus resembling their mother.

FLIGHT: The flight feathers, or primaries, of the young ducks are the last ones to be formed, and so it is two months before they are capable of flying.

While the female takes care of the young, the male goes into seclusion and, during his eclipse molt, sheds his flight feathers. He loses his beautiful, brilliant colors and saucy tail curl and for a

Beating its wings against the water, a mallard springs into the air in its characteristic takeoff.

time looks almost like his mate. This camouflage is Nature's way of compensating for his flightlessness.

The male regains his flight feathers at about the same time that the young develop theirs. Once the young are airborne, the female molts and becomes flightless.

The mallard duck is a strong flier and can easily reach speeds of 60 miles per hour. With a strong tail wind, it has been clocked at almost 85 miles per hour. When taking off from the water, it beats its wings against the water and springs directly into the air. It can swerve abruptly, it can dodge, it can actually fly backwards and even upside down to elude danger.

Mallards have been known to fly 2,000 miles practically nonstop. They fly in large flocks during migration, usually in the famous V formation. When the lead bird tires, it drops behind, and another forges ahead as leader. Sometimes the flight line becomes straggly and appears as a lopsided V.

MIGRATION: The mallards' spring migration is so timed that their appearance in the north nearly coincides with the break-up of the ice. The height of the migration occurs about the last week in March, when they flood into Canada's prairie provinces.

The migration south starts about the first of September, peaks around the first of October and is usually concluded by about the middle of November. These dates, of course, depend upon the icing conditions up north and the distance and destination of the ducks' journey.

HABITS: The mallard duck is extremely sociable and the male particularly so during the breeding season. The drake mates with just about anything that will hold still or can be caught on the move. Hybridization between the mallard and the tame muscovy and the wild black duck is very common, and the offspring of such unions are fertile. The mallard has also been known to cross with the pintail, baldpate and green-winged teal.

Classified as a "puddle" duck, the mallard has centrally located legs and can therefore walk with ease and for considerable distances. It seldom dives beneath the surface of the water to feed. During breeding displays, however, both the male and female plunge beneath the surface, pop up again quickly and splash about with all the wild abandon of ghetto children playing in the spray of a fire hydrant.

A certain Dr. Prang found that although the mallard is a good swimmer, it has a low efficiency ratio in the water. His tests show that only 5 percent of the energy expended by the mallard in swimming is converted to actual propulsion. Most boats are better designed hydrodynamically and achieve a 20 to 30 percent efficiency ratio. However, he concluded that what the ducks lose hydrodynamically they make up for aerodynamically.

In feeding, the duck turns its rump up and extends its neck to feed on the floor in shallow water. To maintain this upended position, the duck has to paddle frantically.

FOOD: Ninety-one percent of the mallard's food is vegetable matter, the remaining 9 percent animal matter. Naturally, in different parts of the country the mallard feeds upon different foods. A total list of all the foods eaten by this duck would be too long to compile.

In the northeastern sector of the country the mallard prefers wild rice, pondweed, smartweed, wild celery, and wild millet. In the southeast it favors wild millet, smartweed, bulrush, duckweed, spike rush, pondweed and rice. In the West pondweed, bulrush, sorghum, horned pondweed and barley are staples. In addition, the mallard feeds extensively in cultivated fields, gleaning grain such as corn, wheat and buckwheat. Acorns are another popular food. One mallard in New York was found to have eaten thirty-four small yellow perch.

LIFE SPAN: The potential life span of the mallard duck is seven to nine years, but about 60 percent of them are killed or die by the time they are two years old. The longevity record goes to a mallard that lived to be twenty-five years old on a farm pond in Bucks County, Pennsylvania.

ENEMIES: The crow ranks as one of the mallard's main enemies. The number of nests destroyed and eggs eaten by these black predators is almost beyond belief. Skunks, raccoons, opossums, foxes, and snakes all eat the eggs of the mallard and the young, too, if they can catch them. Some of the western ground squirrels destroy the nest by either eating the eggs or just rolling them out of the nest in play. The snapping turtle takes both the young ducks and the adults by catching them by the leg and pulling them under the water till they drown. Fish, such as large-mouth bass, pike and pickerel, muskellunge, are all deadly to ducks.

The only instance I know of a mallard drake helping the hen to raise the young occurred on a friend's pond. The bass were gulping down the young, and the mallard drake posted himself between the shallow water and the deep. The hen kept the ducklings in the shallow water while the drake dived beneath the surface and chased off any bass that approached.

When I used to guide wilderness canoe trips up in Canada, we had a fish lure in the shape of a little duck. We would tow the lure behind the canoe, where it sent out ripples like a baby duck swimming. Although we never caught many fish, they banged that lure constantly, often throwing it a foot or so up in the air. We had no doubts about the fate of any duckling that happened to swim in those waters.

With owls at night, hawks and eagles by day, fish beneath the water, mink and otter on its surface, raccoons and foxes on land and the gamut of hunters' guns across the continent, it is a wonder any mallard ever lives to breed again. Yet they somehow manage to survive these dangers, plus accidents, parasites and disease.

The impoundment of new ponds has partly compensated for the destruction caused to the mallard's habitat by the draining of potholes for agriculture. But now new threats are appearing. DDE, DDT and DDD pesticide residues have been found to be high in mallards, and at present studies on mercury residues are being conducted. A tremendous amount of experimentation is going on to discover a substitute for lead shot. Ducks are killed not only when the lead shot is fired at them and hits them, but also when they ingest the spent lead shot with their food. The lead, when ground up by the gizzard and exposed to the duck's digestive juices, creates a fatal toxin. It is estimated that between five hundred thousand and one million five hundred thousand ducks, most of them mallards, are lost annually through lead poisoning.

TABLE FARE: It is universally agreed that the mallard duck provides excellent eating. It is the standard against which all other ducks are judged, whether it be in sporting qualities or as table fare.

Black Duck

Anas rubripes

As I paddled my canoe noiselessly through the Quebec wilderness, the only sounds that shattered the silence were those of the straining pinions and frantic quacking of the flock upon flock of black ducks that exploded into flight when I hove into view. It was early September, and I was about 50 miles from the source of Canada's Ottawa River. The black ducks do not nest in the taiga area where I found them; they were merely using it as a resting spot in their migration to the south. I flushed thousands of blacks that morning, and, if only for a short while, I experienced the thrill, so common to our early explorers, of encountering seemingly endless numbers of ducks.

I have seen larger concentrations of blacks along New Jersey's east coast because this state boasts one of the largest wintering concentrations known: as many as sixty-five thousand or more in good years. However, the thrill of seeing so many black ducks out in the wilderness was greater to me because the black duck is primarily a wilderness wood duck.

DESCRIPTION: There is currently an argument going on as to whether the black duck should be considered as a species separate

63

Black Duck

from the mallard or merely as a subspecies. The black duck is slightly smaller than the mallard, having a body length of about 23 inches and a wingspan of 3 feet. A drake may weigh a little over 3 pounds, while the hen weighs slightly under.

The black duck's plumage is similar to that of the hen mallard but considerably darker brown. The light head of the black duck is much more conspicuous because of its dark body. The white underwing feathers flash silver when the bird is in flight, and, according to Allan Cruickshank, they are this duck's most conspicuous field mark. The secondary feathers of the wing, the speculum, are bluish purple, edged with black and tipped with white. The drake's bill is yellow, while the hen's is olive-green; the bill's nail tip is dark on both sexes. The feet of the black duck are usually a light brownish or reddish orange.

Those who advocate subspecies status for the black duck point out the increasing hybridization of the mallard and the black duck. They claim that the black duck is a melanistic mallard whose dark color is an adaptation to the bird's dark forest habitat. They also claim that as the black duck nests increasingly in marsh areas, mingling and breeding with the mallard, its dark coloration will eventually be phased out, reverting to a more typical mallard coloration.

DISTRIBUTION: The black duck is an eastern species. It breeds from the Ungava Peninsula in Canada south to Illinois and Mary-

64

land; and from Wisconsin east to the Atlantic Ocean. Its wintering range overlaps the southern portion of its breeding range and extends from the Great Lakes to New England and south to Texas and Florida. The black duck is the most important duck in the east of the United States as it is the most common freshwater duck.

COMMUNICATION: Both sexes of the black duck quack, but the female's voice is more strident and raucous. The blacks also hiss and occasionally make a whistling sound.

BREEDING AND NESTING: The black ducks pair up during the winter, and when their time instinct so dictates, they migrate northward in pairs. The fact of being already paired in no way affects their courtship process, which must still be adhered to.

The black duck's courtship is a proving of physical ability or rather of durability. It appears to be a game of tag or a race, in which each member of the pair is doing its best to outfly the other. Flying at a speed of 45 to 50 miles per hour, the ducks zip up and down the length of the pond or lake that they have chosen for their breeding ground. Occasionally they plop down onto the water and almost as soon take off again—and so the merry chase goes on. At last the female decides that the male is a worthy suitor, and the pair settles down on the water, where she accepts his advances.

The black duck's nest is usually built on the ground, although I have read of three instances where the duck had utilized a nest in a tree. The typical nest is carefully hidden from view among high grasses or under low, brushy growth. It is seldom located more than a few yards from water. The female forms the nest well with her body, using the weeds, mosses or grasses which are in the area. Further grasses or vegetation are usually added, and a nest is rarely considered complete unless it contains a copious amount of down. The quantity of down increases with the period of incubation because the female usually idly picks at her breast and body as she sits on the nest.

EGGS AND YOUNG: The black duck usually lays a clutch of eight to ten eggs, although on occasion she may lay as many as twelve. The eggs are smooth, and their color varies from a dull white through different shades of cream to a pale buff that may have greenish tinges. The eggs are almost oval, averaging 59 millimeters in length by 43 millimeters in diameter.

Incubation, which takes twenty-six to twenty-eight days, is performed by the female without any assistance from the male.

Indeed, the female is usually abandoned by the male as soon as breeding ceases with the completion of the set of eggs. When the female leaves the nest to go to water and to feed, she carefully covers the eggs with a mixture of down and nesting material.

All the fertile eggs in the black duck's nest usually hatch within an hour or so of the start of the hatching activity. After hatching the young remain in the nest for a couple of hours until they have all dried their down and regained the energy expended in freeing themselves from their shells.

The young black duck has a yellow face, throat and belly, a mottled breast and dark head, back of the neck, back and upper wings. It looks almost exactly like a young mallard except that the mallard duckling does not have the mottled breast.

When the young have dried off, the mother leads them to water. This is usually a short trip as the nest is always in the proximity of water. On the rare occasions when a drought has dried up the nearby pothole, the female unerringly leads her brood to whatever water is in her area. If the trip is long or arduous, it is made with as many stops as the little ones need to rest. During these rest periods the ducklings usually huddle under the mother for warmth.

The mother black duck is a gallant defender of her young. Like many wild mothers, she uses the decoy ruse of simulated injury to lure a potentially dangerous intruder away from the vicinity of her young. At the first alarm note from her, the ducklings scatter and hide under any vegetation or debris that is handy.

FLIGHT: The fledgling period of the black duck lasts about fifty to sixty days. The down is replaced by feathers, and the wing primaries are fully developed by the end of this period so that flight becomes possible.

The black duck is a very strong and speedy bird in flight. When surprised on the water, it can spring directly into the air, the first wing strokes actually beating against the water which, by its resistance, affords the duck greater purchase than air. The black duck climbs rapidly and usually travels in rather small flocks in a V formation or a long skein. During the periods of winter concentrations the birds may fly in large flocks, but this is not the usual pattern.

The black duck has been clocked at speeds of 45 to 50 miles per hour and more, but much of this flight speed depends upon the wind direction.

In its postnuptial molt, the black duck sheds all its flight feathers at one time and cannot fly. It is during this period that the males gather together on large, marshy areas where they can hide among the grasses. The female is busy with her young now, and by the time they can fly, the adults' flight feathers are also fully developed, so that flight becomes possible for all the ducks.

MIGRATION: The black duck uses the Atlantic flyway in migration. The trek north starts in late March, peaks in mid-April, and most of the birds are on their breeding grounds by the third week in April. The fall migration starts during the last two weeks in September and continues into the middle of November. The birds seem to be reluctant to leave their inland streams and lakes and only do so when they freeze up. Then the birds congregate in the estuarine marshes along the coast. Some black ducks migrate as far as 1,000 miles from their breeding grounds to their wintering sites.

HABITS: The black duck is one of the wariest of all ducks. It seldom if ever drops to the water without first circling the area several times while it checks the terrain below. The flare from an upturned human face probably scares off more ducks than any other single mistake a duck hunter could make.

The legs of the black duck are centrally placed on the body so that this duck can walk easily. The position of the legs places this duck in the "puddle" or "dipper" duck category, which means that it usually feeds in shallow water by tipping its body. The food is picked up by the bill and water runs out through the strainer serrations while the food is retained and swallowed.

During the winter the black duck often feeds under cover of darkness and then flies out to the open waters of the bays or ocean to rest during the daytime. Increased hunting activity almost precludes its feeding in the shallows during the day. Extensive freeze-ups, however, force a reversal of this pattern because the ducks simply cannot obtain sufficient food during the hours of darkness. Fortunately, such freeze-ups usually occur after the hunting season is over, so that the increased daylight feeding does not expose the duck population to an additional hazard.

FOOD: The black duck eats a much larger proportion of animal life than the mallard. On an annual basis animal life accounts for between 25 and 35 percent of the total food intake. However, there are periods when the black duck feeds almost exclusively on the salt-marsh snail. It also eats small clams, crustaceans, insects and occasionally small fish. Of the plant foods available, pondweed, wild rice, cordgrass, bulrush, smartweed, naiad, algae, widgeon grass and spike rush are the most important.

LIFE SPAN: The average life span of the black duck is figured at five to six years, although the majority of the ducks are killed by the end of their second year. The banding of birds, that tremendous wildlife research tool, has provided concrete proof that the longest lived duck on record was a black duck.

This particular black duck drake (number C-617-405) was banded on December 3, 1933, by W. B. Large at Durand Eastman Park, Rochester, New York. Number C-617-405 certainly led a charmed life because it escaped the many hazards of nineteen years of migration and nineteen hunting seasons, not to mention the natural predators to which it was exposed. Number C-617-405 was finally brought down by hunter Russell Haring in York County, Pennsylvania on October 15, 1953, at the ripe old age of twenty years.

The second oldest duck was also a black. This duck was banded on September 9, 1932, at Jones Beach State Bird Sanctuary on Long Island, New York, and was found dead on January 22, 1951, at Great South Bay, Long Island, New York, at the age of nineteen years.

ENEMIES: Life for the black duck is fraught with danger. Marsh fires during the nesting season constitute a hazard. Floods and excessive tides may inundate the nests and drown the young. Drought may dry up potholes and sloughs, necessitating long trips overland for mother and young. Heavy icing can reduce food availability and so cause starvation. Skunks, raccoons, opossums and crows eat the eggs. Snapping turtles and fish gobble up the young. Mink, otter and foxes eat the eggs, young and adults if they can catch them. Hawks, owls and eagles add ducks to their menus when possible. Parasites, both internal and external, sap the bird's vitality, and diseases take their toll. Botulism also is found in areas where the water renewal is not sufficient to prevent the production of this extremely deadly toxin. And then there are just plain accidents, for instance when the ducks fly into objects or get caught in traps set for muskrats. In some years as many as 175,000 to 250,000 black ducks are legally harvested by hunters.

TABLE FARE: The black duck is considered one of the most delectable of the waterfowl. This high opinion is lessened only when the duck is feeding exclusively on animal matter, which may impart an unpleasant taste to the meat. When the bird is feeding on vegetable matter its flesh ranks with the best.

Pintail

Anas acuta

Poxono Island is a 1,000-acre tract of virgin timber in the middle of the Delaware River. At its southern end sprawls a large pond, the existence of which even many area residents are unaware. Every spring, the pond becomes a mecca for ducks in migration.

For years, I have photographed these visitors from blinds along the shore. The most common species at this pond is the pintail, one of the best known and farthest ranging of all gamebirds.

Pintails breed mainly on the Alaskan tundra and the Western Canadian prairie, but they migrate to winter ranges throughout the lower United States and Central America. In fact, these ducks are such strong fliers that some regularly migrate between Alaska and the Hawaiian Islands—a non-stop flight of more than 2,000 miles.

DESCRIPTION: The pintail is one of the sleekest, neatest-looking ducks gracing our continent. Its two long central tail feathers earn it its common name of "pintail" and the name "sprig" that you hear applied to it in the southern swamps. Although the pintail has a greater total length than the mallard, in actual body length, discounting its tail, it is slightly smaller. The male pintail duck averages 27 inches in length, has a wingspan of 34 inches and weighs about 2 pounds. The male has a blue-gray bill and feet, and its head and throat are a rich, dark brown. The neck, breast and belly are white, the tail black. The drake's back and side feathers are grayish with darker vermiculations. The top wing surfaces are grayish brown, the speculum green with a leading brown border and a trailing black border edged with white. The underwing surfaces are lighter than the top. The male pintail is one of the easiest ducks to identify.

The female pintail closely resembles the female mallard, but her overall brown coloration is slightly darker. Her bill is blue-gray, whereas the mallard hen's bill is orange, spotted with green. The speculum on the female mallard is blue-purple, like the male's, while the female pintail's speculum is a light shade of brown. The female pintail has a longer neck than any of the other brown ducks.

DISTRIBUTION: The pintail is the most widespread duck in North America and ventures farther into the Arctic than the mallard. It is common in the East but even more abundant in the West. Its winter range is roughly the lower two-thirds of the continental United States, from ocean to ocean. Its breeding range extends from the northern third of the continent up to the Arctic Ocean. It is probably the duck with the largest population on the Canadian prairie provinces and is found in even larger numbers up on the tundra, especially in western Alaska.

COMMUNICATION: The drake has a low, soft whistle that is heard primarily during the breeding season. This call is often described as a "mewing" sound. In flight or when disturbed, the male also makes a sound that is not quite a quack. The female has a rough-sounding quack and in the breeding season calls with a soft *rrr-rrrr*.

BREEDING AND NESTING: The pintails pair up after they have arrived on their breeding grounds. Some female pintails appear to be particularly attractive to the opposite sex, and such a female may be the center of attention of as many as five or six drakes. Each one circles about and displays, putting on his best show in an attempt to win the female's favors. He bends his neck sharply forward and throws water up and back in a flashing arc. In his next act he lifts his head erect, raises the rear portion of his wings and fans his tail out and up. He then turns about, keeping his head toward the female, and swims slowly away, presumably in the earnest hope

Pintail Ducks

that she will follow him. And if she is interested, she will. At other times the action is much faster, and the courtship is done on the wing. The hen flies at top speed and swiftly turns, rolls and banks. The drake flies as close to her as possible, sometimes beneath her but so close that their wing tips touch.

Only by flying over Alaska's tundra area can one realize what a vast number of potholes of water there are in that area. These potholes are the home of the breeding pintails.

The nest is made on a tussock or some slight elevation that will keep it above the water level. It is constructed from the sedges, grasses, etc., that grow in the area. More noticeable than the plant material is the down that the female plucks from her body to line the nest. The down is mixed with the grasses to form a cover that is rolled over the eggs when the female is not in attendance.

In the prairie provinces, the pintail often nests as much as half a mile from the nearest water. One nest discovered near Crane Lake in Saskatchewan was over a mile away.

EGGS AND YOUNG: The pintail does not as a rule have a large clutch of eggs, eight being the average number. The eggs average 54 millimeters in length by 38 millimeters in diameter. In color they range from pale olive to pale brownish olive.

Incubation requires twenty-two days and is done by the female. Unlike most drakes, the male pintail usually stays in the vicinity of the nest and may even be of some help in raising the young. This may be due to the fact that the pintail nests out on the tundra, where the male can hide anywhere since the entire countryside looks alike.

The mother pintail sits exceptionally tight on her nest. This bravery is further demonstrated after the young hatch. One female, with young, was disturbed and in defense of her young flew at the head of the person disturbing her. Then she splashed down on the water nearby and made a great commotion. This whole show was to divert attention away from her young, which crept into hiding under the vegetation along the shore.

It may seem strange that if a waterfowl that cannot fly is disturbed, it will forsake even a large lake to seek shelter among whatever vegetation is available. In most cases, when the lake is large enough, it would be impossible to catch the ducks on the water. Yet they do not like to be exposed on the open water and instinctively head for cover. This reaction, which is typical of both freshwater ducks and geese, is probably a holdover from their youth.

The downy young of the pintail duck are easily distinguishable from the young of other "puddle" ducks because they are gray and brown instead of yellow and brown.

When the young start to feather out, both sexes have the uniform coloration of the mother. As soon as the birds are capable of flying, at about two months of age, the young males molt out their feathers and begin to assume the plumage of the adult male. Some young males appear as adults in December, while others do not reach that advanced stage until the following spring. In any case, it is over a year before the young male is as sleek and as long-tailed as the adult.

FLIGHT: The pintail duck is perhaps the fastest flier of any of the North American ducks. Its graceful lines lend themselves to speed. This duck is also exceedingly agile on the wing and can perform rolls and banks that would do credit to a fighter plane. It has been clocked at over 65 miles an hour, and with a strong tail wind speeds of 90 miles per hour or more are possible.

The female loses her flight feathers after her young are fledged,

Fastest on the wing of all the ducks, pintails migrate in large flocks which travel in irregular formations at high altitude.

and it takes about three weeks for her to become airborne again. It is generally conceded that she flies less fast than the male.

When landing, the pintail drops rapidly on set wings, levels off as it nears the water and sometimes rises slightly before going into a long glide to alight.

In migration, the pintails frequently travel in large flocks and at a considerable height.

MIGRATION: Regardless of the weather, the pintail starts its migration at a very early date. The northward trek is often under way by the middle of February, the birds arriving in the north so early that the migration may be held back awaiting the breakup of the ice. As they are among the earliest of the migrants and nesting birds, the pintails have first pick of the tundra ponds and potholes.

Eager as the pintails are to rush the spring migration, they seem just as anxious to forsake their breeding grounds when fall comes. The first of September finds the birds on the wing starting their long trek south.

HABITS: The legs of the pintail duck are located in the center of the bird's body, thus enabling this duck to walk very easily. Because of its leg placement, it is considered a puddle duck, and it usually feeds by tipping its rump up and its neck down. However, it can dive and often does so, more to escape from danger than for the purpose of feeding.

Frank Noble tells of wounding a large pintail drake that dived beneath the water. When the drake did not reappear, a boat was rowed out to the area where it was last seen. Through the clear water the pintail was clearly visible holding on to an underwater plant with its bill, using the plant as an anchor. The duck remained motionless until touched and then, although it kicked its feet furiously, it did not let go of the plant. It had to be forcibly pulled loose. There are accounts of both pintail and other ducks actually drowning in this way when wounded rather than allowing themselves to be taken.

The pintail takes off from water with ease by beating against the surface with its wings and so catapulting straight up into the air. It is the pintail's flight speed, plus its proverbial wariness, that makes it such a challenge to hunters.

Pintails can be decoyed and respond to a good caller using the feeding-gabbling call of the mallard. Being sociable, the pintail is often found in mixed flocks along with mallards, teal, baldpates, etc.

FOOD: Eighty-seven percent of the pintail's diet is vegetable matter and the remaining 13 percent animal matter. The latter includes mollusks, crustaceans, snails, water beetles, small fish, frogs and marine worms. The pintail's favorite plant foods are bulrush, smartweed, pondweed, wild millet, wild rice, musk grass, glasswort and widgeon grass. It also feeds upon domestic grains such as rice, barley and corn, whenever these are available. Acorns, too, form part of its diet.

LIFE SPAN: The potential life span of the pintail is seven to eight years, but most of them do not live beyond their fifth year. The longevity record is held by a pintail that lived to be seventeen years old.

ENEMIES: Breeding farther north than many of our other common ducks, the pintail is exposed to more northern predators. The raven takes eggs and the jaeger, chicks. Hawks, owls and eagles take their toll. The Arctic and the red fox, the wolf and the wolverine feed on the eggs, the young and the flightless adults if they can catch them. The Eskimos and Indians harvest these ducks in their flightless stage. Disease, parasites and accidents take their toll.

TABLE FARE: Because the pintail feeds primarily on vegetation, its flesh, like that of the mallard and black duck, is considered a delicacy.

Gadwall

Anas strepera

In the course of an Alaskan trip, on my way to the Alcan Highway, I drove through the heart of Canada's prairie provinces, which are the country's chief duck-rearing region. Potholes, ponds and lakes abound, and the surface of every one of them was stippled by the movement of myriads of ducks.

Early records speak of the gadwall as a very common duck, with large concentrations in some regions. I had never seen more than two dozen gadwalls together in all the time I had spent afield. And I didn't see that many together during my Alaskan trip, but in total I saw thousands of the birds. It seemed that every one of the countless bodies of water that I passed had at least one pair of gadwalls on it.

DESCRIPTION: The gadwall male averages 20 inches in length, has a wingspread of about 34 inches and weighs about 2 pounds. Its basic coloration is grayish brown. It has a dark bill and bright yellow feet. The head and neck are dark brown, while the chest and breast appear scaled with gray-black markings. The belly is white. The side feathers have very fine, light brown vermiculations, and

Gadwall

the back, tail and wings are dark brown. The speculum has three white feathers, making this the only "puddle" duck with white in its speculum. There are also some black speculum feathers as well as dark coverets in front of the speculum.

The female gadwall is slightly smaller, lighter in weight and definitely browner in coloration than the male. Her brown color is mottled rather than vermiculated. Her bill is slightly lighter in color than the male's, but her feet are just as yellow. Her wing color is identical to the male's.

DISTRIBUTION: Nowhere very common, the gadwall is usually found in mixed flocks with the pintail and widgeon. Its greatest concentrations occur in the Canadian prairie provinces during the breeding season. It winters in the United States in a crescent-shaped range that extends from Washington State down the Pacific coast, through the Gulf of Mexico states and up the Atlantic coast to New Jersey. I usually find a few gadwalls whenever I visit the Brigantine Wildlife Refuge across from Atlantic City. Most of the gadwalls winter in Mexico. The gadwall is found throughout the world in the North Temperate Zone, but records seem to indicate that it is not a common duck anywhere.

COMMUNICATION: Like the female mallard, the female gadwall has a much louder voice than her mate. In fact, it is hard to distinguish between the loud quacks of the female gadwall and the female mallard, even though the gadwall's call is higher pitched. The male gadwall has a low, reedy *cack, cack* call. He also has a shrill, whistled call that is used most frequently during the breeding season.

BREEDING AND NESTING: The gadwall is a southern duck and always seems reluctant to go north. Perhaps in time, through evolution, it will stay in its beloved southland, like many individuals of other species, notably Canada geese, that have become nonmigratory.

It is not known whether the gadwalls are paired up when they arrive on the breeding grounds, but they probably are, like most other ducks. There is always a considerable courtship display, which takes place both on the water and in the air.

When on the water, the male faces the female, extends his neck and gives a "burp" call. The female does a lot of very loud quacking, which stimulates the male to greater efforts. One of the actions is head-bobbing, with the head pumping up and down like a piston. The male also raises the rear portion of his folded wings. By raising his head and then bringing his bill down on his chest, he "bows" to the female. When he thinks she is interested enough, he swims away slowly, turning his head to watch her. If the female is interested, she turns her head sideways, gabbling all the while, as she swims after him.

The courtship flight usually involves two males and one female, which is why there is some doubt about the gadwalls being paired before they arrive on the breeding ground. As the two males approach the female on the water, she takes to the air but flies slowly. The males follow with a great deal of calling and whistling. Taking turns, one of the males flies in front of the female, sets his wings and shoots up in front of her, displaying the beautiful markings of his speculum. Then he drops back and the other performs the same display.

This isn't really a "gentlemen's" agreement worked out between the males because one male usually gets in more display turns than his rival and is then chosen by the female. When the flight is over, the female settles down on the water with her chosen mate. He approaches her, bowing and pressing his breast against her body. With his bill, he takes gentle nips at her feathers. When she is sufficiently stimulated she submerges her body and copulation takes place.

The gadwall always hides its nest very cunningly in or under the most dense vegetation in the area. The nest is seldom far from water but is usually placed in a dry spot well above the water level. It is a shallow depression made by the bird with her body and feet. Pieces of the local vegetation are used in its construction. The lining of down becomes heavier as the duck continues to brood because she is always plucking more down from her body and adding it to the nest.

EGGS AND YOUNG: The gadwall has a large clutch numbering from ten to twelve. These are a dull, creamy white and average 55 millimeters in length and 39 millimeters in diameter. Incubation takes twenty-eight days and is done entirely by the female. If disturbed while incubating, the gadwall is more than likely to abandon her nest altogether.

The baby gadwall's down is dark on the top of its head and the back of its neck. The top of its wings and the upper part of its body are also dark. The face, neck, breast and belly of the baby gadwall are a pale yellow. Its bill is yellow, its feet are pink. As it grows older, all of its down becomes paler, almost as if it were being bleached by the sun.

The young feed on insects when first hatched, but they soon convert to vegetation. As their down is replaced by feathers, they assume the quiet colors of the female. The fledgling period for the gadwall extends from fifty to sixty days.

At about the time the young are hatching, in the second half of June, the adult male gadwall goes into his eclipse plumage. Soon after, he loses his flight feathers.

FLIGHT: Since the gadwall is a "puddle" duck, it takes off by springing directly into the air. It hits a flight speed of about 45 miles per hour and habitually travels in an almost straight line and in a small flock of not more than a dozen or so birds.

MIGRATION: As already mentioned, the gadwall is a "southerner" at heart. It is one of the last ducks to head north, seldom arriving on its breeding grounds before May. It is also one of the first ducks to head back south and arrives back on its wintering grounds in early October.

HABITS: The gadwall is a sociable duck, and since it is comparatively scarce, it is often found mixed in with flocks of baldpate and pintails. It walks well because of its central leg placement and is often found walking about and feeding in grainfields and in the more open forests. It has been said that it was the breaking up of the original prairie sod that reduced the gadwall's numbers. The bird formerly nested extensively on the virgin prairie, and although it benefits from the cultivated grains that have replaced the virgin sod, this food value does not compensate for the loss of nesting sites.

FOOD: The gadwall is more of a vegetarian than any of our other puddle ducks, such food making up 98 percent of its diet. The 2 percent of animal matter is composed of insects and their larvae, small fish, beetles, tadpoles, crustaceans and mollusks. The percentage breakdown of the vegetable matter is as follows: pondweeds 42, sedges 20, algae 10, coontail 8, grasses 8, arrowheads 3, cultivated grains and miscellaneous plant food 7 percent. This duck feeds by tipping its rear end up in the manner of all puddle ducks. As the records show, it is more interested in leafy plant foods than in seeds.

LIFE SPAN: The gadwall normally has a potential life span of seven and a half years, but the longevity record goes to a bird that lived to be sixteen years old.

ENEMIES: The crow is probably the chief enemy, after man, and it preys mainly on the eggs. In the case of man it was the plow rather than the gun that did the greatest damage to the gadwall population. Magpies also destroy gadwall eggs. The raccoon, fox, coyote and skunk destroy nests by eating the eggs while the weasel, mink and otter take the young. Hawks, owls and eagles take the adults as well as the young. Disease, parasites and accidents also claim victims.

TABLE FARE: I have never eaten a gadwall, and I find that the consensus among other writers is split. Some claim that the flesh is good, although not on a par with that of the mallard. Others claim that the flesh is edible but not desirable. Most vegetarian creatures have highly palatable flesh, and there seems to be no reason why this should not be so in the case of the gadwall.

American Widgeon

Mareca americana

The American widgeon has two common names that are used interchangeably, widgeon of course being one, while the other is baldpate. Apart from about another dozen localized or colloquial names, the bird has one most appropriate nickname, "poacher."

The baldpate—the name I prefer to use—is a "puddle" duck which does most of its feeding in shallow water by upending itself on the surface. It has a special fondness for the roots of the wild celery plant, which grow at a considerable depth. Since it does not like to dive, the baldpate "poaches" the roots of the wild celery from the diving ducks, such as the canvasback, that can reach them more easily.

Not content to feed upon such pieces of the wild celery as the canvasback may drop, the baldpate tries to snatch the entire root when the canvasback surfaces. The canvasback is larger than the baldpate so it is most unlikely that it surrenders its food through fear. It is probably because of the persistence of the baldpate and the good nature of the canvasback that this pilfering is permitted.

DESCRIPTION: The first sight of the male baldpate shows why this, too, is such an appropriate name for this duck. The top of its head has white feathers that contrast markedly with the rest of its plumage and in fact suggest a bald head.

Behind the male's eye is a broad, bright green stripe. The cheeks, throat and neck are off-white, heavily spotted with black. The back, breast and sides have pinkish brown feathers that are finely marked with wavy black lines. The belly and the forepart of the wing are white. The speculum is green with a black upper border, and the primaries are brown. The bill is grayish blue.

The female does not have a bald pate. Her crown is dusky brown, and she lacks the green head stripe. Her cheeks, neck and throat are similar to the male's. Her back is a dusky brown, each feather having a light tan edge, and her sides are light brown. Her white belly shows more conspicuously than the male's when she is on the water because her side color does not extend as far down toward the belly as the male's. Her forewing does not have the bright white patch that the male displays but is a mottled brown and white. The speculum is a darker shade of brown than her primary feathers. Her bill and feet are a darker blue-gray than the male's.

DISTRIBUTION: The American widgeon has a large range that covers, at some season, all of the United States and most of Canada and Alaska. Its winter range extends along the fringe of the Pacific, Atlantic and Gulf coasts, Texas, New Mexico, Arizona and Old Mexico. Its breeding range reaches roughly from the Rocky Mountains east to the Mississippi River, from Wyoming north through Canada's prairie provinces, British Columbia, the Yukon and into Alaska.

COMMUNICATION: The male baldpate sometimes quacks, but his usual call is a fairly high, three-note whistle that sounds *whew, whew, whew.* The female has a hoarse quack and also makes a guttural *qurr, qurr, qurr* sound that warns the little ones of danger.

BREEDING AND NESTING: The baldpates do not pair up on their wintering grounds, arriving north on their breeding ground in small flocks. There is much rivalry among the males for the favors of the females.

Although there is almost a fifty-fifty ratio between the sexes, during the breeding season as many as five or six males court the same female. It could be reasonably conjectured that one female is more receptive to the males because her egg-laying processes are more advanced than those of her sisters. It would be natural for an early breeder to get the first attention. Then, as the other females' bodies become ready, they begin to be courted. There is almost no surplus of unmated males or females during the height of the breeding season.

The males gather on the water in a circle about the desired female. They are loud in their proclamations of love, and their *whew-whew-whew* calls fill the air. Each male displays by keeping his wings folded but elevating the rear portion. Both male and female also partially extend their wings and preen behind them. This displays the male's beautiful speculum.

The courting flight of the baldpate is similar to that of the gadwall but much swifter. The baldpates twist and turn through the air at high speeds, the male zooming under, then up in front of the female to display before dropping back again.

There is actually very little body contact between rival males, but quite a bit of threatening and a great deal of noise. When the female has selected one of the available males, she follows him about on the water, and both the male and female engage in the head-bobbing ritual. Almost immediately after, the pair retire to whatever pothole or pond the male has selected as his individual territory. This territory is then defended by the male against any other duck of the same species, male or female. Quite frequently, the male baldpate will tolerate no other duck of any species on his territory if it is a small one.

The baldpate's nest is often built at a considerable distance from water—and inexplicably so. This duck insists upon a dry location for its nest, but it often disregards ideal nesting sites that are close to the water. The nest may or may not be concealed. It is usually in a depression in the earth, made of leaves or stems and lined with down.

EGGS AND YOUNG: The baldpate's clutch of eggs usually contains between nine and eleven eggs. They are creamy white in color and average 53 millimeters in length by 38 millimeters in diameter. Incubation takes twenty-four or twenty-five days and is performed by the female alone.

The down of the baby baldpate is light yellow on the belly and a darker brownish yellow on the breast and face. The top of the head, back of the neck, back and wings are dark brown. The feet and bill are grayish blue.

The hazardous trip from the nest to water is started as soon as the young baldpate's down is dry. The female baldpate is a courageous mother, and if her young are threatened or disturbed, she puts on a diversionary display to allow the little ones to escape. She flops around, drags her wing as if it were broken and splashes about if she is on water. When she has decoyed the danger away from her young or feels that they are safely hidden, she flies from the area, returning only when this does not endanger the young.

The fledgling period for the young baldpate from hatching to flight lasts about two months.

FLIGHT: At about the time that the female starts her incubation, the male goes into his eclipse period. He loses his bright head color and his flight feathers. The males usually gather together during this flightless period on some fairly large body of water that has ample vegetation cover. The male acquires his flight feathers at about the same time as the young. The female goes into her post-nuptial molt later than the male and so is flightless for a period before and after her young are starting to fly.

The baldpate is a strong, swift flier capable of hitting speeds of 50 or 55 miles per hour. Its wings make a very audible whistling sound in flight. The birds fly in small, compact flocks that can be identified at a distance by their constant turning, twisting flight pattern. The baldpate seldom flies at a great height even during migration.

MIGRATION: The baldpate has a very leisurely migration, seldom arriving on its breeding grounds before the end of May. Although it may start south around the first of September, it dawdles and does not reach its wintering grounds until late November.

HABITS: The baldpate is a favorite with hunters because its speedy, twisting flight presents a real challenge. The bird is naturally wary, and exposure to gunning soon convinces the baldpate that it should move somewhere else, very smartly.

Apart from the canvasback, a favorite target for the baldpate's piracy is the American coot, which also feeds upon deep-growing water plants. Apparently the baldpate sees the coot coming up from the bottom because when it breaks the surface of the water, the baldpate is there to share its prize. The coots give little indication that this pilfering really bothers them, perhaps because they themselves are constantly stealing food from other coots. They seem to have a true communistic approach to life; everyone shares in what anyone has.

FOOD: Vegetable matter makes up 93 percent of the baldpate's diet, animal matter the remaining 7 percent. Mollusks, insects, their larvae, beetles, crickets, grasshoppers and leeches are consumed by the baldpate, the young ones eating more of this material than the adults. The vegetable matter is rated at the following percentages: pondweeds 43, grasses 3½, algae 7, sedges 7, wild celery 6, water milfoils 3½, duckweed 2, smartweed 1½, arrow grass, water lilies, coontail and other miscellaneous vegetation making up the balance.

LIFE SPAN: The baldpate has a potential life span of about seven years, the longevity record being held by a bird that lived to be nine years and four months old.

ENEMIES: Prairie fires, drought, disease, parasites and accidents are all factors that control the baldpate population. Predators that destroy the eggs, such as the crow, raccoon, skunk, fox, coyote, and those that kill the young and adults, such as hawks, owls, eagles, mink and otter, are further contributing but not controlling factors.

TABLE FARE: The baldpate is rated very high as a table bird.

OVERLEAF ▶

Surface-Feeding Ducks

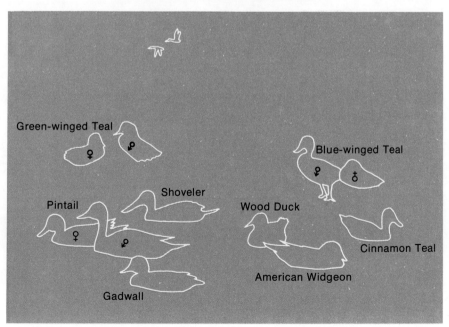

Shoveler

Spatula clypeata

Often one wonders how a certain creature came by its name. For example, why is the small bird called a dickcissel so named? On the other hand some names are just so fitting that they go unquestioned. A perfect example of that is the shoveler duck. Both its common and its Latin name *Spatula* take into account the tremendous size of this duck's bill. The duck in fact uses its bill as if it were a shovel as it scoops up its food.

DESCRIPTION: The male shoveler duck is an average 20 inches in length, has a wingspread of 32 inches and weighs 1⅓ pounds. Its bill is much longer than its head and much wider at the tip than at the base. This duck is a regular "old ski-nose." The bill is dark bluish gray in color. The male's head and neck are dark green with a purplish iridescence. The breast is white, the center of the back bluish brown, each feather having a lighter tip. The rump and the tail are blackish green. The forepart of the wing is blue, the speculum green, bordered top and bottom by white, the primaries grayish brown. The belly and sides of this duck are chestnut brown. The eye is orange, and the feet are red.

The female shoveler is slightly smaller in size and lighter in weight than the male. She is a brown duck, her head and neck being grayish brown, streaked with dark brown. Her back, sides, rump and upper tail coverts are dark brown with light buff edgings and markings. Her breast, belly and under tail coverts are a buff brown with lighter brown markings. Her feet are orange. Although her bill is large, like the male's, it is a lighter blue-gray.

DISTRIBUTION: The shoveler duck is world-wide in distribution, being found in North and South America, Europe, Asia, Africa and even in Australia. It is a common bird throughout its wide range and, because of its spatulate bill, easily recognized and noted.

Shoveler

In North America it visits all the forty-eight contiguous states during some of the seasons and most of the Canadian provinces except the Arctic. It winters along the Pacific coast from Washington south and right through Arizona, New Mexico, Texas, along the Gulf states and up the Atlantic coast as far as New Jersey. It is a very common winter resident at the Brigantine National Wildlife Refuge. The majority of shovelers winter in Mexico.

The summer breeding range extends from California east through Wyoming, Nebraska, Iowa to Wisconsin, and north through the prairie provinces of Canada to the Yukon and Alaska. There are breeding records, too, for Ohio, Pennsylvania and New York.

COMMUNICATION: The shoveler is not a talkative duck. Both male and female have a quack that is much softer than that of the female mallard. The male also has a low, guttural *woh, woh, woh, woh* call. It may not be termed communication, but the most commonly heard sound of the shoveler is that of the water being pulled into its mouth and then forced out through the bill's lamellae as the duck feeds. This noise can be heard from afar.

BREEDING AND NESTING: When traveling to its breeding grounds, the shoveler duck flies in small flocks, and apparently mate selection takes place after the birds have arrived there.

The shoveler is not a very demonstrative duck, and both male and female carry on a courtship that is almost "stuffy" in its propriety. Maybe the ducks do not want to call attention to what we humans might call their "aberrant" sexual relations. The shovelers engage in polyandry.

The male faces the female, giving out a little "burp" call, and then pretends to feed. Next he flies toward the female, making a rattling sound with his wing pinions. When he lands near her, both male and female go through the head-bobbing ritual that precedes copulation.

The shovelers sometimes engage in a courtship flight. This usually occurs only when there are two males present. The flight may well occur when the attentions of the two males create too much pressure for the female on the water. The flight would then be more of an escape than a display.

The female takes off from the water closely pursued by the two males, and the ensuing flight is proof of their mastery of the air. Twisting, turning, rolling, banking, the ducks zoom back and forth, high and low, until one of the males, usually the younger, finds himself outclassed and drops behind. Then the ducks drop down to the water, where copulation takes place. Even though one of the drakes may have dropped behind in flight, he shares in the copulation; he has to wait his turn, however.

Where two males are "married" to one female, there seems to be little animosity between the males. Apparently that drab little female is a feathered "sex bomb" capable of satisfying two males. Frequently one of the two males is an immature bird that has not found a young mate of its own and so shares the favors of the "older woman" with her husband. This situation is due not to an excess of males in the shoveler duck population but to the fact that many of the year-old females are not mature enough to mate during their first year. In most types of wildlife and even among humans, it is most unusual for the males to reach sexual maturity before the females, but this does happen with shoveler ducks.

The nest of the shoveler duck may be in boggy areas very close to water or it may be a long distance from water on a bone-dry hilltop; there is no universal pattern when it comes to placement. A favorite location, however, seems to be in the cover of high, rank grass in moist areas. Most of the nests are rudimentary hollows scraped in the ground, constructed of grass and weed stems and lined with down.

EGGS AND YOUNG: Ten eggs are an average-sized clutch for the shoveler duck, although nests have been found with as many as fourteen or fifteen eggs. The eggs vary in color from a pale gray-green to a pale olive-buff that is very similar to the color of mallards' eggs. In size the eggs average 52 millimeters in length by 37 millimeters in diameter.

When the clutch is complete, the males leave the female to her chore of incubation, which takes twenty-one to twenty-three days.

When the ducklings hatch they are easy to recognize because from the start there is evidence of the oversized bill which is their claim to fame. Their down is dark brown over the top of the head, down the back of their necks and their backs. There is also a brown eye stripe. The ducklings' face, cheeks, neck and breast are brownish yellow, and the belly is a lighter yellow. The feet are yellowish orange, while the bill is grayish at the base, pale yellow on the forepart and has a pinkish tip.

The young are shepherded by the female to the pond, where they feed heavily upon insect life.

FLIGHT: The fledgling period for the ducklings is about two months. The adult male has gone through its eclipse period and regained its powers of flight by about the time that the young ones are experiencing the thrill of being airborne. The female during this period is in her postnuptial molt and is flightless. By September, all the shovelers are flying.

The shoveler duck is a speedy flier and has been clocked by automobiles at 53 miles per hour without the duck exerting itself. If really pushed, it could probably do 60 to 65 miles per hour and much more with a favorable tail wind. Its flight can be extremely acrobatic and dexterous, like that of the teal.

In migration, the shovelers fly in small flocks and comparatively low. Their flight is usually steady unless disturbed.

MIGRATION: Like the baldpate and the gadwall, the shoveler duck lingers on its wintering grounds until the northern sloughs and ponds are entirely ice-free. Although it may start north at the end of March, it does not reach its northern breeding ground for another five or six weeks. In the fall the migration south starts as soon as the birds can fly, and they arrive on their wintering grounds by the middle of October.

HABITS: The shoveler duck is not a saltwater bird. It much prefers to feed in fresh water, particularly where the ponds and streams are shallow and muddy. It is found along the coast in winter, but in areas where the fresh water remains unfrozen. Its dislike of salt water has determined the bird's winter range, forcing it to go far enough south to find ice-free fresh water.

The shoveler is a "puddle" duck with centrally placed legs that facilitate walking. It springs directly into the air on takeoff and then levels off into its swift flight.

The birds are very sociable, and although they are often in company with their own kind, more frequently they associate with other species of ducks. As it is sociable, the shoveler is comparatively easy to decoy, coming into the blocks set out for other ducks. Though not an exceptionally wary bird, if shot at and missed, it soon learns and may change its habits, feeding exclusively under cover of darkness.

The shoveler duck usually feeds by skimming food from the surface of the water. When in the company of other species of ducks, it usually tags along behind them, its bill going like a vacuum cleaner, picking up food particles that some of the other ducks may have dropped. It also seines off food from the surface of the water that the other ducks can't touch. The shoveler sometimes tips up to feed but almost never dives below the surface to secure food.

The oversized bill of the shoveler is a very efficient separating device. The lamellae, or tooth-like serrations, that are present in most ducks' bills, are so enlarged in the shoveler that they form bristly protuberances. Like the bird called the skimmer, the shoveler has a beak especially adapted for feeding. The shoveler's tongue is endowed with sensitive taste organs which tell the duck what to retain as food and what to reject as waste material. This duck almost always sits on the water with its body inclined forward so that its rump is considerably higher than its head. It thoroughly enjoys walking about on the mud flats, cramming its bill down into the ooze in a search for food particles.

FOOD: Sixty-six percent of the shoveler's diet is vegetable matter, and the remaining 34 percent is animal matter. Mollusks, crustaceans, insects and fish make up the latter, while the duck's favorite plant foods are pondweed, bulrush, spike rush, salt grass, algae, water lily, sedge, widgeon grass, wild millet and duckweed.

LIFE SPAN: The shoveler duck has a potential life span of about seven years, yet the oldest shoveler on record lived to be only five and a half years.

ENEMIES: Of the shoveler's many enemies, some eat the eggs, others the young, others the adults and some take their prey in all three stages. The predators include snapping turtles, raccoons, skunks, foxes, coyotes, opossums, crows, hawks, eagles and owls. Disease, parasites and accidents take their toll.

TABLE FARE: The high incidence of animal material in the shoveler's diet affects the taste of the flesh and so makes this duck less than desirable for human consumption. When the shoveler is on a vegetable diet, it is much more palatable.

Thin white ring around the neck is the identifying mark of the mallard drake.

Crest erected, the hooded merganser drake displays a white cockade behind his eye. His bill is long, narrow and toothed.

Shoveler duck is distinguished by its long bill that is wider at the tip than at the base.

Blue-winged Teal

Anas discors

It is interesting to read the reports of our early naturalists and hunters on the flight speed of the blue-winged teal.

John James Audubon, in 1840, said: "The flight of the blue-winged teal is extremely rapid and well sustained. Indeed, I have thought that, when traveling, it passes through the air with a speed equal to that of the passenger pigeon."

Doctor Yorke wrote in 1899: "They travel at the rate of about one hundred thirty miles per hour, exceeded only by the green-winged teal."

Dr. L. C. Sanford, in 1903, describes how "at the approach of evening the first line [of blue-winged teal] appears over the tops of the rush grass, flying low and with a speed possessed only by a teal. Another minute and they have passed; the rush of their wings told how closely they came; but no one but an old hand could have stopped one."

Mr. Dwight M. Huntington, in 1903, writes: "I was almost in despair, when I fired at a passing flock, holding the gun a yard or more before the leading birds, and at the report a single teal, some distance behind the others, fell dead. I at once began shooting long distances ahead of the passing ducks, and before long I had a large bag of birds."

The blue-winged teal is a fast-flying duck, but its reputation has always flown faster than the bird.

DESCRIPTION: The adult male blue-winged teal is about 15½ inches in length, has a wingspan of roughly 24 inches and weighs approximately 14 ounces. Its most conspicuous feature is a crescent of white that extends from the top of the head to the chin in front of the eye. There is also a distinctive white patch on both sides at the base of the tail. The head and neck are slate-gray. The back, rump and tail are dark brown with a buff edging to each feather. The breast, belly and sides are light brown, heavily spotted with black. The lesser and greater coverts of the upper wing are a light, bright blue, which earns this duck its name. A white border separates this color from the speculum, whose center feathers are light green, while the end feathers are dark green. The primary feathers and their coverts are grayish brown. The lesser and greater coverts of the underwing are white. The bill is blue-gray, the eye brown, and the feet are a dull yellow.

The female blue-winged teal lacks the male's facial crescent, but she has a white spot behind the bill and a white throat. Her head and neck are off-white streaked with dark brown. Her back, rump and tail are dark brown with a light edge to each feather. Her breast and sides are brown with a light brown edging, so that the feathers seem to be scales. Her belly is white. Her wings, bill and feet are almost identical to the male's except that the colors are not as deep or vivid.

DISTRIBUTION: The blue-winged teal is found throughout the forty-eight contiguous states and most of Canada. Its winter range is the coast of Connecticut, New York, New Jersey, Delaware, Maryland, Virginia and North Carolina. It also covers South Carolina, Georgia, Florida, Alabama, Mississippi, Louisiana and Texas. Most of the birds winter in Mexico, Central America and portions of South America.

This teal's breeding range extends from Nevada east to Pennsylvania and New York, stops at the Great Lakes and then swings north to the Yukon. Except for strays, the bird does not breed in either the Atlantic or Pacific coastal regions.

COMMUNICATION: The blue-winged teal is usually silent. When in flight it sometimes makes a twittering sound. The female has a weak quack, while the drake emits a hissing, whistled peep.

Blue-winged Teal

BREEDING AND NESTING: This duck is so reluctant to leave the southland where it spends the winter that it is one of the last ducks to arrive on its breeding grounds. This spring lateness practically guarantees that the teal are paired up by the time they reach their breeding destination, and the courtship displays take place while they are migrating northward.

The blue-winged teal have quite elaborate courtship rituals which take place both on the wing and on the water. The flight ritual is more of a pursuit than a display and usually involves three ducks, two males and one female. It is a flight of stamina and ability, as the ducks go through all the acrobatic twisting and turning for which this species is so justifiably famous.

On the water the female may instigate the action by uttering a *rrrr* call note. The male responds by swimming to or with the female and going through a chin-lifting motion, occasionally giving off his soft, whistled notes. He also engages in a very ritualized feeding display for the benefit of the female. When the male up-ends, as if to feed, he shows the female the bright colors of his legs —and color plays an extremely important part in the sexual attraction of birds. Both the male and female engage in a head-bobbing gesture just before copulation takes place.

The female blue-winged teal selects widely varying locations for her nest. The typical nest is a well-formed hollow lined with dry grass and down, set under a clump of grass. Such a nest is exceedingly difficult to find because of the grass "roof." Other possible locations are among clumps of cattails, on hillsides and often on top of or in the side of a muskrat house. One common feature of all the nests is that even if the area is wet, the nest and eggs are dry.

EGGS AND YOUNG: The blue-winged teal, like the green-winged teal, is very prolific. Although some nests have been found with fifteen eggs, the usual number is ten or twelve. The eggs average 46 millimeters in length by 33 millimeters in diameter. The color of the eggs varies from a dull to a greenish white.

Incubation is performed solely by the female, who is abandoned by the male as soon as she begins to incubate. The incubation period may last from twenty-one to twenty-three days. When the female has to leave the eggs to seek food and water, she covers them completely with a blanket of down and grass to prevent detection and a rapid loss of heat.

The young blue-winged teal all hatch within a few hours of each other and stay in the nest for another two to four hours while they regain the strength expended in freeing themselves from their shells. Like all newly hatched birds, the young do not have to eat at once because they have body reserves that tide them over for at least twenty-four to thirty-six hours. However, as soon as they leave the nest they begin to feed upon any tiny insect that moves slowly enough to be captured. They pick at any bright, shiny object and through a process of trial and error learn what to eat and what to reject.

The baby blue-winged teal has a dark crown, back of the neck and back. Its face, throat, neck, breast and belly are pale yellow and its feet and bill light yellow. The young of both sexes in their juvenile plumage, as well as the male in his eclipse plumage, closely resemble the female in coloration.

FLIGHT: The ducklings develop rapidly and are fledged and able to fly after about six weeks. This compensates for their parents' late arrival on the breeding grounds and their early departure.

The blue-winged teal has a normal flight speed of just over 50 miles per hour, but anything above that has to be credited to the wind. The early speed estimates were strictly guesswork because they were made before there was equipment available to clock the actual speed of the ducks. Most records of the speeds of various types of wildlife are established by comparing the creature's speed with the known speed of a moving automobile, train or plane or with a stopwatch over a measured distance.

Although the blue-winged teal is a strong, fast flier, it is not capable of keeping up with some of the larger, heavier and stronger ducks such as the mallard, pintail and canvasback. The gyrations of a massed flock of blue-winged teal help to identify these ducks as teal at even a great distance, but binoculars are needed to identify the particular species.

MIGRATION: As already mentioned, the blue-winged teal is among the last arrivals on its northern breeding grounds. Long before it arrives, the baldpate, gadwall, pintail, shoveler and other ducks have already taken up residence and in most cases set up housekeeping.

The bluewings usually start north after the first of March and seldom reach their northern destination until after the first of May. At the end of August the direction is reversed, and the blue-winged teal leads the migration parade south. Again the journey takes two months or even more.

HABITS: The blue-winged teal does not like a large expanse of water but prefers the smaller potholes, bayous and lagoons. Although it sometimes feeds along the coast, it has a decided preference for fresh rather than saline water. Although not noted as a wary bird, it may prefer the greater protection that small bodies of water afford through the proximity of the shoreline grasses.

The bluewings circle an area repeatedly before they alight, as if checking it out for potential danger. Or it may be that, like a flock of pigeons, they just enjoy their version of "follow the leader" in their swooping, stooping flight.

This teal has adapted better than most of the other ducks to man's encroachment on its habitat. The ditching and draining of so much of its native marshland has cut down its population, yet its numbers have not plummeted as drastically as those of some of the less adaptable species. The blue-winged teal not only has made its abode near civilization, in many cases it nests on lakes right in the heart of towns and cities.

Since the blue-winged teal is a "puddle" duck, it feeds on or near the surface of the water. It may dive under the water to escape from danger, but it seldom does so to feed.

FOOD: Twenty-nine percent of the bluewing's diet is animal matter such as small mollusks, insects and their larvae, crustaceans, snails, worms and tadpoles.

The 71 percent of its diet that is made up of plant material can be broken down in the following percentages: sedges 18, pond-weeds 12, grasses 12, smartweed 8, algae 3, with water lilies, water milfoil, bur reeds and other miscellaneous plants making up the balance. Cultivated grains such as rice and corn are also favorite foods.

LIFE SPAN: Most blue-winged teal do not live out their potential life span of about seven years. The longest substantiated life record for this teal appears to be four years. There must, however, be a number of unbanded birds that live longer than this.

ENEMIES: Raccoons, skunks, foxes, coyotes, ground squirrels and crows destroy a great many blue-winged teal nests by consuming the eggs. Fleet as this teal is in flight, it is preyed upon by hawks and eagles. Disease, parasites and accidents take their toll.

TABLE FARE: The blue-winged teal, like the green-winged teal, grows very fat on the abundant food that is available to it. Its flesh is highly praised by gourmets and is eagerly sought by thousands of hunters who do not claim to have an educated palate.

Cinnamon Teal

Anas cyanoptera

The naming of the cinnamon teal has led to quite a bit of confusion. Its commonly accepted English name of "cinnamon" is most apt. However, the latter part of its Latin name *cyanoptera* means "blue-winged," and again this is most apt. But this bird cannot be called the blue-winged teal because there is already a duck with this common name, although its Latin name *discors* means not "blue-winged" but, quite unaccountably, "out of harmony."

The blue patterning of the blue-winged teal's wing is identical to that of the cinnamon teal's wing. If anything, the blue-winged teal has a bit more green on its wing secondaries than the cinnamon teal, but it can't be called a green-winged teal because there is already a teal of this name. And, once again, the green-winged teal's Latin name does not mean "green-winged." All this nomenclature is certainly very confusing and incongruous!

DESCRIPTION: The adult male cinnamon teal is 15¾ inches in length, has a 24½-inch wingspan and weighs about 12 ounces. The bird is well named because its plumage is a rich chestnut-cinnamon. This color is found on the bird's head, neck, shoulders, breast, belly and flanks. His back and rump are a mottled brown, his tail is plain brown. The greater and middle wing coverts are a bright powder blue, the lesser coverts are white, and the speculum is bright green. The primary wing feathers are brown. The legs and feet are orange-yellow, the eye is orange and the bill black.

During the male's eclipse period, the rich cinnamon color of his plumage is replaced with a soft, mottled brown. In this phase, the male cinnamon teal and male blue-winged teal are almost identical, the cinnamon teal being slightly browner and the blue-winged slightly grayer.

The adult female cinnamon teal is about the same size as the male and therefore slightly smaller than the female blue-winged teal. The latter has a white chin and a speck of white behind the bill which the female cinnamon teal lacks. It is very difficult to tell these two ducks apart.

The female cinnamon teal is a softly mottled brown over her entire body. Her wings are almost identical to the male's except that her primaries are lighter in color.

DISTRIBUTION: The cinnamon teal is strictly a western duck; it is almost never seen as far east as the Mississippi River. Its winter range is the western half of Old Mexico with perhaps a few of the ducks lingering on in southern Arizona.

The cinnamon teal's breeding range includes Arizona, New Mexico, California, Colorado, Utah, Nevada, Wyoming, Montana, Idaho, Oregon, Washington, British Columbia and Alberta. The duck is quite common within the confines of its range. I saw large numbers of this teal on the impounded waters of Shasta Dam in northern California. It is unique in that it is very common in South America, having a breeding and wintering range on that continent. The birds of North and South America do not intermingle.

COMMUNICATION: As is common with ducks, the female of this species is much more vocal than her mate. However, neither sex is really very noisy, their main call being a soft, weak quack that sounds *gach-gach-ga-ga*. The male has been heard to give a low, rattling, chattering call.

BREEDING AND YOUNG: During the courtship period, both the male and female engage in the head-bobbing display. The male is much more active than the female, his head bobbing up and down like a valve tappet. When the female bobs her head, it usually signifies acceptance of the male.

The competition between the males is fierce, and they swim at each other with extended necks and open bills. Even after the female has made her choice and accepted a mate, the unmated males continue to display for her. The mated male must constantly chase his rivals away and is usually successful in doing so; his problem is rather keeping them away. Sometimes the female joins her mate in driving off the unwanted males, while at other times she just swims docilely behind him as he does his best to eliminate the competition.

Occasionally, the males of two mated pairs join together in a game that contains no animosity and seems to be a duck's version of leapfrog. One male swims at the other, and when he gets close, flies up and over the other male. It always looks as though the duck were jumping, but it is highly improbable that, without the use of his wings, he could leap over his companion.

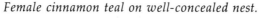

Female cinnamon teal on well-concealed nest.

The cinnamon teal's nest is constructed by the female of whatever grasses are found in the area. It is usually on dry land but as near to water as the availability of good cover allows. This teal does her utmost to provide good concealment for the nest, utilizing dense stands of grass or hiding it under bushes with low-growing branches. Only rarely is the nest located where it can become damp. The bowl of the nest is usually at least 6 inches in diameter and about 3 inches in depth. Copious amounts of down are added to the lining of the nest, more for warmth and as a covering for the eggs than for softness.

EGGS AND YOUNG: The cinnamon teal lays a large clutch of eggs. Although some nests have been found with as many as fourteen eggs in them, the average clutch numbers ten to twelve eggs. The shells vary in color from pure white to a light pinkish buff. The eggs average 47 millimeters in length by 34 millimeters in diameter.

Incubation requires twenty-three to twenty-four days and is done exclusively by the female, although the male does not entirely desert the female at this time. There have been many recorded instances where the male has assisted the female in the rearing of the young. This is a most unusual occurrence among ducks. In some cases, the male became more solicitous of the young's safety than the female. When danger came near, it was the male that became agitated, while the female seemed to be not in the least concerned. When the male was nearby and on guard, the female went on with her feeding or preening or whatever activity she was engaged in. If no male was in the area, then the female remained on the alert.

If danger approaches, the adult ducks use the broken-wing ruse in an attempt to call attention to themselves, thus providing the little ones with a chance to escape undetected. The young are quick to take advantage of the slightest diversion, and in the blink of an eye, they disappear under whatever vegetation is in or on the water. Neither do they hesitate to abandon the water and hide among the dense vegetation that usually clothes the banks and shorelines.

The baby cinnamon teal is a vividly colored duckling with a bright yellow face, throat, neck, breast and belly. The yellow is less bright on the belly than on the head, but the shading is gradual and subtle. There is even a yellow cast to the brown down of this duckling's back. The top of the head, back of the neck, back, wings, rump and tail are a light reddish brown. There is a distinct brown stripe that passes through the center of the duckling's eye. The feet and bill are pale yellow.

The ducklings feed exclusively on insects when they first hatch, but at a very early age, they begin to pick up the seeds of the various types of water weeds. Soon, they are feeding on vegetation.

FLIGHT: The young cinnamon teal are capable of flying about six weeks after hatching.

All the teal are good, strong fliers, and the cinnamon teal is no exception. It jumps up from the water into the air and is off on the twisting, erratic flight that is typical of all the teal. As it is a comparatively small duck, its speed is not as great as it is usually reputed to be. It can fly at speeds of up to 45 miles per hour. It is only during migration that this teal flies in fairly large flocks. Most of the time it is found flying only in single family groups.

MIGRATION: The cinnamon teal does not have an exceptionally long migration flight. It is apparently in no great hurry to get to its breeding grounds, and the main northward migration does not get under way until the latter part of March of the first part of April. It is equally slow in getting started on the southward trip in the fall, which does not begin until the end of September or the first part of October.

HABITS: The cinnamon teal cannot be considered a sociable duck because it is seldom, if ever, found in large flocks of its own kind and rarely mixes with other duck species. Yet it decoys well as it is rather tame and unsuspicious.

This teal likes the shallow edges of the ponds and sloughs that it inhabits. It does not care for deep water and does all its feeding on the surface. It is not recorded as ever diving underwater to feed and in most cases does not tip up as most of the "puddle" ducks do. Its feeding habits are very similar to those of the shoveler duck in that it strains most of its food from the surface of the water and likes to poke about in the mud at the very edge of the water. Some experts claim that the cinnamon teal is an evolutionary link between the shoveler duck and the rest of the teal family.

FOOD: Eighty percent of the cinnamon teal's diet is composed of vegetable matter. Its favorite foods are the seeds and various parts of sedges, pondweeds, bulrush, horned pondweed, salt grass, widgeon grass, smartweed, dock and spike rush.

The 20 percent of its diet that is made up of animal matter consists of mollusks, beetles, dragonfly and damselfly nymphs, snails, and some bivalves.

LIFE SPAN: The cinnamon teal has a potential life span of from seven to nine years. The only longevity record that I can find for this duck falls far short of its potential, since the banded individual in question lived to be four and a half years old.

ENEMIES: Predation on all ducks is heavy and constant. The cinnamon teal, however, is noted as a persistent nester, and although its nest is often destroyed by predators, the female makes a second and even a third attempt until at last she is successful in hatching her brood. Coyotes probably rank about as high as crows on this teal's list of enemies. Foxes, raccoons, skunks, opossums, magpies, hawks, eagles, owls, snakes and turtles make an impressive line-up of enemies, yet the teal can overcome their combined onslaught. The draining of the breeding sloughs and ponds, however, it cannot overcome, so that man is as usual at the head of the destructive forces arrayed against this duck. Disease, parasites and accidents also take their toll.

TABLE FARE: During the season that the teal is hunted, it is feeding almost exclusively on vegetation, and so its flesh is at its peak. This duck ranks high as table fare. Because of the southern location of its wintering range, the cinnamon teal is hunted mostly in Mexico.

Green-winged Teal

Anas carolinensis

The green-winged teal is frequently found on the ponds formed by beaver dams. In Yellowstone National Park there is a small stream where the beaver have made a series of step dams that do not flood the surrounding land but create a succession of deep pools. While photographing some of these step dams in the course of a wildlife expedition I discovered a female green-winged teal. It was early September, and she was alone, her family having already flown away. Her flight feathers were not yet fully developed, and she could not fly. She therefore sought refuge in the dense vegetation that grew along the sides of the stream. Once I had found her and worked with her, taking some photographs, she became quite tame and actually paid little attention to me unless I moved.

DESCRIPTION: The green-winged teal is, with the bufflehead, the smallest North American duck. The adult male is 14 inches in length, has a wingspread of 23 inches and weighs about 12 ounces.

The male ranks second only to the wood duck in beauty of plumage. His head and neck are a rich cinnamon brown. There is a wide, bright iridescent green stripe on his head that starts in front of the eye and goes to the nape of the neck. His shoulders, back and side feathers are light gray with very fine, dark vermiculations. The breast is light brown with darker brown spots, and the belly is white. A vertical white line separates the breast color from that of the sides. The upper wing coverts and primary feathers are brownish gray. The speculum has four or five feathers that match the bright green stripe on the head. The rest of the speculum feathers are dark green with a white border on the trailing edge. There are white patches on the underwing coverts. The bill is dark bluish gray, while the feet are light gray.

The female green-winged teal is slightly smaller in size and lighter in weight than her mate. Her head has a dark crown, her throat, chin and a spot behind the bill are white. The rest of her head, her neck, breast, back and side feathers are light to dark brown with a white edging. Her belly is white. On the top of the wing, the lesser and middle coverts are gray and the secondary coverts white. Half the feathers of the speculum are bright green, while the others are a very dark green. The trailing edge of the speculum is bordered with white, and the primary feathers are gray. On the underwing the lining is white, except for the leading edge, the speculum and the primaries. The feet and the forepart of the bill are bluish, whereas the base of the bill is pinkish.

Occasionally the European common teal is found on the east coast of the United States. The male common teal is almost identical to the male green-winged teal, except that the American teal has a vertical white line behind its breast, while the European teal has a horizontal white line above the wing.

DISTRIBUTION: The winter range of the green-winged teal stretches from the state of Washington down the Pacific coast into Old Mexico. Its eastern limit runs in an arc down through Montana, Wyoming, Kansas, Oklahoma, Arkansas, Mississippi, Alabama, Georgia and swings up to include South Carolina, North Carolina and Virginia.

The breeding range extends from California east to Iowa, north to Canada's Arctic region and west to Alaska.

In migration, these little ducks touch most of the other forty-eight states.

Green-winged Teal

COMMUNICATION: The voice of the green-winged teal fits its size. The male chirps and has a short, high-pitched whistle; the female has a soft quack. During the breeding season the male has a soft *pheep, pheep* call.

BREEDING AND NESTING: The green-winged teal are usually paired up before they reach their northern breeding grounds. The birds start their migration early and take so long to get to their final destination that most of the courtship rituals are done during migration.

In the performance of their courting rites, the male greenwings look like animated toys. The rite is very stylized and almost appears to be choreographed. One male follows directly behind another as they swim slowly and deliberately about the female. Uttering their *pheep, pheep* call, the males begin to bob their heads up and down as they swim. At intervals, one of the males lifts his wings and with wildly thrashing feet, stands upright on the surface of the water. When one male tires he sinks back into the water and the other male goes through the same procedure. This performance is repeated a great many times. Although the female does not seem unduly impressed by the males' display, she eventually chooses one of them as a mate.

When the teal finally arrive on their breeding grounds, they promptly select a nest site and the egg-laying gets under way. The nest may be constructed of the long grass that grows along the edge of the prairie potholes. Hidden among such grass, the nest is very difficult to locate. It is frequently built at a considerable distance from water on a dry hillside and is sometimes hidden among the trees of the taiga forests. In this case it is usually in a slight depression in the ground and is built of grass and leaves and lined with down. The green-winged teal seems to build its nest in as many different sites as the mallard duck. In keeping with the bird's diminutive size, the nest is only about 6 inches in diameter.

EGGS AND YOUNG: The green-winged teal lays large clutches of eggs. Although ten to twelve eggs constitute an average clutch, there is a record of one female teal that had eighteen eggs. The eggs range in color from a dull off-white to a pale olive buff. They average 45 millimeters in length by 34 millimeters in diameter.

The incubation is done by the female over a period of twenty-one to twenty-three days. The male's contribution to the family is the fertilizing of the eggs, and he leaves the female as soon as she starts to incubate.

The young green-winged teal has a darker yellow down on its face, neck and belly than most other ducklings. Like them it has a single dark stripe that runs through the eye and beyond, but it also has a second stripe running through the cheek. The crown, back of the neck and upper half of the body are covered with dark brown down. The feet are gray-blue, and the bill has a dark center with a lighter edge.

The green-winged teal has a fledgling period of about six weeks from the time it hatches until it can fly.

The female green-winged teal is a very courageous mother and employs many ruses to decoy danger away from her young. It is only after her young are capable of flying that she goes into her postnuptial molt and becomes flightless.

FLIGHT: The green-winged teal is a "puddle" duck that can take off amazingly fast by jumping directly into the air. It is a strong flier, but it is not as fast as is commonly thought. Because of its small size it gives a false impression of speed. It can fly at speeds of up to 50 miles per hour and even faster with favorable winds. It travels in rather large flocks, which are noted for their erratic flight, the whole flock twisting and turning in unison.

MIGRATION: The green-winged teal is a hardy bird and leaves its wintering grounds long before the ice has melted on the more northern ponds. It works its way north as the weather turns warmer. It may leave the south as early as the first of March but arrives in Alaska only at the beginning or in the middle of May. This two-month span is dictated solely by the weather.

In the fall, the green-winged teal is loath to leave its breeding ground. Storms and cold weather may make the ducks restless, but it is only the icing up of the inland waters that forces them to take to the wing and head for warmer climes in a search for open water.

HABITS: The green-winged teal is a sociable duck and decoys well. Its erratic flight and speed make it a challenge to the hunter. However, the duck has a streak of curiosity that works to its disadvantage. Quite frequently, even when the teal have been shot at, they circle the area as if to take a look at what has caused the noise and disturbance. This return circle often puts them within range of the hunter's gun again. Moreover the fact that they fly in compact flocks gives the hunter a chance to hit more than one bird at a time.

These teal are frequenters of mud flats and long river gravel bars where they can sit, preen and rest with little chance of danger sneaking up on them unseen. They are freshwater birds, and although sometimes seen near the coast, they frequent only those areas where fresh water is available.

FOOD: An investigation was conducted on the stomach contents of 653 green-winged teal to determine their food preferences. It was found that 91 percent of their diet was vegetable matter and 9 percent animal matter. The plant material was broken down into the following categories and percentages: sedges 39, pondweeds 12, grasses 11, smartweed 5, algae 5, duckweeds 2, water milfoil, arrow grass and bur reed 3, with miscellaneous plant food making up the remaining 14 percent. Insects accounted for 5 percent and mollusks for 4 percent of the birds' diet.

Surprisingly, the green-winged teal feeds on the rotting, maggoty flesh of the spent salmon that litter the western river banks when the salmon runs are finished. It also feeds on such cultivated grains as corn, rice, wheat, buckwheat and oats.

LIFE SPAN: The green-winged teal has a potential life span of about seven years. The record longevity for an individual green-wing seems to be eight years.

ENEMIES: It is amazing that any duck is ever able to reproduce itself, so numerous are its enemies. The crow is probably the chief enemy at nesting time. From its elevated perch in an old tree, it marks the nest location as soon as the female moves. Crows eat not only the ducks' eggs but the ducklings as well. In the destruction of the eggs, the crow is joined by the raccoon, skunk, opossum, fox and coyote. The adult green-winged teal, swift as it is, still falls prey to hawks, owls and eagles. Disease, parasites and accidents also take their toll.

TABLE FARE: Except for the period when the green-winged teal is feeding upon putrid salmon flesh, its own flesh is considered a gourmet's delicacy.

Wood Duck

Aix sponsa

No other duck in North America can compete with the spectacular beauty of the wood duck. This duck's Latin name takes into account its beauty. *Sponsa* means betrothed, as if this bird were plumed in all its bright array for its wedding. Yet, the wood duck is not conceited; far from flaunting its beauty, it is a shy, retiring denizen of woodland lakes and streams.

When I was a boy, during the 1930s, the wood duck was so scarce that it was given absolute protection wherever it was found. The closed season in both the United States and Canada lasted from 1918 to 1941. In one of our back fields we had a tree-lined pothole that usually hosted a pair of these beauties each year, but it was years before I saw these ducks anywhere else.

Fortunately, the wood duck has been brought back from the verge of extinction, and today it is common. It was not only the legal protection afforded the duck that saved it, but also the tremendous effort made by the United States Government, state governments and private individuals. This effort was concentrated on making homes available to the remaining wood ducks and in some cases, hand-rearing the birds.

The overshooting of the wood duck in the early 1900s coincided with the destruction of potential nesting sites. Widespread tree-felling during World War I deprived the wood ducks of their nesting hollows, and their population plummeted. The construction of tens of thousands of nesting boxes — more of which are still needed — was an important factor in stemming the decline of the wood duck. This illustrates the fact that our loss of many types of wildlife today is due to a lack, or destruction of, habitat rather than to the gun.

Dr. Donald C. Carter, of the New York Museum of Natural History, probably did more than any other single individual to save the wood duck. His home near Butler, New Jersey, is prime wood duck country with its ponds and streams nestled in the wooded valleys. Dr. Carter obtained wild wood duck eggs under federal permit and hatched the eggs in incubators. In a short time he was raising and releasing hundreds of wood ducks a year.

Today, the wood duck has been saved, but much more could be done to increase its numbers. Its range can support much larger numbers than are now found there.

DESCRIPTION: The beauty of the wood duck beggars description. The male is about 18 inches in length, has a wingspan of 24 inches and weighs up to 1½ pounds. Its bill is short and orange-red and black in color, its eye blood-red. The male sports a long crest that is a metallic green with shadings of blue and purple on the sides. Two thin white lines run through the crest, which is rarely erected. The throat patch and belly are white. The breast is brownish purple flecked with little darts of white. A white and black band separates the breast from the buff-colored side feathers. The tail is quite long and dark. The wing primaries are a sooty gray, while the coverts and secondaries are shades of purple, green, and blue. The feet are yellow.

The female wood duck must be considered drab compared to her mate, yet even she is much more colorful than any of her female counterparts. She is smaller than the male. Her bill, wings and feet are almost identical to the male's. Her crest is shorter and grayish green in color. The eye ring, throat and belly are white, the breast and sides brown with rows of white spots. The rest of her body is grayish brown.

DISTRIBUTION: The wood duck is found only in North America. Although it frequents parts of California, Oregon and Washington, it is an eastern bird. Its breeding range extends from just north of the Great Lakes and just west of the Mississippi River east to the Maritime Provinces and south to the Gulf of Mexico. Its winter range extends from the Carolinas through the Gulf Coast states.

COMMUNICATION: The main call of the wood duck is a whistled note that rises at the end. It also makes a soft guttural sound.

Wood Duck

BREEDING AND NESTING: The wood ducks usually arrive back on their breeding grounds in March, in flocks of perhaps ten to twenty birds. Courtship appears to be carried on only after the birds have returned north. Not only is the wood duck beautiful, he is gentle. Even during the courtship period he displays none of the rowdy fighting that is common among many species of birds.

Two males may stab at each other with their beaks a few times, a few feathers may be pulled from a rival, but that is usually the extent of the contest. The males are more interested in displaying their beauty before the female than they are in battling other males.

The female often instigates the courtship by pointing her bill toward the water and whistling a courtship note. She also caresses the male's white throat patch with her bill.

The male has a movement called "preening behind the wing" which presents his colors in display to the female. In another display, he faces the female, tucks in his chin and erects his crest and tail. Wood ducks seem to show more affection toward each other than many of the other ducks.

As soon as the pair formation is completed the male and female fly off to search out a nesting site. They check every knothole, cavity and tree hollow in the woodland. To be acceptable, the opening hole has to be at least 3 inches in diameter, and the cavity should have at least 50 square inches of floor space. Abandoned pileated woodpecker nest holes are often used and sometimes those of the flicker. Although the male does not brood the eggs, he helps to check out possible nest sites, clambering in and out of the hole experimentally. No additional nesting material is carried into the hole, although the female adds down plucked from her body.

There are several records of the wood duck entering a barn through a knothole and laying its eggs on the hay inside. Audubon relates that he once found a wood duck's nest in a rock fissure.

EGGS AND YOUNG: A good friend of mine, Art Wilkens, had a lovely home on the bank of the Delaware River. On an island in the river was a large sycamore tree that had a hollow where a rotted limb had been torn off. This nest site was used year after year by wood ducks. In the early morning the male and female would fly up to the nest cavity. The female would enter it while the male landed on the river a short distance away. The job of egg-laying usually took about an hour, after which the female would fly down to join the male. The pair would then feed and disport themselves in the water for the rest of the day.

The wood duck has a large clutch, laying as many as twelve to fifteen eggs. These are off-white, and the shell is quite glossy. In size they average about 51 millimeters in length by 38 millimeters in diameter. The incubation is done by the female alone and requires twenty-eight to thirty days. Unlike many other species of ducks, the male woody stays in the vicinity of the nest until the eggs hatch.

For a long time arguments raged about how the baby wood ducks got down from the nest cavity. No less an authority than Audubon has described—in company with other observers—how the mother wood duck carries her young down from the nest in her beak. According to a number of other reliable witnesses, the young are carried down on the mother's back. Today there are photographs and movies that show the young jumping from the hole by themselves. Art Wilkens saw this procedure in two successive years, and each year it was the same.

The female flew out of the hole and then turned around and flew back to it, putting the front part of her body in the hole. She made a soft, calling note. Then she withdrew and flew to a nearby limb, where she sat and continued to call. Finally she flew down to the water below, all the while continuing to call.

Shortly thereafter, a duckling appeared at the entrance of the hole and jumped out, its feet wide spread, its tiny wings beating furiously. In a short time another duckling plopped out, and another and another. Some of the ducklings landed in the water, but others fell on the stream bank—apparently none the worse for the experience. It has been calculated that falling ducklings have 1 square inch of body surface to every 3.2 grams of weight, which means that they actually have very little impact upon landing.

Observation of many wood duck nest boxes where the hatching time could accurately be determined has shown that the ducklings usually remain in the nest until the following morning. The young have strong, sharp claws and also use their beaks as an aid in climbing.

The young ducks feed exclusively on insects because of their high protein content but later change to a predominantly vegetarian diet.

The ducklings have a fledgling period of about two months. The female raises the young without any help from the male, who meanwhile molts his breeding plumage and sheds his flight feathers.

FLIGHT: About the time that the young wood ducks begin to fly, the male completes his second molt and, again sporting his bright adult color, is able to fly once more. Only when the young ducks no longer need the female for protection or instruction does she go into her postnuptial molt and become flightless.

The wood duck's flight speed is between 45 and 50 miles per

hour but seems greater because usually the bird is flying through stands of trees. Probably no other duck can match the dexterity of the wood duck's flight. Few other ducks fly through such an obstacle course as the timbered areas that are home to the woody.

The wood duck probably does more walking than any of the other ducks because it frequently seeks food on the dry forest floor. If surprised, whether on land or water, it springs into the air and swiftly flies away.

In migration wood ducks fly high, in small flocks.

MIGRATION: The wood duck also bears the nickname of "summer" duck. This is because it does not remain on its northern breeding grounds much after the end of summer. Usually most of the birds are back in the Gulf coast area by the end of October. I saw some wood ducks at Brigantine Wildlife Refuge in New Jersey on November 16, 1971, but this is unusually late for them to be so far north. The reason was probably that the fall of 1971 was a particularly mild one. The wood duck usually starts its migration north about the middle of March.

HABITS: The wood duck is a perching duck. It seems to be more agile with its legs than any other species. It walks well on land and can easily scramble up inclined branches or sloping tree trunks and land and perch on small branches. It usually feeds like the "puddle" ducks by merely tipping up its rear end, yet it can and often does dive beneath the surface of the water like the "bay" or "diver" ducks.

It is seldom found in the company of other ducks with the exception of the hooded merganser, with whom it seems to get along extremely well.

The wood duck is not an overly suspicious duck, and it was this trusting attitude that allowed its numbers to be so decimated by hunters in the early part of this century. It also facilitated the bird's comeback, however, by allowing it to be easily tamed and therefore successfully hand-reared.

FOOD: The food of the wood duck is 90 percent vegetable and 10 percent animal matter. The latter consists of whatever insects the duck can catch without much effort.

Acorns are one of the wood duck's preferred foods. One male wood duck bagged by a hunter was found to have thirty-three acorns in its crop. The seeds or nuts of the dogwood, elm and hickory are also of great importance to the wood duck. Wild rice, pondweed, bur reed, smartweed, arrow-arum, duckweed and water lily are its favorite plant foods.

LIFE SPAN: The longevity record for a wood duck appears to be eight years, four and a half years being the average life span.

ENEMIES: The raccoon is the main pilferer of wood duck nests. The bird's nesting habits remove it from the many dangers to which the ground-nesting ducks are exposed. Tree-climbing snakes, such as the black rat snake, are a menace. Otters, mink and, in the south, alligators take the ducks and the young when they are on the water. Winged predators, such as hawks and owls, take their toll, and parasites, disease and accidents claim many victims.

TABLE FARE: The wood duck usually has an unlimited amount of food and so is normally quite plump. The vegetation upon which it feeds produces a flesh so tasty that the wood duck is classified as one of the finest table ducks.

OVERLEAF

Surface-Feeding and Diving Ducks

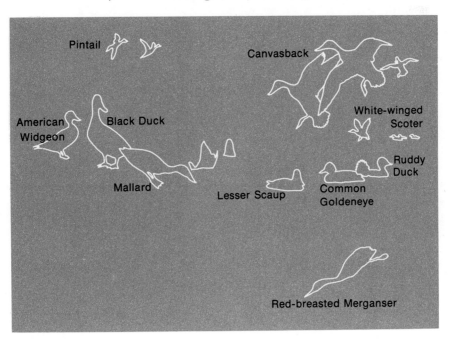

DIVING DUCKS
(Subfamily Aythyinae)

Redhead
Aythya americana

In 1970, Governor Cahill of New Jersey signed into law a "wet-lands" bill to prevent the devastation of the remaining marsh, bay and estuarine areas of this state. The destruction of the New Jersey coast had been proceeding at a constantly accelerating pace. The shoreline was being either filled in or dredged out by developers, both processes being highly destructive to the myriad forms of wildlife that inhabited those areas.

Although the redhead duck is still found in goodly numbers along the New Jersey coast, the records show that today's seemingly large flocks are just remnants of the former population found there.

In 1925 the Manasquan Inlet and Bay Canal was opened to facilitate boating. This allowed the sea water to course into the head of Barnegat Bay, making the water of the bay saline, whereas before it had been brackish or almost fresh. This change reduced the numbers of both the redhead and canvasback ducks by destroying the wild celery grass on which they feed.

It is this destructive ditching and dredging that is ruining so much of the wildlife in Florida today.

DESCRIPTION: The redhead duck is well named because its head and neck are a bright, rusty chestnut color. Whereas the canvasback's bill slopes from above the eye to the tip of the bill, the redhead's forehead is prominent, and its bill has a downward turn before sloping out to the tip. The breast, lower part of the neck, upper back, rump and upper and lower tail coverts of the redhead are black. Its back, scapulars, sides and flanks are white, finely barred with black. The wing coverts are gray, the speculum pale gray with a trailing white edge. The belly is white, the rear portion marked with thin black barring. The legs and feet are blue-gray, and the bill is bluish with a white ring behind the black tip. The eye is yellow. The adult male redhead duck has a total body length of 19½ inches, a wingspan of 32 inches and weighs about 2½ pounds.

The female redhead has a brown head and neck. She has a white facial marking behind her bill and a pale line behind the eye. Her bill is lighter in color than the male's. Her breast, back, rump and tail are dark brown with a lighter edging to the feathers. Her sides are light brown, her belly is whitish, and her wings are similar to the male's but lighter in color. Her eye is brown, and her feet are paler than the male's. She is smaller in size and lighter in weight than her spouse.

DISTRIBUTION: The redhead duck is fairly common throughout the United States during migration. Its breeding range is concentrated in the prairie states of Nebraska, Iowa, North and South Dakota, Minnesota and sections of Montana, Idaho, Washington, California, Nevada, Oregon and Utah. In Canada, it is found in British Columbia, Alberta, Saskatchewan and Manitoba.

The duck winters in a very restricted range along the Pacific coast from Washington south to Mexico and along the Atlantic coast from New Jersey south to Mexico.

COMMUNICATION: The redhead duck is quite noisy, the female uttering a loud *squack,* which is much higher in pitch than the call of the female mallard. During the breeding season, she also makes a rattling *que-e-e-k* call. The male redhead has a call that can be rendered as *me-ough* or *whee-ough.* It is a loud, deep, cat-like call.

BREEDING AND NESTING: The redhead duck heads north at an early date and most of the pairing up is probably done on the breeding grounds. The female may initiate the courtship ritual by giving out a soft *errrr* note and then gently pecking at the feathers of the male she has selected. The male responds by a display in

Redhead Duck

which he throws his head back until it touches his tail. As he brings his head back up, he calls to the female. He also pretends to preen behind his wing. Then, turning around, he swims away with his head turned toward the female. Before copulation, both the male and female dip their bills into the water and swim about with their necks erect but their bills pointing down.

There is fierce rivalry between the males, who lower their heads, extend their necks and swim at each other with a great show of force.

The redhead's nest is made on a platform of dead reeds and rushes that is built up by the duck to raise the nest above the water level. The nest is usually well hidden in the dense cover of reeds and cattails. Normally it is built in shallow water, but it has been found in a water depth of about 2 feet.

The nest is large, with an outside diameter of about 16 inches. Its top may be 10 to 12 inches above the water level. The cup of the nest is quite deep, and the female lines it with down plucked from her breast.

There are records to prove that some female redheads don't go to the trouble of building up their own reed platform but utilize old muskrat houses instead.

EGGS AND YOUNG: The redhead duck lays a large clutch of eggs, and although twelve to fifteen eggs are commonly found, some nests may contain as many as twenty-two eggs. The eggs average 61 millimeters in length by 43 millimeters in diameter. The color of the redhead's eggs varies from light olive brown to a more marked brown. The shells are thick and very strong. The female does the incubation with no assistance from the male. It takes between twenty-two and twenty-four days for the eggs to hatch.

When the young redhead's down dries off, there is noticeably less contrast between the light and the dark areas than there is on any other duckling. The head, back of the neck and back are a light yellowish brown. The face, neck, breast and belly are very light yellow. The feet and legs are gray, while the bill is two-toned, with a blue center and pink edges.

The redhead ducklings, because they hatch out over water, probably go swimming much sooner than the ducklings of the mallard, baldpate and other "puddle" ducks whose nests are often a considerable distance from water. Although no comparative records are available, the redhead ducklings' chances of survival would seem to be much greater because of the elimination of the long and extremely hazardous overland trip.

FLIGHT: The young redheads are slow in feathering out completely. They have all but their flight feathers by the time they are six or seven weeks old, but it is at least another two weeks before they can fly.

The adult male redhead goes into his eclipse plumage in August and does not drop his primary flight feathers until the middle of the month. The female drops her flight feathers about the same time or slightly later, so that for a period late in August, almost all the redhead ducks, both young and old, are unable to fly.

When the redheads do fly, they rocket along at speeds of between 50 and 60 miles per hour. Since they are "bay" ducks, their legs are placed toward the rear of the body, with the result that they are awkward walkers. To take off, the redhead has to run along the surface of the water to build up momentum before becoming airborne. In flight, it has a very rapid wing beat and is swift but erratic. These ducks usually travel in large flocks that seem thoroughly to enjoy flying. Often, for no apparent reason, the flocks take off and course back and forth, the birds twisting and turning in unison. They usually adopt the V formation or a variation of it. Sometimes they fly so high that they are almost out of sight. When the redheads decide to land, they drop down from the heights very rapidly, turning their bodies sideways, the wind slipping along the upper wing side so fast that the feathers make a rattling sound. As they near the water, they set their wings and glide in for a splashdown.

MIGRATION: The redhead duck has a fairly long distance to travel in migration. The first flights north usually get under way by the first of March, and almost all the ducks of this species are on the breeding grounds by the middle of April.

The fall migration, because of the young's long development period, does not get under way until the middle of September and is not concluded until the first part of November.

HABITS: The redhead duck has its counterpart in Africa called the African pochard. The African duck does not have the bright red head of the American duck, but the rest of the markings are similar. It is amazing how alike these birds are in habits as well as looks. Both the species are diving ducks that feed in the depths. While they are swimming, their tails almost touch the water. The feet give the diving impetus. The duck raises the forepart of its body, inclines its head forward and with a mighty push from its feet, arcs cleanly below the surface. It does not appear to use its wings for propulsion while under water but holds them tightly against the body to keep it streamlined.

The redhead duck is not a very wary bird and can be decoyed and called in rather easily. Some hunters take advantage of its curiosity by tolling floating rafts of the birds to within gunshot. This is done in some places with a tolling dog that is especially trained to play with a stick on the beach. The dogs are usually small, yellow, long-haired dogs that resemble a fox. The ducks are curious about the dog's antics, swim toward the shore to get a closer look and soon find that they are within gun range. If the hunter has no dog, he may wave a red handkerchief on the end of a long stick.

Redheads are sociable ducks and are often found in mixed flocks with other ducks, notably the canvasback or baldpate. The redheads benefit from the baldpates' extreme wariness, which may prevent the redheads from flying or swimming into the gun range of the hunters.

These ducks frequently feed throughout the night, particularly when there is a full moon.

FOOD: The redhead's diet is 90 percent vegetable matter and 10 percent animal matter. It feeds upon snails, mollusks and insects such as grasshoppers. Its preferences in plant foods are for pond-weed, wild rice, wild celery, bulrush, widgeon grass, and musk grass.

Not being a fussy eater, the redhead eats the leaves, stalks and even the bulbs or roots of the plants that it pulls loose from the bottom of bays. When it pops to the surface, it often trails the greenery behind it so that it looks like someone eating uncut spaghetti.

LIFE SPAN: The redhead duck's potential life span is seven to nine years. While most redheads succumb to some sort of misfortune long before this time, there are band records for redheads that lived to be ten, eleven, twelve, fourteen and sixteen and a half years old.

ENEMIES: The redhead's habit of building its nest out in the marsh over water helps to protect the eggs from such predators as skunks, opossums, foxes, coyotes and ground squirrels. The raccoon finds the water no hazard, the proof being that it frequently takes up its abode in an abandoned muskrat house. The crow is very destructive to the redhead's eggs. Fish are also natural enemies. Disease, parasites and accidents claim other victims.

TABLE FARE: The redhead's flesh is highly rated, particularly when the duck has been feeding exclusively on vegetation.

Canvasback

Aythya valisineria

New Jersey is famous as a wintering haven for ducks and geese, and I try to get to Barnegat Bay and Brigantine National Wildlife Refuge as often as I can to study and photograph waterfowl. Barnegat, in years gone by, was famous for both redhead and canvasback ducks. The numbers of both of these ducks have greatly diminished over the past years. Bombay Hook in Delaware is a good birding area, but it is Chesapeake Bay that holds the greatest rafts of canvasbacks. My main regret is that I seldom get a chance to get down to the Bay.

DESCRIPTION: The canvasback's common name derives from the very fine gray and white vermiculations on its back, which give the impression of the weave of threads in a piece of canvas. Its most conspicuous features are its dull red head, coupled with its long, sloping black bill.

The canvasback male averages 21 inches in length and has a wingspan of 33 inches and a weight of about 3 pounds, which makes him one of our heaviest ducks. His breast, wing primaries, rump, tail and under tail coverts are black. His scapulars, secondary

Canvasback

and wing covert feathers are the same color as his canvas back. The flank feathers graduate from gray to white on his belly. The feet are blue-gray.

The female canvasback has the same long, ski-sloped bill as the male, but hers is a bit lighter in color. Where the male canvasback has a dull red head, the female's is light brown. Her wing coloration is similar to the male's but several shades lighter. Where the male is black, the female is a medium brown. Her gray and white areas are much lighter and brighter than the male's.

When the male goes into his eclipse plumage, he is almost identical to the female. To confuse the situation even further, the female is just about the same size and weight as the male. There are, however, two small points that distinguish the male from the female at this stage. The male canvasback, even in eclipse, has a darker head than the female, and his eye is red while hers is yellow-brown.

DISTRIBUTION: The breeding range of this duck has been greatly reduced owing to the draining of many of the potholes of the prairie states where it nests. Formerly most of this drainage was undertaken for agricultural purposes, but today much of it is done under mosquito control programs. At some time of the year, some of the canvasbacks cross almost all the forty-eight contiguous states.

The breeding range of the canvasback includes the Canadian provinces of British Columbia, Alberta, Saskatchewan, Manitoba and a portion of the Northwest Territories. In the United States, it nests in Washington, Oregon, Utah, Idaho, Montana, Wyoming, North and South Dakota, Nebraska and Minnesota. These ducks also nest in the fantastic waterfowl breeding grounds of the Yukon River drainage basin in Alaska and the Yukon. This entire area was threatened a few years ago when the Rampart Dam was being considered.

The duck's winter range extends along the seacoasts from the state of Washington to Old Mexico in the West, and from Rhode Island to Old Mexico on the Atlantic and Gulf coasts.

The canvasback is known as a bay duck, and rightly so, because it usually winters on both the saline and freshwater bays and coves of the coastal regions.

COMMUNICATION: Canvasbacks make a wide variety of sounds. The male peeps, growls, has a harsh, guttural croak, and makes a cooing sound during the breeding season. The female quacks, makes a *cuck, cuck* sound and when frightened gives out a strident *currow* call.

BREEDING AND NESTING: The canvasback is a hardy duck that follows the receding ice northward in the early spring. The ducks travel in large flocks, and the pair formation usually takes place on the breeding grounds.

The male displays for the female by throwing his head back until it touches his back. As he brings it forward again to the normal position, he makes his cooing sound. The female answers with her *cuk-cuk* call. Often the male approaches the female with his head lowered, his neck looking as though it had a kink in it. If the female pays little attention to the male, he often lowers his head close to the water and sneaks up behind her in an attempt to mount her. The female has no trouble in escaping from one male, and when the attentions of several males are forced upon her, she eludes them by taking to the air.

After she has selected a mate, the pair of canvasbacks often flies together in a nuptial flight. The male follows close behind the female and attempts to grasp her tail feathers with his bill as they fly. The female twists and turns to thwart this attempt. Then the pair drops down to the water, where the male bends his head forward and approaches the female, dipping his bill into the water as he does so. When the female is ready to accept his advances, she lowers her body in the water so that copulation can take place.

The canvasback builds a large, bulky nest among tall reeds in sloughs and potholes. The nest is usually built up from the floor of the pond even though the water may be 10 to 15 inches deep. It is well made out of dead reeds and in some instances its top portion would probably float away if it were not anchored to the surrounding reeds. The nest is usually raised about 8 inches above the water. It is about 18 inches across, with a cavity 4 to 6 inches deep by 8 to 10 inches across. There is seldom much down in the nest lining. The nest is not easy to locate because it blends so well with the reeds and because the female canvasback sits tight and does not betray the nest's location by a wild escape flight.

EGGS AND YOUNG: The canvasback usually lays between eight and ten eggs to a clutch. The eggs are large, measuring 62 millimeters in length by 43 millimeters in diameter. They are a drab, dark olive color. The smaller eggs that are sometimes found in the canvasback's nest probably belong to either the redhead or ruddy ducks. The female performs the incubation without any help from the male, in a period of about twenty-eight days. While the females are incubating, the male canvasbacks gather together in bachelor flocks on some of the larger lakes.

The down of the canvasback duckling is a light, bright yellow on the cheeks, throat, breast, belly and rump. The crown of the head, back of the neck, back, wings and tail are light brown.

FLIGHT: The young grow very rapidly, but their weight is probably a handicap for flight, and it is usually nine to ten weeks before they are able to fly.

The canvasback needs a long running start before it can become airborne. It raises itself out of the water, and with both feet and wings beating at full speed, it finally launches itself into the air. Once in flight, it really gets moving and is credited with being the fastest-flying duck in North America. Without the benefit of a tail wind, canvasbacks have been clocked at 72 miles per hour. Their wing beat is strong, rapid and noisy.

The canvasbacks often fly in large flocks of several hundred birds and at considerable heights. When migrating they usually assume the typical V formation, but on short flights they often bunch up or fly in irregular lines.

MIGRATION: The canvasback loves its northern range and heads north so early in the spring that its journey is often delayed because the ponds and sloughs are still covered with ice. The main spring migration takes place in March. In the fall the canvasback is loath to leave the north and is finally forced out only by the freeze-up.

In migration the canvasback uses the Pacific, Mississippi and Atlantic flyways. Fewer of these ducks are using the Mississippi flyway than formerly; now more of them swing east and follow the Atlantic coast south.

HABITS: The canvasback, since it is a sociable duck, comes into decoys fairly easily, but the blocks of decoys have to be quite large. Sometimes a hundred or more decoys are used at one time. The canvasback population has been greatly reduced by the ditching and draining of the duck's nesting areas and by overshooting. The canvasback was one of the most sought-after ducks in the days of market hunting and can still challenge the mallard's distinction of being the most hunted duck. Growing hunting pressure has made these ducks quite wary, and they tend increasingly to feed and sleep well out in the bays away from lurking hunters. If the hunting pressure becomes great enough, the ducks fly out to sea to sleep during the daytime, feeding in the bays at night.

The canvasback's legs are set behind center on its body, which facilitates diving. This bird is an excellent swimmer and diver.

When wounded, it dives underwater, where it can swim such long distances that it is almost impossible to catch up with it.

FOOD: Eighty-one percent of the canvasback's diet is made up of vegetable matter, most of it gathered in the depths of bays, ponds and sloughs. The Latin word *valisineria* in this duck's name derives from the fact that its preferred food is the wild celery *Vallisneria spiralis.* Wild celery constitutes the main attraction of the Chesapeake Bay area for this duck. As the wild celery seems to be spreading both north and south, the wintering concentrations of the canvasback ducks will probably do likewise.

Wild celery is also called eelgrass because of its long, slender, wavy fronds. It has a succulent white root, which is the portion eaten by the canvasback. This duck will dive as deep as 20 feet to pull up this plant, root and all. Coming to the surface, the duck cuts off the long green stems of the plant and eats just the root. The green fronds are left to collect in masses and float away. It is the root that the baldpate duck tries to steal from the canvasback, although it eats some of the greenery as well.

The canvasback's other favorite plant foods are pondweed, arrowhead, water lily, bulrush, wild rice, musk grass, algae, widgeon grass, bur reed and water milfoil.

The 19 percent of the canvasback's diet that is made up of animal matter consists of insects and their larvae, mollusks, crustaceans and fish. This duck also eats the rotting bodies of spent salmon that are found along streamsides.

LIFE SPAN: The average life span of the canvasback duck is about ten years. However, one banded canvasback nearly doubled that span by living to be nineteen years old.

ENEMIES: The crow steals the eggs of the canvasback because the water surrounding this duck's nest is no deterrent to it. Most of the four-footed predators are thwarted by the nest's location. Mink, otter, fish, turtles, hawks, owls and eagles take the young and the adults whenever possible. The adult canvasback flies so fast that it often escapes pursuit by even the swiftest winged predator. Disease, parasites and accidents may be lethal.

TABLE FARE: Except for those canvasbacks that have been feeding on rotting salmon, this duck is considered an epicure's delight. The canvasback always fetched the highest prices for the market hunter and is still one of the most coveted ducks.

Ring-necked Duck

Aythya collaris

The American Southeast, sprinkled with countless bodies of brackish water, is one of the major winter ranges of the ring-necked duck. This plump bird is considered to be excellent table fare, and for good reason: It passes the winter gorging on the vegetation that is rife in the region's myriad ponds, marshes, swamps and rice fields.

Unlike most duck species, the ring-neck usually develops a favorite feeding haunt, which it returns to time after time. Even if it is shot at repeatedly near this spot, the habit is so deeply ingrained that the bird will continue to return, bypassing seemingly similar ponds in the neighborhood.

DESCRIPTION: The adult male ring-necked duck is 17 inches in length, has a wingspan of 27 inches and weighs about 1¾ pounds. This duck is frequently confused with the scaup ducks, to which it is related. Actually the name ring-necked is misleading because the narrow rusty band around this duck's neck is hard to see. A better name would have been ring-billed duck because two white rings—one right behind the tip of the bill and the other separating

the bill from the head—make conspicuous and reliable field identification marks. The rest of the bill is blue like that of the scaup.

The ring-necked duck has an iridescent purple head. The
feathers on the crown of the head are a little longer than the rest,
forming a short crest which gives the head a triangular appearance.
There is a small white chin mark. The breast, scapulars, back, rump,
upper and under tail coverts and tail are black. The belly is white,
but the rear portion and the sides have thin black lines crossing the
white. The wing coverts are blackish, the primaries brown, and
the speculum is grayish white with a trailing white edge. The
underwing lining is whitish. The eye is bright yellow, and the legs
and feet are blue-gray.

The female's bill is similar to that of the male, but the blue is less
bright. The crown of her head and the back of her neck are brown.
The brown eye is circled with white that extends as a stripe separating the crown from the sooty-white cheek. The throat and neck are
whitish and lack the collar of the male. The back, rump and tail are
dark brown, the sides and flanks are light brown, and the belly is
whitish. The female's wings are similar to the male's but lack their
richness of color. Her legs and feet are blue-gray.

DISTRIBUTION: The ring-necked duck is common and has a widespread range. It winters along the Atlantic, Gulf and Pacific coastal
regions, although it much prefers freshwater ponds to saline conditions. This is why, weather and icing conditions permitting, it will
be found wintering in the interior of most of the southeastern
states. During its migration period it is found in most of the forty-
eight contiguous states.

Its breeding range is centered around the prairie provinces of
Canada and the prairie states of the United States. In lesser numbers, however, it is found in all the Canadian provinces and the
states of the border region from the Atlantic to the Pacific.

COMMUNICATION: The male ring-necked duck makes a *purrrr*
sound and has a deep, resonant whistle. The hen is usually silent,
but during the breeding season she, too, makes a soft *rrrrrr* call.

BREEDING AND NESTING: These ducks usually migrate in small,
mixed flocks, and the pairing up seems to be done on the breeding
ground.

The female incites the male by whistling her soft call. The male
responds by raising his head in a kinked-neck position and erecting the feathers of his short crest. He, too, then sounds his whistled

Male Ring-necked Duck

call. The male also goes through the headthrow movement where the head and neck are bent backward until the head rests on the back. It is then snapped forward to a perpendicular position, the bill traveling in a 180° arc.

Occasionally both the male and female engage in the preening-behind-the-wing display. If and when the female accepts the male, both of them go through the display of dipping the bill into the water before copulation takes place. The male stays with the female until the nest is built and the complete set of eggs has been laid. Incubation severs the pair formation, and the male leaves the female to seek out the bachelor company of other males.

The female builds the nest out in marsh or slough areas among vegetation that grows in 8 to 10 inches of water. The nest is made up of the reeds or cattails that prevail in the area. It is built up from the bottom of the pond until it is about 8 inches higher than the water level. Its diameter is usually 12 inches, the actual nest cavity being 6 to 8 inches across and at least 3 or 4 inches in depth. In fact occasionally the eggs are actually wet from the water beneath them.

The nest is usually hard to locate because it blends in well with the background vegetation and the female sits very tight and so does not betray its location.

Female Ring-necked Duck

EGGS AND YOUNG: Nine to twelve eggs are an average clutch for the ring-necked duck. The eggs vary in color from creamy green to buff and average 57 millimeters in length by 39 millimeters in diameter. Incubation takes from twenty-four to twenty-six days.

The baby ringnecks' down is the common duckling yellow on the cheeks, neck, breast and belly. The crown of the head, back of the neck, back, wings and tail are dark brown with yellow spots behind the wings and on the rump. The bill, legs and feet are slate-blue.

Since they hatch over water the little ones are swimming about in a matter of hours after hatching. Their diet is an all-insect one and therefore high in protein value. The ducklings are interested in anything mobile that is small enough to be eaten. The sloughs and ponds that are home to the ring-necked ducks are also the habitat of myriad types of aquatic insects and their larvae. The ducklings take advantage of this situation, and their days are filled with flurried activity as they dart in all directions snapping up, or at least snapping at, whatever insects they chance upon.

FLIGHT: The ducklings grow rapidly, on their rich diet and within six to seven weeks they are fully fledged and capable of flying. The adult male ring-necked duck grows out of his eclipse plumage at about the same time as the young learn to fly. The female, her job of raising the young over, enters her postnuptial period and becomes flightless. By September, all the ring-necked ducks are back in the air.

The ring-necked duck is a strong flier. To become airborne, however, it must run along the surface of the water to build up the momentum needed to take off. Once in the air it rapidly gets up to a speed of about 45 miles per hour. It is able to twist and turn as adroitly as the scaup. Unlike the scaup, the ring-necked duck does not fly in compact flocks but prefers a more open, loose formation. It does not fly at great heights. When these ducks fly into an area they usually land without the preliminary circling common to many other ducks.

MIGRATION: The ring-necked duck does not believe in rushing the season, neither is it a laggard. It starts its northward migration about the middle of March, so that it arrives on the breeding grounds late enough to insure that the ice is off the ponds. It starts south again in September and arrives on its wintering grounds by the end of November.

HABITS: The ring-necked duck may sometimes be found in the company of the scaup ducks. It is not a gregarious bird, however, and prefers to be with its own kind and then not in large numbers. I have never seen more than twelve or fourteen ringnecks at one time, but I have not seen them on their main southern wintering grounds, where perhaps they flock up more.

This duck may be decoyed successfully, but most hunters take advantage of its preference for certain well-known feeding locations. Blinds are built on the passageway to the feeding area which offers the hunters good pass shooting.

The ring-necked duck is a diving duck that feeds in relatively deep water. When diving and swimming underwater, it keeps its wings tightly against its body and uses just its feet for propulsion.

FOOD: The diet of the ring-necked duck consists of 81 percent of vegetable matter and 19 percent animal matter. Its favorite plant foods are pondweed, water shield, musk grass, smartweed, wild rice, coontail, duckweed, spike rush, water lily, naiad, bulrush, widgeon grass and bur reed. It eats various parts of the plants such as the leaves, roots, stems or seeds. In its main wintering grounds, in the southeastern states, the ring-necked duck feeds more on water shield and water lily, particularly the bulbous roots, than do any of the other ducks.

The animal matter it consumes is just as varied as its plant food. It feeds upon minnows, tadpoles, small frogs, crayfish, snails, dragonflies, damselflies, caddisflies and all types of water beetles, mollusks, crustaceans and worms.

LIFE SPAN: The ring-necked duck has a potential life span of from seven to nine years. The only banded ringneck that I can find on record bettered that span by living to be ten years old.

ENEMIES: For any of the ducks that breed and nest on the prairie provinces of Canada or the prairie states of the United States the dragline and ditching plow are the greatest enemy. The destruction of their natural habitat deprives them of their vital nesting grounds and so reduces their population more drastically than all their other enemies combined.

Crows are the most destructive of the ring-necked duck's winged predators because they flock to the potholes and sloughs in the spring to feed on ducks' eggs. The nest's location over water discourages most of the four-footed predators, although raccoons still destroy some of the nests. Mink and otter feed on the young ducklings and on any adults they can catch. Hawks, owls and eagles take both the young and the adults. Parasites, disease and accidents claim further victims.

TABLE FARE: The ring-necked duck is considered a fine table bird, particularly when it has been feeding strictly on vegetation, especially water-lily bulbs. When it has been feeding on animal matter, its flesh is considered less desirable.

Greater Scaup
Aythya marila

My first encounter with the greater scaup took place in my youth, while I was on Christmas vacation in Florida. One day I was taken to visit the municipal pier at St. Petersburg. Although I had only a box camera, I was busily trying to photograph the gulls and the pelicans that sat on all the pilings. My attention was then attracted by a crowd that had gathered at the end of the pier. When I worked my way to the edge of the pier, I almost dropped my camera overboard. There below me was the largest concentration of ducks I had ever seen. The water was covered by swimming ducks and roiled by diving ducks. They were greater scaup ducks, and there were thousands of them. I didn't know what kind of ducks they were at first but I soon found out because I took notes on their appearance.

DESCRIPTION: The male adult greater scaup is 17¾ inches in length, has a wingspan of 30 inches and weighs about 2 pounds. It has a bright blue bill which has earned it its common name of "bluebill." Its bright yellow eye contrasts sharply with its dark, metallic green head and neck. The breast is black, the flanks and

Greater Scaup

belly are white. The back also is white with thin black vermiculations crossing it. The rump is black, but the tail and under tail coverts are dark brown. The upper wings are mainly dark brown, although the secondary feathers are white, with a trailing edge of brown. The underwing surface is white, and the feet are blue-gray.

The female greater scaup has a blue bill like her mate's, but it is slightly lighter in color. On the front of her face, behind the bill, she has a white patch that is a very conspicuous field mark. Her eye is yellow, and her head and neck are brown. Her breast, back, tail and flanks are various shades of mottled brown, while her belly is white. The female greater scaup's wings are identical to those of the male except that they are several shades lighter in color. Her feet, too, are blue-gray.

In his eclipse plumage the male greater scaup is actually duller in color than the female because he becomes as brown as she is but lacks the white flank feathers and white facial markings.

DISTRIBUTION: The greater scaup is not as common as the lesser scaup and has a much more restricted range. Its winter range ex-

143

tends from Alaska to southern California along the Pacific coast. It is found along the Atlantic from Texas along the Gulf coast, around Florida, north to Maine and along the Gulf of St. Lawrence.

Its breeding range is restricted to the far north: the tundra areas of the Hudson Bay area, the Northwest and Yukon Territories and Alaska.

Although it does not breed in saltwater areas, it definitely prefers such areas during the winter.

COMMUNICATION: The greater scaup duck does not usually make much noise. Its standard call is a harsh *scaup, scaup, scaup* sound, from which it derives its name. During the breeding season, the male has an expanded repertoire of soft cooing notes that can be described as *week-week-whew, pa-whoo, chup-chup* or *chup-chup, cherr-err.*

The female has an alarm call that is a form of the *scaup* call but sounds *scaar, scaar*. During the breeding season, she has a soft *tuck-tuck-turra-tuck* call.

BREEDING AND NESTING: The greater scaup duck migrates north in rather large flocks, and the pairing up is usually done on the breeding grounds.

The male greater scaup's most common display during the breeding season is known as the "cough." In this performance, the male makes the coughing *week-week-whew* call and flicks his wings and tail rapidly. He also throws his head back until the bill touches his rump. He then snaps his head back into an upright position as he utters the *pa-whooo* call.

If the female is interested in the male, he swims in front of her, leading her on, while she follows uttering her soft call. Both sexes preen behind the wing and just before copulation takes place, dip their bills into the water repeatedly. The female then lowers her body into the water to receive the male.

The greater scaup duck's nest is usually located near water on top of one of the tussocks or hummocks commonly found in the tundra regions, where the usual covering of very high grass provides excellent camouflage. The nest is usually in a hollow lined with fine pieces of broken grass. Occasionally it is built over water, and if it is not on a hummock, the base is built up like that of the redhead duck's nest.

The bowl of the nest is 6 to 8 inches across and 2 to 4 inches in depth. This duck is reported to use very little down for lining the nest.

The greater scaup are colony nesters, and the nests are sometimes only a couple of feet from each other.

EGGS AND YOUNG: The greater scaup's clutch usually numbers between eight and ten eggs. In color the eggs vary from a deep olive-buff to a lighter yellow-green. They average 62 millimeters in length by 43 millimeters in diameter.

The male greater scaup is in close attendance on the female until her eggs have been laid. As she begins to brood the eggs, his interest in her wanes, and while he is still able to fly, he heads out to sea or to some large lake, where he joins the other males. Shortly after, he assumes his eclipse plumage and loses his flight feathers.

Incubation takes twenty-four to twenty-six days.

The greater scaup ducklings are rather dull in color at first. The top of the head, back of the neck, rump, back and wings are dark, almost chestnut brown. The face and cheeks are tan, the breast and belly dull yellowish white. The feet are yellowish green, and the bill is bluish.

The female greater scaup is a good mother but not a very demonstrative one. When danger threatens, she leads her young away if possible and hides them among the rankest vegetation she can find. She does not, however, make use of the decoy or wounded ruse.

FLIGHT: The fledgling period for the greater scaup duck is about seven to seven and a half weeks. The female loses her flight feathers after the young have developed to the point where they are no longer dependent upon her.

The greater scaup fly in a bunched, wedge-shaped formation. They have to run along the surface of the water, heading into the wind, in order to take off. Once airborne, they are rather speedy fliers, reaching speeds of up to 50 miles per hour or more. Their wing beat is rapid and makes a loud, whistling sound. They usually fly at considerable heights during migration and at about 30 feet above the water on regular flights.

MIGRATION: The greater scaup is a hardy duck, and, as already noted, some of the birds winter along the Alaskan coast. For these ducks the migration is a short one. Those that travel to the southeast of the country have a distance of about 3,000 miles to cover.

The main flight to the northern breeding grounds takes place about the middle of March unless the migration is delayed by an unusually long and icy winter.

In the middle of September the greater scaup are forced to head south again by the oncoming winter.

HABITS: The greater scaup duck is very sociable. It travels, feeds and nests in flocks and is also shot in flocks because it is easily decoyed. As the hunting pressure increases, it begins to stay out at sea all day and come in under cover of darkness to feed. It is a very strong swimmer and is undismayed by the most violent winter ocean storms. It is an excellent diver and swims with just its feet, its wings held tightly to the body to streamline it. It has been known to stay underwater for as much as a minute. It is not a particularly wary bird and while diving for food is most lax about posting guards. Sometimes the entire flock will be underwater together, and at such times an enemy can easily sneak up on them. While feeding, the scaup really makes the water bubble and fly as it dives again and again. If wounded, it is almost impossible to catch because it simply disappears underwater and swims away. It can surface and get another lungful of air without betraying its position.

FOOD: Fifty-three percent of the diet of the greater scaup is animal matter, and the remaining 47 percent is vegetation. The scaup usually feeds in fairly deep water, where it must dive to obtain its food. Its favorite foods are salt-water mussels, clams, oysters, barnacles, crabs, fish, tadpoles and snails. Its vegetable food includes the stems, leaves, roots and seeds of pondweed, widgeon grass, musk grass, wild celery, naiad, coontail, eelgrass, smartweed and bulrush.

LIFE SPAN: The greater scaup duck has a potential life span of from seven to nine years. There appears to be no individual longevity record.

ENEMIES: The greater scaup duck runs the gamut of enemies from the denizens of the Arctic to those of the temperate and near-tropical zones. It has enemies that take the eggs, the young, the adults or all three. Crows, gulls, jaegers, hawks, owls, eagles, foxes, mink, otter, turtles and fish are only a few of its predators. Disease, parasites and accidents claim further victims.

TABLE FARE: This duck is not the most desirable table duck. When its diet is primarily animal matter, its flesh is unpalatable, but when it is on a vegetable diet, it is considered edible.

Lesser Scaup

Aythya affinis

The duck-hunting season in the United States varies according to the location of the states, those in the north opening up the earliest so that their hunters have the opportunity to hunt ducks before they have all migrated south. Some states such as New Jersey have a split season. It opens up to catch some of the early migrators and then closes only to open again when some of the late arrivals, such as the lesser scaup, come in.

Most of the lesser scaup winter in the southeastern and Mississippi River states. By the time the birds are on their wintering grounds the rice crop has been gathered, and the ducks flock in to glean any remaining grain. They thrive on this rich fare, but it is such a lure that the ducks are easily hunted. They return again and again to such spots, providing the hunters with both pass and decoy shooting.

DESCRIPTION: The adult male lesser scaup is so similar to the male greater scaup that it is hard to tell them apart. There are differences between them, but they are not readily noticeable. The lesser scaup has the same bright blue bill, feet and legs as the greater scaup. However, his head is a little more angular, due to his short crest feathers, and his head and neck are purplish black rather than green. His breast is black. He does not have the clean white and black markings of the greater scaup. His white feathers verge on gray, and his dark feathers are brownish instead of black. He is also slightly smaller, being 17½ inches in length, with a wingspan of 27½ inches and a weight of 1¾ pounds. The lesser scaup also has a smaller "nail" on the tip of its bill than the greater scaup.

The female lesser scaup is a smaller edition of the female greater scaup except that she lacks the partly white primary feathers.

DISTRIBUTION: The lesser scaup is much more abundant than the greater scaup. It avoids the saltwater areas whenever possible, much preferring fresh water for all its activities. Both its breeding and wintering ranges are much more extensive than those of the greater scaup.

The wintering range of the lesser scaup is a coastal belt about 200 miles wide, stretching from the state of Washington south right round the perimeter of the United States, up to Connecticut and Rhode Island. An extension of the range also reaches up the Mississippi River as far as southern Illinois.

The breeding range of the lesser scaup includes the states of Nebraska, North and South Dakota, Minnesota, a piece of eastern Alaska, and the provinces of Manitoba, Saskatchewan, British Columbia, Yukon and the Northwest Territories. During their migration period these ducks virtually blanket the United States.

COMMUNICATION: Like its larger cousin, the lesser scaup is not very vocal. It has a somewhat similar *scaup, scaup* call, but it is not as clearly enunciated. The male also makes a cooing sound and has a low, whistling *whee-ooo* call. The female's voice is much harsher, and she makes a *kerr-urr* sound.

BREEDING AND NESTING: The lesser scaup does not need to head north as early as the greater scaup because it has a more southern breeding range. The ice has usually melted from the ponds and sloughs shortly before these ducks arrive. Consequently the pair formation takes place on the wintering grounds.

The male displays before the female of his choice by bowing his head to her, and then, opening his bill wide, he makes his *scaup* sound. Sometimes the female initiates the advances by coquettishly swimming around the male with her head erect and lifting her bill upward with short, jerky motions. She may also bite at the male gently and he responds in a similar manner. Both sexes also preen behind the wing to display the white feathers in the speculum.

The male coughs and flicks his wings and tail very rapidly. Like the greater scaup, this scaup also throws his head backward to touch his tail. However, he performs this display so fast that it may be missed if the preliminary head-shaking movements are not noted in advance. This display is accompanied by the whistled *whee-ooo* call.

When the male has convinced the female that he would make an ideal mate, she follows behind him as he swims slowly away, turning the back of his head toward her. Copulation takes place only after both the birds have signaled that they are ready for it by dipping their bills into the water.

Even after the lesser scaup are paired up and on their breeding ground, they seem to be reluctant to get down to the job of nest-building. Because of this propensity to dawdle, they have a slightly longer breeding season than most of the ducks.

These ducks prefer the smaller ponds, potholes and sloughs, leaving the larger lakes to the greater scaup. On occasion, the nest may be built up in the water, fastened among the reeds and rushes, but most of the nests are built on dry land. The selection of a nesting site varies with the natural cover in the different areas. The nest may be in among high grass, under bushes, hidden among large rocks or even out in the open. The nest itself is usually just a hollow scraped out in the ground, lined with grass and down.

EGGS AND YOUNG: The male lesser scaup, when the long honeymoon is over, abandons the female and flies out to join the rest of the "boys" on some of the larger ponds. There the males go through the eclipse stage and become flightless.

The female lesser scaup, meanwhile, completes her clutch of nine to twelve eggs and begins the task of incubation, which takes about twenty-four to twenty-six days. Her eggs are dark olive-green to greenish buff in color. They average 57 millimeters in length by 39 millimeters in diameter.

The down of the newly hatched ducklings is a fairly dark brown on the top of the head, the back of the neck, the wings, back and tail. The face is tan and has a brown eye stripe. The breast and belly are yellow; the feet are yellowish green, and the bill is blue.

The lesser scaup ducklings travel in compact groups while feeding, and if threatened by danger, they do not scatter but attempt to swim away as a group. Only if they feel they can no longer escape by swimming on the top of the water do they resort to diving. Then it is every duckling for itself as they scatter beneath the surface. As soon as they pop up again, they regroup and again take off as a single unit. This grouping action is very common among many animals as well as birds and offers much more protection than scattering. A predator almost always attempts to catch any individual that splits off from the main group.

FLIGHT: It takes the lesser scaup ducklings about two and a half months to acquire their primary feathers and learn to fly. About the time that they are able to take to the air, the female sheds her primary feathers and becomes flightless.

The lesser scaup duck runs along the surface of the water to build up the momentum needed to launch itself into the air. It is swift and lively in flight. It can attain speeds of up to 50 miles per hour but always appears to be going much faster because of its erratic twisting and turning.

These ducks fly in large, compact groups, which makes them a favorite among hunters because usually more than one duck can be bagged with one shot. If undisturbed, they fly fairly low over the water. When shot at, they hurtle up, twisting and turning even after they are out of the hunter's range. Their wing beats are rapid, producing a whistling sound as they fly. During migration they may fly at considerable heights.

MIGRATION: The lesser scaup's northward trek usually starts about the middle of March and may last into the beginning of June. Their flight south is usually delayed until the ice has formed on the smaller ponds and sloughs. When feeding becomes difficult, the lesser scaup fly just far enough south to find ice-free ponds. Their southern migration is leisurely, and it may take them until the latter part of December to reach their wintering grounds.

HABITS: The lesser scaup's sociability often costs it its life because it decoys easily, and to reach its wintering grounds it has to run a gauntlet of duck hunters the length of the continent. Those birds that survive the migration south grow much warier in the process. If the hunting pressure is severe, this duck seeks out large bodies of water during the daytime and ventures into the shallows to feed only under cover of darkness.

As it is a "bay" or diving duck, the placement of its legs toward the rear of the body makes it awkward in the little walking that it does. It is an excellent diver and feeds primarily by securing its food beneath the surface of the water.

FOOD: The lesser scaup is more of a vegetarian than the greater scaup, about 60 percent of its diet consisting of vegetable matter. Its favorite plant foods are wild celery, pondweed, widgeon grass, wild rice, naiad, horned pondweed, bulrush, arrowhead, musk grass, water milfoil and smartweed.

The 40 percent of animal matter in its diet consists of mollusks, small fish, tadpoles, snails, worms, crayfish, and the adults, nymphs and larvae of many types of water insects.

LIFE SPAN: The lesser scaup has a potential life span of from seven to nine years. The longevity record for this species is held by a duck that lived to be ten years old.

ENEMIES: The enemies of the lesser scaup duck are crows, hawks, owls, eagles, turtles, large fish, raccoons, foxes, otter and mink. The relentless ditching and draining of their habitat does them more harm than any natural enemy. Prairie fires are a danger, and disease, parasites and accidents take their toll.

TABLE FARE: The lesser scaup is more eagerly sought as food than its larger cousin because it feeds more often on vegetable matter. When the birds are glutting themselves in the rice fields, they become very fat and succulent.

OVERLEAF ▶

Diving Ducks

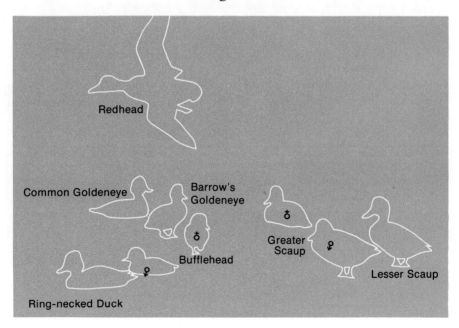

Common Goldeneye

Bucephala clangula

"Soon a small flock of five (goldeneyes) comes in, the shrill whistling of their wings sending a thrill of pleasure through our chilled
veins (as) they scale down toward the decoys," recalled naturalist
Arthur Cleveland Bent of a memorable winter morning shoot.

The common goldeneye's characteristic whistle, generated by
its rapid wing beats, is familiar to most North American hunters,
for this duck ranges across much of the continent. It is a sound that
often inspires poetic descriptions.

"Of all wing music, from the droning of the rufous hummer to
the startling whirr of the ruffed grouse, I know of none so thrilling
sweet as the . . . wing-note of the Golden-eye," wrote William
Dawson in 1909. "A pair of the birds have been frightened from the
water, and as they rise in rapid circles to gain a view of some dis-
tant goal they sow the air with vibrant whistling sounds."

DESCRIPTION: The goldeneye is well named, for its eye is a bright
golden yellow. The adult male common goldeneye is 18 inches in
length, has a wingspan of 28½ inches and weighs about 2 pounds.
His head and the upper part of his neck are black with a greenish
tinge. The bright yellow eye is very noticeable against the contrast-

ing head. There is a large white spot on the lower face behind the blackish bill. This spot is one of this duck's main identifying field marks. The lower neck, breast, belly and flanks are white, while the back, rump and tail are black. The wings are darkish brown with some white middle and greater wing coverts and secondaries. The feet are orangy red.

The female goldeneye has the golden yellow eye but a brown head, and she lacks the white facial disk. Her bill is two-toned, being bluish-black at the base but orange at the tip. She has a wide white collar. Her breast and flanks are grayish brown, and her belly is white. Her back, rump and tail are ash-gray. Her wings are identical to the male's in patterning but lighter in color. Her feet are yellow. The female is slightly smaller than the male.

DISTRIBUTION: The common goldeneye is a widespread duck, and its wintering range embraces almost all the forty-eight contiguous states and extends up along the Pacific coast to Alaska. It winters in large numbers on the Great Lakes.

This duck breeds primarily in Canada, below the Arctic Circle, from Newfoundland west to Alberta and up into Alaska. It is not found north of the tree line because it is a tree-cavity nesting bird.

COMMUNICATION: The common goldeneye is not noted as a conversationalist. The male, during the courtship season, makes a double-noted *zzee-at* call in a harsh, rasping voice. His other call can best be rendered as *cur-r-rew*. The female's voice cannot be considered more melodious as she also makes a harsh *grrrk* call.

BREEDING AND NESTING: The common goldeneyes pair up while they are still on their wintering grounds. The gradual lengthening of the days stirs the amorous instincts in the males and also their belligerency toward the other males. The drakes chase and fight with each other in an attempt to reduce the competition and impress the females.

These ducks have one of the most elaborate breeding displays of any of the ducks. If more than one male is present, the more aggressive one flattens his head and neck out along the water in a sneak position and chases after his rival.

In performing before the female, the male common goldeneye uses the headthrow maneuver, whereby he throws his head back until it touches his tail. However, unlike most of the other ducks, the goldeneye adds a special fillip of his own. As he brings his head forward again, he kicks backward with both feet, sending the water

Common goldeneye female with young.

flying in a cascading curtain. This is also the time when he utters his *zzee-at* call.

Quite often the male raises his head and neck straight up to the sky and calls. At other times, he points his head and neck straight out in front of his body, but without touching the water, and pushes them forward and backward. While he does this, the female's reaction is often to pump her head up and down, usually prior to her pre-copulatory display. When the female is ready to accept the male, she floats on the water with her head and neck outstretched, looking for all the world like a dead duck. The male then swims behind her and, in mounting her, holds on to her head feathers with his bill, his body weight pushing her completely underwater. When copulation is over, the male still does not release the female's head. The female comes to the top of the water and pivots in several small circles until her head is released by the male.

The common goldeneye nests in hollow trees or other natural cavities. Some of these nests are at a considerable height above the ground. Ideally the nest tree is as close to the water as possible. The perennial shortage of nest sites is a limiting factor to the common goldeneye population.

EGGS AND YOUNG: No extra material is brought into the nesting cavity. The eggs are bedded down on the soft, rotted pieces of wood, some down being used occasionally.

The common goldeneye lays a large clutch containing an average of ten to twelve eggs. These are a pale bluish green and average 59 millimeters in length by 43 millimeters in diameter. Incubation is performed by the female alone and takes about twenty-eight days.

The young ducklings usually stay in the nest cavity until the day after hatching. This delay may be to give them a chance to regain enough strength to clamber up to the opening of the nest cavity, or it may be to ensure that all the fertile eggs are given a chance to hatch.

When the young are ready to abandon the nest, the female flies down to the water or the earth below and calls to her babies. There is usually no hesitation on their part. Responding to her call, they clamber up to the entrance hole and jump out. The entire brood has usually vacated the nest site in a matter of minutes. The fall, no matter how high, does not seem to do the baby goldeneyes any harm. They immediately gather around the female, who shepherds them about in the search for food.

The baby common goldeneye has a dark, brownish black face, crown of the head, back of the neck, back, wings and tail. A brown bib crosses the breast. The cheeks, front of the throat and belly are white. The bill is bluish gray, and the feet are greenish yellow.

FLIGHT: The fledgling period for the common goldeneye is about two months. The adult male goldeneye, who has gone through his eclipse phase, and the young are both capable of flying more or less simultaneously. At about this time the female goldeneye drops all her primary feathers and becomes flightless.

In flight, the common goldeneye's wing beat is so rapid that it makes a whistling sound, which is why this duck is nicknamed the "whistler." It is capable of flying at speeds of up to 50 miles per hour. The goldeneyes fly in small flocks, usually at considerable heights, rising from the water with a running takeoff and spiraling to gain altitude.

MIGRATION: The common goldeneye is a hardy duck and stays as far north as the icing conditions permit. It is often forced far to the south, however, in its search for open water.

The spring migration is under way by the first of March and continues until the end of May. The main direction for this migration is north and northwestward.

The fall migration takes place about the end of September and continues until the latter part of November. Even in the fall migration the common goldeneyes do not travel in large flocks.

HABITS: The goldeneye is a very wary bird. It decoys well but is always suspicious and constantly alert to the slightest sign of danger. If it detects danger, it often flies back and forth over the danger spot several times as if to ascertain the nature of the threat.

After it has been shot at a few times, the goldeneye changes its feeding habits. Ordinarily, these ducks do very little flying at night, but as the hunting pressure increases they forsake their normal diurnal habits and fly and feed only at night. The days are spent far out on the open water, which affords them protection.

The common goldeneye is a superb diver and not only seeks sanctuary under the water, but also feeds there and often dives and splashes about just in sport. While swimming underwater, it normally uses just its feet, but if more speed is needed, it makes use of its wings as well.

FOOD: In searching for food, the goldeneye dives below the surface and systematically turns over all the smaller stones with its beak, devouring whatever insects, larvae, mollusks or crustaceans it finds there. About three-quarters of this duck's diet is composed of animal matter, most of it gathered on the floor of lakes or rivers. The goldeneye also chases and eats small fish.

The bulk of the 25 percent of plant matter in this duck's diet is also collected in the depths. The goldeneye's favorite plant foods are pondweed, wild celery, musk grass, bulrush, smartweed, widgeon grass, eelgrass, waterweed, sedge and wild millet.

LIFE SPAN: The common goldeneye duck has a potential life span of between seven and nine years. There appears to be no individual longevity record for this species.

ENEMIES: The adult goldeneye's flight speed and diving ability help it to elude many of its winged predators. The old, young, sick or infirm individuals are naturally most subject to predation because they are easier to catch.

Aerial enemies such as hawks, owls, eagles, ravens, crows all prey on the goldeneye. Terrestrial enemies such as the fox, coyote, mink, otter, raccoon, skunk and turtle take the goldeneye adults, ducklings and eggs whenever the opportunity presents itself. Parasites, disease and accidents also take their toll.

TABLE FARE: The high incidence of animal matter in the common goldeneye's diet makes it one of the less desirable ducks for culinary purposes. However, the duck's sporting attributes of speed and caution make it a highly prized game bird. Those that are shot are usually eaten.

Barrow's Goldeneye

Bucephala islandica

The industry of a large beaver colony has maintained Horseshoe Lake in Alaska as a cornucopic wildlife sanctuary. The waters impounded by the beaver dams attract many species of mammals and birds — and naturalists as well.

Several summers ago, I visited this lake, which is set in beautiful Mt. McKinley National Park. I spent much of my time photographing the diverse wildlife; it was at that time that I encountered large numbers of Barrow's goldeneyes.

Though they are much like the common goldeneye, the Barrow's species is not nearly as familiar to most sportsmen. This is because their winter ranges are confined to the northern coastlines along the Pacific and the Atlantic.

DESCRIPTION: The adult male Barrow's goldeneye bears a very close resemblance to the common goldeneye. It, too, has a length of 18 inches, a wingspan of 28½ inches and a weight of about 2 pounds.

The most conspicuous field identification differences between the males of these two species are the purplish sheen to the Barrow's head and its distinctive white facial crescent between the eye and the bill. The bills of both birds are black, and their eyes, of course, are yellow.

The Barrow's neck, breast, belly and flanks are white. The back and rump are black, and the tail is a dark grayish brown. The Barrow's wing has less white in the coverts and secondaries than that of the common goldeneye. The primaries are grayish brown. The feet are orangy yellow.

The female Barrow's goldeneye looks very much like her counterpart, the female common goldeneye. The most conspicuous difference between the females of the two species is that the common goldeneye's bill has a blackish base and an orange tip, while the bill of the Barrow's goldeneye is bright yellow with a dark nail tip. The Barrow's female also has a much more rounded head than the female common goldeneye, which has an angular sloping head.

DISTRIBUTION: The Barrow's goldeneye is primarily a western duck, and only there is it fairly common. It is found only in North America and has two distinct ranges with no migration between the birds of the east and west coasts.

Barrow's Goldeneye

Along the Pacific, its wintering range extends from Alaska and British Columbia south to the northern half of California. Its breeding range extends from the interior of Alaska to the Yukon, British Columbia, Alberta, Washington, Oregon, California, Montana, Wyoming, Colorado and Utah.

On the Atlantic coast, the wintering range of the Barrow's goldeneye covers both sides of the Gulf of St. Lawrence, New Brunswick, Maine, New Hampshire, Vermont, Massachusetts, New York, Connecticut and Rhode Island. Its breeding range is the northeast coast of Labrador and the south coast of Greenland.

COMMUNICATION: Neither sex of the Barrow's goldeneye is very vocal. The male's main call is a hoarse, croaking sound. During the breeding season, he also utters a soft, mewing cry.

BREEDING AND NESTING: The Barrow's goldeneye arrives on its breeding grounds as soon as the ice has begun to break up. The birds arrive in small flocks, and the courtship rivalry is a dominant activity. Males chase after one another and often engage in battles where they rise up and flail out at each other with their wings.

Like the common goldeneye, the male Barrow's goldeneye, in displaying for the female, performs the headthrow, tossing his head back until it touches his tail. As the head is brought forward, the feet are kicked backward and up with enough force to send an arc of water flying backward for a distance of up to 2 feet.

The male also erects his head feathers, showing off their purplish iridescence to the best advantage. Then, stretching his head and neck out before him, but without touching the water, he chases after the female. If she is willing to accept his advances, she engages in a ritual of bill-dipping or make-believe drinking. The male, too, then goes through these actions.

The female, before copulation, relaxes and floats on the surface of the water as if she were dead. The male floats near her and stretches out his wing and leg. Then, erecting his neck to its fullest extent, with his bill pointing downward, he swims to her, grasps her head feathers and mounts her. After copulation, the male retains his hold on the female's head while they rotate in a circle on the surface of the water.

Nest selection depends on where the Barrow's goldeneye is found. It prefers to nest in a tree cavity, and on its western range such sites are comparatively easy to locate. It utilizes any natural cavity or abandoned woodpecker hole that is large enough to admit it.

No extra material is brought into the nest cavity. The material that has been found in the nesting cavities of the Barrow's goldeneye was undoubtedly brought in by previous tenants, such as flying squirrels.

The goldeneyes that breed in the upper reaches of Labrador and along the coast of Iceland are not able to nest in trees because there are none. These ducks place their nests in splits and fissures in rocks, under boulders or in whatever cavities they can find in the banks of streams and rivers. The ducks nesting in the rocks use more down in the lining of their nests than those nesting in trees.

EGGS AND YOUNG: The Barrow's goldeneye has a large clutch, ten to fifteen eggs being commonly found. The eggs vary in color from olive- to blue-green. They average 61 millimeters in length by 44 millimeters in diameter. Incubation requires twenty-six to twenty-eight days and is performed exclusively by the female.

The males, prior to going into their eclipse plumage, completely forsake the females and gather together on the larger lakes or out on the ocean.

The female, while on her eggs, sits very tight and, according to various observers, sometimes has to be lifted off the nest if the eggs are to be seen.

When the ducklings hatch, those in the trees remain in the nest for a period of twenty-four hours after hatching. Those which hatch among rocks leave the nest as soon as their down is dry.

The Barrow's goldeneye duckling has a black head and face down to a line below the eye. A wide white patch extends from the rear of one cheek across the throat to the rear of the other cheek. The back of the neck is black. The duckling's back, rump, tail and wings are dark brown or almost black. A wide brown band extends across the chest. The breast and belly are white, the bill is black, and the feet are yellowish green.

The young feed on insects, an eating habit they never outgrow. This rich protein diet produces good growth, and in about eight weeks the young are fully fledged and capable of flying.

FLIGHT: Because of the rear placement of its legs, the Barrow's goldeneye is classified as a diving duck. Like the other diving ducks, it has to run along the surface of the water before it can take off. It lumbers into the air rather heavily and usually flies low over the water unless it is frightened. If alarmed, it spirals upward, rapidly gaining altitude.

This duck has a very rapid wing beat and, with the common

In a shower of spray, a Barrow's goldeneye runs along the water's surface to gain speed for the takeoff.

goldeneye, shares the name of whistler because of the sound produced by its beating wings. It is capable of flying at speeds of up to 50 miles per hour. In migration, it flies at considerable heights.

MIGRATION: It is only during the spring migration or the breeding season that large flocks of these ducks can be seen together. Most of the western Barrow's goldeneyes migrate only a short distance. In fact, some of them actually breed in the area where they have wintered. The migration of the eastern Barrow's goldeneye, although longer than that of its western cousin, is short when compared with the journeys undertaken by most other species of ducks.

The northward migration gets under way in late February and continues until May. The fall migration starts in October and continues into December, according to the extent of the freeze-up.

HABITS: The Barrow's goldeneye is among the least wary of the ducks. Much of this tameness is due to the duck never having seen a human being in much of its wilderness breeding range. Although this goldeneye is not a sociable duck, it comes into decoys fairly easily. However, these must be set in calm water because this duck seems reluctant to land on fast-running water.

The rear placement of its legs allows the goldeneye to dive with skill and ease. It prefers to feed in comparatively deep water. Its diving ability is also used to escape from whatever danger presents itself.

FOOD: The diet of the Barrow's goldeneye is 26 percent vegetable matter and 74 percent animal matter. The duck's favorite plant foods are pondweed, algae, widgeon grass and horned pondweed. To find crayfish, which it avidly eats, the goldeneye dives to the bottom of a stream or pond and turns over with its bill whatever stones it can move, seeking its elusive prey. It also eats snails, mollusks, crustaceans, insects and their larvae and some small fish whenever the opportunity presents itself.

LIFE SPAN: The Barrow's goldeneye has a potential life span of from seven to nine years. A search for longevity records for this species has proved fruitless.

ENEMIES: Gulls, jaegers, skuas, crows, ravens, hawks, owls, eagles, foxes, coyotes, mink, otter, large fish and turtles prey on the Barrow's goldeneye whenever possible. Disease, parasites and accidents take their toll.

TABLE FARE: This duck is nowhere very common and is therefore not excessively hunted. Often, because of its limited ranges, it never gets into areas where it could be hunted. Its flesh is considered palatable when the duck is feeding on vegetation, but undesirable when it is feeding on various types of animal matter.

Bufflehead

Bucephala albeola

Some years ago I lived at the Boy Scout Camp of Pahaquarra, which was on the Delaware River opposite Poxono Island. Below the island the river ran over some rocky shallows, producing a long riffle. This spot, which remained free from ice all winter, was always frequented by American mergansers, American goldeneye and bufflehead ducks.

The arrival of the bufflehead ducks, usually in December, was always quite an event, because we knew that within the next two days the bald eagles would be back, following their prey as they had done for years.

The eagle's modus operandi in hunting the little buffleheads never varied. The eagle would soar out over the river and the flock of buffleheads would scatter, some taking to the wing, others plunging beneath the water's surface. The eagle would then concentrate on one of the diving ducks, slowly flying overhead as it watched the duck swimming underwater. When the bufflehead needed more oxygen, it would pop to the surface, only to dive again as it was met by the stoop of the eagle. This procedure would continue until the duck could no longer dive. The eagle would then snatch up its prey with a killing talon and fly off to eat its meal.

DESCRIPTION: The bufflehead duck is the smallest wild duck found in North America. It has a total length of 13 to 14 inches, a wingspan of 24 inches and may weigh up to 1 pound. The bufflehead male is primarily white, although it has a black back, rump, tail, tertials and primary feathers. Its head is as round as a butterball—another of the duck's nicknames—and is a metallic greenish purple on the front and lower portions. The cheeks, crown and upper back of the head are pure white, like a cockade. The bill is bluish, and the feet are orangy red.

The female bufflehead is slightly smaller and is a much more demure creature than her mate. Her head, neck, back, rump, tail and wings are a soft brown, while her chest, breast and belly are off-white. Behind and below her eye she sports a white cheek patch. Part of her speculum is white, and her feet are gray.

DISTRIBUTION: The bufflehead duck is found throughout the forty-eight contiguous states and most of Canada and Alaska. Its breeding range extends from north of the Canadian border up into Alaska and is concentrated in the wooded western half of Canada. The bufflehead winters from Maine to Alaska, along the coasts, south to the Mexican border. It is a duck of the woodland lakes and streams in the summer and primarily of the coastline in the winter. Where the interior rivers in the north of the United States are not frozen over, the bufflehead resides.

COMMUNICATION: The male bufflehead's call is a thin, squeaky whistle, while the female has a soft, hoarse quack. These calls, however, are seldom heard. The birds evidently have another method of communicating because when part of the flock is feeding below the surface, it seems to be warned of any impending danger by the ducks that are still on the surface.

BREEDING AND NESTING: The courtship of the bufflehead is quite aggressive. The males become very antagonistic toward one another at this time, frequently chasing and darting at each other.

To impress the female the male erects his head feathers and with his bill pointing upward swims toward and around the females in the flock. He often dives beneath the female, and when he emerges, lowers his bill into the water and shakes his head vigorously from side to side, sending up a fine spray of water. If the female does not appear to be interested, the male flies over to another female who may be more favorably inclined to his attentions. Eventually he succeeds in separating a female from the flock, and the pair then flies off to seek out a nesting spot.

The bufflehead is a cavity-nesting duck, and its nest is usually found in abandoned flicker holes. Failing these, the duck uses any suitable natural cavity; it never makes its own cavity. No additional nesting material is brought into the nest hole, but down from the female is added to whatever rotted wood fragments the hole may already contain. The height of the hole above the ground seems to have no bearing on its acceptability. There are records of these ducks utilizing abandoned kingfisher nest holes in a steep bank if a tree site cannot be found. A major requirement of the nest site is that it be located close to water.

EGGS AND YOUNG: Ten to twelve is the usual number of eggs in a bufflehead clutch. The eggs average about 48 millimeters in length by 34 millimeters in diameter. The most common colors are shades of off-white ranging to buff. Incubation takes twenty-two days and is performed by the female without any help from the male.

The young bufflehead has a dark top half to its head, a dark neck, blending to a deep brownish color on its back and wings, and a light brown collar about the lower neck. Its cheeks, throat, breast and belly are white, and there are also white spots on its wings.

The downy young have no difficulty in leaving the nesting cavity. At their mother's urging, they climb up the inside of the cavity and then just fall or jump out of the opening to the ground below. One would expect this operation to be very damaging to the young ducklings, but apparently this is not so because they simply pick themselves up and scramble after the mother to the water.

Upon losing their down, the young bufflehead of both sexes assume a plumage that is very similar to that of the female. The male's eclipse plumage during his flightless stage is likewise dull. The young male does not acquire its adult coloring of contrasting black and white until it is one and a half years old.

FLIGHT: The young learn to fly usually about two months after hatching.

The bufflehead, because of its small size, gives a deceptive impression of speed in flight, 40 miles per hour being its average top speed. However, it is unique in that it is the only one of the "bay" or "diving" ducks that can take off by springing directly from the water into the air like the "puddle" ducks. The bufflehead sometimes resembles a Polaris missile because it is actually flying as it rises from beneath the surface to burst into the air. Traveling in small, compact flocks of about twenty-five to thirty, the buffleheads fly just above the surface of the water. It is only during migration that the bufflehead flies at any height, and even then it seldom goes above 1,000 feet.

MIGRATION: Despite its energetic, bouncy nature, the bufflehead seems to be reluctant to leave its summer breeding grounds in the fall and just as reluctant to leave its wintering grounds in the spring. Its spring migration may conclude as late as May and, as mentioned earlier, it usually arrives in New Jersey in December.

HABITS: The bufflehead is a common little duck, but in no area is it considered plentiful. The flocks are small and are usually composed of two or three family groups that have affinities with each other. They are sociable little ducks, however, and often consort with other similar species such as the goldeneyes. They in fact seem to get along well with whatever waterfowl or water birds are in their area.

FOOD: Seventy-nine percent of the bufflehead's food consists of animal matter and the remainder of vegetable matter. It prefers to feed in the shallow bays of either the large inland lakes or the ocean. Most of its food is obtained by diving beneath the surface. The bufflehead usually remains submerged for about twenty seconds and then bobs up again for air before plopping down into another dive. As the ducks usually feed in flocks, they churn up the water with their constant popping up and down.

Insects—particularly caddisfly larvae and dragonfly nymphs—form the main portion of the bufflehead's diet. It is an avid consumer of all sorts of water beetles and other insects and also eats small mollusks, crustaceans and fish. Its preferred plant foods are naiad, pondweed, wild celery, wild rice and widgeon grass.

LIFE SPAN: Although it has a potential life span of five to seven years, the bufflehead is very fortunate if it reaches the first figure.

ENEMIES: This duck is probably hunted by an unusual number of predators, both airborne and terrestrial, because its small size makes it more vulnerable than its larger relatives. It, too, is plagued by parasites, disease and accidents.

TABLE FARE: The high incidence of animal matter in the bufflehead's diet makes its flesh most unpalatable. This unpalatability provides the duck with a large measure of protection by discouraging most human hunters.

SEA DUCKS

(Subfamily Aythyinae)

Harlequin Duck

Histrionicus histrionicus

The 800-mile ferry trip between Haines, Alaska, and Prince Rupert, British Columbia, is a beautiful ride along the famed inland passage, through a wilderness of steep cliffs and the forested mountainsides. Storms are ever present in this coastal region, and the enveloping fog is almost constant.

For most of the trip I remained glued to the rain-splattered windows of the ferry because whales are commonly seen in these narrows. As our ship split the curtain of fog, flocks of ducks would either skitter aside and dive for safety or heave themselves into the air to become lost in the mist. It was here that I saw my first harlequin ducks.

The harlequin duck gets is name from Harlequin, the clown, a stock character in the Italian Commedia dell 'Arte. In these old plays Harlequin always appeared wearing a mask and tights of many bright, highly contrasting colors, to which the harlequin duck's plumage can justifiably be compared.

DESCRIPTION: The beautiful and unique markings and coloring of the adult male harlequin duck make its identification easy. It has an overall length of 16¾ inches, a wingspan of 25 inches and a weight of 1¼ pounds.

It is a basically dark duck with conspicuously contrasting stripes. Its head has a dark, blue-black crown. A white line runs vertically in front of the eye and then horizontally, separating the crown from the blue face. There is a white spot behind the eye and a white crescent behind and below the spot. A white collar with a black line below it circles the neck. A vertical white line with black borders fore and aft separates the slate-blue breast from the chestnut flanks. The belly and tail are both brown. The back, rump and upper wing coverts are slate-blue. The outer secondary feathers of the wing are purplish blue, and the inner ones, like the scapulars, sport white lines. The wing primary feathers and underwing surfaces are brown. The bill, legs and feet are bluish gray, and the eye is reddish brown.

When the male goes into his eclipse plumage, he retains all his markings, but the blue color becomes grayish and quite drab. He looks at this time as if he had been thoroughly laundered too many times.

Beside the male's striking coloration, the female's is nondescript. During the breeding season she is basically dark brown with three conspicuous white spots on her head. One spot is in front of and slightly above the eye, another lies behind the eye, and an elongated white patch extends from the bill back through the cheek. The belly is whitish, and the feet, legs and bill are a lighter blue-gray than the male's. The eye, like his, is reddish brown.

When the female goes into her postnuptial molt, she just becomes a lighter, drabber shade of brown, and her white belly becomes grayish.

DISTRIBUTION: There are two distinct subspecies of the harlequin duck, the eastern and the western, which do not intermingle. However, apart from their range differences, nothing distinguishes one from the other.

The harlequin duck of the Pacific areas winters from the Aleutian chain of islands south to California, on or near the coast and the unfrozen rivers. Its breeding range stretches almost as far but reaches inland to a distance of 1,000 miles wherever there are quick-flowing rivers.

The east coast harlequin winters along Greenland's southern coast and from the mouth of the St. Lawrence River south to New Jersey along the Atlantic coast. Its breeding range extends from Labrador to the straits of Hudson's Bay, across to Baffin Island and up into Greenland. Here, the harlequin nests not only along the fast-flowing rivers but along the coast as well.

The western range of this duck is much more extensive than the eastern range, and although it is nowhere a common duck, the bulk of the population is found on the western waters.

COMMUNICATION: The harlequin duck is a noisy bird with quite a repertory of sounds and calls. The most common call is a high-pitched, two-note whistle that descends to a much lower note in a long trill. The male has a hoarse, croaking call that sounds like *heh, heh,* while the female makes an *ek, ek, ek, ek* call. During the breeding season the male has a call that can be rendered as *oy, oy, oy, oy, oy,* and during this season both sexes call *gi-ak, gi-ak.*

BREEDING AND NESTING: The pairing up of the harlequin duck usually takes place on the breeding ground. At such times, the pugnaciousness of the males quickly manifests itself as the rivals swim at each other, hissing loudly. The males often join in actual battles and pull out beakfuls of their rival's feathers.

A common threat display, done for the benefit of the other males, is known as the water-twitch. The male lowers his bill into the water and shakes his head vigorously from side to side, sending the water flying in both directions. Sometimes the male rises up and flaps his wings at his rival.

Both the male and female nod their heads back and forth, and the male then carries this performance further by throwing his head backward and calling loudly as he brings his head forward again. Both sexes also engage in bill-dipping or ritualized drinking before copulation takes place. Then the male rushes over to the female, who, if she is willing to accept him, assumes a prone position in the water.

The nest site selection is determined by the type of habitat that the country affords. Those harlequin ducks that breed near forested areas utilize hollows in trees, whereas those that breed beyond the tree lines nest on the ground among the rocks or weeds. These ducks more than any other species are adapted to living on the swift-flowing northern streams, and many of them are found nesting quite far inland.

The nests that are hidden among the grasses or bushes are usually composed of the same type of material. The nest itself is perhaps 10 to 12 inches in diameter by 2 to 3 inches in height. Finer pieces of grass are used in the lining of the nest, and this liner is further softened by the addition of down from the mother's breast.

EGGS AND YOUNG: The five to six eggs of the harlequin duck's clutch are greenish buff in color. They average 57 millimeters in length by 41 millimeters in diameter. They are rather pointed to prevent them from rolling.

Incubation is performed solely by the female over a period of about twenty-four to twenty-six days.

After the breeding season is over and the female begins to brood, the males usually leave the nesting area to gather in bachelor flocks on the nearby sea.

The young harlequin ducks are covered with dark brown down on the top of the head, the back of the neck, the back, rump, tail and wings. Their cheeks, throat, breast and belly are white. They also sport a white spot above and in front of the eye. The bill has a bluish base and a yellow tip, and their feet are blue-gray.

The ducklings feed on, or are fed, insects as a basic diet during the first weeks of their lives. As they begin to pick up food for themselves, they begin to feed on whatever animal matter they can catch.

FLIGHT: It takes about eight weeks for the young harlequins to become fully fledged and capable of flying.

The harlequin duck is a diving duck and so must run along the surface of the water to build up the momentum needed to get into flight. The birds usually fly low over the water. Their wing beat is rapid, and they can fly at speeds of 40 to 45 miles per hour. Except during migration, they fly more in family groups than in large flocks. They usually fly in an uneven string rather than in the more regular V formations.

MIGRATION: For many of the harlequin ducks migration is seldom more than a seasonal shift away from the ocean to the rivers, streams and lakes farther inland. The eastern harlequins travel much farther than their western counterparts.

The eastern harlequins start their migration north in late February and are usually all on the breeding grounds by late May. The fall migration gets under way in October and is usually completed by the end of November

HABITS: The harlequin duck is unique among the ducks of North America in that it prefers to live around and feed in the very fastest of rushing rivers. In South America there is a duck with similar habits known as the torrent duck. Many of our western streams are frequented by a small bird called a water ouzel that dives beneath the swift water and walks around on the bottom searching for food. The harlequin duck has exactly the same feeding habits.

No water is too swift for these ducks. Even those that are swept through rapids and over small falls seem none the worse for the experience. Along the coast they ride the breakers as buoyantly as corks, apparently unconcerned about the possibility of being dashed against the rocky shore.

Harlequin ducks submerge for an underwater meal.

FOOD: The harlequin duck feeds almost entirely on animal matter, almost all of which is secured by diving. The black mussel found along our seacoasts ranks as perhaps its favorite food. It feeds also on crustaceans, mollusks, gastropods, insects and their larvae, small fish, tadpoles, frogs, etc. At low tide, these ducks become particularly active feeding among the exposed kelp beds or in shallow water on the food that is then more readily available to them.

LIFE SPAN: The harlequin duck has a potential life span of from seven to nine years. However, because it is not a popular sport duck, records and observations concerning it are incomplete, and no individual longevity records appear to be available.

ENEMIES: This duck has a unique enemy in the form of the black mussel, its favorite food, large specimens of which have been known to trap the duck and cause it to drown. The harlequin is also subject to predation by all the more common predators such as hawks, eagles, owls, jaegers, skuas, ravens, crows, mink, otter, foxes, etc. Disease, parasites and accidents take their toll.

TABLE FARE: The harlequin duck is seldom hunted for food by any except Eskimo and Indian hunters. Because of the harlequin's food preferences, its flesh is not coveted by most sportsmen.

Oldsquaw

Clangula hyemalis

In 1969, I spent part of the fall on Canada's Ungava Trough, along the George River. Every day I hiked for hours on end over the bald, knobby ridges of the area in search of caribou. During all that time, I glimpsed only one—but on the river, I observed many an oldsquaw, that duck famous for its call and for its aquatic abilities.

So resonant is the voice of this bird that the fur traders of the Upper Yukon called it the "organ duck." And so strong a diver is the oldsquaw that it has been known to escape predators and hunters alike by diving into water, swimming a long distance submerged, and finally erupting from the water in full flight.

DESCRIPTION: The adult male oldsquaw duck has such conspicuous body markings that it is very easy to identify. It is one of the few ducks found anywhere in the world to have a spring breeding plumage. Its two center tail feathers are so long and carried at such a jaunty angle that they stick out like a handle. These ducks should have been called "long-tailed" because no other duck's tail feathers begin to approach theirs in length, not even those of the pintail duck.

The adult male has a total length of 21 inches, a wingspan of 28½ inches and a weight of about 1½ pounds. In its winter plumage, the male has a white neck, throat and head. There is an elongated, vertical dark patch on the side of the neck and a buff-colored patch around and behind the eye. The breast, back, rump and upper tail coverts and the two long tail feathers are a dark brownish black. The wings are a slightly lighter brown, while the speculum is light brown. The belly, flanks, scapulars and tail feathers are white. The legs and feet are bluish gray. The bill is dark at the base and tip, the rest being a pinkish color. The eyes are reddish brown.

In spring, this plumage changes, and the males that go through this mutation first are the ones that are ready to breed first. In his breeding plumage, the adult male has a dark brown head, neck and breast. A large white facial disc surrounds the eye. The white scapulars are also replaced with brown, the rest of the duck remaining the same color as it was in the winter.

The adult female oldsquaw duck is 16 inches in length, has a wingspan of 28½ inches and weighs about 1½ pounds. The female is not much smaller than the male, the difference in her total length being due to the absence in her case of the long center tail feathers.

In her winter plumage, the female, too, is basically white in color. Her head, throat and neck are white with a light brown mottling on her crown and on the back and sides of her neck. Her lower breast, belly and flanks are pure white, and some of her scapulars are whitish. Her upper breast, back, rump, tail and wings have a shading of light and dark brown in each feather. Her feet and legs are bluish gray, and her bill is gray-brown.

The female adult oldsquaw also goes through a prenuptial molt, but the change in her case is not as conspicuous as it is in the male's. She retains most of her basic body coloration, but the small light brown patches on her head and neck become much larger in area and darker in color. Her whitish scapulars also turn dark.

DISTRIBUTION: The wintering range of the oldsquaw duck is concentrated in three main areas. In the East, it is found along the Atlantic Ocean from the Gulf of St. Lawrence south to North Carolina. In the central area, this duck is found around all the Great Lakes. Its Pacific range extends from the Alaskan panhandle down along the coast as far as Oregon.

This duck's breeding range is extensive. It nests in the tundra coastal areas of Alaska, right across Canada and around Hudson's Bay, north to the Arctic islands and Greenland, and east to Iceland.

This is probably the most northern nesting species of duck in the world.

COMMUNICATION: The Cree Indians are responsible for giving this duck its commonly accepted name of oldsquaw. This duck's constant chattering and calling reminded them of a garrulous old woman. It is probably the most vocal duck on this continent. Whereas most waterfowl try to be secretive, the oldsquaw constantly calls attention to itself with the racket it creates.

The oldsquaw's most common call is a yodel-like *ow-owdle-ow* and *ow-ow-owdle-ow,* with the call rising on the last note. The call is sometimes rendered as *ow-ow-ly* or *ow-owly.* The nickname of "ow-owly" given to this duck comes from this call.

Most of this duck's calls are rich, clear and melodious, although it also has a hoarser quack and makes a short *ah-ah-ah* sound and one that can be described as *ong-ong-onk.*

Both the calls and actions of the oldsquaw give the impression that this is a happy duck.

BREEDING AND NESTING: The pairing up of the sexes takes place on the breeding grounds. Usually the male oldsquaws arrive on the breeding grounds a week or more in advance of the females. When the females arrive, those that have the most advanced breeding cycle are besieged by suitors. Often as many as fifteen drakes will pay court to one female, completely ignoring, and being ignored by, the unresponsive females. These females are not rejected; their turn will come, since many of the males are also geared to a later sexual cycle.

With so much competition, the males do a lot of fighting among themselves. They chase one another about on and under the water and in the air. Occasionally, they lock fast with their beaks while flying and tumble out of the air to land with a splash in the water, where the fray still continues. It is unlikely that any of the rival males are seriously injured in these fracases, but this is not because of any lack of malicious intent.

In the display that he does most frequently for the female the male erects his neck and head vertically and calls again and again. It looks and sounds almost like a hound baying at the moon. At other times, he erects his head and neck and then brings them down almost to the water level, at the same time elevating his tail vertically and kicking out backward with both feet, showering out water behind. This action, like almost all those performed by these ducks, is accompanied by loud calling.

Throughout the males' fighting, displaying and calling, more males come in, attracted by the commotion.

The female oldsquaw is a rather passive partner but may go through a bill-lifting sign of approval. Her main response, and the one the male is most interested in, is to remain prone in front of the mate she has chosen, allowing him to mount her.

Most of the breeding displays are done on pools and ponds that are situated just a few miles in from the sea. After the birds have paired up, the selected male drives all the other ducks, both male and female, off the pond.

The nest is made by the female of the grasses that are found in the area. It is usually concealed under a bush or among rank, standing grass. Heavy grasses are used for the bulk of the nest and fine grasses for the bowl. The female adds a copious lining of down, plucked from her breast and mixed in with the fine grasses. She uses this "blanket" to conceal her eggs when she is not on her nest.

Although the male does not help in the incubation, he remains in the vicinity of the nest during the brooding period.

EGGS AND YOUNG: Although some oldsquaw nests have been known to contain as many as seventeen eggs, the average clutch numbers six to eight eggs. These average 53 millimeters in length by 37 millimeters in diameter and range in color from olive to greenish buff. They are much more pointed than the eggs of most of the other ducks.

The female oldsquaw is a close sitter, allowing potential danger to approach very closely before she abandons her nest. Incubation requires twenty-four to twenty-five days.

Oldsquaw ducklings have a dark brown, almost black, face, head and back of the neck. A wide white throat patch extends from cheek to cheek. The upper breast, back, tail, wings and flanks are a uniform dark brown. The lower breast and belly are white. The feet, legs and bill are blue-gray, the bill being slightly darker.

The female is a very determined mother and uses all sorts of ruses to decoy danger away from her family. She has even been known to flutter right up to a human being to draw attention away from her young and give them a chance to escape.

The young attempt to escape from danger by diving, but at an early age they are not too successful in this, as they can remain under water for only four or five seconds. Adults can stay under for as long as a minute.

As soon as possible after the ducklings hatch, the female forsakes the small ponds and takes her family down to the open sea.

FLIGHT: The fledgling period for the oldsquaw ducklings is about two months, and when they can fly, the female becomes flightless. The male oldsquaw does not go into an eclipse plumage, but he becomes flightless while the female is incubating the eggs.

The oldsquaw is a restless bird and often takes to the wing for no apparent reason. The birds also have an un-ducklike characteristic of rising from the water as a large flock and "towering," in other words flying in tight, ascending spirals to heights where they are almost out of sight. Then, just as quickly, they drop down out of the sky to land with loud plops in the water.

Unlike most of the diving ducks, the oldsquaw can rise from the water vertically without having to run along the surface. It usually flies low over the water when moving from spot to spot, but even this flight is characterized by a constant twisting and turning of the entire flock. If it is attacked by an aerial predator while in flight, it plummets into the water like a dropped shot, swims under the surface and comes up some distance away, bursting up from the water and into the air without any hesitation.

The oldsquaw is a swift flier, capable of a speed of 45 miles per hour, and its wing beat is so rapid that it creates a whistling sound. The duck's speed and erratic flight pattern make it a most elusive target for a hunter.

MIGRATION: During the spring migration, the oldsquaws fly in large flocks that are usually segregated according to sex. The males, as already stated, start north first. The main northward migrations take place in April, May and June.

The fall migration is made in mixed flocks, the birds flying at considerable heights. The oldsquaw has a protracted breeding season, and so the fall migration is not as clearly defined as it is

An alert and protective mother, the oldsquaw hen keeps a sharp eye out for danger as she escorts her ducklings on a short swim.

with many species of ducks. However, the bulk of the oldsquaws migrate southward during the months of September and October.

Habits: The oldsquaw is a sociable duck and is usually quite tame. A sometimes fatal curiosity makes it decoy easily. The fact that these ducks fly so tightly bunched is also detrimental to them because a single, well-placed shot often drops a number of the birds. Whereas most ducks remain on the water if the weather is good, the oldsquaw is constantly taking to the air and making several turns aloft before dropping back again in almost the same spot. And it does this whether it is disturbed or not.

Although the oldsquaw can rise from the water vertically, it is a true diving duck and has the rear placement of the legs needed for depth-diving. When it dives, it frequently uses its wings underwater. It has been caught in fishnets that were set as deep as 180 feet. This is an exceptional depth for a duck, although it is fairly common for the loons.

Food: The oldsquaw's diet is composed of 88 percent animal matter and 12 percent vegetable matter. Almost all its food is taken by diving, although the ducks are quick to take advantage of the food that is exposed at low tide. The black mussel is a favorite food, and as these bivalves open up to feed on food particles brought in by the incoming tide, the oldsquaw is there to pluck them from their shells. It feeds also on all sorts of small mollusks, crustaceans, insects and their larvae and small fish.

The oldsquaw eats some types of seaweed, pondweed, pickerel-weed, duckweed, water plantain, blue flag and moss, all of which it gathers in the water. It feeds on some types of land grasses.

Life Span: The oldsquaw has a potential life span of from seven to nine years. Although some individuals undoubtedly live beyond this age, there are no authenticated records of a greater longevity.

Enemies: The gulls, skuas and jaegers of the far north are the oldsquaw's principal enemies. Hawks, owls, eagles, ravens and polar bears also prey on it, and foxes destroy many of the nests. Disease, parasites and accidents take a further toll.

Table Fare: Because of the high animal content in this duck's diet, its flesh leaves much to be desired. Although it is often shot by hunters who are out after scoters, it presents as much of a challenge to a cook as it does to a wing shot.

Common Scoter

Oidemia nigra

Surf Scoter   *Melanitta perspicillata*

White-winged Scoter   *Melanitta deglandi*

Up until a few years ago, all three species of scoters were classified as a single genus, but today they have been split up. The common scoter, which was formerly called the American scoter, is of the genus *Oidemia,* while the surf and white-winged scoters share the genus *Melanitta.* Along the coast of New England, where scoter-hunting is a very popular sport, these birds are commonly called "coots." However, these sea ducks should not be confused with the much smaller, rail-like *Fulica americana* that is commonly called the American coot.

Because these scoters look alike and have similar habits and overlapping ranges, all three will be discussed in this one section, the differences between them being pointed out.

DESCRIPTION: The adult male common scoter is the only entirely black duck found in North America. The only splash of color on this bird is the large, fleshy, golden-yellow protuberance on the basal portion of the upper bill. The rest of the bill is black, and even the feet and legs are dark. The adult male is 19 inches in length, has a wingspan of 32½ inches and weighs 2½ pounds.

The adult female common scoter is about the same size as the male but is a predominantly brown bird. The top portion of her head and the back of her neck are solid brown. Her bill is black. The cheeks, throat, sides and front of the female's neck are ashy white. The breast and belly are a speckled mixture of white and brown, which is lightest in the center and grows darker on the flanks. The rest of the female's feathers are a two-toned brown, each feather's darker center and lighter edges creating an overall mottled appearance.

The adult male surf scoter is slightly smaller than the common scoter, having a length of 19 inches and a wingspan of 32 inches and weighing about 2 pounds. This scoter is also entirely black except for two very conspicuous white patches on its crown and at the nape of the neck. Its bill is long and thick, swollen at the base and brightly colored with black, white, yellow and orange. Its feet also are a bright pinkish red.

The adult female surf scoter is slightly smaller than the male and differs from the common scoter female by having a much browner coloration. She lacks the white throat and neck of the common scoter, having instead a white facial patch right behind her bill and another one on the rear portion of the cheek.

The adult male white-winged scoter is the largest and heaviest of the three scoters. Because of this extra size and weight it moves much more sluggishly than the other two scoters. It measures 21 inches in length, has a wingspan of 37½ inches and weighs up to 3½ pounds. This scoter also is basically black, but it is easy to recognize because of its pure white wing speculum and a small white patch extending behind the eye. Both the male surf and the male white-winged scoter have white eyes, while the females of all three species and the male common scoter have brown eyes. The bill of the white-winged male has a swollen black base and is basically orange with purplish sides and a reddish tip. The feet and legs are also gaudy, being a purplish pink on the outside that shades to orange on the inside.

The adult female white-winged scoter also has the white wing speculum as her most distinguishing field mark. Her feet and legs are orange. She is larger and darker than the female surf scoter but otherwise very similar in appearance.

Sometimes when the white-winged scoters are swimming on

the water, the white specula are not visible, and at such times it is very difficult to tell the female surf and white-winged scoters apart.

DISTRIBUTION: The common scoter has a smaller population and a more restricted range than the other two scoters. It is more of a maritime bird than they are. Its winter range on the Pacific coast extends from the Alaskan panhandle and Aleutian Islands and British Columbia down to the state of Washington, with a few stragglers reaching Oregon and California. Its winter range on the Atlantic coast extends from the Canadian Maritime Provinces south to North Carolina. Its breeding range runs along Alaska's Bering Sea and Beaufort Sea coasts and into Canada's Yukon and Northwest Territories.

The surf scoter also is found along both coasts in the winter. On the Pacific coast its range extends from Alaska's panhandle through British Columbia, Washington, Oregon and California, down to Baja California. Along the Atlantic coast the range extends from Canada's Maritime Provinces south to North Carolina. The surf scoter's breeding range is located inland in western Alaska, the Yukon, the Northwest Territories and as far south as northern Alberta.

The white-winged scoter's wintering range is the same as that of the surf scoter. Its breeding range also overlaps that of the surf scoter but extends much farther south. It reaches the Beaufort Sea and west to Alaska, embraces the Yukon and the Northwest Territories and extends south to British Columbia, Alberta, Saskatchewan, Manitoba and northern Montana and North Dakota.

COMMUNICATION: The scoters have a variety of calls that are common to all three species. Their plaintive *cour-loo* or *whee-loo* call is a one-note, musically whistled call that is perhaps the one most frequently heard. They also make a harsh, short, croaking sound.

In some of the eastern areas, the white-winged scoter is referred to as a bell coot because of the bell-like sounds that it makes. There has been some confusion as to whether these sounds were made by the bird's voice or wings. Its wings whistle in flight, but the bell-like notes are a vocal sound. This is why the bird is sometimes called a bell-tongued coot.

BREEDING AND NESTING: The scoters, even though some of them have overlapping ranges in both the winter and the breeding seasons, seldom migrate together. They may associate in mixed flocks in the winter and may arrive on the breeding grounds about the same time, but they usually migrate in flocks according to their species.

The scoters are sociable birds and spend most of their lives in flocks. Pairing is done before the birds arrive on their breeding grounds, judging by the lateness of their arrival and the small amount of courtship display that is seen there.

The courtship is usually performed while the birds are gathering before their northward flights. The males concentrate on the females who have undergone the most advanced hormonal changes, and who will therefore breed and lay their eggs first. The rival

Gregarious scoters spend most of their lives in flocks.

males chase each other about, but there seems to be very little actual body contact. With their necks outstretched, they swim at one another at high speed, one usually giving way by veering off or diving beneath the surface.

In displaying for the female, the males rise up on the top of the water, wildly flapping their wings. The female preens behind her wing. When the males press their suit too hard, she dives beneath the surface of the water, only to be followed by all the males. When she pops to the surface, the males also pop up.

Occasionally one of the males flies off to a distance of about 75 feet. Upon alighting on the water, he swims back toward the female like a ship steaming along at full speed. The male also engages in bill-dipping, and sometimes while his bill is in the water, he shakes his head from side to side very rapidly, sending the water flying.

When the female has selected a male, she helps him drive off the rival males as well as other paired ducks if this is possible. Most of the displays of both the male and female are done to the accompaniment of their low, whistled call.

The scoters' nest is usually well hidden in among high grasses, low bushes or rocks. It is close to water and is usually a hollow scraped in the ground lined with leaves, grasses and down. Occasionally the nest is in a small mound built up of the same material. There is usually enough extra material to form a blanket that is used to cover the eggs before the female is ready to sit or after she is sitting and has to leave the nest for food and water.

EGGS AND YOUNG: The common scoter and the surf scoter lay between six and ten eggs to a clutch, while the white-winged scoter lays between nine and fourteen. The reason for this discrepancy in numbers is probably that the first two scoters nest farther north and along the Arctic Ocean, while the white-winged scoter nests in the heart of Canada, where it is subject to more predation. The larger clutch of eggs would therefore be designed to offset the higher mortality rate, since every bird living in the wilds lays eggs enough to maintain its species' population.

The eggs of all three of the scoters are the same bright pinkish buff color. Those of the common scoter and the surf scoter are the same size, averaging about 61 millimeters in length by 42 millimeters in diameter. The eggs of the white-winged scoter are slightly larger, being 65 millimeters in length by 45 millimeters in diameter.

The incubation of the eggs requires from twenty-eight to thirty days. The males of all three species abandon the females as soon as all the eggs have been laid and the female starts to sit. The males retire to the coves and bays of the sea or to large inland lakes, where they concentrate in big flocks.

The young of the three scoters have similar color patterns but different degrees of shading. In all three species, the young have a blue bill with a reddish nail tip. The top half of the head and face and the back of the neck are dark. The lower cheek and throat are white. A brown bib encircles the top of the breast, and the back, wings, rump, tail and thighs are also brown. The lower breast, belly and under-tail portion are white. The feet are pinkish green.

The young white-winged scoter is the brightest white and, living up to its name, it has a white speculum. The surf scoter is an intermediate grayish white, while the common scoter is the darkest of all three, being sooty in color.

FLIGHT: The young scoters have a long fledgling period of as much as nine weeks before they are capable of flying.

The adult male scoters do not go into an eclipse plumage, but they do shed their primary flight feathers in August and become flightless. The females' postnuptial molt is later than the males', and they are flightless in the last part of August and the first part of September.

All the scoters seem to have difficulty in taking off from the water, but once they are airborne, their flight is swift and direct. Their wing beats are rapid enough to produce a whistling sound, and their flight speed is between 50 and 60 miles per hour. Because of their comparatively large size, the scoters appear to be flying more slowly than is actually the case.

The scoters travel in large, grouped flocks or in long strings. If not disturbed, they fly very low over the water. When the weather is bad and the wind strong, these ducks fly along the troughs between the large waves, which provide shelter from the wind.

MIGRATION: As already mentioned, the scoters migrate northward very slowly, gathering together in ever-increasing numbers. When at last they lift off on the final leg of their journey, it is so late in the season that they can be assured of finding open water when they arrive on their breeding grounds. The last lap of the spring migration does not take place until the latter part of May or the beginning of June.

The scoters, particularly the common and surf scoters, dislike flying overland at any time and usually fly a longer route following the coastline. The white-winged scoter has to fly overland to reach its nesting grounds in the interior.

The fall flight is also somewhat delayed by the scoters' long fledgling period, so that it seldom gets under way until the end of September and is at its peak in the middle of October.

HABITS: Being sociable ducks, the scoters decoy readily. One of the most famed areas for scoter-hunting is Merrymeeting Bay, Maine. The Chesapeake Bay area also offers great sport.

The scoters are not particularly wary until they have been exposed to hunting pressure. After being shot at, they change their daily habits, feeding inshore at night and flying out by day to the safety of the open sea, where they raft up by the thousands.

Scoters habitually take a morning flight. Often, for no apparent reason, they rise up from the water en masse, fly about for half an hour or more and then settle down again in the same spot from which they took off. This is, perhaps, their daily constitutional.

The scoters, being sea ducks, are excellent swimmers and divers. They normally use their wings when swimming underwater. They can dive deeply and often stay submerged for a minute or more. They are rarely seen on land and come ashore only to nest.

Food: The common scoter's diet is 10 percent vegetable matter and 90 percent animal matter. The surf scoter's diet is 12 percent vegetarian and 88 percent animal matter. The white-winged scoter eats 6 percent vegetable and 94 percent animal matter.

All the scoters obtain most of their food by diving for it or feeding in the shallows exposed by the receding tide. They all feed on the same items. The vegetable part of their diet is composed of eelgrass, widgeon grass, algae, kelp and musk grass. The animal matter is made up of mussels, barnacles, rock clams, oysters, crustaceans, amphipods, insects and fish. The shells of some of their food are broken up by the small stones that they ingest for just that purpose. The shells, in turn, help to grind up other softer foods that they eat.

Life Span: The scoters have a potential life span of about nine to twelve years. Unfortunately, no individual longevity records are available for any of the three scoters.

Enemies: The scoters run the full gamut of predators because of the extreme ranges of their breeding and wintering grounds, which stretch from the Arctic to the temperate zones. Gulls, ravens, crows, skuas, jaegers, hawks, owls, eagles, bears, foxes, raccoons, skunks, coyotes, otter, mink, turtles, etc., all prey on these ducks according to where they are found at what time of the year. Disease, parasites and accidents add to the mortality rate.

Table Fare: The scoters are avidly hunted because they are found in such large numbers in some parts of their wintering ranges. The high incidence of animal matter in their diet does not make them very desirable table fare. However, most of the sportsmen who hunt the scoters, which are rated high as a sporting game duck, do eat them. The young ducks of the year, of course, are the most sought after because they are the most tender. The young scoters are usually roasted, but the older birds have to be stewed.

Common Eider

Somateria mollissima

King Eider   *Somateria spectabilis*

Spectacled Eider   *Lampronetta fischeri*

Steller's Eider   *Polysticta stelleri*

The sea was rough, as it always is in Cook's Inlet in Alaska when the tide is flowing in. As I sat on a huge rock, shrouded under a tent of camouflage material, I noticed far out in the inlet some objects bobbing about on the rough water. Even with binoculars it was difficult to see what they were, but at last I was able to identify them as an adult duck and her partially grown young.

As each wave crested beneath them the ducks were lifted into sight but were just as quickly hidden when they slipped down into the trough. It seemed incredible that even ducks could swim in such waves, but, despite slow progress, they successfully reached the shore and swam out of sight under the rock where I was sitting. They then busied themselves swimming among the rocks of the shoreline feeding upon various types of sea life that were clinging to the rocks. By this time I had identified them as a mother common eider and her brood.

DESCRIPTION: The adult male common eider duck is 24 inches in length, has a wingspan of 42 inches and weighs about 4½ pounds. Its forehead and bill profile is similar to that of the canvasback duck. A fleshy extension of the yellow bill goes up the forehead almost to the eye. The top of the head to below the eye is black. The back of the head is green, the cheeks, throat and neck are white.

Common Eiders

The lower breast is a cream color, and the back, scapulars and middle coverts of the wing are white. The rest of the wing and the belly, rump and tail are black. The feet are a dull yellowish color.

The female common eider is smaller than the male. Her basic coloration is a deep brown, her feathers having black bars that create a lined and scaled appearance. The edge of her greater wing coverts and her secondary feathers are white.

The adult male king eider is 22 inches in length, has a 37-inch wingspread and weighs 3¼ pounds. His head is striking in appearance because the yellow bill extends into a black-edged frontal shield that reaches to the top of the forehead. The top and back of the head down to the eye are blue. The cheek, throat and neck are white, and the breast is a cream color. The forepart of the back, the middle wing coverts and part of the flank feathers are white. The rest of the wing, the lower back, belly, rump and tail are black. The feet are dull yellow.

The female king eider is almost identical with the female common eider, although it is slightly smaller.

The adult male spectacled eider is 21 inches in length, has a wingspan of 36 inches and weighs about 3½ pounds. This duck's eye is surrounded by white feathers that are separated from the green head by a black line. The bill is yellow. The bird has a white throat, neck, back, scapulars and middle wing coverts, and the rest of its body is black. Its feet are dull yellow.

The female spectacled eider has a faint "spectacle" of brown instead of white. Her basic brown color is more reddish than that of the common eider. Except for these two points, she is almost identical in markings with the female common eider.

The adult male Steller's eider is the smallest of the four eiders, with a length of 18 inches, a wingspan of 29 inches and a weight of 1½ pounds. This bird's bill is blue and shaped like that of a regular duck rather than like the typical eider bill. The head is whitish green with a bright green tuft at the base of the crown. The throat, neck, back, rump and tail are bluish black. The wing coverts are white, the secondaries bluish with white trailing edges, and the primary feathers black. The breast and belly are a cinnamon brown that darkens toward the tail. The feet and legs are blue-gray.

The female Steller's eider is the smallest of the eiders and in basic appearance is similar to the female common eider except that her greater wing coverts are edged with white and her secondary feathers are blue-gray edged with white. Her feet also are blue-gray.

DISTRIBUTION: The common eider is the most abundant of the four eiders, but even this duck is rarely seen in the United States. It winters along the southern Alaskan coast and in upper British Columbia in the West. In the East it winters from James Bay and Ungava south along the coast to New England. It is most commonly seen in the United States at Chatham, Massachusetts, where it congregates in huge rafts that blanket the ocean. Its breeding range is the northern coast of North America and the Arctic islands.

The king eider's range is basically the same as that of the common eider, but this duck ventures a little farther south on the Pacific coast in the winter, sometimes reaching Washington and Oregon.

The spectacled eider is very rare in North America, being found only along Alaska's western and northern coasts. It is common along the coast of Siberia. The only time I have ever seen this eider was during my stay at the Eskimo village of Tununak, Alaska, on the Bering Sea. The Steller's eider is even rarer than the spectacled eider. Because these two ducks are so rarely, if ever, seen by sportsmen, further discussion will be confined to the other two eiders, which they in any case resemble in their life habits.

COMMUNICATION: The male common eider makes a soft cooing sound that can be described as *ah-hoo* or *ah-ee-oo*. He also makes a harsher, moaning sound. The male king eider makes a vibrating, cooing sound. The females of both these ducks have a coarse *cuck, cuck, cuck* call.

BREEDING AND NESTING: The male common and king eiders head north for the breeding grounds about two or three weeks before the females, so that all the courtship and pairing up is done on the breeding grounds.

The very similar courtship displays of these two ducks are a showy performance because of the birds' striking coloration and patterning. When the drakes display for the female, they keep up a constant cooing. As they approach the female, they lean forward and extend their bodies, necks and heads full length. Then they snap back to an upright swimming position. In order to present their showy bellies, they extend their bills skyward, and by flapping their wings and treading water they almost succeed in walking on top of the water.

The female encourages the male by swimming against him and following him about. She incites him to copulation by submerging most of her body as she swims about him.

The eiders are gentle ducks, and there is very little fighting between the males.

The common eider is a marine bird and builds its nest on the ocean shore or coastal islands. It is a colony bird, and often the nests are only a couple of yards apart. They are built on the ground, well above the high tide mark. While some of the nests are in the open, hidden among the rocks, others are concealed under grasses and bushes.

The king eider always nests near the ocean, but its nesting preference is for freshwater areas. Like the common eider, the king eider may build its nest on the bare beach or hidden under whatever vegetation is handy.

Spectacled eider hen on her nest. These eiders are rarely seen in North America except in parts of coastal Alaska.

The nests of both of these birds are made up of seaweeds, grass, moss and sticks. The eider duck is world-famous because of the fantastic insulating qualities of its down, which it always uses copiously for its nest. Each nest yields about 1 to 1¼ ounces of this extremely light down. The natives who gather the down take only a little of it until the female has finished with the nest. Then it is completely collected. In Europe the eiders are encouraged to nest unmolested and "duck farms" are set up to collect the down.

Eggs and Young: The average clutch of eggs for both species comprises five to six eggs. The eggs of the common eider are pale olive-green splotched with white. They average 76 millimeters in length by 50 millimeters in diameter. The king eider's eggs are dark olive-buff in color and average 67 millimeters in length by 44 millimeters in diameter.

Incubation in the case of both eiders is done exclusively by the female and takes twenty-eight days. At this time the male eiders usually fly out to sea, where they raft up in large flocks. The female eiders are often quite belligerent in the defense of their nests.

The eider ducklings are easy to recognize because of their sloped bills. The two species are similar in appearance, except that the common eider's bill is longer than that of the king eider.

The ducklings have brown heads, necks, breasts, backs and wings. Their throats and bellies are white. The common eider duckling has blue-gray feet and legs, while the king eider duckling's legs and feet are a dull yellow.

The down for which the eider ducks are famous stands the ducklings in good stead. As soon as they hatch and can move their mother takes them to the nearest body of water, which usually has ice floating about on it. The young seem impervious to the cold, and this hardiness is necessary since the eiders are ice-fringe residents.

FLIGHT: A period of sixty to seventy days elapses before the young eiders have developed enough to be able to fly.

The eiders fly well but have chunky bodies that are not built for speed. Their flight speed is about 45 miles per hour. They often fly in long lines, usually low over the water. To get into flight, the birds run and spatter along the surface for a considerable distance before becoming airborne.

MIGRATION: The migration distance for most of the eiders is comparatively short. They are usually pushed south by the ice formation in winter and closely follow its break-up in the spring. During the break-up, the ducks fly into every open lead of water they can locate.

On July 23 and 24, 1969, I was at Point Barrow, Alaska, which is the largest Eskimo village in the world. Both the common and king male eider ducks were migrating west from the Beaufort Sea breeding grounds to the Chukchi Sea, where they go into their eclipse stage. The females and young follow at a much later date. As the ducks pass over the narrow spit of land on which the village lies, they are hunted by the Eskimos. Records show that this site has been used by the Eskimos for hunting for more than 1,500 years. The ducks that are killed are stored for food for the winter.

HABITS: The eider ducks are very shy and wary, perhaps as a result of the intense hunting pressure of the Eskimos, who have no closed season on the eiders. During the limited periods of time each year that the ducks are in their vicinity, the Eskimos hunt them whenever and wherever possible.

The eiders are excellent divers because of the rear placement of their legs. Often, if disturbed, they attempt to escape by diving rather than by flying. They use their wings under the water as well as in the air.

I have never seen an eider duck on land. Although they come to the shoals and shallows to feed, they retire to the ocean to rest. There they gather in large numbers and sleep even though they are being tossed about like a bunch of corks.

Food: The eiders' diet is almost entirely made up of animal matter. They particularly favor the edible mussel. They also feed on small fish and all sorts of mollusks, crustaceans, insects and their larvae, starfish and some plant food.

Life Span: The eiders have a potential life span of nine to ten years. The only longevity record appears to be for a common eider that lived to be five years old.

Enemies: In the far north, along the sea coasts, gulls take the place of the crow as the greatest destroyer of nests and young. The polar bear, Arctic fox, wolf, raven and jaeger take the eggs and young, and the larger predators take the adults, too, if they can catch them. Killer whales also feed on the eiders, although the ducks are no more than an hors d'oeuvre for them. Disease, parasites and accidents take their toll.

Table Fare: Man, as is so often the case, has to be considered the eiders' greatest enemy. The eiders are a staple food for the Eskimos and are constantly hunted by them. However, their flesh is considered unpalatable by most sportsmen, who therefore seldom, if ever, hunt them.

STIFF-TAILED DUCKS

(Subfamily Oxyurinae)

Ruddy Duck

Oxyura jamaicensis

Found only in North America, the ruddy duck is, in many ways, a unique species. The male is easily identified, as he is the only duck that carries his tail erect. He also boasts the most impressive of all duck courtship displays, and is the only male among all the ducks that helps in raising the young. As if these achievements were not enough, the male ruddy duck is the only member of the duck clan with a bright-blue bill and one of the few with distinct plumage for summer and winter. To compete with her mate, no doubt, the female ruddy duck establishes her own uniqueness by violating the general tendency of her sex (among ducks) toward noisiness; she is almost totally silent.

DESCRIPTION: The ruddy duck is a small, fan-tailed duck. The male usually carries his long tail feathers fanned out and erected at a jaunty angle much like a strutting tom turkey's tail.

The male ruddy duck averages about 15 inches in length, has a wingspread of 22½ inches and weighs about 1¼ pounds. He is one of the few ducks that don't have an eclipse plumage but two com-

Ruddy Duck

pletely different plumages, one during the breeding season and one in the fall and winter. In his breeding plumage, which is the best known, the lower rear part of the male's head, his throat, back, breast and flanks are a bright rufous red. The top of his head is black, and he has a wide white cheek stripe. His rump is dark brown barred with black. The tail and the top surface of the wings are a plain dark brown. The underside of the wing is white, as are the under tail coverts. The white belly has brown and black barrings. The feet are blue-gray, and the long, upturned bill is sky-blue.

In his winter plumage, which for some reason is not considered an eclipse plumage, the male looks very much like the female. His bright red color is replaced by a dark mottled brown. Even his wings become a darker brown, and his white cheek patch turns sooty white. The bill changes to a dull dark blue.

The female ruddy duck also has long tail feathers but never appears to erect or fan them out. Her bill is long, upturned and dark blue. The top of her crown is dark brown, but her cheeks and throat are a dull white with a brown splash of a cheek patch. Her wings and tail are dark brown, and her underwing lining has a row of sooty white feathers. Her breast, flanks and belly are a dull brown mottled with white. Her feet are blue-gray.

Both the male and female ruddy ducks have the lobed rear toe that is common to all the diving ducks.

DISTRIBUTION: The ruddy duck is a common duck with a very wide distribution. It winters along the coastal fringe of the United States from Washington south to California, east to Florida and north to New Jersey and Long Island.

Its Canadian breeding range is in Alberta, Saskatchewan and Manitoba. In the United States, North and South Dakota, Minnesota and Nebraska are its main breeding range, although some of these ducks nest in portions of Colorado, Montana, Idaho, Wyoming, Utah, Nevada and California.

COMMUNICATION: The female ruddy duck is silent or almost so, her only known call being a weak clucking sound. The drake is hardly more vociferous; his slightly louder clucking sounds *ip-ip-ip-ip-cluck, cluck.*

BREEDING AND NESTING: The little male ruddy duck is as proud as a tom turkey, and although he doesn't strut about on land, he certainly does so while swimming about. He puffs out his air sac, which erects the breast feathers and greatly increases his size. His tail is fanned out and brought forward vertically so that it resembles the forward-curving, feathered headdresses worn in the Mummers' parade. As he approaches the female, he raises the feathered "horns" on his head and inclines his bill forward until it touches his breast. He then beats his head up and down against his breast, forcing the air out of his tracheal air sac and so producing the clucking sound already described. This same pumping action forces air out of his breast feathers, thereby forming bubbles.

Rivalry among the male ruddy ducks is strong, and if an interloper appears on the scene, the first male opens his bill wide, extends his neck, fluffs out his feathers and swims over to chase away the rival or engage him in battle. Sometimes the two males actually disappear under the water in a frenzied, churning, pecking and grabbing fight. The victorious male, usually the one that was first with the female, returns to her as soon as he has routed his rival. Turning away from her, the male again raises his tail vertically, displaying its white underside for her benefit.

The female ruddy duck is extremely shy during the nesting

season and seeks out sloughs and potholes that have deep water and high, rank shore vegetation. In among the reeds and rushes, the female weaves a nest that is made up of these materials and is fastened to the growing stalks. It is built about 6 inches above the water level. To facilitate entry to the nest, a ramp is made of vegetation. This allows the female to slide in or out of her nest with a minimum of effort and disturbance. The nest is always difficult to find because it matches its surroundings very well, and the female usually leaves it so surreptitiously that she does not disclose its whereabouts.

EGGS AND YOUNG: The ruddy duck normally lays a clutch of eight to ten eggs. Exceptionally large clutches are usually the result of two females laying in the same nest. The female ruddy has been known to lay her eggs in another duck's nest, and the eggs of both the redhead duck and the canvasback have been found in the ruddy duck's nest. It is difficult to determine if these rare occurrences are accidents or cases of parasitism.

On the rare occasions when a ruddy duck's nest is found, it is seldom credited to the proper duck because although this duck is small, its eggs are exceptionally large. They average 62 millimeters in length by 45 millimeters in diameter. Since they are cream-colored, they are easily stained a darker hue as the incubation period progresses. The shell of the eggs is very thick and has a rough exterior.

The male ruddy duck does not share in the incubation, which takes the female about thirty days. He does, however, remain in the immediate area, and he helps the female raise the young. Neither parent does much in defense of the ducklings, as they dive out of sight when danger threatens. The young ruddy ducks are extremely precocious, as would be expected from the large egg size, and they plop into the water to swim about, dive and feed very soon after hatching. When threatened, the young dive underwater like the parents, and when they have to surface, they hide among the vegetation.

The ruddy ducklings have gray-black down on the crown of their heads, the back of their necks and on their backs, wings and tails. Their white cheek patch has a black stripe. Their breasts and flanks are a light gray-white, and their bellies are white. The bill is slate-blue, and the feet are gray-blue, tinged with green.

FLIGHT: It is about two months before the young ruddy ducks are fledged and capable of flying. The ruddy ducks, young and

Ruddy duck hen on her nest of typically large eggs.

adults alike, have great difficulty in building up enough speed to become airborne. They run along the surface of the water, their feet wildly splattering and their wings beating frantically. Their wings are short and rounded, and their wing beats are so rapid that they produce a buzzing sound like a large, angry bumblebee. Once it is in the air, the ruddy duck flies at a speed of about 40 miles per hour.

The ruddy duck flies low over the water and even in migration does not fly high but prefers to follow river and stream courses. When this duck lands, its chunky body drops into the water with a splash.

MIGRATION: The ruddy duck's spring migration gets under way about the first part of March so that by May the birds are on their breeding grounds. The fall migration starts in September and is usually concluded within a month. In migration, the ruddy duck usually flies in the early morning, late in the evening or at night.

HABITS: The ruddy duck's feet are placed so far back on its body that the bird has great difficulty in walking. On the rare occasions when it takes to the land it stands almost perpendicular, using its stiff tail to help brace and support its body. It hitches itself forward by moving both its feet simultaneously. This means of locomotion may seem unusual to anybody who does not know that the ruddy duck, unlike most of the other ducks, does not use alternate feet while swimming but paddles with both together.

The ruddy is an excellent swimmer and a superb diver. It actually acts more like a grebe than a duck when it is in the water. It often dives beneath the surface, but it just as often silently sinks out of sight, exactly as the grebes do.

Flying is a last resort to a ruddy duck. When threatened, it disappears under the water to hide among the shoreline vegetation or to creep out among the vegetation on the bank. It can swim long distances underwater. While doing so, it seldom uses its wings unless it needs maximum speed. Most of this duck's food is obtained by diving for it.

FOOD: Seventy-two percent of the ruddy duck's diet is made up of vegetable matter such as the seeds, roots, stems and leaves of pondweed, bulrush, wild celery, widgeon grass, naiad and muskgrass. The 28 percent of its diet that is made up of animal matter is composed chiefly of insects and their larvae such as caddisflies, horseflies, water boatmen and midges. It also eats crustaceans and mollusks.

LIFE SPAN: The ruddy duck has a potential life span of from seven to nine years, but no individual longevity records are available.

ENEMIES: The ruddy duck's habit of building its nest over water protects the eggs from the depredations of many of the four-footed predators. Crows are probably the chief enemy. Large fish and turtles take the ducklings. Hawks, owls and eagles feed on the adults, although these ducks usually stay near dense vegetation into which they can escape at the first sign of danger. Disease, parasites and accidents take their toll. The draining of prairie potholes has reduced the population of these ducks by depriving them of nesting areas.

The ruddy duck is shy and wary during the nesting season but does not seem to be so at other times of the year. It was a combination of the destruction of its nesting areas and overshooting that caused its population to hit an all-time low during the 1920s. Fortunately, today the ruddy duck population is on the increase.

TABLE FARE: Although the ruddy duck is small, it is a good feeder and is usually quite fat and succulent.

MERGANSERS
(Subfamily Merginae)

American Merganser
Mergus merganser

Red-breasted Merganser   *Mergus serrator*

In the wilderness areas of Quebec, Canada, where I used to guide boy scout canoe trips, both the American and the red-breasted merganser ducks were very common. It was an almost hourly event, while paddling around a sharp bend in the Ottawa River, to startle a mother merganser and her family. As the young were flightless, there was some squawking and a great deal of flurry as the young rushed up the stream ahead of us, frantically beating the water with their wings as they tried to run on its surface. Sometimes we had three or four families of mergansers running ahead of us at one time.

For years I had a standing offer of $1.00 for any boy scout who could catch a baby merganser and bring it to me so that I could photograph it. Although countless boys tried, all failed. They would race after the ducks, which at first scooted ahead as a family. When the canoes got close and the boys thought that victory was theirs, the young ducks would invariably scatter and dive.

DESCRIPTION: Two of the species will be dealt with in this one section because although these species look slightly different, their range, their habits and almost all their characteristics are the same. The data given apply to both these mergansers unless otherwise noted.

The adult male American merganser is about 25 inches in length, has a wingspread of 36 inches and weighs about 3¼ pounds. This duck has a thin, pointed, blood-red bill with serrated edges that facilitate the grasping of fish. These serrations are slightly larger than those of the red-breasted merganser. The drake's head has a metallic green sheen, much like that of a mallard drake. His breast, sides and belly are white. His back, rump, tail and wing primary feathers are black, as are the lesser wing coverts and the three outside secondary feathers. The feet are bright orangy red.

The adult male red-breasted merganser is about 22 inches in length, has a 32-inch wingspan and weighs about 2½ pounds. The head is as green as the American merganser's, but this male has a crest that can be erected. His breast is a rusty red spotted with dark brown. His belly is white, and his gray sides are separated from the breast feathers by two rows of white, black-bordered feathers. The back, rump and tail, the three outside secondary feathers and the wing primary feathers are dark brown. The sides have a white base with black vermiculations. The feet and bill are orangy red. The lesser coverts, or the leading wing edge, are white, but there is a black border between the lesser and greater wing coverts.

The females of these two species are almost identical, although the female American merganser is slightly larger, with a length of 25 inches, a wingspan of 36 inches and a weight of about 3¼ pounds. The female red-breasted merganser is 22 inches in length, has a wingspan of 32 inches and weighs about 2¼ pounds. Their color patterns are identical, although the coloring of the red-breasted merganser is several shades lighter than that of the American merganser.

The female mergansers have red bills and feet. Their heads are brown with a white throat and a white patch in front of and below the eye. The breast and belly of both are white. Their backs, rumps, tails and sides are light gray. The lesser coverts of the wings are gray, the greater coverts black with white tips. Six of the secondary feathers are white, while the first three outside ones, like the wing primary feathers, are dark gray.

DISTRIBUTION: The ranges of these two species of mergansers overlap considerably. The winter range of the American merganser is roughly the middle third of the United States, from the Atlantic to the Pacific coast. Its breeding range is the upper third of the United States and the lower half of Canada, with a spillover into Alaska.

The red-breasted merganser is more of a coastline bird in the winter, being found along the Pacific coast from British Columbia south to Baja California, and from the province of New Brunswick south to Texas along the Atlantic coast. Its breeding range is a little farther north than the American merganser's. Its range starts at the Great Lakes and extends north to Canada's Arctic islands.

COMMUNICATION: I have never heard either of the mergansers utter any sound except a hoarse squawking made by the frightened young that we chased with the canoes and a soft *doorr, doorr* sound made by the males during the breeding season.

BREEDING AND NESTING: The courtship of the male mergansers is energetic. I have seen the males do quite a bit of fighting, seizing each other with their bills and pulling each other's head feathers out. They also stab at one another with their strong, pointed bills and ram each other in an attempt to drive their rival away. To display for the female, the male often extends his neck and fanned-out tail, letting his breast sink into the water. During this display, he lifts the rear of his wings up and away from the body, while emitting his *doorr* call. At other times, the male rises up out of the water with wings outstretched as if he were sitting on the surface.

Most of the time the female appears to pay no attention to the display. However, if too many of the males become too ardent, she may swim at them and chase them all away. When she has selected a mate, she swims over to him and touches or caresses him with her bill. Before copulation, she lowers her body into the water until she is almost submerged. When the male mounts her, she is forced completely underwater.

The American merganser may nest in a hollow tree or, failing that, on the ground. The red-breasted merganser nests on the ground, usually in, around or under large boulders. I have never seen the nest of the American merganser but have seen a number of red-breasted merganser nests on Kodiak Island and Nunivak Island, both in Alaska.

On Nunivak, the Eskimos I was with were hunting for the eggs for food. They would walk among the rocks and every so often peer under some of the flatter rocks. They also tried to catch the female but without success. All the nests that were discovered had several entrances. As the Eskimos reached in one way, the duck went flapping out at the other side.

The nests are made up of grasses, sedges, moss, etc., but the main ingredient is down from the female's breast. If the female has the time, she covers over her eggs completely when she gets off the nest to feed or exercise. This covering is done more for warmth than for protection against predators. The nest is usually hidden under the rocks and so would not be seen. However, the temperature up north in the shade under the rocks is always very low even if the sun is shining warmly. The eggs must be covered to keep them from becoming chilled.

EGGS AND YOUNG: The mergansers have large broods. The nests that I saw had between twelve and fourteen eggs, and the records show that sixteen to seventeen eggs are not uncommon. The eggs average 64 millimeters in length by 44 millimeters in diameter. They are a light buff color, and the shells are very strong. I know this because the Eskimos cracked one of each set before they took the eggs. Development had hardly started, but I was interested to know if there was a stage of development beyond which the Eskimos would not eat them.

Incubation is done entirely by the female. In fact, in neither Canada nor Alaska did I ever see a male merganser of either species anywhere in the area after the eggs had been laid. Of course soon after breeding the males go into their eclipse plumage, but I also saw females with young later on without ever seeing any of the males.

The mergansers' incubation period is twenty-eight days. The young American mergansers that hatch out in a tree jump out in the same fashion as young wood ducks.

The young of both these mergansers are basically very similar. The top of the head, back of the neck and back are dark brown with a couple of white spots on the wings and rump. Both species have rusty red patches around the eye and on the rear of the cheeks and sides of the neck. The red-breasted merganser duckling has a single dark line through the eye, while the American merganser has one dark line through the eye and another below it. The chin, throat, breast and belly of both birds are white. The red-breasted merganser young have a yellowish bill and feet, while those of the American merganser are blue-gray.

The ducklings can not only swim almost at once but also dive at a very early age. The female mergansers try to lead their young away from danger and, as already described, the young ducks dive beneath the surface when hard-pressed.

FLIGHT: It is about two months before the young mergansers can fly. When running away from danger, they skitter along the surface of the water, frantically flapping their wings. At first the wings are used like oars, pushing against the water. It must come as a surprise when the young duck finds that its primary feathers are strong enough to support flight, and it becomes airborne.

The mergansers always flap along the surface of the water to build up enough momentum to take off. Once in the air they are strong fliers, capable of traveling at 50 miles per hour. They usually fly low over the water and follow the river course instead of rising up higher and flying over the tops of the trees. In flight they have a characteristic silhouette in which the head is greatly extended and usually held slightly below the body, giving an air of stream-lined efficiency.

Mergansers do not appear to fly in large flocks even during migration. Twenty-five birds—in other words a couple of family groups—seem to be about the limit.

MIGRATION: The mergansers are exceptionally hardy birds and are among the earliest fall ducks to migrate north in the spring. They winter as far north as open water is to be found and follow the recession of the ice in the spring very closely. If there is a hole in the ice of a frozen river, mergansers will be in it. Often in February the birds are already heading north again, not to return until the following November or December.

HABITS: The mergansers seem to prefer to be in the company of their own kind. I have sometimes seen some goldeneye ducks with them but seldom any other kind.

The mergansers are excellent divers, perhaps the best of all the ducks. Their leg placement toward the rear of the body is a help in diving, and they also use their wings underwater, where they can outswim the fastest fish. They often do cooperative fishing, whereby a group of them actually herd the fish into shallow water or other spots that make the capture of the fish easier.

In the winter, the red-breasted merganser shows a decided preference for feeding along the seacoast, while the American merganser prefers freshwater areas.

Hooded Merganser

conspicuous duck despite his diminutive size. The drake averages 17½ inches in length, has a wingspan of 25 inches and weighs about 1¼ pounds. His long, narrow, toothed bill is black like his head and neck. When his crest is erected, the white cockade behind the eye becomes his dominant field identification mark. The breast and belly are white. The back is black, while the rump and tail are dark brown. Two black stripes project downward, separating the breast from the sides, which are a rich brown with fine black vermiculations. This merganser's wings are basically black, but the lesser coverts have a whitish trailing edge. Part of the secondary coverts and the secondary scapulars have white edges. The eye is bright yellow with a dark center, and the feet are a dull yellow-brown.

The female hooded merganser is smaller in size and weight than her mate. She, too, sports a crest, but hers is a rusty red. Her face, neck, breast and back are grayish brown. Her side feathers also are grayish-brown with a light brown edging that gives her a scaled appearance. Her belly is white, and she has a white mark under her chin. Her rump and tail are dark brown as are her wings, with some white on the secondary coverts and feathers. Her bill is brownish yellow, and her feet are brownish.

DISTRIBUTION: The hooded merganser is not a common duck. It has a decided preference for fresh water and is usually found in the quiet, slow-flowing waters of swamps or on woodland lakes and streams.

The hooded merganser's winter range covers the freshwater areas along the Pacific coast from Washington down through California, and from New Jersey south to Texas along the Atlantic and Gulf coasts.

The breeding range of this merganser extends from the deep south states north to the southern fringe of the Canadian provinces, from the Atlantic to the Pacific, from British Columbia and Washington east to Missouri and then south again.

COMMUNICATION: This merganser is not a voluble duck. The regular call note is a low-toned, rather hoarse croak. The female makes a *croo, croo* alarm note for her young when danger is near.

BREEDING AND NESTING: Some of the hooded mergansers breed and nest on their wintering grounds, and so the pair formation is fairly constant. Even those hooded mergansers that migrate pair up before heading north.

The beautiful white cockaded crest plays a very important part in this merganser's courtship rituals. The male pursues the female both on the water and in the air. On the water he approaches the female and raises his body out of the water with his crest depressed. As he drops down to the water, the crest is suddenly expanded to its fullest. The male also extends his neck up as high and straight as possible in order to show his erected crest to its best advantage. He then throws his head backward and allows the rear portion of his body to submerge. The female is a most passive participant during the courting display. When she approves of a mate, both she and the male go through a ritualized drinking display before copulation takes place.

The wood duck and the hooded merganser are in direct competition during the nesting season because these ducks inhabit the same area and both are tree-nesting species. Sometimes the hooded merganser nests in a low stump, but its preference is for a hollow in a tree at least 20 feet above the ground. Occasionally the wood duck and hooded merganser fight for the possession of a desirable nest site. The merganser invariably wins because it is the larger duck. On the other hand, these ducks have been known to share the same nest site, each laying its eggs in a communal nest. Even the chore of incubation may be shared by the two females.

No additional nesting material is carried into the nest site, but down from the female's breast is used.

EGGS AND YOUNG: Ten to twelve eggs constitute an average clutch for the hooded merganser. The eggs average 53 millimeters in length by 44 millimeters in width. They are pure white, and the shell is glossy and very hard. The incubation, performed exclusively by the female, requires thirty-one days.

The young hooded mergansers have dark brown down on the top half of the head, the back of the neck, the back, rump, tail and wings. They have light brown cheeks and sides of the neck. The chin, breast and belly are white. The feet are greenish.

Like the baby wood ducks, the baby hooded mergansers usually stay in the nest until the day after their hatching, and they leave the nest in the same fashion as the baby wood ducks: they jump. Whatever the height of the nest site, the little ducks just bounce when they hit the ground, pick themselves up and scurry over to where the female is calling to them.

The young feed mainly on insects. The mother is very courageous in the defense of her young and puts on a real show of being crippled. She utters her hoarse, croaking sound to send her young scampering to safety among the vegetation of the shoreline. Splashing and fluttering about, she attempts to decoy the danger away from her young or to give them enough time to hide safely.

FLIGHT: It is about two months before the young hooded mergansers are fully fledged and capable of flight.

These mergansers do not fly in large flocks. The small groups that are seen are usually single family groups that have not yet split up.

The hooded merganser flies with its neck extended, its crest flattened and its head, neck and body on the same plane. It usually flies low above the water and can reach speeds of 45 miles per hour.

The hooded merganser is unique among the mergansers in that it can take off by leaping straight up in the air like a "puddle" duck or it may run along the surface of the water like the other diving ducks. The wing strokes of the hooded merganser are short and fast. These ducks usually fly in single file formation.

MIGRATION: Many of the hooded mergansers breed and winter in the same area and therefore do not migrate. In the fall, those hooded mergansers that do migrate do not linger on the breeding grounds as long as their two larger cousins. They are usually in migration from the middle of October to the middle of November. The migration north in the spring usually occurs during the month of March.

HABITS: The hooded merganser is a very shy and wary duck, yet in spite of these characteristics it is not common. Apparently it was never abundant even when there were more suitable nesting sites available to it than there are today.

When swimming, the merganser appears to be very buoyant. When submerging, the bird may rise up, tilt forward and dive beneath the surface with a plop, or it may just slowly and silently sink out of sight.

When swimming underwater, the bird uses its wings as well as its feet and has no difficulty in outswimming the fish that it feeds upon.

FOOD: The hooded merganser feeds on all types of small fish, as well as on tadpoles, frogs, snails, crayfish and water insects and their larvae. It also, on occasion, eats some of the seeds of aquatic plants.

LIFE SPAN: The hooded merganser has a potential life span of from seven to nine years. There appear to be no individual longevity records for this species.

ENEMIES: The eggs of this duck are subject to predation by the raccoon, tree-climbing snakes and squirrels. Their location in a snug cavity high in a tree provides excellent protection for the eggs.

The young and adults are vulnerable to the regular predators such as large fish, turtles, mink, otter, foxes and raccoons, as well as hawks and owls. Disease, parasites and accidents take their toll.

TABLE FARE: The hooded merganser is seldom, if ever, hunted for food. Its flesh is considered unpalatable because of the preponderance of animal matter in its diet. It is sometimes shot by hunters in mistake for a bufflehead or goldeneye.

Upland Birds

Order Galliformes

Grouse, Ptarmigan, Prairie Chickens (Family Tetraonidae)

Quail, Partridge, Pheasants (Family Phasianidae)

Turkeys (Family Meleagrididae)

Pigeons and Doves (Order Columbiformes; Family Columbidae)

Introduction

Our main upland game birds, the pheasants, quail, grouse and turkey, belong to the Order Galliformes and to the Tetraonidae, Phasianidae and Meleagrididae families.

The Family Tetraonidae embraces the grouse, ptarmigan and prairie chickens. There are eighteen species in the world, of which the ten found in North America will be discussed here.

These are short-legged, chicken-like birds with a short bill and feathers around the nostrils. Some have feathered head crests, some have eye combs, some have erectable neck feathers, some bare, inflatable neck sacs. The wings are short and cupped. The tail is a good length and is used for displaying during the breeding season. The legs are short and the tarsi feathered, but not spurred. In some cases the toes are feathered, in others there are seasonal scales on the toes. In some species male and female look alike, whereas in others there is a great diversity.

The flight of these birds is strong but cannot be sustained. None of the species is migratory. Some feed on the ground and others in trees; some sleep under the snow in winter.

The males of most of these species have elaborate courtship displays in which they "boom," "dance" and "drum." Some males are monogamous, some polygamous. The nests are usually rudimentary and built on the ground. With the exception of the ptarmigan, the incubation and raising of the young is done by the female. The young are precocious. The birds communicate by clucking, cackling and whistling.

They are primarily vegetarians but also eat some insect and animal life.

The Family Phasianidae contains the quail, partridge and pheasant, of which there are one hundred and sixty-five species in the world. Nine of the species found in North America will be treated here. The partridges and pheasants have been imported to this continent, whereas the quail are native. Our domestic chickens are of this family, and all are also imported birds. None of them is discussed here.

The male pheasants are among the most gaudily marked of all birds, and the females are drab in comparison. With the quail and partridge the sexes are very similar. Some of the species have feathered crests, some have facial wattles. Their bills are typical of chickens, the quail's being particularly short. Their bodies are all rounded, their legs are short to medium long, some being heavily spurred, and their tails are very short to exceptionally long. Their wings are strong, cupped or rounded and not built for sustained flight. None of the North American species is truly migratory.

Most of these species are gregarious except during the breeding season. Some species are monogamous, others polygamous. Most feed on the ground, some roost in trees. Some of the species scratch for food with their feet, but some use their bills. They communicate by whistles, crowing, cackling and clucking.

Most species are seed-feeders, although some feed on other plant matter; insects and some animal matter are also eaten.

The nests are rudimentary and located on the ground. The female in most species does all the incubating and in many species raises the young alone. The young are precocious.

The Family Meleagrididae has only two species of turkeys, both of them found in North America but discussion will be limited to the one species found north of Mexico.

The turkey is a stout-bodied bird with a short bill. The skin of the head and neck is bare and has a caruncle and wattles. The color of these areas can be changed at will. The neck is long, the wings are strong and cupped, and flight is strong but not sustained, the birds being nonmigratory. The legs are long, the tarsi bare but heavily spurred. The tail is long, full and rounded. The female is quite similar to the male.

Turkeys are gregarious, although during the breeding season, the old males have a harem and are pugnacious.

These birds feed mainly on the ground and chiefly on vegetation, although they also eat some insects and animal matter. They scratch strongly with their feet and are good runners. Most of their activities are terrestrial, but they do roost in trees.

Their nests are rudimentary, usually well concealed on the forest floor. The young develop fast.

The remainder of our upland birds are the pigeons and the doves, which belong to the Order Columbiformes and the Family Columbidae. There are two hundred and eighty-nine species in the world, of which three species found in the United States will be discussed.

These birds are small in size as game birds go, and their plumage is iridescent. The bill is slender and has a fleshy cere at the base. Their heads are small, their necks short, their bodies compact, their wings long and strong. They are excellent fliers, and most are migratory.

The Columbidae have moderately long to long tails. Their legs are short, their tarsi unfeathered, and they have no spurs. Both sexes are identical.

These birds range from solitary to extremely gregarious. Males, particularly during the breeding season, are very pugnacious. They may feed on the ground or in trees, and they always nest and roost in trees. They are unique among birds in that they drink by suction. The young are fed regurgitated "pigeon's milk." The birds communicate by cooing and whistling vocally. Their pinions whistle in flight and make a clapping sound at takeoff. They feed mainly on seeds, fruit and other plant matter. They occasionally eat some insects or other animal matter. Their nests are rudimentary platforms of twigs in a tree.

GROUSE, PTARMIGAN, PRAIRIE CHICKENS

Family Tetraonidae

Dusky Blue Grouse

Dendragapus obscurus

Sooty Grouse   *Dendragapus fuliginosus*

I was photographing bighorn sheep in the mountains of western Montana when I saw my first blue grouse. As I walked down an old logging road, there was a commotion in the roadside bracken. With a great clapping of wings, some grouse rocketed up out of the vegetation and took off into the forest. One bird, however, landed in the outermost branches of a nearby tree, where it stretched out its neck and looked at me with great curiosity. It probably had never seen a human being before. The curiosity was mutual, for I had never seen a blue grouse before. It was the darkest large-sized grouse I had ever seen, and it was immediately apparent why this bird is also referred to as the dusky or sooty grouse.

Until very recently the names dusky, sooty, blue, gray, mountain and pine grouse all referred to the same bird. There were eight subspecies of *Dendragapus obscurus*. Now, taxonomists recognize the dusky and the sooty grouse to be two distinct species, even though they are all but identical. There are three subspecies of

D. obscurus, the dusky grouse, and four subspecies of *D. fuliginosus,* the sooty grouse. But for general purposes, they are all still classed together as "blue" grouse, which is how they will be treated here.

DESCRIPTION: The adult male blue grouse is about 20 to 22 inches in length, has a wingspan of about 28 inches and weighs up to 3½ pounds. The male has a black bill and a dark eye. The top of his head, back of his neck, back, wings and rump are grayish brown, and the tail is a dark slate-black, with a gray terminal band. There is a white line running through the eye, and the throat is white. The bird's face, breast and belly are a slaty blue-gray. Its flanks and under tail coverts have grayish brown feathers, edged with white. There is a bright yellow comb above the eye. Hidden by the feathers

Dusky Blue Grouse

on each side of the neck are golf-ball sized orange air sacs. When these are displayed, the neck feathers are laid flat, forming a feathered disc or rosette that completely surrounds the air sacs. The sacs and feathers look exactly like a fried egg.

The female blue grouse is considerably smaller than the male and lighter in weight. The name blue grouse is applicable only to the male because the female is a brown bird. She has a dark bill and eye and she also has the white line passing through the eye and the white throat. However, the top of her head, her neck, breast, back, wings and rump have mottled brown and white feathers, with black barring. Her tail is a dark slate-black with a gray tip. The feathers on her belly and flanks are arranged in vertical rows and are brown, edged with black against a white background. The female does not have the air sacs or the comb.

The adult male sooty blue grouse is identical to the dusky blue grouse male except that it is 2 inches shorter in length, has about 1 inch less wingspan and weighs perhaps ½ pound less. The female sooty grouse is correspondingly smaller.

DISTRIBUTION: The blue grouse is a woodland, mountain bird. It is found from the deciduous forests of the foothills up to and occasionally above the timber line. The dusky blue grouse is found in the Rocky Mountains in New Mexico, Arizona, Colorado, Utah and Nevada. The sooty blue grouse is found in the Rocky Mountains, the sierras and the coastal range of Wyoming, Montana, Idaho, California, Oregon, Washington, British Columbia, Alberta, the Yukon and southeastern Alaska.

COMMUNICATION: The blue grouse are not very vocal except during the breeding season. Everyone who has heard the males' "booming" or "tooting," as it is sometimes called, remarks on its ventriloquistic qualities. Some say it sounds like a growling or groaning. The call is given in a group of from four to six notes and can best be described as *hoooo, hoot, hoot, hoot, a-hoot, hoot* or various combinations of these sounds. The male also has a single-note call that sounds *oop* or *ulp*. The female makes a cackling sound and has a sharp, single-note alarm call that is a warning to her chicks. The chicks peep.

BREEDING AND NESTING: The male blue grouse starts to descend from its mountain-top winter range in March. The small groups of males now split up as each seeks out a mate.

When the male first starts to call, he usually does so perched on

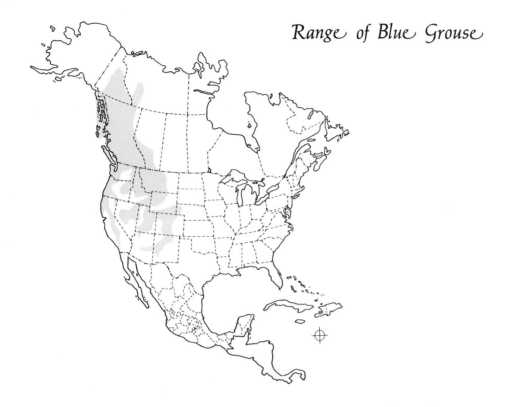

Range of Blue Grouse

a large limb at the top of a tall tree. This is a good vantage point which allows him to see everything that moves in his area. The added height also allows his calls to travel farther. Turning about on the limb, the male suddenly droops his wings, fans out his tail and inflates his air sacs. With outstretched neck, he gives out his hooting call. The call is lower in tone than the somewhat similar call of the great horned owl and actually sounds louder at a distance than from close up.

When a female is attracted to the male's love song, she responds with her own cackling call. The male is quick to seek her out. If the female is on the ground, the male struts before her, his drooping wings now touching the ground like a tom turkey's. As he approaches the female, his twenty black tail feathers are fanned out vertically, making a black background for his face and head. Turning from side to side as he advances, the male makes sure that the female has a chance to be impressed by his orange air sacs and the white feather rosettes. He quickly runs toward the female, then stopping just before a collision becomes inevitable, he burps a single, deep *oop* call.

Often the female is not ready to accept the male's advances at once so that this whole procedure is repeated time after time. When the female yields, she turns from the male and squats in front of him, thereby facilitating copulation.

It is generally agreed that the blue grouse is monogamous.

The blue grouse makes a most rudimentary nest. It is usually just a hollow scraped out in the forest floor with dead grass or pine needles used as a lining. It is normally hidden under a fallen log, under brush or up against a stump. Because of the inaccessibility of much of the blue grouse's habitat, its nest is seldom found by man.

EGGS AND YOUNG: A normal blue grouse clutch consists of from seven to ten eggs. These average 49 millimeters in length by 34 millimeters in diameter, dimensions which are rather small considering the size of the bird. The eggs range in basic color from pinkish buff to buff and are thickly and uniformly covered with clay-colored spots.

Incubation requires twenty-one to twenty-four days and is performed by the female alone. The young are precocious, and are led from the nesting area by the female as soon as their down is dry. If threatened by danger, the female tries to intercept the intruder. She feigns injury, calls attention to herself in every possible manner, does anything to give her chicks a chance to hide or remove themselves from the immediate area.

There have been several instances of the male blue grouse being seen with the hen and the young chicks. Although this is a common occurrence with ptarmigan, it is a rarity among grouse.

The young blue grouse feed on insects at first and then turn vegetarian like the adults.

FLIGHT: By the time the young are two weeks old their wings have developed enough to allow them to make short jump-flights. At the age of one month, they are able to fly up into a tree to escape enemies that could catch them on the ground.

The blue grouse is capable of flying at speeds of 25 miles per hour or more on the level. This speed is usually more than sufficient for the bird to disappear quickly behind intervening trees. The short, cupped wings of the blue grouse allow it a rapid takeoff, and after reaching its top speed, it soars for as long a distance as it needs before landing. Probably the blue grouse does not have a fast flight because, being a forest bird, it flies mostly twisting and turning around trees and branches. As this grouse is usually found on the side of a mountain, it can greatly increase its flight speed by just pitching down to the valley below.

MIGRATION: The blue grouse does not migrate, although it is subject to seasonal shifts of habitat. It was once commonly thought that this grouse hibernated in the winter because after the first deep snow, the bird was not seen again until the following spring. Actually, it had simply shifted its feeding range. Curiously enough, whereas all the creatures of the western mountains descend to lower elevations as the temperatures drop and the snow depth increases, the blue grouse works its way higher up into the mountains. Here the birds congregate in the tops of the huge fir trees which provide them with both food and shelter.

HABITS: Probably most of the blue grouse roost in trees during the winter because there are only a few records of the birds roosting under the snow like the ruffed grouse. The records, however, are sketchy because so few people get up into the mountains when the snow is deep. With the tremendous interest in cross-country skiing that is sweeping our country, more knowledge may soon be available about the winter habits of many wild creatures.

It is the blue grouse's roosting habits that have earned it the nickname of "fool hen." The bird is safe enough from a fox or a coyote while perched in a tree, but not from a man with a gun. Yet it often just sits there until it is killed, no matter how many shots are fired at it. The sobriquet of "fool hen" could in fact be applied to almost any of the real wilderness grouse, the ruffed grouse included. Where they never see human beings, the grouse have no fear of them. The blue grouse, however, like the ruffed grouse, has the ability to learn from experience and can become as elusive as an educated ruffed grouse.

There is never a shortage of water in the mountains where the blue grouse lives. Every hollow will have at least a trickle of water seeping down it. In the winter, the grouse eats snow.

In areas where the forests have been cut and farming introduced on some of the higher plateaus, the blue grouse leaves its beloved forests long enough each day to feed on some of the cultivated crops. The blue grouse develops a special affinity for its own particular corner of the world. Despite encroaching civilization, as long as there are some stands of conifer trees left, the grouse will stay.

Food: The adult blue grouse is almost wholly vegetarian, feeding on only a very small percentage of insects in the summer and fall. It feeds mainly on the seeds, fruit, buds and leaves of the following trees and plants: Douglas fir, pine, eriogonum, blueberry, cat's-ear, bearberry, cherry, pussytoe, spruce, willow, mountain ash, vetch, clover, larch, hemlock and serviceberry.

The blue grouse eats grasshoppers, ants, leaf beetles, sawfly larvae, leafhoppers and scarab beetles.

Life Span: The blue grouse has a life expectancy of from ten to fifteen years, the longest of any game bird.

Enemies: The blue grouse, its young and/or its eggs are preyed upon by ravens, magpies, foxes, bobcats, lynxes, martens, hawks, owls and eagles. Predation, however, seems to be a rather insignificant factor with these birds, primarily because the altitudes that they frequent do not harbor many of the predators. Disease, parasites and accidents take a few grouse.

Table Fare: In the summer and fall, when the blue grouse is feeding on various kinds of berries and leafy vegetation, its flesh is considered superior to that of any of the other grouse. During the winter the grouse's resinous diet makes its flesh decidedly unpalatable.

Spruce Grouse
Canachites canadensis

In 1965, I was on Alaska's Lake Iliamna. One day I took a skiff and ran up some of the tributary rivers looking for Alaskan brown bear. As the salmon run had not started yet, no bear were to be seen along the river banks, but I did notice a hen spruce grouse with a covey of chicks. When I approached the hen, she gave an alarm call, and the chicks scattered into the dense, knee-high underbrush. The female then flew up into a nearby spruce tree. As I walked around the tree, the female hopped from one branch to another, circling right along with me. When I stopped, she stopped. When I walked away, she would walk down the limb in my direction. When I approached, she retreated back toward the trunk of the tree. In all probability, she had never seen a human before, and she showed absolutely no fear. It is this lack of fear that has earned this wilderness grouse the name of "fool hen."

On another occasion, years earlier, on Lac Pikianikijuan in Quebec, Canada, I actually caught a male spruce grouse with my hands. The bird was sitting in a stand of young jack pine, and I just moved up as slowly and as quietly as I could until I was finally able to reach out and snatch the grouse off its perch. After taking a couple of photographs of the bird, I released it.

DESCRIPTION: The adult male spruce grouse is 17 inches long, has a wingspan of 22 inches and weighs about 1½ pounds. The male has a darkly mottled gray or brown and white back and a very conspicuous black face, throat and chest patch or bib. The belly is white with black bars, the tail black with a dark brown

Blue Grouse

terminal band. The bird's legs are feathered down to its toes. The male sports a bare patch of orange-red skin and a small comb above each eye. The female is smaller in size, lighter in weight and is a mottled buffy brown and white in color. The spruce grouse lacks the crest feathers that are so prominent on the ruffed grouse.

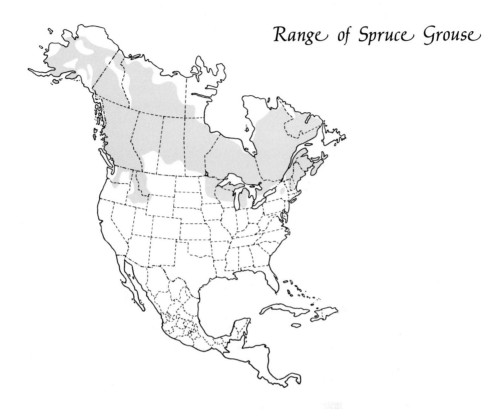

Range of Spruce Grouse

DISTRIBUTION: The spruce grouse is found from the Atlantic to the Pacific in a large arc that extends from Labrador to Alaska, just below Hudson's Bay and as far north as the tree line. The bird's range extends into the United States in the Rocky Mountains and coastal ranges, in Minnesota, Wisconsin, Michigan and in the northern part of New York, Vermont, New Hampshire and Maine. The spruce grouse is strictly a forest bird and has been pushed back over quite a bit of its range by man's destruction of the wilderness.

COMMUNICATION: The only calls I have heard the spruce grouse make are deep, clucking *putt* or *chuck* sounds. I have heard the female make both sounds but have only heard the male make the *putt* call. The female makes a *kruck, kruck, kruck* sound of warning to her chicks. The male also makes a sound similar to the drumming of the ruffed grouse, but he produces the sound in a different manner. A young male spruce grouse was recorded making a wailing, whistling *weeo, weeo, weeo* sound.

BREEDING AND NESTING: In April, during the courtship period, the male spruce grouse displays for the female and proclaims his territorial rights with his "drumming." Whereas the ruffed grouse drums by beating the air with his wings while his body is held rigid, the spruce grouse combines his drumming with an aerial display. The ruffed grouse usually drums from some favored spot, while the spruce grouse puts on its display anywhere within his chosen territory. With the female in attendance, the male flies to the top of a tall spruce or tamarack tree. Assured of an audience, he then flutters out of the tree and with a tremendous flapping of his wings, produces the drumming sound while in flight.

There are several variations of the spruce grouse's drumming procedure. Instead of flying out of the top of the tree, the male may fly from the limb of one tree to the limb of another nearby tree, fluttering his wings and drumming as he goes. He descends to the ground by passing back and forth from tree to tree, performing all the way down. At other times, the male may fly straight up in the air and, without landing in any tree, performs while he is descending. He may do this many times. Yet another variation has been recorded where the spruce grouse fly-walked up an inclined tree, drumming all the way up. When he reached the thicker branches near the top of the tree, he flew to the ground, only to start back up again.

When the male spruce grouse is on the ground, he displays and struts for the female like a miniature tom turkey. His feathers are shaken loose so that they stand up on end, the wings are drooped, and the head is held up and back. The grouse's glory, of course, is his tail, which is fanned out to its very fullest and raised almost vertically.

Although the drumming sound made by the spruce grouse would not impress a ruffed grouse female, it satisfies the spruce grouse female, and breeding shortly ensues.

The spruce grouse's nest is very difficult to locate because it is usually hidden in a dense tangle of brush or up against the base of a spruce tree, where it is hidden by the drooping branches. The nest is a rudimentary one, being little more than a hollow scraped in the earth or moss, lined with whatever leaves, evergreen needles or grasses happen to be in the area.

The mother spruce grouse's camouflage is so perfect that her presence does not give away the nest's location. She sits so tight on the nest that at times she will actually be stepped on before she moves, thereby revealing the nest's whereabouts.

EGGS AND YOUNG: The spruce grouse usually lays a clutch of from ten to twelve eggs, but some nests have been found with as many as sixteen. The eggs average 43 millimeters in length by 31 millimeters in diameter. Their basic color ranges from cinnamon- to cream-buff. The eggs are usually handsomely marked with both large and small spots and blotches of rich reddish browns.

Usually an egg is laid each day, although occasionally a day will be skipped. The laying normally takes place early in the morning, the female sneaking onto the nest, laying the egg and then leaving the immediate area for the rest of the day. When the clutch is complete, the female begins the incubation, which requires seventeen or eighteen days and is done entirely by the female. After incubation begins, the male usually withdraws from all contact with the female and spends his summer days in seclusion.

Young spruce grouse are precocious and are led from the nest area by the mother only a few hours after their down has dried. The chicks' down is a yellowish buff color with a few black markings.

The female spruce grouse is a very good mother and does everything possible to protect her young from danger. While they scatter at her alarm call, she tries to decoy the danger away. If one of the chicks should peep, the mother disregards her own safety to come to the chick's aid.

I saw an excellent example of this on Alaska's Kenai Peninsula in 1966. I met a young biologist there who had made a tape recording of a day-old grouse chick peeping. If he wanted to study, catch or examine any female grouse he saw with chicks, all he had to do was to play his recording. The female would immediately scatter her brood and fly over to look for her "lost" chick. Apparently a recording of a day-old chick worked most effectively. The older the chick when its peep was recorded, the less appeal it had for a female grouse. By the time a chick was two weeks old, a recording of its voice would be ignored by the female.

FLIGHT: The young grouse develops very rapidly, and within five or six days their primary wing feathers have grown out far enough for them to fly short distances. By the time the chick is a week old, it is strong enough to fly up into low bushes. At two to three weeks of age, it can fly away from its ground-based enemies.

The spruce grouse has the short, cupped wings that are typical of all members of the *Tetraonidae* grouse family. These wings are designed for a fast takeoff but are not suitable for sustained flight.

The spruce grouse seldom has to fly fast or far. Its maximum flight speed is about 30 miles per hour. Its aerial activity is usually confined to flying from the ground to the top of a tree or vice versa. When performing his spring drumming display, the male flies more than at any other moment in his life.

The only time a spruce grouse really needs speed and power in flight is to escape from winged predators, such as hawks and eagles, by flying into dense cover. Owls are discounted because they hunt at night, and flight is of little benefit to the grouse in the darkness. Against most of the four-footed predators, the grouse needs only to fly up from the ground to a safe perch in a tree.

MIGRATION: The spruce grouse does not migrate, although it is subject to seasonal shifts that are due to food requirements rather than to extremes of weather. Unlike the ruffed grouse, which buries itself under the soft snow in cold weather, the spruce grouse seeks only the shelter that it can find among the dense growth of swamps and evergreen trees.

HABITS: Everyone who has ever seen or had anything to do with the spruce grouse makes the same kind of comment on its approachability. Unlike the ruffed grouse, it has not been able to learn that man is an enemy. In the deep wilderness, this trusting behavior causes the grouse no grief. But as our wilderness goes, so does the spruce grouse. It is not adaptable and cannot compete with human encroachment.

Spruce grouse do not flock up as some of the other grouse do. The birds have a tendency to be solitary, perhaps paired, but seldom, if ever, more than a single-family group.

The spruce grouse's feet are feathered right to the claws of the toes. These feathers act as snowshoes, effectively doubling the grouse's foot area and so enabling it to walk across the top of even soft snow.

In the summer, spruce grouse enjoy a good dust bath as a means of controlling ectoparasites. Often they dust in the rotted powder of a long-dead tree.

FOOD: The spruce grouse is well named, for it prefers to live in and around spruce trees, which provide one of its staple foods.

During the late spring, summer and early fall, the spruce grouse may eat an occasional insect. It also eats various types of berries, such as the blueberry, bearberry and bunchberry. However, the largest part of its diet is made up of conifer needles from the various spruces, pines, firs and larches or tamaracks. It also eats the buds of the white birch trees, salal, wood fern, Christmas fern, sedge and some mosses.

Life Span: There are no longevity records available for the spruce grouse, but judging from the records that exist for the ruffed grouse, it would appear to have a life expectancy of from five to seven years.

Enemies: Foxes, coyotes, wolves, bobcats, lynxes, mountain lions, marten, fishers, wolverines, bears, crows, ravens, hawks, owls and eagles—some or all of these predators are found in the various regions of the spruce grouse's range. They take the eggs, chicks or adults whenever possible.

Disease, parasites and accidents further raise the spruce grouse's mortality rate.

Table Fare: The spruce grouse is considered good eating when it has been feeding on berries in the late summer and early fall. However, as soon as it goes back to a diet of conifer needles, its flesh acquires an unpleasant taste. Even so, the native people eat the spruce grouse throughout the year, whenever they can obtain it.

Ruffed Grouse

Bonasa umbellus

Just as the sun had dispelled the morning haze, there was a quick pit-pattering of feet and then the thunderous explosion of wildly beating wings. The ruffed grouse hidden beneath a tangle of fox grapevines had flushed out behind the hunter. The grouse's cupped wings rocketed its body through the woodland as it twisted and turned in its elusive flight. The hunter whirled, but the intervening brush effectively hid the grouse from view, and silence soon reigned again. Yet the missed shot did not matter, for the hunter had nonetheless obtained that which he had come for: he had flushed a grouse, the "King of the Gamebirds," from cover.

DESCRIPTION: The ruffed grouse is a small, chicken-like bird that measures about 19 inches in length, has a wingspan of 25 inches and weighs up to 1¾ pounds. Superficially, the male and female ruffed grouse resemble each other, with their somber-hued plumage of browns, black and white. The female, however, is slightly smaller and slimmer than the male. Moreover the black outer band on the male's tail is continuous, while that of the female is broken by two brown central tail feathers. The male's

Ruffed Grouse

tail measures over 5¾ inches in length, whereas that of a female is usually under 5½ inches. The male has much longer feather crests and a far longer, darker and more complete ruff around its neck. Both sexes have the comb-like pectinations that grow out of the sides of the toes each fall and effectively double the size of each toe. These scales allow the grouse to walk on the top of soft snow as if it were wearing snowshoes. In the spring, the scales are no longer needed and drop off.

The ruffed grouse is a bird of North America's colder regions, and its legs and feet right down to the toes are completely covered with feathers.

The ruffed grouse's basic plumage color varies widely. Some birds range from ashy gray through dark gray to almost black, while others go from the palest buff through browns to almost chocolate. There are ten subspecies of ruffed grouse in North America, and in some of the species the color may be more consistent, while in others the widest degrees of shading are found. Dichromatism is the rule rather than the exception.

DISTRIBUTION: The ruffed grouse is closely related to the forest. Its largest population concentrations occur along woodland fringes rather than in the mature forest. It has the largest range of any of the different types of grouse, being found in woodland areas from the Atlantic to the Pacific; from Alaska down to California, in the Cascade, Sierra and Rocky Mountains; from Hudson's Bay south through Michigan and Wisconsin into Illinois; and from Labrador south to Tennessee and South Carolina along the Appalachian Mountains.

COMMUNICATION: In the spring the woodlands reverberate with the muffled drumming of the male ruffed grouse. This "drumming" —one of the best-known features of the grouse—serves to attract the female and also presents a challenge to rival males. It is usually done from a large, fallen log, but the grouse may also use a rock, a stump or even drum while sitting on the ground. High-speed motion picture cameras have shown that the sound is made by the grouse's cupped wings beating against the air. It starts with a few complete thumps and then blurs into a roll; thump, thump, thump, *thmm-thmm-thmm-thmm-thmm-thmm* thump. The sound is ventriloquistic, and although it carries well, it is hard to locate. It is produced at forty cycles per second, which means that it is easily heard by other grouse but is too low to be heard by the great horned owl.

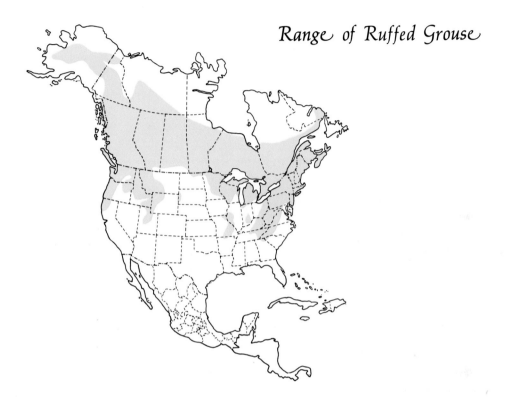

Range of Ruffed Grouse

The most common vocal sound of the grouse is a series of *putt-putts*. This is usually made by the female and seems to serve the purpose of holding her brood of chicks together. The young have a *tsee-tseeee* answering call.

BREEDING AND NESTING: The drumming of the ruffed grouse announces not only to other ruffed grouse but to the world in general that the grouse's breeding season is at hand. Some of the old drumming logs have been used continuously for decades by successive generations of grouse. In addition to drumming from the log, the male grouse uses it as a stage for displaying. He erects his neck ruff, erects and fans out his tail, droops his wings and struts from one end to the other.

The female that is summoned by the drumming and impressed with the male's display accepts his advances. A rival male is quickly challenged and a bloody fight may ensue, the weaker of the two males being driven from the area.

The nest of the ruffed grouse is usually located only a few feet from some path or trail that passes through the woodland. Invariably the nest itself is up against the trunk of a tree, stump or clump of bushes. This typical location gives the female protection from the rear but also means that there is a blind side from which a predator may approach. The advantages must outweigh the disadvantages because over 90 percent of the nests are in such locations.

The nest is just a depression formed out of whatever leaves happen to be on the forest floor. There is no evidence that any extra material is added in its construction, the few feathers that it contains being merely the result of shedding.

EGGS AND YOUNG: Usually one egg is laid per day until the clutch of nine to twelve eggs is completed. The eggs are 32 millimeters long by 29 millimeters in diameter. Their pale brown color usually matches the material of which the nest is composed.

The brooding of the eggs is done exclusively by the female. While she broods, she often picks up nearby leaves and places them on her back. If danger approaches, she sits tight on the nest and usually escapes notice because of her camouflage plumage. If the hen feels that she is about to be discovered, she flies from the nest, and some of the leaves may settle over the eggs.

Brooding takes between twenty-one and twenty-three days, the variation being determined by the time that the female spends off the nest to feed and get water.

Baby grouse are about the size of a golf ball when first hatched. They are precocious and are ready to leave the nest as soon as their down has dried. The hen herds her brood to the edge of the forest, where the supply of insects is much greater. She is quick to spot potential danger, and her warning call immediately scatters the chicks into hiding. If the danger draws close, the mother resorts to the "broken-wing" ruse. She flops on her side, beats her wings and makes a mewing sound. A predator is quick to follow her as she flops about on the ground, at the same time increasing the distance between herself and the chicks. This tactic is kept up until she feels that the chicks are safe. Then, springing into the air, she flies a circuitous route back to where she left the chicks. There her *puck* call reassembles the brood, and they leave the area with all possible speed.

FLIGHT: The grouse chicks' primary wing feathers grow very rapidly, and in four to five days the young are fluttering around and within a week can fly short distances. A few days later the chicks begin to roost up in trees, thereby gaining greater protection than they had enjoyed on the ground.

Although the ruffed grouse usually makes short flights, it has been known to fly over 1 mile at a time. Most people know the sound of the frantic wingbeats of a startled grouse. However, if it has ample time to escape from danger, it can fly without making a sound by beating its wings at a slower rate.

The top speed of the ruffed grouse is about 50 miles per hour, but it usually flies at speeds of between 25 and 35 miles per hour. A grouse flushing before a hunter often gives a deceptive impression of speed because it twists and turns its body to dodge the heavy thickets and underbrush that are its chosen habitat. Dexterous as the grouse is, it often collides with branches and sticks, sometimes with fatal results.

MIGRATION: The ruffed grouse does not migrate but is famous for its "crazy" flights, as the fall shuffle or dispersal flights are often called. Usually in the month of September, the summer broods of young grouse begin to break up and scatter to find a home range. This break-up usually precedes a storm. Although most of the birds walk the ½ to 3½ miles that are traversed during this period, some of them fly. Often those that fly crash into buildings, where they frequently break windows and usually kill themselves in the process. In the past couple of years I have had two grouse crash into my kitchen windows. Many theories have been put forward to explain this phenomenon, for instance that the grouse are intoxicated from eating fermented berries, are scared by falling leaves, or fail to realize the presence of the glass. Much study is being done on these flights, but so far no definite answer has been provided.

The fall dispersal flights are usually undertaken by the young birds, but there is also a slight spring shuffle in which some of the adults participate.

HABITS: Although ruffed grouse split up in the fall, there is a temporary regrouping in the winter, when flocks of four to eight grouse may sometimes be seen. This regrouping may be the result of a search for greater protection from cold winds and more abundant food.

The snow cover during the winter offers valuable protection to the ruffed grouse. In the southern part of its range the grouse roosts in trees, preferably conifers. In the central part of the range, where the snow may be wet, it roosts either in trees or on the top of the snow. Where the temperatures really drop and the winds are sharp, the snow is usually deep and powdery. Under these conditions the grouse roosts under the snow. The temperature 6 feet above the ground may be 40°F below zero, but with a 25 mile-per-hour wind, the actual chill factor is 104°F below zero. The insulating quality of the snow is such that the grouse sleeping beneath it actually finds temperatures above zero.

The adult male does very little traveling after it has acquired a home territory. It participates in the spring shuffle only in order to move up through the social system and acquire a more desirable territory, if the previous dominant male has been killed and the territory is vacant.

The ruffed grouse is a cyclic bird. This is not a habit but an occurrence that is neither fully understood nor fully controllable. The ten-year cycle is prominent in the north and almost absent in the south. It may not occur with equal intensity in the same range, in the same year or under the same conditions, but the fluctuations are widespread, peak populations occurring in the second or third year of each decade. It has been found that some 70 to 80 percent of all grouse do not survive a full year and that hunting has little or no effect on the cycle. A maximum grouse population is considered to be one bird to 4 acres of land. Ruffed grouse will not tolerate a higher population build-up, and even that ratio is reached on only the best of habitats.

Food: The ruffed grouse has been known to eat over 600 different items, and it very rarely lacks for food. The bulk of its diet is vegetable matter such as buds, leaves, berries, nuts, some grain and insects. A grouse may eat 1,300 buds in one day and a quarter of a million in one year. Yet it seldom does any real harm to the tree that it is feeding on because it does not sit still long enough to eat all the buds on one branch. Instead, like a grazing animal, the grouse moves from one branch to another, always working from the lower limbs toward the top of the tree.

Both the ruffed grouse and the white-tailed deer are browsers and are therefore in direct competition with each other. In fact, where deer are too plentiful, the numbers of grouse are curtailed.

Life Span: In the wild a ruffed grouse may live to be three or four years old. Captive grouse often live to be four or five, and some reach six years of age.

Sign: The most common sign of the ruffed grouse is its droppings. Since the food that the grouse eats is of low nutritional value, it has to consume vast quantities of it and so excretes much waste material. The droppings are about ¾ to 1¼ inches long by ⅜ of an inch in diameter and are composed of fibrous material. I have seen as many as seventy-three droppings from a single grouse in a single night.

Dusting spots used by the ruffed grouse may be seen in old wood roads, in the rotted wood of old stumps or on anthills. Usually a few fallen feathers help to identify such spots.

ENEMIES: The ruffed grouse is subject to predation by many creatures such as the great horned owl, the barred owl, the snowy owl, the gyrfalcon, the goshawk, the Cooper's hawk, the sharp-shinned hawk, foxes, bobcats and lynxes. During the brooding period snakes, skunks, opossums, raccoons, weasels, mink, etc., take the eggs, the chicks and the adults if possible.

TABLE FARE: The flesh of the ruffed grouse during the fall is a delight to the palate and fully justifies the hard hunting involved. In midwinter, when the grouse may feed upon conifer needles, the flesh is less tasty.

OVERLEAF ►

The Grouse of North America

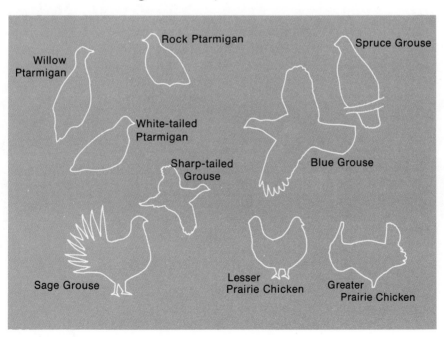

Sharp-tailed Grouse

Pedioecetes phasianellus

The brushlands are alive with the sound of booming — spring has come to sharptail country. For a cacophony of low, hollow *boooms* signals the noisy and frenetic mating ritual of this game bird.

Like its relative the prairie chicken, the sharp-tail is attached to a specific mating area. This turf, usually located atop small knolls, is commonly called a dancing ground.

Shortly after first thaw, as many as seventy-five of these grouse will swarm to their dancing ground for day-long frenzies. In addition, sharp-tails seem to stay near their ground throughout the year. Banding studies have shown that although male and female sharp-tails travel considerable distances in search of forage and shelter, they usually keep within fifteen miles of their mating turf.

DESCRIPTION: At a quick glance, the sharptail could easily be confused with the prairie chicken. The northern part of the prairie chicken's range overlaps the southern portion of the sharptail's range. In fact, it is even difficult for the birds to tell themselves apart. These two species not only strongly resemble each other, they are so closely related that they often interbreed. In most cases, the offspring of these crosses resemble the prairie chicken more closely than the sharptail.

To confuse the issue further, the male and female sharptail are so similar in appearance—although she is smaller in size—that unless the bird is in the hand, sexing is extremely difficult. The black on the male sharptail's center tail feathers runs lengthwise, while the female's usually runs crosswise. She also lacks the inflatable air sacs on the neck. At first glance, the sharptail could also be confused with the hen ring-necked pheasant; the distinguishing feature here is the sharptail's shorter tail.

The adult male sharptail has a length of about 17½ to 19½ inches, a wingspan of about 20 inches and a weight of between 1¾ and 2 pounds. There are six subspecies of the sharptail, which vary slightly in size, although the main difference among them is their range.

Sharp-tailed Grouse

The sharptail is basically brown. The top of its head, the back of its neck, its back, and rump are predominantly brown, although the feathers have a black edging and some white mottling. The center tail rectrices are dark, long and pointed, hence the name sharptail; the rest of the tail feathers are white.

There is a black line starting behind the bird's bill and running through the eye. The cheeks and throat are white. The breast has white feathers with a brown edge that gives them a dart or arrow-point pattern. The belly and flanks are basically white with some black darts, and the underside of the tail is white. The wings are dark brown with white splotches. The tarsi are covered with brown feathers down to the toes. A yellow comb is located above each eye in the male, and on each side of his back is a lavender-colored, inflatable air sac, surrounded by white feathers. These sacs are not as large as the prairie chicken's nor are they as prominently displayed. When they are not inflated, they become invisible.

DISTRIBUTION: It must always be remembered that the sharptail is a bird of the brushlands. It is found in areas where brush is permanent and temporarily in areas that are in transition between grasslands and forest.

The sharptail is found in Colorado, Wyoming, Nebraska, South and North Dakota, Minnesota, Wisconsin, Michigan, Montana, Utah, Idaho, Oregon, Washington, British Columbia, Alberta, Saskatchewan, Manitoba, Ontario, Quebec, the Northwest Territories, the Yukon and central Alaska. In some of these states, the populations are small and confined to restricted areas of the state.

COMMUNICATION: The sharp-tailed grouse has a wide range of calls. Both the male and female almost always cackle when they are flushed. Another call that the birds give when disturbed can be described as *whucker, whucker, whucker.* In the spring, the male has a low *cack, cack, cack, cack* call that resembles that of a turkey. On the dancing ground, the male also makes a hollow, boooming sound. The female has a high-pitched alarm call that effectively causes her chicks to scatter to find shelter. The chicks call to their mother and to each other with a plaintive *peeep.*

BREEDING AND NESTING: In early April, as the snow retreats, the sharp-tailed grouse begins to gather in even larger numbers on their "dancing" grounds. Whereas throughout the winter the male sharptails may have paid periodic visits to these spots, now their presence there is mandatory.

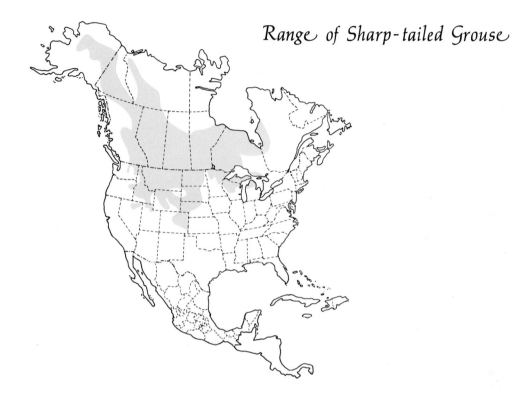

Range of Sharp-tailed Grouse

The sharptail engages in the most energetic display of all of the grouse. Its performance is a frenzied flurry of activity. The males gather to perform before dawn, dance for several hours and then retire into the brush to feed and rest until about two hours before sunset, when they stage a repeat performance.

The average number of males gathered on one dancing ground is about twelve, but as many as fifty or more males have been seen in one area. When they first gather, they stand quietly as if waiting for their cue. One male suddenly droops his wings until the tips touch the ground. He then erects his tail vertically over his back, so that the white underside shows very conspicuously. The tail is vibrated sideways so that it makes a rustling noise, the neck feathers are erected, and the eye combs are inflated.

With his neck extended forward and downward, the male rushes forward a short distance. Then he blurringly stamps his feet, sometimes turning in a little circle, all the while vibrating his tail and uttering his low-toned call. Finally, he "freezes" tensely in his display position, looking as if someone had suddenly turned off his motor switch. After resting in that manner for a few moments, the sharptail spins off into another dance. Usually the activity of one male triggers a response in the rest of the males, and all of them whirl into action.

Sometimes one of the males singles out another male as a dancing or fighting partner. Then the two males dance for each other. Seldom is a fight a physical one; usually one male tries to "psych" the other into giving way or turning aside. The few real fights are of short duration and involve only the loss of a few feathers.

The appearance of a hen on the dancing grounds makes the activity even more hectic. The hens at first ignore the dancers by remaining on the edge of the area, but as they become more receptive, they walk out onto the stage and squat down before the male of their choice. Copulation follows immediately.

The sharptail's nest is not an elaborate construction. With her feet, the female digs a shallow depression in the soil and adds some dried grass or leaves as a liner. Usually the nest is concealed under a bush or clump of grass, but sometimes it may be located right out in the open.

EGGS AND YOUNG: The sharptail's clutch usually contains about twelve eggs, but occasionally there are more and sometimes less. The eggs average 42 millimeters in length by 32 millimeters in diameter. Their basic color is dark brown with purple shadings, and most of the eggs also have small dark spots. They gradually lighten as the color is worn off by the female sitting on them and constantly turning them. The female is difficult to locate while on her nest because she blends in so well with her surroundings.

The hen performs all incubation activities, which require twenty-one days. The males continue to dance until the latter part of May. By then, all the hens are sitting on their eggs, and none of them visit the dancing grounds at this time. Gradually the dancing activities lessen, and the males finally scatter to lead a sedentary and solitary existence for most of the summer.

The nest of any of the ground-nesting birds is most vulnerable to predation just before and during the hatching period. As soon as her brood has dried off, the female leads it to a safer spot among the heavy vegetation. It is fortunate that most vegetation is approaching its most luxuriant growth at about the time that the vulnerable young of the various birds are hatching. The female uses all her wiles to decoy danger away from her chicks, but there is little she can do to give them actual physical protection.

The young grouse feed primarily on insects, and on this rich protein diet they grow exceedingly fast. At two months of age, they are large enough to take care of themselves and the brood break-up begins.

FLIGHT: The young sharptails can fly for a short distance when they are ten days old. At one month of age, they are almost fully feathered and can fly well.

The sharptail is a strong flier, capable of springing into the air and reaching a speed of 35 to 40 miles per hour in a matter of seconds. Its cupped wings whistle as the pinions cleave the air. It varies its flight by alternately flapping and soaring. When it has reached its desired speed or height, it sets its wings and glides for long distances. The bird's flight is usually direct, its purpose being apparently to put distance between the sharptail and whatever disturbed it rather than to perform a twisting, evasive action.

MIGRATION: The sharp-tailed grouse does not migrate except for making seasonal shifts that are forced on it by food requirements at different seasons.

HABITS: During the summer, the sharp-tailed grouse spends all its time on the ground in such activities as feeding, nesting and sleeping. This practice continues until the first snow of the season. The grouse then switches from being a terrestrial creature to being arboreal. It still sleeps on the ground, plunging into the snow to spend the night. Here the insulating blanket of snow keeps it most comfortable. Even a freezing rainstorm does not have the same ability to seal the snow's surface in the brush and woodlands as it does in the more open areas.

But the grouse now spends its daylight hours up in the trees, feeding on the buds, flying from tree to tree and dozing there for a midday siesta. The bird becomes exceedingly wary at this time of the year because it feels the loss of its camouflage and the lack of the protective vegetation that it enjoys during the rest of the year. From its vantage point up in a tree, it usually spots danger at a distance and wings off to find shelter before the enemy gets any closer.

FOOD: The food intake of the sharp-tailed grouse has been carefully analyzed. Laboratory tests have shown that 90 percent of its diet is composed of vegetation and the remaining 10 percent chiefly of insects. Grasshoppers are the sharptail's favorite insect food, and beetles, caterpillars and other small insects make up the balance of this part of its diet. Of the vegetable matter, 31 percent consists of leaves, flowers and buds, 27 percent is fruit, 20 percent grain, 7 percent weed seeds, and the balance is miscellaneous plant material. The grouse's favorite foods include white birch, wheat, mountain ash, clover, dandelion, prairie rose, sunflower seeds, chokecherry, wild rose, wild cherry, willow, poplar, alder, alfalfa and maple. Wild rose hips are a special favorite, the bright red hips remaining above the snow and readily visible. One sharptail is recorded to have eaten over a thousand wheat grains.

LIFE SPAN: The sharp-tailed grouse should have a life expectancy of about five years. No banding records are available for this species.

ENEMIES: The destruction of its habitat to make more land available for farmland has been the prime reason for the decline in the numbers of the sharp-tailed grouse. When the brushland goes, so does the sharptail. Crows, magpies, badgers, ground squirrels, snakes, foxes, coyotes, feral dogs and cats, hawks, owls and eagles all prey on the sharp-tailed grouse and its young or eggs. Parasites, disease and accidents further reduce its population.

TABLE FARE: The sharp-tailed grouse is eagerly hunted. It has all the attributes of an ideal game bird, since it flushes well, flies strongly, and its flesh is delicious.

Sage Grouse

Centrocercus urophasianus

Sagebrush is a woody shrub with grayish green, aromatic foliage that is found mainly on the arid upland plains and lower mountainsides of our western states. In many of these states, the sagebrush is spreading, largely owing to poor range management practices. Overgrazing leads to the natural range grasses being wiped out as a result of erosion. When this occurs, the sagebrush takes over the land. Although sagebrush is not a good food for livestock, it provides valuable food, shade and shelter for many wild creatures, particularly the sage grouse.

DESCRIPTION: The sage grouse is the largest member of the grouse family to be found in North America. A large adult male may measure 30 inches in length, have a wingspan of 36 inches and weigh up to 7 pounds or more. It is a basically grayish brown bird with a dark belly and a stiff, long-pointed tail. The bird's bill is short and black-tipped. The top of its head, the back of its neck, its back, tail, flanks and upper wing coverts are a mottled grayish brown, black and white. The primary feathers of the wing are brown, the under coverts white. There is a small yellow comb-like process above each eye. A white line starts behind the bird's bill, goes through the eye and runs down to form a border under the black throat patch. The white is in turn bordered by a wider black band that starts behind the eye and circles above the breast. There are extra-long white filoplumes on the sides of the neck. The breast is covered with scale-like white feathers that conceal a pair of orange-colored, nonfeathered air sacs, which are seen only when the bird is displaying. The belly is black. The legs are feathered down to the black toes. Altogether, this is the most strikingly plumaged member of the grouse family.

The female sage grouse is only half to two-thirds the size of the male, largely because of her much shorter tail. She is also a

Male sage grouse on the strutting grounds in spring.

Range of Sage Grouse

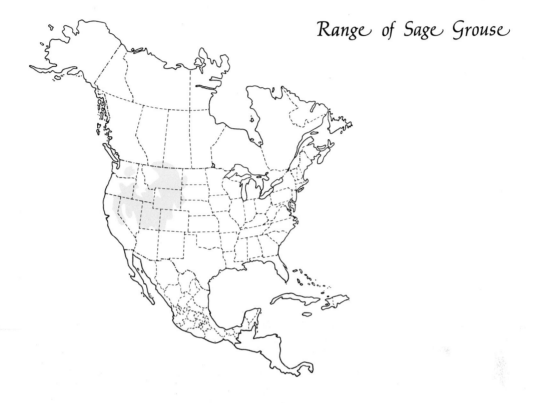

duller looking bird, her throat and breast being mottled instead of black and white like the male's. She lacks the long neck filoplumes and the air sacs.

DISTRIBUTION: The sage grouse is found only where sagebrush is plentiful. It is estimated that although the grouse's range has shrunk, it is still found on about 130 million acres of Montana, Wyoming, Colorado, Idaho, Utah, Nevada, Oregon, Washington, Nebraska, North and South Dakota. The last four states have only a limited sage-grouse range and population.

COMMUNICATION: During his elaborate breeding display the male sage grouse makes sounds like a huge cat purring, together with a low, staccato, grunting sound. When the sage grouse is flushed into flight, it has a higher pitched cackle. The male's regular call is a guttural *cuck, cuck, cuck,* while the hen's voice sounds like that of our domestic hen. The chicks peep.

BREEDING AND NESTING: The sage grouse is gregarious by nature and is almost always found in a flock or in close proximity to its own kind.

In April and May and sometimes even into early June, the male sage grouse all gather together on a communal "strutting" ground. Some of these areas have been used by the sage grouse year after year from time immemorial. A strutting ground may vary in size from a couple of hundred square feet to several acres. Although these grounds lie on comparatively flat plains, they are all on the highest elevation in the area and are usually free of high or clumped vegetation. The number of males using any particular strutting ground may vary from a dozen up into the hundreds.

The twenty feathers on the male's tail are very stiff and pointed, and when he starts to display, the tail is spread fan-shaped and erected to a completely vertical position. His head is held high and back so that the filoplume feathers of the neck stand out. His wings are brought forward with the wrist held straight up, the tips of the wings almost touching the ground. Then the male gulps in air to inflate his neck sacs. The bright yellow-orange sacs, once inflated, are raised forward and upward until they are clearly visible and make the white neck and breast feathers stand on end like a wreath. The male then quickly runs forward for a short distance, rubbing his wings up and down against his breast feathers. The sound produced is similar to that made by a displaying peacock when he vibrates his feathers. After the third run, the male suddenly stops and, bouncing his air sacs up and down, produces a popping sound. At the height of the breeding season, a male may perform a display like this four or five times an hour.

Odd as it may seem, this performance is apparently done more to intimidate the lesser males than to impress the females because it goes on whether there are any females present or not. Often, if the females are around, they pay no attention to the display at all. Yet the performance must also serve a breeding purpose, since the larger males, who do most of the displaying and some of the fighting, are the ones that do the breeding. When a female is ready to be bred, she comes to the strutting ground and selects one of the dominant males. There may be two hundred males on a given ground, but a dozen or so dominant males do all the breeding.

The females come to the males early in the morning and after being bred retire into the sagebrush to a spot they have chosen for a nest. If the sage grouse population is high, the nests may be as close as 200 feet from each other. Some of the spots selected for the nests may be used year after year.

The sage grouse's nest is usually a bowl scraped out by the female in the earth under a cluster of sagebrush. It is a very rudimentary affair, lined with a few leaves or grasses. The female is very inconspicuous when she sits on her nest, her coloring allowing her to blend into the landscape.

EGGS AND YOUNG: The sage grouse's clutch averages from seven to nine eggs, the smallest number laid by any of our native grouse. The eggs average 55 millimeters in length by 38 millimeters in diameter. The shells are smooth and vary greatly in basic color, even within one clutch. They range from deep brown, through yellow, to white, always with a green tinge. The dark brown spots are small and usually evenly distributed over the entire shell.

Incubation, which requires twenty-five days, is performed entirely by the female. Knowing instinctively that she is camouflaged, she allows herself to be approached very closely before flushing from the nest.

The chicks are precocious and are led from the nest a few hours after their down has dried. They are a mottled gray-black in color. The female is a very good mother and tries to decoy danger away from the young by feigning a broken wing. If she fails in her ruse, she may fly at the intruder with a lot of hissing and cackling. This commotion is usually enough to deter all but the largest, most determined predators. At the first warning cluck from the mother, the young scatter like chaff in the wind.

As there are often a number of broods in one area, the chicks may shift from one female to another. This does not seem to cause any consternation among the females because the broods appear to get along amicably. Besides, the females can't count so that the loss or gain of a chick or two means nothing to them.

The females take care of the chicks for about two months. Long before this time, the young can fly, but the brood break-up is not complete until about the end of August or the beginning of September. At about this time, the males reinsert themselves into the lives of the chicks. As the flocks tend to merge and concentrate in the fall, the males rejoin the group or form bachelor groups consisting of the older males.

FLIGHT: The sage grouse is a strong flier, although not as fast as most of the other grouse. It appears to be willing to fly greater distances to reach food. When flushed, it flies farther than other grouse, perhaps because the other grouse, except for the sharptail, are woodland birds to whom heavy cover is instantly available.

The cupped wings of the sage grouse allow it to spring up into the air in full flight but are not suited for long-distance flight.

Usually this grouse tries to run from danger and will sprint ahead of a hunter for a long distance before flushing. When it finally breaks into the air, it almost always does so with a pheasant-like cackle. Its takeoff is rather heavy, but once it gets speed up, it is an efficient flier. After reaching top speed, it soars on set wings, and if the distance it intends to travel is considerable, it alternates flapping and soaring. The sage grouse usually flies to its favorite watering places.

MIGRATION: The sage grouse does not migrate in the strict sense of the word. Weather or sometimes food conditions may cause it to shift slightly from one area to another. However, the sagebrush provides it with both food and shelter. The grouse tends to be at higher elevations in the summer, drifting down into the valleys in the fall and winter.

HABITS: The sage grouse is an early riser. Usually it goes to water to drink within an hour after the sun is up. It then feeds away from water until its crop is full. Then the grouse retires to rest, to dust itself in summer and to sit in the sun in winter. Activity picks up again about 2 p.m., when the grouse starts to feed once more. It often goes to water again before settling down for the night. Sage grouse roost on the ground at night. It is claimed that they sometimes roost in circles in the manner of bobwhite quails.

There have been reports of a sage grouse sitting up on a sagebrush bush, but this is not usual. There is very little need for the grouse to leave the ground. It can easily reach all the food it needs without flying up into a tree, which, if the tree is in the open, would expose it unnecessarily to danger. Creatures that have as good a camouflage as the sage grouse know their advantage instinctively and are quick to use it. The gray of the sage grouse allows it to blend into the sagebrush so that it is possible for a human to be in the midst of a flock of these birds and not discover them unless they move.

FOOD: The sage grouse's main foods are the leaves and blossoms of the sagebrush. This one plant provides 71 percent of its year-round diet. The grouse also eats dandelions, alfalfa, clover, gilia, pussytoe and agoseris. Its diet further includes a few ants, beetles and chinch bugs.

LIFE SPAN: The average life span for the sage grouse is five years. One adult female lived for seven years after banding.

ENEMIES: The ground squirrel is the greatest predator of the sage grouse's eggs, followed by the badger, magpie and coyote. All these predators also feed on the chicks and adults if they can catch them. They are joined in this activity by skunks, weasels, mink, bobcats, cats and dogs, hawks, owls and eagles. Fire is a tremendous hazard, and the rancher's mowing machine also takes its toll. The sage grouse, like all other creatures, is subject to disease and parasites.

TABLE FARE: Tastes differ on the subject of the sage grouse's flesh, some people liking it and others finding it slightly bitter. Some of this bitter taste can be removed if the bird is dressed and drawn as soon as it is shot.

Greater Prairie Chicken

Tympanuchus cupido

Lesser Prairie Chicken   *Tympanuchus pallidicinctus*

I have always been fascinated by the early explorers' reports about the wildlife that they encountered in regions where they were the first white men to set foot. These reports describe both the long and the short grass prairies stretching to the horizon. Bison herds dotted the landscape, deer thrived along the watercourses, and the prairie chickens existed in flocks uncountable. Just as no one thought that the bison could be diminished, it was also believed that the supply of prairie chickens was inexhaustible. Both suppositions have proved wrong. Today, the future of the bison is secure, but unfortunately the same cannot be said of the prairie chicken. The last heath hen, an eastern prairie chicken, died in 1931, and the future of both the greater and the lesser prairie chicken is insecure.

DESCRIPTION: The male adult greater prairie chicken is about 18½ inches in length, has a wingspan of about 27½ inches and weighs up to 2½ pounds. The top of his head, the back of his neck, his back, his upper wing coverts and the top of his tail are reddish brown, barred with black and shot through with some white. The primary and secondary wing feathers are gray, white and black. The tail has a wide band at the tip, although the extreme edge is light brown. The bird has a white line over the eye, a black line through the eye and part way down the neck and a white throat. Long, stiff feathers called pinnae stick out from the side of the neck. These can be erected to make a small fan behind the male's head when he is displaying. It is from these feathers that the prairie chicken came to be called the pinnated grouse. There are small yellow combs or sacs above each eye and two large yellow inflatable air sacs on each side of the neck. The bird's eye is hazel-brown. Its breast, belly, flanks and the underside of its tail are basically white, or buffy white with darker brown bars. The legs and feet are feathered right down to the toes. The feet are yellow.

The female prairie chicken is both smaller in size and lighter in weight than the male. She is lighter in color, and the end of her tail is barred instead of being banded like the male's. She lacks the air sacs, and her pinnae neck feathers are much shorter than the male's.

The adult male lesser prairie chicken measures 15 to 16 inches in length, has a wingspan of about 23 inches and weighs about 1¾ pounds. In addition to being smaller than its big cousin, the lesser prairie chicken is lighter in color. Whereas the greater prairie chicken has a lot of black in the barrings on both its back and its breast, the lesser prairie chicken does not. The lesser prairie chicken does have some black on its wings, however, and it has the same large black band on its tail. The absence of the black barring gives this bird a distinctly reddish appearance. The combs above the eye are yellow, but the lesser prairie chicken has lavender-colored air sacs. The two birds could easily be confused, but their ranges do not overlap.

DISTRIBUTION: The greater prairie chicken's range has been greatly reduced. It is found today in parts of Michigan, Wisconsin, Illinois, Indiana, Minnesota, Iowa, Missouri, Oklahoma, Texas, Kansas, Nebraska, North and South Dakota, Manitoba and Alberta.

The lesser prairie chicken is found in Kansas, Oklahoma, Texas and New Mexico. In all four states, its range is limited and consists more or less of scattered pockets.

Greater Prairie Chicken

Market hunting took a heavy toll of the prairie chickens, thousands of barrels of them being sold on the market. However, it was not the gun but the plow that decimated their populations. When the first farms were carved out of the prairies, they raised a variety of crops. The prairie chicken proved itself adaptable enough to add the cultivated grains, particularly wheat and corn, to its diet. For a short period, farming actually increased the number of prairie chickens. It was only when the farms switched mainly to one crop, wheat, that the prairie chicken was doomed. Research has shown that these birds cannot survive in any area, regardless of the availability of food, if more than 60 percent of the grassland is converted to cropland. Moreover the birds have to have high grasses for protection while roosting and nesting and for winter cover.

Lesser Prairie Chicken

COMMUNICATION: Most of the sounds made by the prairie chicken are heard mainly during the breeding season. Some of them are vocal, others are physical. The cooing note of the male is a loud *c-a-o-o-o-o-o-o, hoo, hoo*. This is a three-note call with each note one step up the musical scale. It has been claimed that his call can be heard for a distance of 2 miles or more. The male also has two different cackling calls that can be described as *ka-ka-ka-ka-a-a-a-a* and a long-drawn *q-u-a-h*. When the males fight, they give vent to a low-pitched whine.

The female's usual note is a hoarse cackle. When the young are struggling to free themselves from their shells, she encourages them to greater effort by calling *brirrrb-brirrrb*. When she is shepherding her chicks about, she warns them of impending danger by giving a sharp, short, shrill call. The chicks peep.

Range of Prairie Chicken

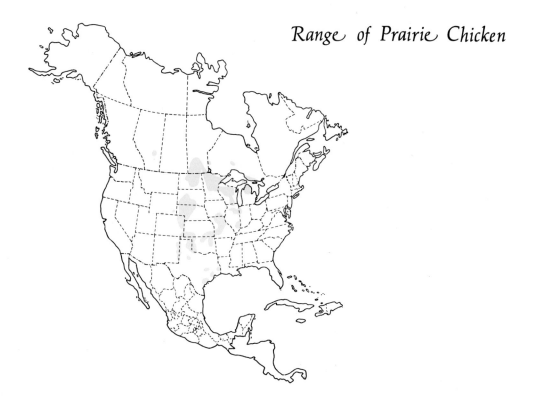

BREEDING AND NESTING: One of the most interesting courtship displays performed by any of our native birds is that of the prairie chicken.

All the breeding of both the lesser and greater prairie chicken takes place on the "booming" ground. This is a spot selected by the males to perform their courtship displays. Its location may be shifted from year to year, owing to intrusive farming activities, but in some cases the same grounds have been used since the arrival of the first white men. The ground is usually located on the highest rise to be found on the prairie, and the vegetation must be short.

The male prairie chickens occasionally resort to the booming ground throughout the winter. Under the influence of increased hormones in their bodies, they visit the grounds more frequently in the months of February and March and do so religiously throughout April, May and even into June. The number of male prairie chickens that utilize a particular ground depends upon many factors such as the number of males and booming grounds in the entire area. As many as forty or as few as two males may utilize a booming ground, but the average number is ten to twelve in a stable chicken population. Only the males visit the booming ground in the early spring, the females coming in only to be bred. The males often walk to the booming ground but usually leave it on the wing. They are on the booming ground before dawn. They remain active for about two hours after sunrise, leaving only to return about two hours before sunset, when they stay until dark.

In performing, the male holds his body, neck and head horizontal to the ground and runs forward for 10 or 15 feet, then stops suddenly. Next he stamps his feet on the ground so hard and so swiftly that he creates a noise which can be heard at quite a distance and which is very similar to the sound made by blowing across the opening of an empty bottle. Some of the plains Indians' dance steps are patterned after the prairie chicken's foot stomping. While stamping his feet, the male usually turns his body, sometimes in a full circle and occasionally even jumping up in the air. As the prairie chicken dances, his bright orange or lavender-colored air sacs are inflated to their fullest, and he makes the long pinnae feathers on his neck stand upright like a stiff collar. His wings are slightly drooped so that although the primaries are all pointing to the rear, they are separated. He spreads his tail out like a vertical fan and then snaps it partially closed.

The males dance to intimidate their rivals because during these dances, the dominant males lay claim to the area in the center of the booming ground. Each individual's territory is small, about 15 square feet, and the choicest territory is in the center of the ground because this is where the bulk of the breeding takes place.

Often two males run at each other, only to stop when they are about 2 feet apart and walk away from each other. When the males do fight, they peck at each other, sometimes jumping up into the air so that they can strike out at each other with their feet. Some of the males even try to jump up high enough to be able to drop down on top of their rival. Fights are usually of short duration, a few feathers being lost and perhaps some scratches inflicted.

The females begin to visit the booming grounds in late March, coming in singly. As a female approaches the area, all bedlam breaks loose as the males do their utmost to impress her with their individual performances. All this comes to naught as it is still too early for the female to breed, and she is just reconnoitering.

During April all the females gather each morning near the center of the booming ground. Now territorial rights are strictly observed by the males. The dominant males hold the best center territories, and they are the ones that do the breeding. The males on the periphery of the booming ground get little out of all their performing except exercise. Their day will come as the dominant males die off of old age or fall before a predator, and the outside birds move up in the hierarchy.

The females are now receptive to the attentions of the males, who are displaying continuously, and they show their acceptance by remaining on the chosen male's territory. Social amenities must be observed, however, so the male goes through an elaborate bowing display before the female. With wings outstretched and his bill touching the ground, he prostrates himself before her. She responds by squatting down and, slowly fanning her raised wings, presents herself to the male, who loses no time in mounting her.

Most breeding occurs in the first two weeks in April. After that the females' visits fall off, although the males continue to perform for another month or so.

A prime requirement for the nest is that the grass be high enough to give protective cover. In the virgin prairie areas, of which so few are left, this was no problem. Today, the prairie chicken has to resort to hedgerows, marshy swales or ungrazed pastures.

The nest is seldom more than a form hollowed out in the grass. Where the cover is high, the nest appears to be roofed over. The prairie chicken may use some additional dead grass in constructing a nest bowl about 7 or 8 inches in diameter and 2 or 3 inches deep.

EGGS AND YOUNG: The prairie chicken is prolific and fertile. It has a large clutch of from twelve to sixteen eggs and is usually successful in hatching the entire clutch. The eggs are 44 millimeters in length by 33 millimeters in diameter. They vary in color from buff to grayish olive. Some are unmarked, while others are flecked with tiny brown spots.

Incubation requires twenty-three days and is performed entirely by the female. During the first few days of incubation, the hen flushes from her nest rather easily. As time goes on, she becomes increasingly attached to her eggs and has to be almost stepped on before she will flush.

The chicks usually hatch over a twenty-four-hour period. They are precocious and ready to leave the nest as soon as their down dries. The mother frequently has trouble keeping the first chicks that hatch under her so that she can continue incubating the remaining eggs. The chicks' down is light brown with black spots.

As soon as all the chicks are hatched, the female leads them away from the nest. They quickly learn to catch the insects that are their main source of food. At about two weeks of age, seeds of various kinds of plants are added to the chicks' diet and soon become the dominant food.

The mother prairie chicken attempts to decoy danger away from her young. At her danger call, the young scatter and remain hidden until the mother calls them out again.

FLIGHT: The primary feathers develop very rapidly, and by the time the young prairie chickens are two weeks old, they can make short flying hops; when they are four weeks old, they are able to fly away from land-based predators.

The prairie chicken, like all members of the grouse family, has short, cupped wings that allow a speedy takeoff but not sustained flight. However, the prairie chicken probably flies more than any of the other members of this family.

The prairie chicken flies when leaving the booming ground, going to its feeding grounds and roosting areas and escaping from danger. Its flight is usually quite speedy, up to about 30 or 35 miles per hour, and is normally low and fairly direct. It consists of alternating flapping and soaring.

MIGRATION: The prairie chicken used to migrate, sometimes for hundreds of miles. Today, it cannot be said to do so. There are seasonal shifts due to weather, food or breeding, but most of its activities could be encompassed by an area 5 square miles.

HABITS: The prairie chicken is an early riser; it is up before the sun and flies out to feed. It can usually pick up enough food in two hours to fill its crop. Then it lazes around through the middle of the day. Feeding is resumed in midafternoon.

During the summer months, while the female is tending the chicks, the males remain solitary or join together in small groups. After the brood break-up in late August, all the chickens gather together in large flocks, the sexes being segregated. Some of the fall flocks contain as many as a hundred individuals. The males fight among themselves for territory and many perform on the booming grounds in November. Winter storms put an end to most of this activity, but the flame is only banked, not extinguished, and the booming ground remains the focal point of the male's life.

To rid itself of parasites, the prairie chicken takes frequent dust baths. Its need for water is scant because it can usually slake its thirst by obtaining moisture from the vegetation that it eats. It supplements this by drinking drops of dew and eating snow in the winter.

The prairie chickens fly into their roosting areas in a flock just before the sun goes down. Upon alighting, the birds scatter over quite a large area if there is an abundance of good cover. Each bird then hollows out a form in the high grass and sits facing into the wind. Although the birds may use the same general area for roosting each night, they do not use the same form.

FOOD: The bulk of the prairie chicken's diet is vegetable matter. The percentages vary according to the season and the availability of food. In the winter 97 percent of its diet is vegetation, in the spring 99 percent, in the summer 70 percent and in the fall 78 percent. The birds feed primarily on seeds and fruits but also browse on buds and leaves. Their favorite foods are ruellia, oats, corn, knotweed, wild rose, blackberry, buttonweed, ragweed, blue-eyed grass, spurge, goldenrod, quaking aspen, apple, wheat, clover, sorghum and bristle grass. Of the animals they eat, grasshoppers head the list. They also eat beetles, caterpillars and ants.

LIFE SPAN: The prairie chicken has a life expectancy of about five or six years.

ENEMIES: All ground-nesting birds are subject to all local predators that are large enough to overcome them. The following predators take the prairie chicken, its young or its eggs: snakes, ground squirrels, skunks, badgers, bobcats, foxes, coyotes, house dogs and cats, magpies, crows, hawks, owls and eagles. Diseases, such as blackhead, parasites, such as body lice, and accidents, such as those caused by mowing machines or automobiles, also take their toll.

TABLE FARE: In the 1800s, the prairie chickens were marketed and sold by the thousands of barrels on the commercial markets. Local people ate so many they tired of them. Prairie chicken-hunting today is limited, and the birds are considered a delicacy. The taste depends upon many factors.

Willow Ptarmigan

Lagopus lagopus

The willow ptarmigan has been chosen as Alaska's state bird. The first ones I ever saw were on the brush-covered flats that lie between Alaska's Lake Iliamna and the Chigmit Mountains. At every turn in the road, we could see broods of ptarmigan chicks being led or herded by the parent birds. I would have loved to visit those same flats just before the snow covered them, when the young birds would have been almost full grown. It would have been unfair to take a pointing bird dog because he would have been on point in every direction at once, but this would have been prime country for my springer spaniel. It was one of the greatest concentrations of game birds that I had ever seen.

DESCRIPTION: The willow ptarmigan is the largest of the three ptarmigan, being 15 to 17 inches in length, with a wingspan of 22 inches and a weight of about 1¼ pounds. This is a bird of the Arctic regions and has very fine feather "hairs" entirely covering the leg, foot and toes. Unlike the ruffed grouse, which loses the scales on its toes in the summer, the ptarmigan retains its toe covering at all times. The toenail covering, however, is shed annually. These

Willow Ptarmigan

claws are used by the bird to scratch down through snow and ice
to secure food.

In the winter both sexes turn white except for their dark bills,
eyes and outer tail feathers. At this time the male and female are
similar in appearance, whereas their summer plumage differs
considerably. The male retains the white wings, belly, legs and feet
in summer, while the rest of his plumage turns reddish brown. The
hen's underparts also stay white, but the upper parts of her body
become a mottled brown. The tail in both species remains black,
as it was in the winter. The male has a small comb (a bare patch of
bright orange-red skin with an upper serrated edge) above each
eye. The comb may be hidden from sight or revealed when the
bird is alarmed or displaying.

Range of Willow Ptarmigan

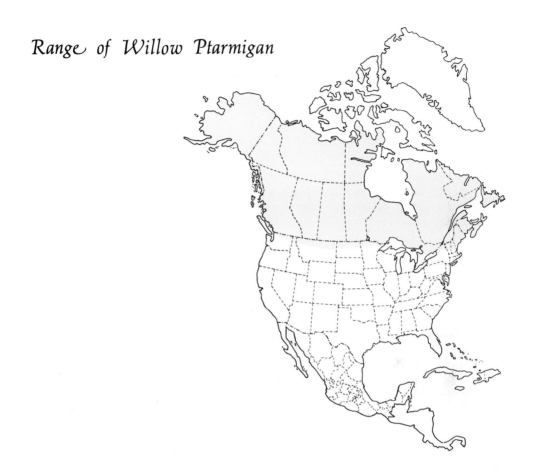

DISTRIBUTION: The willow ptarmigan has the widest range of the three species, being found from the Atlantic to the Pacific and from the fringe of our northern states up to Canada's Arctic islands.

COMMUNICATION: All the ptarmigan make some of the weirdest sounds in the bird-call repertoire. The willow ptarmigan's most frequent call is a very deep-toned, stuttering sound like the croak of an oversized bullfrog or toad.

BREEDING AND NESTING: By May the ptarmigan have scattered over their summer range and are on their breeding grounds. There is much defiant calling among the males. They frequently fly up into the air and then glide down in a broad spiral on set wings to where the female is all but hidden below. The ptarmigan is monogamous, and there is a great deal of rivalry between the males. Although the males often chase each other around, there is very little actual contact. Each male's territory is restricted, but it is apparently important that it contain a small patch of clear ground.

I saw my first willow ptarmigan's nest on the side of the road in Mount McKinley National Park. A road crew had been cutting brush along the roadside and had flushed the female. The nest was hidden under some dwarf willows. It was well formed, the surrounding grasses being the only material used in its construction. The cup was 4 to 5 inches deep. As we approached, the female did not fly from the nest but crept off through the dense underbrush.

Eggs and Young: The eleven eggs in the nest were almost perfectly round and measured 33 millimeters in length by 29 millimeters in breadth. The splotches on the eggs were a very rich purplish red and looked as if they had been generously applied by dripping the color on. Ten to twelve eggs are an average clutch, and one egg is laid every day until the clutch is complete. Frequently the female covers over her eggs after she has added a new one, to keep them hidden from sight until she comes back the following day. Incubation requires twenty-two to twenty-five days. Although the female does all the brooding, the male is always in very close attendance. In fact, he becomes very pugnacious in defense of the young after they hatch.

The young are able to leave the nest within an hour of hatching. Both parents care for the young. I found this surprising because I was accustomed to the female ruffed grouse doing the job by herself. In all three species of ptarmigan, I found the males helping with the family chores. As I tried for photos of the chicks, the female would herd the little ones away while the male stationed himself between me and his departing family. With erected eye comb, fluttering wings and raucous calling he did everything short of actually attacking me to protect the chicks.

As the family moves about among the thick underbrush, they keep in contact by the parents constantly clucking and the chicks peeping in response. Although this serves to keep the family together, one would expect it also to call the predators' attention to its whereabouts.

At first the chicks are on an almost exclusively insect diet, but within two weeks they have shifted to vegetation.

FLIGHT: The chicks begin to flutter about after four or five days, and within eight to ten days they can fly quite a distance. A willow ptarmigan's main mode of travel is to walk from place to place, its wings being used only as a last resort. Because it frequents open areas, it undoubtedly flies more than forest grouse do. Its flight is strong, and it can probably reach speeds of 40 to 45 miles per hour.

MIGRATION: The willow ptarmigan does not migrate but does have very pronounced seasonal shifts in territory. In the fall the birds concentrate in the densest willow flats and draws, where they can find ample cover and food. Sometimes a flock will number from fifty to a hundred birds or more. In the spring the birds scatter widely to establish their individual breeding territory.

HABITS: The willow ptarmigan is apparently well aware of the camouflage value of its plumage. In the winter, when the ground is covered with snow and the bird is in its white feathers, it sits huddled right out in the snow. The black tail feathers are kept hidden by the white ones, and unless it moves its black bill or eye, the ptarmigan is almost invisible. In the spring, when the bird is changing from white to brown, it prefers to remain on or near snow-covered areas. As soon as its summer plumage has grown in, it is quick to take advantage of it by keeping hidden in among thick brush.

The male ptarmigan shows more concern for the female than the other grouse and often perches on a bush or rock to stand guard duty while she feeds.

FOOD: The willow ptarmigan spends its life surrounded by the food it eats. The vegetation of the tundra areas that it inhabits consists mainly of dwarf willows, birches and alders, and the ptarmigan feeds on the buds, leaves and twigs of these woody bushes. It eats all types of seeds as well as the great variety of berries that are found in the northland. Insects form only a small part of its diet.

In the winter the wind frequently drifts the snow, covering the vegetation that the ptarmigan feeds on. It is at this time that the long scratching claws are put to good use to dig down through the snow.

LIFE SPAN: Three to four years are a good average life span for a willow ptarmigan living and breeding in the wild. The bird has a potential life span of about five to six years.

SIGN: The willow ptarmigan is a browser, and a close examination of the tips of shrubs may disclose where it has been feeding. The concentration of droppings will be heavy where the birds have flocked up. It is rather eerie to be in an area where there are known to be ptarmigan and yet be unable to see them because their white plumage matches the snow. On a sunny day it is often easier to detect their presence by their shadows than by the birds themselves.

ENEMIES: The willow ptarmigan is one of the most common game birds of the north and is therefore the victim of concentrated predation by foxes, wolverines, weasels, hawks, falcons, owls, gulls, ravens, magpies and jaegers. Most of the predation is against the eggs and chicks because some of the smaller predators cannot successfully take an adult.

This ptarmigan is also heavily hunted by the Eskimos and Indians as a food staple, as well as being hunted for sport.

TABLE FARE: The willow ptarmigan rates high as table fare, particularly in late summer or fall. In the winter the birds are forced to feed on very dry vegetation, and their flesh becomes bitter and less succulent.

Rock Ptarmigan

Lagopus mutus

The ptarmigan's generic name *Lagopus* is a Latin word meaning rabbit-footed. This stems from the fact that the outgrowth of feathers on the ptarmigan's feet, which is retained all year, is similar in appearance and function to the stiff hairs that enlarge the foot of the snowshoe rabbit. This special characteristic enables both these northern creatures to travel over soft, deep snow without sinking in. I certainly needed snowshoes the first time that I tried to follow the rock ptarmigan across the drifted swales of snow in Alaska's McKinley Park. The ground was half bare and half covered with snow, but the ptarmigan carefully avoided the bare ground. Even though they were in the process of changing from their white winter plumage to their brown summer coats, they were well aware of being still more white than brown. What helped their camouflage even further was that the snow was soiled in places and therefore matched their coloring.

DESCRIPTION: The rock ptarmigan is smaller than its big cousin, the willow ptarmigan. It is about 15 inches in length, has a wingspan of about 20 inches and weighs about 18 to 19 ounces. The

ranges of these two ptarmigan overlap, and without a scale by which to measure them, it is sometimes difficult to distinguish between them. If the birds are in their white winter plumage, the males can easily be told apart because the male rock ptarmigan has a black line extending from its bill through the eye and beyond that the male willow ptarmigan lacks. The male rock ptarmigan retains its white wing and black outer tail feathers year-round just as the willow ptarmigan does. However, in the summer its breast is not solid brown like that of the willow ptarmigan but is heavily splashed with white. The bare red patch of skin and the comb above the eye are as conspicuous on the rock ptarmigan as they are on the willow ptarmigan.

The female rock ptarmigan is slightly smaller than the male, white in the winter and mottled brown and white in the summer. She and the female willow ptarmigan are identical except for the species' size difference.

DISTRIBUTION: The rock ptarmigan is circumpolar, with a range lying about and above the 55° parallel. The name rock ptarmigan is a good one, for the bird inhabits the more open, stone-covered areas of its range, whether they be vertically rising talus slopes or flat, wind-swept stone fields.

COMMUNICATION: The rock ptarmigan's most widely heard call is its call of alarm, which is a series of very loud, guttural *cuck, cuck, cuck, cuck*s. At other times the ptarmigan gives the same sort of call much more softly, as though it were talking to itself.

BREEDING AND NESTING: Mike Smith and I had been attracted by the disappearance of a female ptarmigan behind a clump of grass. It was early in June, and she was still in her white winter coat and extremely conspicuous against the brown of the tundra. We had been watching her from the road that runs through McKinley National Park in the area of the wind-swept Highway Pass. Sure that we had located a nest site, we grabbed our cameras and, making a circuitous approach, came in below the clump of grass behind which she had disappeared. Before we could locate the hen, we heard the guttural call of a male overhead. Looking up, we saw a male sailing on a long spiral about 600 to 800 feet

Rock ptarmigan's winter plumage provides concealment in the snow.

Range of Rock Ptarmigan

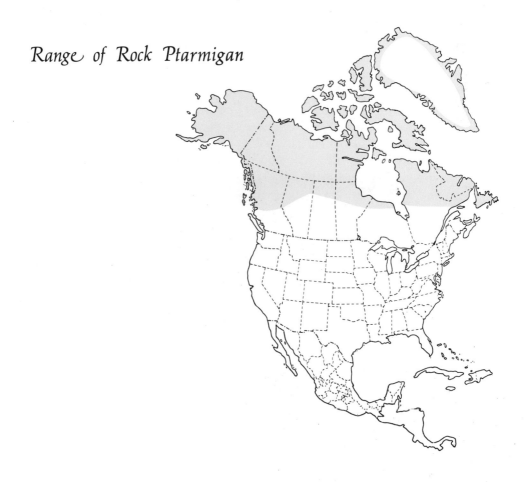

above us. Much to our surprise, the bird made one and a half circles and came to land about 50 feet from us, but only about 6 feet from where the females sat hidden under a bower-like clump of grass. On alighting, the male flared out his tail and ran about the female, first on one side of the grass and then on the other. We are still not sure whether we were witnessing a part of the breeding display or a protective display on the part of the male. However, we suspect the former because the high, sailing flight and the tail-flaring are also typical of the willow ptarmigan's breeding display. Eventually, when the male was within a foot or so of the female, she arose and joined him, and they both flew off.

We went up to see if the female had been on a nest. There were no eggs, but there was a body-shaped hollow in the grass which could not possibly have been made in just the few minutes that the female had been there. We felt that we had discovered the spot that the ptarmigan intended to use for a nest, but we were never able to get back to see if our supposition was correct.

EGGS AND YOUNG: Eight to twelve eggs are considered an average clutch for the rock ptarmigan. The eggs are about 38 millimeters in length by 32 millimeters in width. Their basic color is buff, richly splashed on the large end with a deep reddish brown. The eggs are laid over a period of two weeks, after which an incubation period of twenty-one to twenty-two days is required.

The young are precocious and are able to leave the nest within an hour after hatching. Their protective coloration renders them almost invisible except when they are in motion. They scramble over and through the grasses and sparse dwarf willows and birch. They are very energetic and can jump quite well at an early age. They flap their wings rapidly when they jump, and within a week the primaries provide enough lift for the chicks to fly short distances. The parents are very protective and attempt to decoy danger away from the young or else become pugnacious and actually attack the aggressor.

The chicks feed on insects for the first couple of days but then start to eat the same vegetation as their parents.

FLIGHT: For a grouse, the rock ptarmigan is an exceptionally strong flier. As I have already mentioned, I have seen it fly 600 to 800 feet up into the air, which is six to eight times higher than I have ever seen a ruffed grouse fly. I was walking across an extensive tumbled rock area in the Alaskan range when some rock ptarmigan flew out and headed for the denser cover of the dwarf willows that fringed the area below. Some of the birds flew for a distance of at least 2 miles and just disappeared from sight. As the birds had flushed more wildly than my presence warranted, I was puzzled at their alarm. When I could discern no apparent danger on the ground I checked the sky. There, so high as to be a mere speck, a golden eagle wheeled. I have since seen such wild and long flights on several occasions, and each time they have been caused by eagles.

MIGRATION: In A. C. Bents' book, there is an incomplete statement concerning the rock ptarmigan's spring migration. The notes were made in northern Labrador and tell of thousands of these ptarmigan flying high across Hudson's Straits, heading north toward Baffin Island. There are no records of where the birds had wintered. Alfred Bailey noted that the birds were common at Wales, on Alaska's Seward Peninsula, in the spring and summer but did not winter in the immediate vicinity. I can find no other records of these ptarmigan making a long migration flight. The inference is that this was not a migration but a typical seasonal shift from high land to low land, although the birds usually prefer high land in summer and low land in winter. In the winter the rock ptarmigan often mixes with the willow ptarmigan.

HABITS: The rock ptarmigan's mottled plumage blends in especially well with the fragmented rock areas it favors. Even when the males sit on some projecting slab or boulder, they are hard to see. Such males are doing guard duty and are very alert, their alarm notes being heard usually long before the birds are located.

The habitats of these ptarmigan are usually so remote that often the birds spend their entire lives without ever seeing a man. Although they are quick to sound the alarm call at the slightest unfamiliar movement in their territory, they can be approached rather closely by a man. Often their reaction is to sound the alarm but their curiosity keeps them riveted to the spot. When the birds do retreat, they may fly right out of the area or walk away using an agonizingly slow pace that allows their plumage to blend with the surrounding rocks.

FOOD: The rock ptarmigan eats insects, but this is only a small part of its diet. The buds, leaves and twigs of the dwarf willow and birches are its main food items. It also eats seeds, grasses, mosses and berries.

LIFE SPAN: Although this ptarmigan's potential life span is perhaps six years, the bird that lives to be three or four years old in the wild can consider itself fortunate.

SIGN: The accumulated droppings where the ptarmigan have spent the night are the most common sign.

ENEMIES: I was once amazed to see a hen rock ptarmigan fly up out of the grass to meet the attack of a long-tailed jaeger. The ptarmigan was the heavier of the two birds, and the few times that contact was made, the jaeger definitely got the worst of the encounter. The jaeger was trying to snatch up one of the ptarmigan's young chicks but did not succeed in doing so, although we watched the proceedings for about one and a half hours. The jaeger usually hung in the air about 200 to 300 feet away, but occasionally would slide in for an attempted attack. Each time it was driven off by the female.

Not only jaegers but also gulls, ravens, hawks, falcons, owls and foxes prey on the rock ptarmigan. Any of the meat eaters will take the eggs, chicks or adults if possible.

TABLE FARE: Like all the grouse family, the rock ptarmigan is good to eat. In the summer and fall it is at its tastiest, its flesh becoming slightly bitter and drier after the bird goes on its diet of twigs and other winter vegetation.

White-tailed Ptarmigan

Lagopus leucurus

The white-tailed ptarmigan is a bird of the high country that shares the alpine peaks with mountain sheep and goats. I first encountered it in the Waterton Mountains in Alberta, Canada. I had camped for the night on the edge of a small glacial lake nestled just below the 8,000-foot ridges. In the morning, as I went to the small feeder stream to get water, I heard a soft clucking sound, and suddenly there were the ptarmigan. The following week I again saw the birds on the ridge top not far from the visitor center at the top of Going to the Sun Highway in Glacier National Park, Montana.

DESCRIPTION: The white-tailed ptarmigan is the smallest of the three ptarmigan, measuring 12 to 13 inches in length, with a wing-span of 18 inches. The outstanding characteristic of this ptarmigan is that, unlike the other two species, it does not have any black tail feathers. In the winter both the sexes are pure white except for their dark eyes and bills. In the summer the birds' backs, necks, heads and upper breasts change to a brown or grayish color, although the bellies, wings and tails stay white. Even in their summer plumage, the male and female whitetails look alike, al-

White winter plumage camouflages the white-tailed ptarmigan against the snow; its summer plumage allows it to blend with the vegetation.

though the male has a bare, orange skin patch and comb above the eye which the female lacks.

In its pure white winter plumage, the whitetail blends in well with its surroundings, and on an overcast day it is virtually impossible to see. On a bright, sunny day, it still blends in with the white snow, but its black shadow betrays its presence.

The white-tailed ptarmigan sheds its winter plumage between April and June. The bird is in its mottled summer plumage from June to mid-September, when it starts to turn white again.

The bird is very conscious of its color at all times. While in its white plumage, it sits on the snow; in its brown plumage, it abandons the snow even though some areas remain covered with snow all year. When the bird is in the transition stage, half brown and half white, it frequents the areas at the edge of the snow.

The female usually starts to molt about two weeks after the male but molts faster so that she quickly catches up with him.

White-tailed Ptarmigan

The Latin word *Lagopus* means rabbit-footed and refers to the feathered snowshoes with which all the ptarmigan are equipped. The feathers cover not only the legs but also the entire foot right down to the toe nails. These feathers are shed one at a time so that enough of them are retained to give the bird support on the snow at any time of the year. These toe feathers, or filoplumes, are quite hair-like.

DISTRIBUTION: The white-tailed ptarmigan is the only one that breeds in some sections of the forty-eight contiguous states. It is found on the mountain tops of New Mexico, Colorado, Wyoming, Montana, Idaho, Washington, Oregon, British Columbia, Alberta, the Yukon and Alaska. It has the most restricted range of any of the three ptarmigan and is seldom found below 5,000 feet. In good areas up to twenty breeding birds are found per square mile.

Range of White-tailed Ptarmigan

COMMUNICATION: I have already mentioned the clucking sound that the female white-tailed ptarmigan made as she herded her chicks along in the Waterton Mountains. It was a soft, clucking sound very similar to that which a barnyard hen makes to her chicks. It is the only sound I have heard these birds make. According to various records, the male makes the harsh, guttural *cuck, cuck* sound that is typical of the ptarmigan. These birds also hiss.

BREEDING AND NESTING: Not much is known about the breeding displays of the white-tailed ptarmigan because the habitat that it favors is often at inaccessible elevations of 10,000 to 14,000 feet. However, since both the other ptarmigans engage in aerial displays, calling and posturing for the female, it is safe to assume that the whitetail does the same.

Ptarmigan are usually thought to be monogamous, but some white-tailed males have been seen to pair with two hens at one time. The pairing up begins in April, and the egg-laying starts in the middle of June. However, if heavy snows occur in late April, the pairs split up again and go their separate ways until the ground is bare again. This often causes a delay in nesting.

The white-tailed ptarmigan's nest is about 5 to 6 inches in diameter and is made of the fine local grasses, with the possible addition of other grasses from further afield. The nest is in a snow-free area and often in the lee of a small rock or bush. It is usually out in the open, since the birds count on their own camouflaged plumage as protection. Of the three species of ptarmigan the white-tail seems to be the hardest to see, so perfectly does its plumage match its sourroundings.

EGGS AND YOUNG: The female white-tailed ptarmigan does not lay an egg every day but may skip an occasional day. A clutch usually numbers six to eight eggs, although there are records of one bird that laid as many as fourteen eggs.

The eggs are buff-colored, richly spotted with dark brown. They average 42 millimeters in length by 29 millimeters in diameter. If her eggs are destroyed, the female renests. There is only one brood per year. Incubation requires twenty-two to twenty-three days and is performed by the female.

The young ptarmigan are precocious and follow after the mother as soon as they hatch. They are as well camouflaged as the adults. Their basic color is buff, speckled, barred and spotted with black.

The female white-tailed ptarmigan is a very concerned mother, keeping her brood close to her with a constant clucking sound. In defense of her young, she can be quite pugnacious, even flying up at a man to make him keep his distance.

Unlike the willow and rock ptarmigan males, the male white-tailed ptarmigan does not appear to assist the female in caring for the young. As soon as the female begins to brood, the male takes off, sometimes to join other males.

At first the young feed primarily on insects and are quick to pick at any shiny object that moves. Before long, however, they start to feed on the vegetation that will provide the bulk of their diet in later life.

FLIGHT: The young ptarmigan's primary wing feathers develop quickly, and the birds are soon able to make short flights.

The white-tailed ptarmigan is a good, strong flier, but it prefers to sit tight and rely on its camouflage for protection. If this fails, the bird has strong legs and can run well. It is usually found in areas that have cover, either rocks or low bushes, behind which it can run. As a last resort, the birds thunder into the air and then, on set wings, glide for distances of up to 1 mile. They take various evasive actions against the different predators but seldom fly against hawks or eagles.

The white-tailed ptarmigan's cupped wings allow the bird to reach a high speed in a short time, and it can fly at 40 or 45 miles per hour. However, it cannot sustain flapping flight, and if it is flushed repeatedly, it soon tires.

MIGRATION: The white-tailed ptarmigan does not migrate, but it does have seasonal shifts. When the weather becomes too bitterly cold on the ridges, the ptarmigan seeks out the shelter provided by the dwarf willows and birches. At such times the birds often gather together in large flocks, whereas on the wind-swept slopes of their breeding range they establish individual territories.

HABITS: When the snow is soft and deep and the weather is cold, the ptarmigan burrows under the snow to obtain the protection of its insulation. Sometimes it walks long distances under the snow to reappear where it is least expected. Undoubtedly it can also feed under the snow. On sunny days the ptarmigan makes forms in the snow in the lee of a bush or rock where it is sheltered from the wind.

This ptarmigan is quite tame and exceedingly curious. The males, particularly, will sit on a rock outcrop, their bodies erect, their necks craned out to their full extent so that they can see and watch every move a person makes.

I have stood still, after locating a female and her brood, and have had them march up to within 2 or 3 feet of me. They knew I was there but were intent on their feeding, and so long as I made no sudden moves, they disregarded me. In taking photographs of them, I would get ahead of their line of travel and allow them to come up to me and pass me, and then move on ahead and repeat the entire process.

The young ptarmigan stay with their mother until the brood break-up period in late September. Then they scatter widely only to regroup, but not along family lines, as deepening snow forces them onto their winter ranges. The young and female white-tails seek out the lower valley, while the males keep more to the hillsides. As many as sixty white-tailed ptarmigan to the square mile have been counted on their winter range in Rocky Mountain National Park, Colorado.

Food: The willows and birches of the valleys and draws usually protrude above even the deepest snow and provide the whitetail with its main source of food. The ptarmigan also feeds on the buds and needles of pines and firs, heather, blueberry, alpine flowers and some insects.

Life Span: The white-tailed ptarmigan has a potential life span of about eight years, but banding has produced no records over five years.

Enemies: The white-tailed ptarmigan's range protects it from serious predation, since not many predators are found at such elevations. Hawks, eagles and martens are probably the ptarmigan's main enemies. The marten is an alpine mammal, and the ptarmigan often drifts down to the timber line where the marten makes its home. Foxes, bobcats, weasels and bears also take an occasional ptarmigan on its nest.

Table Fare: The white-tailed ptarmigan is considered a table delicacy and is avidly hunted wherever its range is accessible.

QUAIL, PARTRIDGE, PHEASANTS
Family Phasianidae

Scaled Quail
Callipepla squamata

Like all desert dwellers, the scaled quail is rarely seen when the sun is up. Only unusual circumstances will drive it and the other birds, mammals and reptiles of this harsh environment from their daylight shelters.

One day several summers ago, I was driving through the parched Big Bend section of Texas. The temperature was 127 degrees and the nearby Rio Grande was only inches deep. Late in the afternoon, the sky to the west darkened. Lightning flashed, and through what looked like a hole in the heavens tumbled a column of water that widened as it fell, obliterating almost all vision. I have never seen such a torrential rainfall.

Yet, despite its intensity, the storm was over in minutes. The air was cool—the thermometer must have dropped some 50 degrees—and fragrant with the smell of wet earth. This decidedly unusual atmosphere acted like a magnet that drew the desert animals out into the open.

Suddenly, flocks of scaled quail materialized from beneath thickets, and mockingbirds darted and sang; blacktail jackrabbits emerged from under bushes; mule deer and pronghorn antelopes appeared to lap at puddles.

Soon, though, the water ran off and the earth dried. The next day the desert was again an inferno, and its dewllers were again under cover.

DESCRIPTION: There are two subspecies of the scaled quail, of which *C. s. pallida* is the better known because it has the larger range. *Pallida* is also called the Arizona scaled quail, blue quail or blue rocket. The adult male *pallida* is 10 inches long, has a wing-span of about 13 to 14 inches and weighs about 5 ounces. The scaled quail's most conspicuous feature is the pure white tip to its crest, which has earned it the name "cottontop." The base of the crest is brown, the head, neck and cheeks are gray, the throat buffy. There is a distinct black line extending from the bill through the eye and beyond. The *pallida* quail's breast is slate-blue, its belly light buff, and all these feathers have a dark edge that gives the bird a definite scaled appearance. The upper back is a scaled gray, the center back plain gray and the tail slate-blue. The scapulars are white, the wings grayish brown. There are white streaks on the bird's flanks. The eye is brown, and the bill, feet and legs are grayish brown.

Castonagastris, meaning chestnut-bellied, is the name of the other subspecies of scaled quail—and aptly so. Whereas *pallida* has a buff-colored belly, this quail's belly is a rich chestnut color.

The females of both these subspecies are slightly smaller in size and lighter in weight than the males. Their general overall colors are much more subdued than the males', and it is very difficult to tell the subspecies apart by looking at the females. Neither are they distinguishable by their habits, which are identical.

DISTRIBUTION: *C. s. pallida* has a range that extends from western Texas north to Colorado, west to Arizona and south to Mexico. The chestnut-bellied scaled quail frequents the southern Rio Grande Valley of Texas and northeastern Old Mexico.

COMMUNICATION: The scaled quail is often heard without being seen, for it frequents the impenetrable thickets and cactus clumps of the arid regions that are its habitat.

The common call of the scaled quail is a loud, clear *oh-oh, oh-oh, oh-oh,* whistled on two notes. Some ornithologists describe the call as *pe-co, pe-co, pe-co.* It is heard most frequently in the early morning before the heat of the day sets in. Again in the evening, this call rings out as the birds often assemble in large flocks before retiring

Range of the Scaled Quail

for the night. This quail also calls *check-churr, chip-churr* or *check-ah*. The female has a sharp alarm call to warn the young of danger, and the chicks peep like our domestic chickens. When the scaled quail is disturbed, it makes a guttural *oom-oom-oom* sound.

BREEDING AND NESTING: The scaled quail usually pair up toward the end of the winter while they are still congregated in large flocks. Shortly thereafter, each pair splits off from the flock to seek a territory of its own. During the winter months, the males live peaceably enough, but all this changes when a mated pair selects its territory. Once the territory has been chosen and defined, it is defended by the resident male against all other scaled quail males.

In typical quail fashion, the male struts before the female, drooping his wings and tail and parading about her in circles.

Although the scaled quail mate in April, their brooding period is delayed so that the young hatch in June. In this way a supply of water for the chicks is assured, since the rainy season in the southwestern states starts in June. The mule deer of Texas drop their fawns much later than most deer for the very same reason. The quail and the deer are geared not to a warm season but to a wet one.

The scaled quail's nest is a simple affair scratched out by the female in the sand or the dust. The hollow is lined with whatever dry local grasses the quail can find in such arid regions. Most of the nests are well hidden under clumps or tussocks of grass. Arroyos, washes or small, brush-covered plateaus are the sort of location that this quail seeks out as a nesting site.

EGGS AND YOUNG: Twelve to fourteen eggs are an average clutch for the scaled quail. The eggs average 32 millimeters in length by 25 millimeters in diameter. They are off-white or cream and are speckled, spotted or blotched with cinnamon-brown. Incubation requires twenty-one days and is performed exclusively by the female. The male, however, does help with brooding and caring for the chicks. The scaled quail sometimes raise two broods of young per year.

The chicks are primarily buff-colored on the upper portion of their bodies and buff tempered with gray on their underparts.

Scaled quail chicks are precocious and follow after the adults as soon as their down is dry. If danger approaches, the young, at a command from the adults, flatten themselves out and hide under any vegetation that is handy. Their colors blend in exceedingly well with the dry dust and sand of their habitat. The chicks feed mainly on insects at first, but vegetation is included in their diets within a few days.

FLIGHT: The chicks' wing feathers develop very rapidly, and by the time they are two weeks old, the young are able to use their wings.

The scaled quail is a swift, strong flier, but it much prefers to use its legs to escape from danger. It usually flies only a few hundred feet to get out of the immediate vicinity, then lands and takes to running again. Probably more scaled quail are seen flying to escape an oncoming automobile on the highway than under any other circumstance.

MIGRATION: The scaled quail does not migrate, and as the temperatures remain fairly constant in the areas that it frequents, it normally does not even undertake a seasonal shift. Drought is usually the only reason the birds seek another area.

HABITS: The scaled quail is very active at dawn and again in the late afternoon. The midday heat of its arid habitat slows down the activities of almost all living creatures, and the quail is no exception. A siesta is the order of the day. This quail also enjoys taking dust baths, and it lives in areas where there is no shortage of dust or sand.

The scaled quail is quick to take advantage of feed put out for it—since food in its areas is never overabundant—and readily becomes quite tame in the process. Although its water requirements are not high, it is also quick to learn to use the water guzzlers for both livestock and wildlife.

All the quail are sociable creatures, and the scaled quail sometimes build up in flocks numbering fifty to sixty birds or more.

FOOD: The scaled quail eats a larger quantity of animal matter than any of the other quail. It is figured that as much as 30 percent of its diet is composed of such insects as cucumber beetles, grasshoppers, ants, leaf hoppers and spiders.

More than half the vegetable matter in the scaled quail's diet is composed of noxious weed seeds so that this bird is a most useful ally to man. Among its favorite foods are the seeds of thistles, pigweed, bindweed, wild privet, catclaw, tansy mustard, snakeweed, lupine, mesquite, etc. Its water requirements are largely met by consuming wild fruits such as the prickly pear.

LIFE SPAN: The scaled quail has a potential life span of about five years, but there appear to be no longevity records for any individual birds.

ENEMIES: Drought is the scaled quail's greatest enemy. Snakes and skunks are probably most destructive of the quail's nest and eggs. The gila monster, too, feeds heavily on quail eggs. Coyotes, foxes and bobcats take the scaled quail, both adults and young, on the ground, while hawks and owls take them from the air.

TABLE FARE: The scaled quail is a fine-tasting quail, but it is not greatly hunted because it is not considered a very sporting bird. Much of the time, the quail refuses to flush into the air, and many hunters refuse to shoot a bird while it is on the ground. Moreover the bird's habit of seeking refuge under clumps of cactus or in catclaw thickets makes this quail exceedingly hard to hunt.

Brightly colored facial markings of the male harlequin quail are its most distinguishing feature.

Male bobwhite quail can be identified by its white facial markings; those of the female are yellow.

Both male and female scaled quail have a short head crest; the scaled appearance of their body sets them apart from the other western quail.

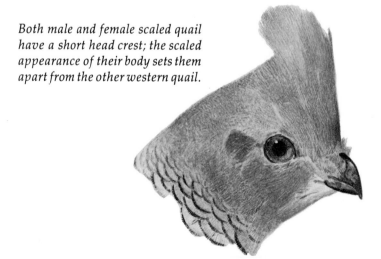

Three western quail that are difficult for the novice to identify (from top): California quail, Gambel's quail and mountain quail. The California and Gambel's have similar facial markings and curved plumes. The mountain quail has a straight, tapered plume.

California Quail

Lophortyx californicus

It was at Tupman, California, that I first saw the California quail. This entire area is a combination of farmland and grazing land that draws life from the irrigation ditches that crisscross the region. The vegetation along the sides of most of the irrigation ditches was rank and lush. Here was a happy combination for the California quail. It had cover, water and food from the weed seeds or spilled grain from the harvested grainfields.

Later, I worked along the California coast on a ranch that is famous for its blacktail deer herd. Again, the conditions that made this a good working ranch and a haven for deer also favored the California or valley quail, as it is sometimes called.

DESCRIPTION: Like all the quail, the California quail is a beautiful little game bird. The adult male is a round-bodied bird that measures between 10 and 11 inches in length, has a wingspan of about 12 inches and weighs about 6½ to 7 ounces. The jaunty black topknot feathers curve forward gracefully over the forehead. The top of his head is a dark brown skullcap with a white border. The California quail's forehead is a sooty white, and his throat is black with a white border. The nape of his neck is blue-gray with white spots, giving it the look of chain mail. This quail has a blue breast and a grayish back and wings; the tail is a darker blue-gray. The forepart of the belly has a scaling of feathers similar to that of the scaled quail. The feathers are white with a dark blue-gray edging. In the center of the belly there is a large brownish spot over the scaling. The bird's flanks are grayish brown with conspicuous horizontal, dark-bordered white splotches. The rear portion of his belly and the underside of his tail are whitish. His bill is black, his eye brown, and his legs and feet are brownish black.

The female's body plumage is similar to the male's but much more subdued in tone. Her crest feathers are not as long, she lacks the white facial markings, and her throat is gray.

California Quail

Range of California Quail

DISTRIBUTION: The ranges of the California and Gambel's quail overlap, although the California quail cannot tolerate such dry regions as the Gambel's quail. The California quail is found in California, Baja California, Nevada, Oregon, Washington and Idaho. Its range has been much reduced more by the destruction of its habitat than by overhunting. However, market hunting also took its toll of the countless thousands of these quail that were once found in the West. It is estimated that up to 100,000 of the birds were sold yearly on the market in San Francisco during the market hunters' heyday in the late 1800s.

The quail has responded well to protection and game management and is making as good a comeback as could be expected of any species against the steamrolling onslaught of human progress.

COMMUNICATION: With the coming of spring and the break-up of the winter flocks, the male's song is heard throughout the day. The call, *ku-kwak-up, ku-kwak-up, ku-kwak-u-k-k-o,* is ordinarily used as an assembly call, but now the male uses it as a proclamation of his marital rights. Sometimes this call is interpreted as *k-woik-uh* or *ca-loi-o*. An unmated male has a slightly different, single-note call that can be described as *cow*. When the birds are running ahead of an intruder through the bush, they have a soft *pit, pit, pit* or *whit, whit, whit* call that informs each member of the flock of the danger. The female has a sharply whistled *kur* alarm note that is used to warn her chicks. The chicks peep with a variety of tones that express everything from contentment to anxiety.

BREEDING AND NESTING: The California quail have usually paired up before the flocks break up in the spring. As soon as each pair has selected its nesting territory, the male advertises his presence and his willingness to fight for his mate by singing. This quail is monogamous so that a mated male's song is not an entreaty to another female but a challenge to any other male. If a female loses her mate, she will respond to the bachelor's rather different call.

The male quail performs for the female by standing as erect as possible. He then runs toward her and around her, occasionally bowing to her. These actions are not to win him his mate, who is already his, but to stimulate a response in her so that coition can take place.

The California quail does not expend much energy in the construction of its nest, which is a slight hollow hidden beneath a clump of grass or under brush or a log. It is lined with dead grass or leaves and is frequently roofed over by growing vegetation.

Unlike most of the other quail, which nest only on the ground, the California has often been recorded as building its nest high up. Some of the nests were located in bushes or trees, utilizing other abandoned birds' nests. Some were built on top of grape arbors, bales of hay or strawstacks, and one was up on the roof of a house. Some of these odd nesting sites are the results of this bird's friendliness and are proof of its ability to adapt itself to man.

EGGS AND YOUNG: Twelve or more eggs are an average clutch for the California quail. The eggs average 31 millimeters in length by 24 millimeters in diameter. They range in color from dull white to creamy buff and also vary widely in their brown markings, some of which are quite large blotches, while others are very fine dots.

During the female's twenty-one-day incubation period, the male remains in the immediate area, singing exuberantly and acting as defender of the nest.

As soon as possible after hatching, the quail parents lead their chicks off into the underbrush. While the female's attention is concentrated on the chicks, the male is constantly on the alert for danger. The alarm note from either parent sends the young scrambling through the vegetation for safety. When possible, the adults try to decoy danger away from their chicks. In whatever manner they can devise, they attempt to call attention only to themselves to give the chicks a chance to slip unobtrusively away. The parents have also been known to attack many of the smaller predators in defense of their young.

The young quail stay in tightly knit family groups until they are eight to ten weeks old. By that time, they are fully feathered and capable of flying and have changed from an insect to a vegetarian diet. As the young birds become more mobile, the various family groups have a greater chance of meeting and intermingling.

FLIGHT: Although the young start to fly at two weeks and are quite adept in the air after four weeks, they much prefer to run rather than fly from danger.

The adults, too, feel much more secure when they are screened by the thick brush and vegetation that they favor as their habitat. When they are flushed, the birds rise up strongly and soon reach an average speed of about 25 miles per hour, a speed that they are capable of almost doubling. Then, on set wings, they glide to safety behind the next clump of vegetation, where they start to run again.

MIGRATION: The California quail does not migrate. The rare seasonal shifts that it makes are usually due to drought or fire.

HABITS: Quail are gregarious birds by nature, and the California quail are often found in exceptionally large flocks. In October, as the food and cover supplies shrink, the coveys begin to grow larger. This pattern continues into the winter, when the coveys reach their largest size, some having as many as 200 birds. Flocks of this size consume a large amount of food per day and so range over a large area, covering perhaps hundreds of acres.

The birds in these large flocks have a better chance of survival because although all the quail are usually alert to danger, the older birds in the flock seem to be designated as sentinels and take turns doing guard duty.

The California quail arises at dawn, and soon after the sun is up it flies down from its perch to forage. It feeds, waters and then seeks shelter to rest, dust itself and just laze about. Later in the afternoon its activity increases until just before sundown. It then retires to a well-protected group of trees, where it roosts for the night. The birds may have a favorite spot or tree or they may take whatever is handy. The one requirement is that the tree be dense and bushy in order to provide them with the maximum protection.

Food: The insects eaten by the California quail are taken almost accidentally. At no time of the year does animal matter—in the form of ants, grasshoppers, beetles and crickets—constitute more than 5 percent of its diet.

According to the season, the quail feeds on the various parts of plants, such as the leaves and seeds. Its favorite foods are filaria, wheat, bur clover, alfalfa, barley, bassia, poplar, sweet clover, corn, turkey mullein, lupine, deervetch, oak, poison oak, pigweed, oats, ryegrass, brome grass, buffalo berry, Russian thistle, bristle grass, black locust, goosefoot and violets.

Life Span: The California quail has a life expectancy of three to four years, but studies show that only 2 percent of the birds live to reach that age. One banded male lived over seven years.

Enemies: The ground squirrel is the quail's chief enemy because of the nest destruction that it causes. Where the squirrels are controlled, the number of quail rises. The squirrels do not seem to hunt for the nests, but in the course of their activities they chance on them and consume the eggs. Intensive studies on this quail show that in some years as many as 82 percent of their nests are destroyed. Of course, many of the quail renest, but it is still figured that 60 percent of all the nests are usually destroyed annually.

During the first two weeks of its life the young quail is extremely vulnerable to adverse weather, predation and accidents. It is figured that 25 percent of the brood succumbs during this period. Under normal conditions another 20 to 30 percent are lost by the end of September. After this time, their chances of survival are much better.

Other predators of the eggs, the young or the adults are the house cat, bobcat, coyote, skunk, fox, California jay, crow, raven, shrike, magpie, snakes, fire ants and hawks, particularly the Cooper's and sharp-shinned.

The quail is subject also to parasites, disease and many kinds of accidents.

Table Fare: The California quail is considered *the* game bird of the Far West. Not only is it a very sporting bird, its flesh is delicious. In 1950 the state of California figured that the food value of this quail in just that state in one year was $906,591.00.

Gambel's Quail

Lophortyx gambellii

I was sitting in a blind one evening at a water hole in southern Arizona, hoping to take photographs of peccary and deer. As the shadows started to lengthen and the saguaros became silhouetted against the darkening sky, I heard a chattering, twittering sound. Running about through the underbrush very cautiously was a covey of Gambel's or desert quail. The birds were coming in for a drink before retiring, and they had every reason to be cautious. In areas where water is scarce, all wildlife is funneled to the few spots where water can be found. All the predators of the region concentrate at these water holes, and the creatures coming to drink are well aware of the danger involved in the undertaking.

DESCRIPTION: The male adult Gambel's quail is about 10 inches in length, has a wingspan of about 12 inches and weighs about 6 or 7 ounces. It is a handsome quail, its colors being subdued rather than somber. Its black topknot plume is its most striking feature. It has a rusty brown skullcap with a white border. The bird's bill is a dark brownish black, its eye brown. Its face and throat are black with a white border. The back of its neck is grayish brown, its back, rump, tail and wings are brownish. The upper portion of the breast is blue-gray, while the lower breast and belly are yellowish white. Right in the middle of the breast-belly area is a large black spot. The flanks of the Gambel's quail are the same rusty brown as its head but laced with heavy, horizontal white streaks. The bird's legs and feet are horn-colored.

The female's coloration is very much like the male's but much duller. She lacks the black breast spot and the black and white coloring of the male's face. Her topknot plume is smaller and lighter in color than the male's. She is slightly smaller in size and lighter in weight than the male.

DISTRIBUTION: The Gambel's or desert quail is found in the desert regions of Arizona, New Mexico, Nevada, southern California and northern Old Mexico.

COMMUNICATION: In proclaiming his individual territory, the male Gambel's quail calls *kaa-wale, kaa-wale*. This is a soft, low-pitched call that carries for a surprisingly long distance. During the breeding season, the male calls *yuk-kae-ja, yuk-kae-ja,* each syllable being very carefully enunciated.

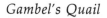

Gambel's Quail

Range of Gambel's Quail

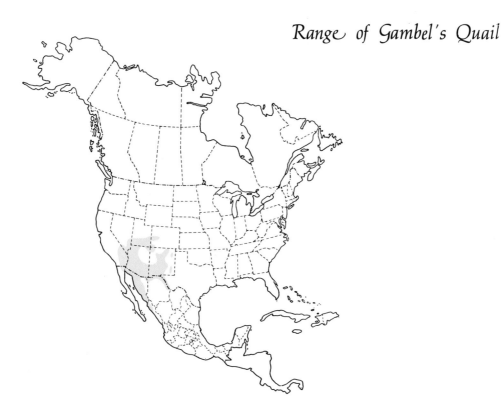

The female has a sharply whistled alarm note which she gives to warn her brood of danger. It sounds like *craer-craer*. A soft, multiple call reassembles her brood after they have been scattered. As the covey moves along feeding, they keep in touch by calling *quoit, oit, woet,* sounds that have been likened to the grunting of a young pig. When the birds are flushed, they have a screeching cackle like that of a startled domestic hen.

BREEDING AND NESTING: Spring comes early in the southwestern desert regions of the United States. The February rains turn the desert into a showplace of blooming flowers. The flocks of Gambel's quail begin to break up, the pairs going their separate ways, and the male's breeding call is frequently heard. The male often calls from some elevated perch within the piece of territory that he claims as his own. Fights between the males are quite common and sometimes bloody, the quail being very pugnacious during the courtship period. When the male is calling, he holds his body stiffly erect, his bill pointing skyward, his wings drooping slightly. His call rings out repeatedly throughout the day.

The male's territorial vigil is interrupted only when his mate wanders into view. Flying down to greet her, he struts around her in a small circle and bows to her very ceremoniously.

The nest of the Gambel's quail is a rather deep hollow scratched out in the sand by the female. Because of the scarcity of vegetation as ground cover, the female cannot just make a nest in the grass. To line the nest, bits of dead grass and leaves must be brought in to the nest site. The nest is usually located under one of the low-growing bushes of the area. This is not only to conceal it from predators, but also to protect it from the heat of the sun.

EGGS AND YOUNG: Like all the quail the Gambel's quail is prolific, and sets of ten to twelve eggs are common, with some clutches containing even more. The eggs average 31 millimeters in length by 24 millimeters in diameter. They vary in color from off-white to buff. The shells are spotted with a variety of large and small dark brown blotches that have a purplish bloom. When the eggs are washed, the purplish tints disappear but reappear again as soon as the shell dries.

Although the female does all the incubating, which requires twenty-one to twenty-four days, the male is always in close attendance. Moreover he helps with the brooding and rearing of the young. As soon as the down on the young is completely dry, the parents lead them away from the nest area, where the smell of the opened shells is an attraction for predators.

The chicks are exceedingly quick and busily snap up every insect that crosses their path. The covey usually travels in a tight little group. An alarm cry from the mother sends the chicks scattering in all directions to seek cover under the nearby vegetation. There they remain motionless until called by the mother from their hiding places. The parents, meantime, will have done all in their power to decoy the predator away from the chicks.

At first the young quail roost on the ground, but after they can fly, they usually roost up in a dense tangle of brush.

Most of the females raise two broods of young per season.

FLIGHT: By the time the chicks are eight to ten days old, their primary wing feathers have grown sufficiently to allow them to take short hop-flights. At three weeks of age, they can fly quite well, and when they are one month old, they start to scatter on their own.

The wings of the Gambel's quail are designed for a speedy takeoff and not for sustained flight. However, this quail in fact flies well, at estimated speeds of 25 to 30 miles per hour, and it flushes fairly easy. When disturbed, it prefers to run from danger if the cover is thick. In desert regions, however, the vegetation is often sparse, and in this case the quail does not hesitate to make an escape flight. When it lands after being flushed, it does so at a run. It zigzags among the vegetation where it is almost impossible for a man to follow. The needle-sharp spines of most of the vegetation found in this quail's area provide it with excellent protection.

MIGRATION: The Gambel's quail does not migrate, nor is it really subject to seasonal shifts. It seems to have to be near a source of water. It may wander out of the area to feed but no farther than is absolutely necessary. Only during periods of extreme drought, when the water holes dry up, does the quail shift its range at all.

HABITS: Gregarious birds are less vulnerable than solitary birds, the main reason being simply that the more eyes and ears there are on the lookout for danger, the greater the possibility of its being detected. It is all but impossible to walk up on a covey of Gambel's quail. The first quail that spots the intruder gives out the alarm call that instantly alerts every quail within hearing distance. The call is picked up and repeated, and all the quail galvanize into action, scattering in every direction. And there is no point in trying to run after them, not only because they can outrun a man, but they run through and under and around vegetation whose thorns and spines prove to be an impassable barrier to humans.

This quail is most active early in the morning, eating and drinking until it retires for the day about 8:30 or 9 a.m. Much of its leisure time is spent dust-bathing or quietly lying in the shade on its side, its legs and wings stretched out. Before twilight, it again has a period of activity.

FOOD: About 93 percent of the diet of the Gambel's quail is made up of vegetable matter, the bulk of which consists of the seeds of the following plants: mesquite, deervetch, Russian thistle, lupine, alfalfa, tansy mustard, spiderling, spurge, bassia, crownbeard, filaria and evolvulus. The 7 percent of its diet that is animal matter consists of beetles, grasshoppers, crickets, leafhoppers, ants and spiders.

LIFE SPAN: The Gambel's quail should have a life expectancy of from four to five years. Four banded birds are known to have lived to be over five years old.

ENEMIES: The Gambel's quail has many enemies. Because it is a desert-dwelling species, it is exposed to what some might consider rather exotic predators such as the gila monster, the roadrunner and the cacomistle. In addition the quail, or its eggs, are preyed upon by skunks, rats, rock and ground squirrels, snakes, coyotes, foxes, bobcats, hawks and owls.

Parasites, disease and accidents take an occasional bird.

TABLE FARE: None of the quail are large enough for a single bird to amount to anything as food. So only a consistent and persistent quail-hunter can get enough of the birds to provide a meal for his family. The Gambel's quail is very good eating, even if it is hard to hunt.

OVERLEAF ▶

The Quail of North America

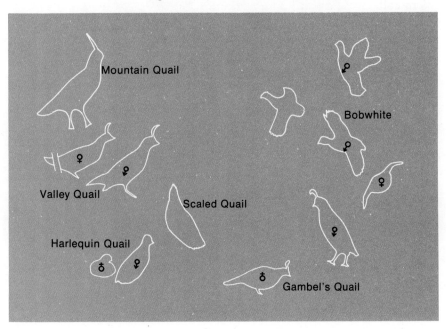

Mountain Quail

Oreortyx picta

There are actually three distinct subspecies of the mountain quail, all of which are almost identical in appearance and habits. Any differences between them lie in their color shadings and their ranges.

The best known mountain quail is *O. p. plumifera* of the central, semiarid mountain regions. The northern form, known as *O. p. picta,* is found in the humid, coastal mountains. This form is paler in color than the central mountain quail, although it has a more olivaceous coloring on its back. The southern mountain quail is *O. p. confinis* and is called the San Pedro mountain quail. This bird resembles the northern rather than the central subspecies. For all practical purposes, these birds are identical and will be treated as such.

DESCRIPTION: The mountain quail is the largest of our native quail. The adult male is about 12 inches in length, has a wingspan of 13 or 14 inches and weighs up to 10 ounces.

The mountain quail is also known as the plumed quail because the two long, thin feathers protruding from the front of its crest

Mountain Quail

are its most conspicuous feature. These jet-black plumes are about 2 inches in length and, although erect, slope slightly to the rear. The crown, the nape of the neck, the upper back and the breast of the mountain quail are a slaty blue color. The bird's throat is a dark, rusty brown. A white patch extends from behind the bill, around the eye and curves sharply downward, separating the throat color from that of the nape of the neck. The mountain quail's wings, back, rump and tail are brown with gray overtones. The scapulars are white. The flanks and belly are the same dark, rusty color as the throat. There are about seven or eight white bars on each flank, and a continuous white line separates the flanks from the wings. The under tail coverts are light brown. The bird has a black bill and eye, and its feet and legs are grayish black.

Although the female is slightly smaller than the male, it is almost impossible to tell the sexes apart because their coloration is identical.

DISTRIBUTION: The mountain quail, as its name denotes, is a bird of the highlands of California, Oregon, Washington, Idaho and

311

Nevada. Originally this bird was not found in Washington but was imported there in 1880 from California. In the spring, summer and fall the bird is seldom found at altitudes of less than 2,000 feet. In summer it is often found as high as 9,000 or 10,000 feet.

The mountain quail favors brushy hill- and mountainsides, particularly areas that have been either timbered off or burned off by forest fires. In these areas the luxuriant regrowth provides both ample cover and an almost limitless supply of food.

COMMUNICATION: The mountain quail's unusually large repertoire of calls is heard much more frequently than the bird is seen. Its most common call is a single-note *quee-ark* or *quee-ilk* that the male whistles with an almost monotonous regularity. This call may be heard every six to nine seconds for a period of five minutes or more. Like that of the bobwhite, it is given from some elevated perch such as the top of a rock, stump or low bush. In calling, the bird first lowers its head, then throws it backward, its plume fully erected. The note is so loud and clear that it can be heard at a distance of ½ to ¾ mile.

The male mountain quail also has a more mournful *too-wook* call that is lower pitched and less sharply given than the *quee-ark* call. Both these calls are associated with the breeding season.

Later, when the quail are shepherding their young, they have a *cree-a-a, cree-a-a* danger call. This call sends the little quail scrambling for cover. When the danger is past, the family is reassembled with a *kow, kow, kow, kow* rallying call. The chicks of course peep, much in the same manner as our domesticated chicks.

BREEDING AND NESTING: Late in March or early in April, the cock mountain quail sends forth his *quee-ark* mating call. The flocks have split up by this time, and the paired birds have selected the territory that they intend to use for nesting. The birds pair up during late winter when they are flocked up at the lower elevations, but the nesting sites are up in the mountains on their summer range.

The male defends the territory selected by his mate and himself against the encroachment of rival pairs. This territory varies in size from 5 to 50 acres, according to the density of the breeding pairs. Each pair of quail tries to claim as much territory as possible but can maintain only the territory that it can defend. If the mountain quail population is high, the individual territories are small.

The male mountain quail's courtship display is similar to that of all of the other quail species. The male droops his wings, fans his tail out and down and struts around the female in small circles.

Range of Mountain Quail

The mountain quail's nest is built on the ground in a hollow that the birds scoop out in the earth with their strong, sharply clawed feet. Sometimes the hollow is 2 to 4 inches deep. The nest is very difficult to locate because it is usually exceedingly well hidden under an overhanging clump of grass or ferns or under brush. Ordinarily the nest is built up against the grass clump or against a stump or log. It is lined with pieces of grass that are broken or cut off to fit the depression, which is usually about 6 inches across. When the bird is brooding the eggs, it is almost impossible to flush it from the nest.

EGGS AND YOUNG: A mountain quail's clutch normally contains ten to fourteen eggs, although there are records of nests containing as many as twenty-two eggs. Undoubtedly, such large clutches are the result of two females laying in the same nest. The eggs average about 34 millimeters in length by 27 millimeters in diameter. They vary in color from pale cream to pinkish buff. Incubation, which requires from twenty-three to twenty-five days, is probably done by both the male and female. Both parents also care for the young, who scramble out of the nest and follow the adults an hour or so after hatching. The chicks' upper parts are predominantly a deep chestnut color, while their underparts are buffy.

The chicks grow rapidly on a diet of insects, and within a few days their wing primary feathers develop. By the time they are a week old, they can fly for short distances.

Both the adult mountain quail are devoted parents, and both are quick to feign injury to decoy danger away from the young. If this ruse fails, the parents attempt everything short of an outright attack on whatever is disturbing their young. While they try to confound the enemy, the chicks rapidly scatter and hide under the surrounding vegetation.

The mountain quail is not overly sociable, and until forced together by severe winter weather, the birds usually confine themselves to their own individual family groups.

FLIGHT: The mountain quail is most reluctant to fly. It much prefers to seek safety in and under the dense thickets and underbrush that are such an essential feature of its habitat. It can run very fast and usually has to run only a few steps before it is hidden from sight. If the bird is flushed, its short, cupped wings allow it to get up to speeds of about 35 to 40 miles per hour in a few seconds. Its flights, however, never cover long distances.

MIGRATION: The mountain quail cannot really be considered migratory, although most of the birds have definite shifts in altitude each spring and fall. The distance traveled is determined solely by the weather and by snow depths. This quail does not come any lower than it is forced to, although it may sometimes be found at elevations as low as 500 feet. When it makes these seasonal shifts, it does not fly but walks either up or down the mountain, according to the season. Sometimes the fall shift is a spiral one, as the birds concentrate on the western slopes of the mountains.

HABITS: The mountain quail is usually quite tame. This is partly due to the fact that it lives mostly far from the haunts of man and is therefore not exposed to dangers of human origin. When hunted, it soon grows wary. Where it is not hunted, it becomes so tame that it often joins domestic flocks of chickens and seeks feed in the barnyard.

This bird requires a supply of water in its range since the local vegetation does not usually contain enough succulence to meet its body's water requirements. If the amount of free-flowing water is limited in its area, its actual range is also limited.

Usually the mountain quail feeds early in the morning and again late in the afternoon. At midday it escapes from the sun's heat under some shade-providing bush. It thoroughly enjoys dust bathing.

FOOD: Ninety-seven percent of the mountain quail's diet is made up of vegetable matter. Its main foods are seeds and grains, but it also eats the roots, stalks, stems and leaves of various plants. Its favorite foods are lupine, clover, brome grass, acorns, deervetch, filaria and wild carrot. It feeds on cultivated grains such as wheat, corn, barley and oats. Most of these grains it scavenges in fields where they have been spilled or missed by mechanical pickers. The 3 percent of its diet that is made up of animal matter consists mainly of grasshoppers, beetles, ants, spiders and centipedes.

The mountain quail cannot be considered injurious to man, and its consumption of weed seeds makes it a most useful ally of the farmer.

LIFE SPAN: The mountain quail has a potential life span of about four or five years. Since it is not an important game bird the records on this quail are meager, and there appear to be no records of individual longevity.

ENEMIES: The gray fox and the bobcat are both very common in the mountain quail's range and are thought to be the bird's main enemies. Coyotes, skunks, snakes, hawks and owls also prey on this quail.

TABLE FARE: The flesh of the mountain quail is considered a real delicacy, but because the bird is not common and almost refuses to fly, it is seldom hunted. Most hunters are not willing to expend the energy needed to get up into the mountains that are this quail's habitat.

Harlequin Quail

Cyrtonyx montezumae

The harlequin quail is the smallest and the least known of our native quail. It is seldom hunted because it is so seldom seen. The bird is difficult to locate and to flush and more difficult to hit because if it does fly, its flight is so short that the bird is usually back down into cover before the hunter's gun is up. When the harlequin is shot, it is usually taken by hunters who were seeking either the scaled or the Gambel's quail and stumbled on the harlequin by accident.

DESCRIPTION: The harlequin is the smallest member of the quail or native partridge family to be found in the United States. The adult male harlequin is 7 to 9 inches in length, has a wingspan of 11 to 12 inches and weighs 3 to 4 ounces. The harlequin has the shortest tail of any of the quail but the largest and heaviest beak, legs, feet and claws. These sturdy appendages are used by the quail in feeding on the roots of some of its food plants, which it has to get by digging 3 or 4 inches in the hard earth.

However, the most striking field characteristic of the male harlequin quail is its bizarre color patterning. The basically black face and throat are overlaid with white streaks so that they have the appearance of a diagram for highway intersections and clover-leaves. The nape of the neck is brown. The bird's back and rump are a medium brown with elongated spots of light buff. The wings are grayish brown with white and black spots and darts. The harlequin's breast is a deep reddish brown, while the belly and under-tail section are jet-black. The flanks are dark gray with dozens of pure white spots. The bill is black, the eyes are brown, the legs reddish brown and the toes almost black.

The female harlequin quail is slightly smaller than the male and much more demure in her plumage. Her facial markings are brown and white but retain enough of the male's patterning to be an aid to identification. The upper portion of her body is almost identical to the male's except that she does not have the grayish tint to her wings. Her underparts are a soft brown with occasional long, dark-bordered splashes of light cream.

DISTRIBUTION: The harlequin quail is a bird of the rocky, wooded slopes of our southwestern mountains. It does not like open areas, preferring to be in or near dense underbrush in which it can hide. It is seldom found below 4,000 feet and is often found as high as 9,000 feet. Winter may cause it to seek lower elevations. The harlequin is found in Texas, New Mexico, Arizona and Colorado, but these states are only the northern extremity of its range. It has a much more extensive range in Old Mexico.

COMMUNICATION: The harlequin quail's call has ventriloquistic qualities that make it exceedingly difficult to locate the bird. The note has been likened to the quavering call of the screech owl. It starts as a low whistle, descending the scale toward the end of the call. It is usually given quite softly, but the sound carries well in the still, quiet air of the arid regions. When the birds are scattered, this call is used to reassemble the flock. It is easily imitated, and it is often possible to call the bird into sight. When the quail is startled or flushed into flight, it makes a soft *chuck, chuck, chuck* sound.

BREEDING AND NESTING: The harlequin quail is monogamous, and the flocks break up in the late winter after the birds have paired up. Often, as the flocks break up, the pairs seek out the higher elevations of their summer range to nest. The males defend their nesting territories against rival males.

Almost nothing is known about this quail's courtship and breeding habits, but it can be presumed that the male struts to impress the female, as all the other quail do. The lack of information

Range of Harlequin Quail

is due to the fact that nowhere is the harlequin quail very plentiful, and most of its range is not near human haunts. In recent years some of these birds have begun to frequent grainfields, and if this habit continues, perhaps more opportunities to study this beautiful little quail will present themselves.

The nest is a depression in the earth which the quail digs out with its strong, sharp claws. Very fine pieces of grass are used as a lining. It is very difficult to find the nest because of the great care that the quail takes in choosing a nest site. The nest may be hidden under the hanging fronds of a clump of grass or under thick brush, or it may be roofed over with long pieces of grass. Some of the nests are under such an expanse of vegetation that they can only be entered through a grassy tunnel.

EGGS AND YOUNG: An average harlequin quail clutch numbers ten to twelve eggs, although sometimes fourteen eggs or more are laid. The eggs average 31 millimeters in length by 24 millimeters in diameter. They are dull white with no splotches of color but soon become stained from the dirt in the nest and on the quail's feet.

The male and female share the task of caring for the young, and it is thought that they also share about equally in the incubation of the eggs. There are even records of several instances where both the male and female were on the nest at the same time. The various species of quail have different incubation periods that range from eighteen to twenty-three days. There appear to be no data on the harlequin quail's incubation period, but it is probably in the eighteen- to twenty-one-day range. The basis for this assumption is that usually the smaller the creature is within a certain species type, the shorter its gestation or incubation period.

The chicks, on hatching, are a reddish buff color on the upper portion of their bodies, while their underparts are grayish white.

If a harlequin quail family is disturbed, both the parents do a great deal of fluttering and flapping about on the ground to draw attention to themselves and away from their young. The young scurry under the nearest piece of vegetation, where they squat down motionless.

FLIGHT: The harlequin quail uses its wings only as a last resort. It much prefers to get from place to place by walking, usually slowly. This quail has the short, cupped wings which are common to all the quail and which are not designed for sustained flight. When flushed, the harlequin gets up speed rapidly, its stubby wings making a *r-r-r-r-r-r-r* sound as it takes off. The flight is short and usually to some dense cover. This quail ordinarily flies in a straight line with no rocking or weaving motions. When it drops back to the ground again, it uses its stout legs to race off to safety.

MIGRATION: The harlequin quail does not migrate, and unless forced to do so by a lack of water or food, it does not even make seasonal shifts.

HABITS: The name "fool hen" is often used for this bird in our southwestern states. Man always has a tendency to call any creature a fool that does not fly or gallop away at his approach. Most creatures are in fact tame and trusting until they learn that man is indeed an enemy. The regions that the harlequin quail frequents are so inhospitable to man that many of these little quail never see a human being.

The harlequin quail seems to know that its black and white

breast and flanks are conspicuous. If danger approaches it squats down, pressing its breast and flanks to the earth so that their patterning cannot be seen. Its brown back closely matches the earth's colors. The bird feels so secure with its camouflage that it will allow a person to walk within a foot or so of it before flying off.

This quail may sit on a rock, stump or log, but it seldom, if ever, lands in a bush or a tree. All its food is picked up or dug up from the ground. Lily bulbs are its dietary staple. It obtains these bulbs by digging 3 or 4 inches into the hard soil to unearth them. The birds have no trouble finding the lily bulbs even if the top portion of the plant has died down or been broken off.

Food: The crops of almost all the harlequin quail that have been examined contained lily bulbs. This quail also eats many piñon nuts and acorns, as well as the seeds, berries, leaves and other parts of many plants. It feeds on some insects, particularly crickets, grasshoppers, caterpillars, ants and spiders.

Life Span: Almost nothing is known about the harlequin quail's longevity, but it probably has a potential life span of about four years.

Enemies: Snakes of various kinds feed on both the quail's eggs and the young. Raccoons, coatimundis, cacomistles, badgers, foxes, bobcats, coyotes, hawks and owls all take an occasional adult quail. Predation, however, is not an important limiting factor as far as harlequin quail numbers in the United States are concerned.

Table Fare: The harlequin quail, like all quail, provides excellent table fare.

Bobwhite Quail

Colinus virginianus

One of the well-remembered sounds of my boyhood, which was spent on a mountain farm in northwest New Jersey, is the cheery whistling of the bobwhite. During the breeding season, the brighter the day, the louder and more frequently would come its delightful *bob-bob-white, bob-bob-white* call. I would always try to seek out each whistling male, and before long I knew the territory of each bird and usually what rock, fence post or stump he would use as his singing perch.

Most of the farms of that area are no longer being farmed and are waiting to be taken over by the urban sprawl. The few that are operating do not have the diverse small grain crops that were once planted. The result is that the quail have left the area.

DESCRIPTION: The bobwhite is a plump-bodied little bird. The adult male measures 10 to 11 inches in length, has a wingspan of 14 to 15 inches and weighs 5 to 6 ounces, and on rare occasions up to 9 ounces. The male's most conspicuous marking is the white throat patch and the broad white stripe above the eye, extending from the bill to the nape of the neck. Both the patch and the stripe

Bobwhite Quail

have a black or dark brown border that accentuates their white-
ness. The bobwhite's breast, back, rump, wings and tail are
reddish brown with black markings. The belly and flanks are basically white, but the dark brown edging of the belly feathers gives
the belly a scaled appearance. Three rows of brown feathers, edged
with black, create stripes on each flank. The bird's bill, eye, legs and
feet are black.

The female bobwhite is almost identical to the male except that
her throat patch and eye stripe are buffy yellow instead of white,
and the border to these areas is dark brown instead of black. She
is also slightly smaller in size and lighter in weight.

DISTRIBUTION: Within recorded times, the bobwhite greatly increased its range, only to be pushed back again and in many places
extirpated entirely. It is a bird of the farmlands and forest fringes.
Its original range extended from Maine west to the upper Mississippi River valley and south to Texas, embracing all of the area east
of that line. However, it was found only in the grasslands of those
areas, on tracts that had been burned off by natural causes or by the
Indians, and along the coastal regions.

The destruction of the virgin forest and the opening up of the
land to farming increased the bobwhite population tremendously.
Around the 1850s, its range had extended north into Canada and
west to take in South Dakota and New Mexico.

Today, the bobwhite is found from eastern Massachusetts down
the coast to New Jersey, across Pennsylvania to the Great Lakes, and
occasionally still occurs in southern Ontario. The line that delimits
its range continues as far west as Iowa and then strikes south to
Texas, east to Florida and up again to New Jersey. Some of the birds
have been successfully introduced into Washington, Oregon, Idaho
and British Columbia, but in some of these areas, the species is
only just holding its own. The bobwhite's eastern range covers a
large area, but the species does not blanket that area. In many
places it has been reduced, and in some it has been wiped out.

COMMUNICATION: The bobwhite is famous for its whistling of
its name, but it also has a wide repertoire of other calls. The regular
bob-bob-white is called loud and clear, but this call is sometimes
changed to a muted *ah-bob-white*. The regular call is heard primarily
in the spring and early summer as it is the mating call whereby a
male seeks a female or proclaims his territory after he has a mate.
He changes to a raspy call which could be interpreted as a battle
cry if another male shows up while he is calling.

Range of Bobwhite Quail

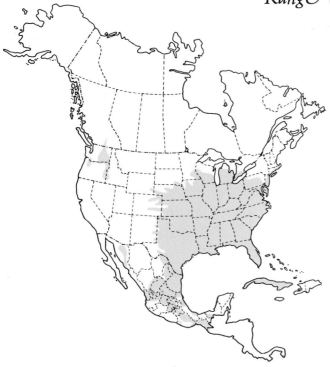

A female, when protecting her young, utters a squealing *tsieu, tsieu, tsieu* call to attract attention to herself so that her chicks can escape. To warn her brood of danger, she calls *toil-ick-ick-ick, toil-ick-ick-ick*. This is the universal danger call and is used by both sexes. After a covey is scattered, they reassemble by calling *wurlee-he, wurlee-he, wurlee-he* or *whoil-kee, whoil-kee*. Both these calls are also given in a conversational tone and are used by a flock of birds to keep in touch with one another as they scatter to feed.

BREEDING AND NESTING: During the winter, the bobwhite stays in coveys for protection and warmth, but in the spring the coveys break up and scatter. Although the males become aggressive toward each other in the spring, fights are not common. With puffed up feathers, one male lowers his head and runs at another male. The second male usually runs away either because the first male is larger or simply because his own hormonal change is not as advanced. When a fight does occur, it is usually simply a "hair-pulling" contest as each of the males attempts to grasp the other's head by the feathers. The scuffling about is usually not serious.

Quail are monogamous, and as there is a larger ratio of males than females in the spring, some of the males remain unmated for that reason. It is thought that most quail remain paired for life. A male that does not mate his first breeding season is almost sure to mate the next year. In his second breeding year, he is older and therefore bigger and stronger than his rivals for the favors of the preceding year's females.

To win a new mate, or to rekindle the flame in his existing mate, a male must go through the courtship proceedings. With the pomposity of a miniature turkey cock, the male bobwhite fluffs out his feathers and droops his wings until the tips drag on the ground. Then, with his tail spread out and down and his head cocked sideways, he charges at the female. Like a coquette, the female gives way before him. Again he charges and again she gives way, never running so fast as to lose him. He chases her until she squats down and submits to copulation.

The pair, having left the covey, seek out an area of their own which they defend against all others. If the weather turns cold, as it can if spring is late, the birds may temporarily give up their territory and flock up again. If not deterred by adverse weather, the bobwhite start to nest a couple of weeks after pairing up. In the deep South, they may be nesting by early March, but in the northern portion of their range, they are not ready to nest until the first part of April.

The male bobwhite is a most devoted mate, seldom leaving the female's side. It is he that builds the nest, usually in a spot where there is a heavy stand of high grasses. He does so by scratching a hollow in the earth, using both his feet and his bill. The lining of the nest is made up of local grasses, leaves, pine needles, etc. The nests are usually well hidden because most of them have a roof formed by the male building under a clump of grass or placing material over the nest.

EGGS AND YOUNG: The bobwhite is very prolific, twelve to fifteen eggs to a clutch being the average. In captivity one bobwhite hen, whose eggs were taken from her, laid over one hundred and fifty eggs in one season.

The female is usually a consistent layer, producing one egg a day, but because of the large size of the clutch, it may be two to three weeks before the clutch is completed and incubation can begin.

Incubation requires twenty-three days and is usually performed exclusively by the female. The male remains in the area but stays away from the vicinity of the nest so as not to attract danger to it. He still sings his cheery *bob-bob-white*. If a predator approaches too close to the nest, the male tries to decoy it away. If the female is killed, the male has been known to brood the eggs and raise the young. If, as sometimes happens, the nest is destroyed, the bobwhite nests again and if need be a third and even a fourth time. Under ordinary conditions, quail produce only one brood a year.

The fertility of quail eggs is high, and if the nest is undiscovered, about 85 to 90 percent of the eggs hatch. The young are precocious and are ready to leave the nest as soon as their down dries off.

Both the parents are in constant attendance on the chicks, teaching them to feed, keeping them together and brooding them when they are chilled. Adverse weather conditions in the form of cold, soaking, protracted rains are the most deadly enemy. Although the mother can keep the chicks warm and dry for a short period of time, hunger forces them to move, and the chicks exposed to the chilling rain are doomed. After a week, the chicks have usually developed enough body feathers for their chances of survival to be much improved.

Either or both of the parents will feign injury to lure a predator away from the chicks. The little ones "freeze" at the first alarm note and blend into their surroundings so well that their detection is very difficult.

The young quail feed exclusively on insects at first and then gradually change over to a mainly vegetarian diet.

FLIGHT: The young bobwhite's flight feathers grow very quickly, and by the time the chicks are ten days old, they can fly for short distances. By the age of three weeks, they can fly away from earthbound predators.

The bobwhite has short, cupped wings that are well designed for a fast takeoff but not for prolonged flights. The quail usually sits very tight until danger is imminent, then thunders into the air, reaching a top speed of about 50 miles per hour very quickly. Then, on set wings, it glides as far as it thinks fit before sailing in for a landing. Upon landing, it may sit tight under whatever cover it can find or it may run to put an even greater distance between itself and the source of danger.

A covey usually scatters widely by flying when threatened but normally reassembles by walking. The quail instinctively know that they are at a disadvantage in the air, where their camouflage coloring is of no use to them.

MIGRATION: The bobwhite quail does not migrate and in most cases does not even have regular seasonal shifts. The birds scatter in the spring, regroup in the summer and fall and only move from one area to another when snow covers their food supply. There are some shifts in population due to the fall dispersal of some of the young to new areas. The normal range of the quail is about ¼ mile in diameter.

HABITS: The bobwhite is one of the most gregarious of the game birds. Flock intermingle with flock, families group, regroup, split up and group again. The birds keep in touch, conversationally, as they feed and move about. When scattered, they waste little time in regrouping again. At night, they form into a tight circle, their tails pointing in and their heads out, ever alert for danger. While in the circle, their bodies are pressed together for mutual warmth.

The flocking circle is an important survival factor because some of the birds are usually awake to detect danger. Even if they are all asleep, the predator has more chance of being heard than if it were stalking a solitary bird. And, if the predator does get close enough to catch a quail, it can usually seize only one at a time, so that while one may die, many will live.

The birds begin to feed at dawn. When there is sufficient moisture in the area, they usually slake their thirst by drinking drops of dew. In areas of restricted water, they go to a watering place to drink. The middle of the day is used for lolling about in the sun in cool weather. In hot weather, the birds seek out the shade. Dusting is a frequent activity as a relief against parasites.

FOOD: About 86 percent of the bobwhite's diet consists of vegetable matter. The seeds of noxious weeds are so preponderant in its diet that the bobwhite is considered highly beneficial to the farmer whose acres it inhabits. One of its favorite foods is ragweed seed. This alone should recommend it to every hay-fever sufferer. Other popular foods are lespedeza, smartweed, corn, sorghum, bristle grass, wheat, beggarweed, acorns, cowpeas, sunflower, doveweed, panic grass, milkpeas, etc. The bobwhite eats the leaves, stems and flowers of these various plants, in addition to the seeds. It does not do much harm to cultivated crops because most of the grain that it eats it picks up by scavenging.

The bobwhite consumes a certain quantity of animal matter, consisting of grasshoppers, locusts, crickets, beetles, ants, caterpillars, spiders, snails, sow bugs, earthworms, centipedes and slugs. Grit is also ingested into the gizzard to be used as an aid to digestion.

LIFE SPAN: The bobwhite quail has a potential life span of from four to five years. However, there is an annual mortality of about 70 to 75 percent of the entire population.

ENEMIES: The bobwhite's greatest enemy is the change in general farming practices. When the quail population was at its peak, a hundred years ago, most of the countryside was occupied by small farms that produced diversified crops in small fields. Today the tendency is to create large fields for more efficient farming by tearing out the hedgerows, thus depriving the quail of potential nesting sites. In many areas today, farms are lying fallow, and many of the fields have gone back to timber. This destroys the quail's habitat completely. Most of the farms that are still in operation are one-crop at the most or two- or three-crop farms, and this specialization deprives the quail of some of its foods.

With a ground-nesting bird like the quail the nest and perhaps the female may be destroyed by such predators as snakes, skunks, opossums, cats, dogs, rats, foxes, bobcats, raccoons and weasels. Hawks and owls catch both the young and the adults. Under normal circumstances, however, predation is not an important factor for the quail population. Accidents and disease take their toll.

TABLE FARE: The bobwhite quail is considered a table delicacy by all who have had the opportunity of eating it. In some sections of the country, notably the southeastern states, the bobwhite is the most important game bird. The yearly bobwhite take is between ten and fifteen million birds.

Chukar Partridge

Alectoris graeca

Near the turn of the century, the first chukar partridges brought to America were released in Illinois. Despite abundant feed and cover, the birds did not survive. A subsequent attempt to introduce them in California enjoyed but limited success.

Then, in 1935, the chukar was set loose on the Nevada uplands. There, in an arid and open habitat that much resembled its native Eurasian ranges, the bird thrived to such a degree that just twelve years later, Nevada permitted an unlimited hunt on it.

Today, the chukar partridge has spread throughout the Rocky Mountain area and occupies a niche as one of the region's most important game birds.

DESCRIPTION: Several different subspecies of the chukar partridge have been imported into the United States, but only the subspecies known as *Alectoris graeca chukar*, which has been the most successful, will be described here. This subspecies comes from Nepal, where the bird is common in the foothills of the Himalaya Mountains.

The adult male chukar partridge is a plump-bodied bird that is smaller than a ruffed grouse but larger than the bobwhite

Chukar partridge wears a unique facial marking: a continuous black band that extends through the eye and across the chest.

quail. It measures about 15 inches in length, has a wingspan of 16 to 17 inches and weighs about 25 ounces. The female is smaller in size and lighter in weight but is identical to the male in coloration. She lacks the short spurs that the male sports.

The chukar is strikingly marked, having a very conspicuous black border around a pure white throat and cheeks. The black extends unbroken through the eyes and around the forehead. The crown of the bird's head is brownish, shading to gray. The bluish gray continues behind the black border and extends down the breast. The rump and central tail feathers are also gray. The bird's back and the inner portion of the wings are brownish gray, the primary feathers dark brown. The chukar's outer tail feathers are a rufous brown. The belly is a rather creamy white, becoming darker in the center. The flank feathers are pure white, barred heavily with black feathers edged with brown. The bill, feet and legs are red. The pupil of the eye is brown with a red ring.

DISTRIBUTION: The chukar partridge has been imported and released in many states, but in most of them the habitat was unsuitable and the releases failed.

The Nepal chukar is a bird accustomed to high, dry country. It cannot stand the humid conditions that prevail in the eastern United States but has fared much better in some of the western states where conditions closely duplicate its native habitat. Talus

Range of Chukar Partridge

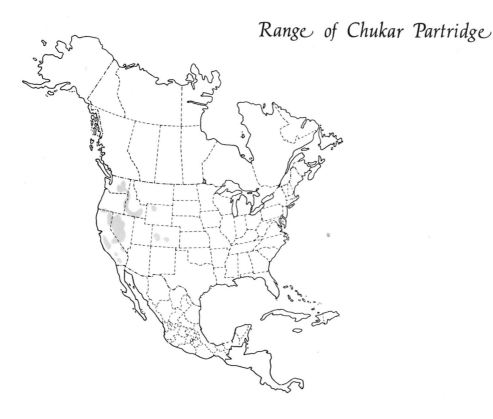

slopes, rocky outcroppings and even desert areas seem to be an ideal habitat for the chukar.

The birds thrive in the foothills of the Rocky Mountains in such states as Washington, Oregon, California, Arizona, Nevada, Utah, Colorado, Idaho, Wyoming, Montana and Canada's British Columbia and Alberta. The population of chukars in most of those states is steadily increasing, and as different strains of chukars are imported, their range will probably expand. The chukar is a most valuable addition to our avifauna because there is practically no competition between it and any of our native species.

COMMUNICATION: The most commonly heard call of the chukar is the *ka, ka, ka* call given by a dispersed flock as it tries to reassemble. This is also the call given by the male when he seeks a mate in the spring. The male also crows his name, calling over and over again *chu, chu, chu-kar, chu-kar*. When startled, the birds give out a loud *cheiou, cheiou, cheiou* cry as they fly off.

BREEDING AND NESTING: The chukar is a sociable bird and is often found in large flocks, especially in late summer and early fall, when its water supply is limited. Some of these flocks contain as many as three to four hundred birds. When the fall rains open up many acres of range that were previously denied the chukars because of the total absence of water, the flocks split into much smaller groups.

In February the chukars begin to pair up, and the males fight for the hens they desire. Competition is keen, and the battles are frequent and sometimes bloody. Even after the pair formation, however, the flock stays intact until the middle or end of March. At this time, the flock breaks up completely, and each pair seeks out its own individual territory.

The courting display of the male does not include any aggressive behavior directed against other males because by this time the fighting is all over. To impress the female, the male ruffles the feathers on his neck, which makes him appear much larger. Then, extending his neck and lowering his head, he drops his wings until they touch the ground. He then runs toward and around the female. This performance is continued until the female squats down and allows the male to mount her.

The chukar's nest is a hollow scratched out in the earth by the female and is usually located near or up against a stump, bush, rock or clump of grass. It is made of the local grasses with the addition of a few feathers plucked from the female's breast.

EGGS AND YOUNG: The chukar starts to lay its eggs in late April, and as the clutch is large, it takes quite a while to complete. The average clutch contains fourteen to sixteen eggs. There is only one brood a year, and late nesting is not proof of a second brood but the result of the first brood being broken up.

The eggs average about 36 millimeters in length by 27 millimeters in diameter. They are basically white with yellowish overtones and have variable-sized brown spots and blotches.

As the hen begins the incubation, which requires twenty-three to twenty-five days, the male usually loses interest in her and drifts away to band together with the other males of the area.

Chukar chicks are precocious and scramble out of the nest and after their mother as soon as their down dries off. Since they inhabit arid regions, they are seldom exposed to the chilling rains that take such a toll of the chicks of other species. When danger threatens, the female feigns injury in an attempt to decoy

Flushed from cover, a brace of chukar partridge flies for the nearest hill-side where it can scramble to safety among the rocks.

the danger away from her brood. The chicks, upon hearing their mother's note of alarm, fade into the vegetation and freeze.

The young feed upon insects at first and then gradually switch to an almost completely vegetarian diet.

FLIGHT: The chicks develop rapidly, and by the time they are two weeks old, they can fly 50 to 60 feet. After another couple of days the whole brood can fly away from any earthbound predator.

Upon being flushed, the chukar usually flies for the steep talus hillsides in its area, where the broken jumble of rocks allows it to play effective "hide and seek" with whatever enemy has threatened it. Although the chukar flies well, it is a short-flight bird and much prefers to run rather than fly away from danger if this is at all possible.

MIGRATION: The chukar partridge does not migrate, although it is subject to seasonal shifts. The birds prefer low-snowfall areas, and any depth of snow will force them to leave a favored area for one which is swept free of snow by the wind. A drought in the summer can cause a similar shift by forcing the birds to concentrate where they can find water. Although the chukar cannot be said to migrate, the expansion of its range shows that it does emigrate.

HABITS: The chukar enjoys the company of its own kind, and in late summer family groups band together in ever larger flocks. The chukar also gets along well with other game-bird species. It is not an aggressive bird and does not compete with the other species. Chukars keep up a constant conversation among themselves when they are flocked up.

During the hot part of the day, the chukar takes life easy under the shade of bushes. Feeding is done in the early evening. In winter, if snow covers its usual foods, the chukar does not hesitate to feed at wildlife grain feeders. Often the birds frequent farms and ranch yards in an attempt to feed on spilled grain. In some areas and in some winters, the chukars may suffer from starvation.

FOOD: The vegetable matter content in the chukar partridge's diet ranges from 85 to 90 percent according to the season. The other 10 to 15 percent of its diet consists of grasshoppers, crickets, ants, beetles and yellowjackets, according to the season.

The chukar partridge is mainly a seed feeder, but it also eats the leaves, stems, stalks, flowers and sometimes the bulbs of various plants. Some of its favorite foods are cheatgrass, wheat, salsify, dandelion, shepherd's purse, equisetum, bunch grass, chokecherry, poison oak, rye, desert parsley, pigweed, sumac and wild rose. It seldom, if ever, does harm to cultivated crops.

LIFE SPAN: The chukar partridge has a potential life span of from five to seven years. A search for longevity records for this bird has proved fruitless.

ENEMIES: Foxes, coyotes, skunks, raccoons, bobcats, hawks, owls and eagles are the chukar's main predators. Any ground-nesting bird is subject to more predation than a tree-nesting bird. Any predator inhabiting the same range as the chukar will prey on the eggs, chicks or adults whenever the opportunity presents itself.

TABLE FARE: The chukar rates high with hunters, not only because it is a sporting bird to hunt, but because its flesh is considered a delicacy.

Gray Partridge

Perdix perdix

The introduction to the United States of exotic game birds has, for the most part, resulted in dismal failure. Such importations started in colonial days and have continued right up to the present time. Of the dozens of species that were tried out, only three have really been successful: the ring-necked pheasant, the chukar and the gray partridge.

The gray partridge is also known as the Hungarian partridge or simply as the Hun because most of the birds imported onto this continent came from Hungary, although some came from Sweden, Germany and Russia.

The earliest releases of these partridges in the United States were made at Lynnhaven, Virginia, in 1899. The first successful importations were made on the west coast. In 1900 about a hundred gray partridge were released in the Willamette Valley in Oregon. After six years, when it was seen that the established birds had begun to breed, more than 5,000 were released. A population explosion ensued, and within a few more years the birds had extended their range to Washington, British Columbia, Idaho and Montana. By 1909 over 45,000 Huns had been imported by the various states.

The greatest success story of the gray partridge, however, was written in the province of Alberta, Canada. Between 1908 and 1909 more than 500 of the birds were released south of Calgary. The success of these releases eclipsed even that of the Willamette Valley. This partridge was originally introduced to supplement or to supplant the diminishing numbers of prairie chickens. In some areas it may have hurried the prairie chicken's demise because of direct competition. Within a few years the gray partridge had firmly established itself in Alberta, Manitoba, Saskatchewan, North and South Dakota and Montana.

DESCRIPTION: The gray partridge is a small bird but larger than any of our native quail. The male and female are identical, except that the female is slightly smaller. The adult male measures about

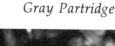

Gray Partridge

Range of Gray Partridge

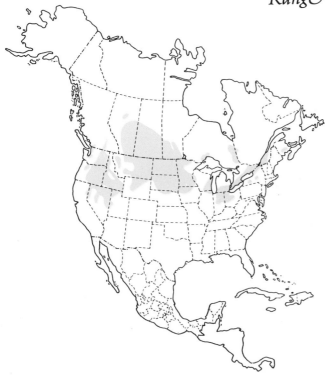

12 to 14 inches in length, has a wingspan of 15 or 16 inches and weighs about 12 to 14 ounces. This partridge has a dark gray cap and a light gray nape, neck and breast. Its belly has a large cinnamon-brown, white-edged patch surrounded by gray. The gray feathers of the flanks have cinnamon-colored tips, making a definite barring. The bird's face, cheeks and throat are light brownish yellow. Its back and rump are mottled gray and brown. The central tail feathers are also gray and brown, but the outer tail feathers are a bright cinnamon brown. The tail is short but well rounded when fanned out. The inner wings are brown, the primaries a dark brown flecked with white. The legs and feet are dark, almost black.

DISTRIBUTION: The heart of the gray partridge country is Alberta, Saskatchewan, Manitoba, North and South Dakota and Montana. There are also good numbers of them in British Columbia, Washington, Oregon, California, Idaho, Nebraska, Ontario,

Quebec, the Maritime Provinces, Illinois and Indiana. The birds have been adapted by nature to survive on the cold, windswept steppes and plains of Asia and Europe. They can withstand the bitter cold and deep snows of winter and the frequent droughts of summer. It is only natural that they should have done best on this continent where the conditions most closely resemble the areas from which they came.

Many other states have experimented with partridge releases with varying degrees of success. In my own state of New Jersey, many releases have been made, and there are some gray partridge, but they cannot be considered a native bird.

COMMUNICATION: Neither sex of the gray partridge has a wide repertory of calls. When the flocks are flushed, they make a rather high-pitched, cackling, squeaky sound. Their regular call, probably an assembly call, is a repetitious, one-note whistle. During the breeding season the females utter a raspy *tur-ip*.

BREEDING AND NESTING: The male gray partridge is monogamous and establishes his territory late in the winter. The battles between the males are common and vicious. The antagonists attempt to pull out each other's head feathers, and there is some wing beating. As these birds have only a rudimentary bump of a spur, they do not use their feet in fighting.

Usually by late February all the birds are paired up and on the territory selected and defended by the male. If, as often happens, a severe, prolonged spell of cold and snow occurs, the birds regroup until the cold has passed.

The gray partridge's nest is a simple affair, usually just a hollow scraped in the earth and lined with the local grasses. It looks like a smaller version of a ring-necked pheasant's nest. It is usually hidden among clumps of grass or beneath the low-hanging branches of bushes.

EGGS AND NESTING: The gray partridge are exceedingly prolific birds, the female laying as many as eighteen to twenty eggs to a clutch. Although two females may sometimes lay in a single nest, such large clutches are usually produced by a single bird.

The eggs are olive-brown in color, without any splotches or markings. They average 33 millimeters in length by 25 millimeters in diameter. The incubation is performed by the female, usually over a twenty-four-day period, although the time may vary from twenty-three to twenty-five days. While the female incubates the eggs, the male is always close at hand. Some biologists think that he may help to brood the eggs, but further study is needed on this point.

Unlike most gallinaceous males, the male gray partridge helps to raise the young after they hatch, even going so far as to brood them during rainy weather or at night. Another habit, quite untypical of other males of this order, is that unmated males, and females, too, will adopt and raise orphaned chicks or will entice some away from the natural parents if the opportunity presents itself.

Although it is thought that some gray partridge pairs raise two broods of young in one season, this is highly unlikely. There is just not enough time for one female to raise two complete broods in one season.

At first the young partridge are brooded beneath the adult birds at night, but as they become larger, they sleep in a circle, like bobwhite quail. With tails in the center of the circle and heads pointed out, the covey is alert to danger from any quarter. This circle provides not only protection against predators but also warmth, as each bird huddles against its nestmates.

The partridge chicks feed primarily on insects at first and only later expand their diet to include vegetation.

FLIGHT: The young partridge develop their wing primary feathers at a very early age. By the time they are eight or nine days old they are beginning to fly, and by two weeks of age, they can cover short distances. Within another week or two, they are good fliers.

The gray partridge is not a sustained-flight bird. It has short, cupped wings that allow it to burst into the air and attain a high speed in a very short time. The pinions are stiff, and the wings make a whistling sound. When a flock explodes into the air, the birds cackle and squeal as they take off. These partridge are capable of hitting speeds of 45 miles per hour or more. After they have attained their top speed, they can set their wings and glide or coast long distances before they land. The birds' flight is not straight because they have a tendency to rock sideways as they fly.

MIGRATION: The gray partridge does not migrate, but during periods of intense cold and deep snows, it may undertake a seasonal shift. It may abandon the more open areas for hedgerows or brushy areas. It does so not only for protection from the wind but for a chance to feed on the buds of the brush. During a severe winter, the birds may move close to farm buildings or to the outskirts of towns. When the weather moderates, they return to their covey's territory.

Although the birds do not migrate, many emigrate. The gray partridge's range is expanding, and the young birds are constantly establishing new territories. This expansion has slowed down but will not stop until all the suitable territory has been occupied.

HABITS: A bird that breaks cover and takes to the air exposes itself to more danger than a bird that can run from danger on the ground. The gray partridge is a master at skulking and sneaking through every bit of available cover. When danger is imminent, it can run almost as fast as a pheasant. A pheasant usually heads for heavy cover and runs in a fairly straight line, whereas the gray partridge prefers to run for whatever cover is available in more open areas and is likely to lay down a maze of tracks. Flying is a last resort. Many good pointing bird dogs are completely fooled, and many are spoiled by the gray partridge's refusal to stand its ground. The only chance a dog has is to make a big circle to get ahead of the running birds.

When shot at, the gray partridge often flies half a mile or more before alighting, and when it does, it runs again. In most cases, a hunter gets the chance to get only a couple of shots off per covey. In Europe, this is often hunted from stands, and drivers force the birds to fly ahead of them in the direction of the stands. The bird can be hunted without dogs or drivers, but most of the shooting will be at long range.

FOOD: The gray partridge is primarily a seed feeder. It feeds both on wild and cultivated seeds and grain. Some of its favorite foods are bristle grass, ragweed, knotweed, brome grass, tarweed, dandelion, alfalfa, clover and other grasses. It eats corn, wheat, barley, oats, buckwheat and sunflower seeds.

The high percentage of noxious weed seeds in this bird's diet more than offsets whatever damage it does to cultivated crops. It also performs a very valuable service to agriculture by feeding on grasshoppers, crickets and many injurious bugs and beetles.

LIFE SPAN: The gray partridge has a potential life span of from five to seven years. Although there must be many banding records, I can find no individual longevity record.

ENEMIES: The gray partridge's greatest enemy is the mowing machine. These birds are residents of the agricultural grasslands. Many of the nesting birds are killed and their nests destroyed by the mowing machine or other farm equipment. Like all ground-nesting birds, they are exposed to more dangers than tree-nesting species. These dangers come in many forms such as rats, snakes, skunks, foxes, coyotes, ground squirrels, cats, dogs, weasels, crows, hawks and owls.

TABLE FARE: The gray partridge is on a par with the bobwhite quail when it comes to fine table quality and is a more substantial bird than the bobwhite.

Ring-necked Pheasant

Phasianus colchicus

The ring-necked pheasant is certainly the gaudiest game bird of North America. It is also one of the hardiest and most adaptable and therefore the most successful of the many importations that have been tried. In the regions that are suitable to the ringneck, it has supplanted most of our native game birds to become the number one game bird. It cannot live in some sections of the country, and the game departments of such states carry on constant experimentation with other strains of pheasants in an effort to emulate the ringneck's success.

The first successful importation of ringnecks into the United States was carried out in 1881 by Judge Denny, who was the American Consul General in Shanghai, China. Judge Denny sent thirty birds to his home in the Willamette Valley in Oregon. The birds did so well that in 1883, the Judge sent over another shipment of birds, which were also released in the valley.

The first successful stocking of pheasants on the east coast took place in 1888 on the Rutherford-Stuyvesant estate at Allamuchy, New Jersey. A Scottish gamekeeper by the name of Dunn had been brought over with his family and his birds. From the first, the venture was a success, and soon many birds that had escaped were breeding in the wild throughout the northern part of the state.

After two successful introductions both state game departments and private individuals across the nation raced to import, rear and release pheasants. Many of these projects were doomed to failure due to lack of expertise in the rearing of the birds or to unsatisfactory habitat. However, where the ringneck became established, its success was beyond the wildest dreams of the early importers.

DESCRIPTION: The cock pheasant is a handsome bird that measures up to 36 inches in length, has a wingspan of 32 inches and weighs up to 4½ or 5 pounds. The tail feathers account for 22 or 23 inches of the total length. The bill is yellow-white, and blood-red cheek patches surround the eye. The head, ear tufts and neck are a dark, metallic green. A white ring almost circles the neck. The back and flank feathers are light brown with dark markings, while the breast and belly are a dark reddish brown or bronze with reddish highlights. The feathers covering the base of the back and tail are almost hair-like and are bluish green in color. The tail is light brown with black bars. The female is about 10 inches smaller in length, weighs 2½ to 3 pounds and has a demure coloring of several shades of light brown with darker markings.

DISTRIBUTION: The pheasant is a bird of the farmland areas and cannot survive in woodlands, mountains, etc. It has done best in a belt stretching across North America roughly between the 38° and 52° parallels in the farmland districts.

COMMUNICATION: It is hard to tell who is more startled, the cock pheasant or the hunter, when the bird suddenly flushes from cover with a loud *cuck-cuck, cuck-cuck, cuck-cuck* that makes the heart pound.

In the springtime especially, the cock crows with a high-pitched double caw that is not unlike the cawing of the common crow. Both sexes also make a chicken-like *puck-puck* sound, which is the main sound of the female.

BREEDING AND NESTING: In April the cock pheasant is in its finest attire. Its cheek patches have enlarged and are the brightest red imaginable. Tests have been made that prove that the cock with the largest cheek patches becomes the dominant male. Like its relatives, the jungle fowl and fighting cocks, the cock pheasant

Ring-necked Pheasant

Range of Ring-necked Pheasant

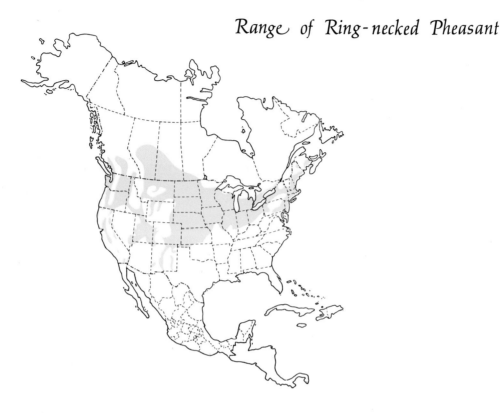

is a scrapper. In gathering together a harem of from four to seven hens, each cock is more than willing and able to prove that he is the better male. The cocks advance toward each other with their heads lowered and suddenly grab with their beaks for their opponent's head, at the same time springing up into the air and striking forward with their needle-sharp spurs. The cocks continue to do battle until one or the other concedes defeat and flees the area or is killed. During these battles the cocks are so intent on each other that they can be closely approached. The hens apparently pay little attention to the fighting of the cocks, yet none of the hens ever goes off with the loser.

At this time the hen selects a nesting site, choosing a spot such as a brushy hedgerow, a hay or grain field or an abandoned field with heavy weed cover. The nest consists merely of a few weeds or blades of grass shaped into a bowl by the hen's body.

EGGS AND YOUNG: Each day, usually early in the morning, the hen sneaks onto her nest to deposit an egg until her clutch of ten to twelve eggs has been laid. The eggs average 38 millimeters in length by 32 millimeters in diameter and are olive-buff in color. The hen does all the brooding, her mottled brown plumage blending perfectly into the background.

After twenty-three days the young hatch. The chicks are precocious, and within an hour they have all hatched, their down has dried and they are ready to follow the mother as she leads them away from the nest site.

The adult pheasant is primarily a seed feeder, but the chicks eat mostly insects because of their need for protein. Moreover, the insects move, and the chick's reflexes are to peck at anything that moves. The hen broods the chicks until they are three or four weeks old, especially during the chilling spring rains.

FLIGHT: The chicks are able to fly a few feet by the time they are six to seven days old. At three to four weeks of age they can escape human pursuit by flying right out of the area.

Hatching ringneck chicks stumble into the bright daylight. Within an hour they'll follow their mother from the nest site.

With rapid beats of its short, cupped wings, a hen pheasant bursts into the air, folding her feet like a retractable landing gear.

A pheasant is not a sustained-flight bird, which explains why its breast meat is white. Its wings are short and cupped in comparison to its body size and weight. The wings are built for sudden bursts of power, and a pheasant soon hits a speed of up to 40 miles per hour. At first its feet trail behind, but within five to seven seconds they are brought forward and folded up like a plane's retractable landing gear. In ten or fifteen seconds the pheasant has hit top speed. It then sets its wings and can glide half a mile with no difficulty. If need be, it will flap its wings once more to gain either more speed or more altitude and then start to glide again.

MIGRATION: The pheasant does not migrate but may shift territory seasonally depending upon the weather. In the mid-western states there are often huge concentrations of pheasants along the brushy hedgerows. The harvesting of the crops and the blanket of snow and ice practically denude the landscape of cover,

forcing the birds to concentrate in any area that can provide protection from the wind and cold. Where possible the pheasant seeks
out marshes and swamps because such areas provide not only
better shelter but also more food.

HABITS: Although a pheasant's flight is strong, running from
danger is its forte. A wary old cock bird knows it is at a disadvantage when it breaks from cover and takes to the air. If possible,
the pheasant sneaks or runs away from whatever it considers
potential danger, and a wise bird often learns to circle around behind a hunter. Many a good bird dog has been ruined by pheasants
because the birds refuse to stay put like a quail. They break cover,
and the dog breaks its point to follow. Before long the dog becomes almost useless for pointing.

Many people are surprised to learn that a pheasant, like most
other birds, can swim. The hunting club of which I am chief
gamekeeper is bounded on one side by the Delaware River. Time
without number I have seen pheasants fly out and land in the
river, where they calmly swam right over to Pennsylvania. They
cannot swim as well as a duck because they lack the webbed feet,
but they are strong swimmers. They have to be, because once they
have landed on the water they apparently cannot take off again.

If the pheasant thinks itself undetected and is free from the
pressure of a dog, it often attempts to sit out the potential danger.
It is remarkable that such a gaudy bird has the ability to hide itself completely in grass or cover no higher than 6 inches. Actually,
when the pheasant pulls it head down so that the white neck
ring does not show, its plumage makes an ideal camouflage.

Over most of its range the pheasant does not compete with
our native species of game birds but rather fills in the void created
when these birds were pushed out of their native haunts by the
advent of agriculture.

FOOD: A pheasant's food is roughly two-thirds vegetable matter
and one-third animal matter, plus a small percentage of useless
material. I once found the empty hulls of five .22 caliber bullets
in the crop of one pheasant and in another, most of the gizzard
space was taken up by a glass marble. Pheasants just like to pick
at shiny objects.

Corn is probably the most important item in the pheasant's
diet, followed by wheat, oats and buckwheat in the cultivated
grains. The pheasant also eats many kinds of berries and fruits
as well as many weed seeds, particularly those of the ragweed.

The animal matter may consist of earthworms, snails, ants, grasshoppers, crickets, most kinds of beetles and some types of caterpillars. I once dressed out one pheasant that had eaten five egg cases of the praying mantis.

LIFE SPAN: In the wild a pheasant may live three to five years but has a potential life span of eight to ten years.

SIGN: The droppings of the pheasant are chicken-like and are easily distinguished from the more fibrous droppings of a ruffed grouse. Like a chicken, the pheasant often scratches the ground to uncover food. These scratch marks as well as dusting spots are readily noticed.

ENEMIES: The pheasant is beset by a host of enemies, and the fact that it can not only survive but readily reproduce itself is a proof of its adaptability. Snakes and crows eat the eggs and the chicks. Hawks, owls, foxes, coyotes, raccoons, skunks, opossums and weasels all prey on the pheasant in varying degrees.

TABLE FARE: The pheasant's flesh rivals that of any other game bird. The meat may have a tendency to dry out if oven roasted. When it is pot roasted on the top of the stove, its juiciness and succulence are assured. It can be made into a one-pot meal, with carrots and potatoes cooked in with the meat. The pot juice is then used in the making of gravy and to flavor the dressing.

Wild Turkey

Meleagris gallopavo

It was to Benjamin Franklin's credit that he thought the wild turkey should be adopted as our national emblem instead of the bald eagle. The turkey was strong, intelligent, wary and, to a certain extent, adaptable.

All these attributes have been needed by the wild turkey to enable it to come back from the very brink of extinction to which it had been pushed. In the early days it was a very common bird, being found throughout most of the country. It was hunted by the Indians for food, but as the woodland Indians were never very numerous, the hunting pressure was not too great.

This pressure greatly increased when the Europeans introduced guns and gunpowder to the New World, and by the end of the 1800s most of the wild turkeys had been wiped out over the greater part of their range. Remnant flocks hid in the southern swamps, the canyon country of the West and in some of the larger woodlands of the East. With the passage and strenuous enforcement of strict laws protecting the turkeys, the importation and release of turkeys in areas where they had been wiped out, and natural and artificial propagation, the birds have made a spectacular comeback.

Wild Turkey

In my state of New Jersey, every turkey had been killed off by the end of the 1800s. Some turkeys have been purchased and released by sportsmen's clubs, but most of the birds now in the state have come over from Pennsylvania, which boasts about 50,000 wild turkeys. Other states with large turkey populations are Texas, Oklahoma, Missouri, Mississippi, Louisiana, Alabama, California, Virginia and West Virginia. And in some other states the numbers are increasing. However, the record area for turkey density is (or was in 1951) the Norias Division of the King Ranch in Texas, where authorities figured there were ninety-four turkeys to the square mile.

DESCRIPTION: The only bird with which the wild turkey can be — and often is — confused is the domesticated turkey. The distinguishing marks of a wild turkey are its black and brown tail feathers, since in the domesticated turkey these feathers are white and black. Our domesticated turkey is descended from the Mexican wild turkey that Fernández and Cortez found being raised by the Aztec Indians.

The wild turkey is a heavy-bodied, stout-legged bird measuring up to 50 inches in length and with a wingspan of about 50 to 56 inches. The average adult wild turkey male weighs between 14 and 17 pounds, while the female weighs between 8 and 10 pounds. The turkey's head and neck are naked except for a scattering of hair-like, bristly feathers. A caruncle, or wart-like fleshy appendage, protrudes from the middle of the forehead. The caruncle can be extended at will and is much larger in the male than the female. There are heavy wattles under the chin that extend down the front of the neck. The color of the head, caruncle and wattles can change, according to the turkey's mood, from white to light gray, deep blue or a fiery red.

The wild turkey's beard has been the source of much argument and the basis for considerable investigation. It is composed of rudimentary, bristle-like feathers that are not shed and continue to grow throughout the bird's life. All the male turkeys have beards, and, surprisingly many of the hens do, too. There are a number of records of old females with beards 8 inches long.

The male's beard begins to grow the first year and is about 1 inch long by November. The second year it grows to about 4 inches, and by the time the male reaches maturity at three or four years, it may be 10 to 12 inches long. There is one record of a male's beard that was 14 inches long. The beards on most females are rudimentary, developing, if at all, when they are about four years old.

The beards wear down as the ends break off through being dragged on the ground. Multiple beards are occasionally found.

One almost exclusively male characteristic is the presence of spurs. There is, however, at least one record of an aberrant female that had this feature. Old records list spurs with a length of 1½ inches. Today a spur length of ¼ to ¾ inch is about average.

The wild turkey's basic coloration can best be described as bronze, with black tips to the feathers. It is the iridescence of its bronze plumage that gives the turkey its great beauty. According to the light, the colors reflect green, gold, brown or red. Once while I was photographing a wild turkey hen from a blind, the sun struck her feathers in such a manner that each one assumed the brilliant, orangy red of a blown-on burning ember. And the female's colors usually have less luster than the male's.

The primary and secondary flight feathers of the wings are white, heavily barred with black. The legs vary in color from a pinkish flesh color through gray to black.

DISTRIBUTION: The wild turkey's range is constantly expanding under game-management programs. The bird is also being introduced into areas that it has never inhabited. Releases in Hawaii, for example, have been successful.

The turkey's original range extended from the Atlantic to the Pacific and from Mexico north to southern Canada in the East. The northwestern and northern prairie states had little or no native wild turkeys.

There are five subspecies of the wild turkey in the United States, but the importation and crossbreeding of these turkeys makes it almost impossible to find one of a pure strain today. The wild turkey is now found in all the forty-eight contiguous states.

COMMUNICATION: Gregarious birds such as the turkey are much more vocal than solitary birds. The turkey has a wide range of calls that convey its many moods or fill its need for communication.

The loud, ringing gobble of the male, particularly during the breeding season, is well known. The call is a many-syllabled *obble-obble-obble-obble*. The female frequently makes a *putt, putt* sound. During the breeding season the female answers the male's gobble with *keow, keow, keow*. It is possible to imitate this call perfectly by using a small diaphragm caller that is held in the roof of the mouth. A wise turkey caller does not call very much be-

Range of Wild Turkey

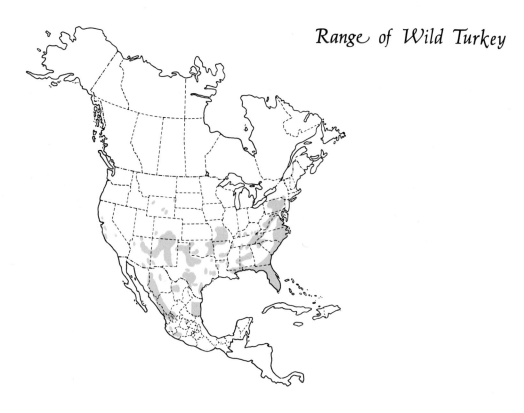

cause a hunted tom turkey becomes very wary and suspicious of all calls.

The male alarm call is *kut-kut-kut,* while the female makes a drawn-out *kwa-a-a-ah* call. The young turkeys respond to such calls with *kee-kee-kee.* The common *yelp* or *yedle* calls are used primarily to keep the flock from straying too far apart while the birds are feeding or to help to reassemble a scattered flock.

BREEDING AND NESTING: The male wild turkey is polygamous, obtaining and maintaining as large a harem as he is able to control. Although a one-year-old male may be capable of breeding, he is seldom given the opportunity to do so because of the dominance of the older males.

The bachelor flocks of tom turkeys begin to break up during the latter part of January and February. Naturally the turkeys in Florida have an earlier breeding season than those in New York state. The peak of the turkeys' breeding activities throughout the country normally falls between March 15th and April 15th, but cold weather can delay the breeding season.

The male turkey is very pugnacious, and fights between the males are common, bloody and sometimes fatal.

The male begins to gobble very early in the morning, often while he is still on his roost, and he sometimes even displays there. After flying to the ground, he begins to display or to strut in earnest. With his wings drooping until they touch the ground, he erects his tail into a beautiful fan, then, drawing his head back, he ruffles his feathers until they all stand on end. He also gobbles or makes a puffing sound by expelling the air from his body.

Although the males often gather to compete with one another on a strutting ground, each adult male has a personal territory of about 4 to 8 acres across. The females are attracted by both the gobbling and the display of the males, whom they actively seek out. The average number of females in a harem is about five hens per tom, although larger numbers have been observed. After the female has chosen a particular tom, she then stays within his territory. Copulation is frequent, the hens seeking out the male's services up until the time that incubation actually commences.

The hen turkey usually selects a nesting spot near the base of a large tree or close to a tangle of heavy vegetation; she apparently wants to be protected at least on one side. The nest is usually just a hollow scraped in the earth, filled in or perhaps

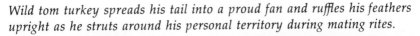

Wild tom turkey spreads his tail into a proud fan and ruffles his feathers upright as he struts around his personal territory during mating rites.

built up slightly around the rim with dead leaves. The hen is very secretive when approaching or leaving her nest. While on the nest she rivals the nearby stones with her ability to remain motionless.

EGGS AND YOUNG: Most of the hen turkeys are laying their eggs by the middle of April. Usually one egg is laid every day until the clutch is complete. The average clutch consists of between eight and fifteen eggs. Larger clutches are usually the joint effort of two hens laying in the same nest. I have seen two hens sitting on the same nest, fighting over the division of the eggs that the nest contained.

There is a great deal of controversy over whether or not the male turkey breaks the clutch of eggs if he finds them in order to prolong the breeding season. Although this may happen, it does not appear to be a common practice.

The eggs measure 70 millimeters in length and 51 millimeters in diameter. They are pale brown, sometimes shading to green, and may be plain or spotted with flecks of darker brown. Incubation requires twenty-eight days. The female is usually very persistent in brooding her eggs, although during the early stage of incubation she may easily be disturbed by human intruders. Like most other birds, the longer she sits, the more attached she becomes to her eggs and the less likely she is to abandon them. Statistics show that about 65 percent of all turkey nests are destroyed before the incubation is completed.

Turkey poults are precocious, and usually within a couple of hours of hatching they are ready to leave the nest. At this time the hen is very solicitous of her poults' well-being and moves very slowly so as not to tire the young ones. She may feed as she shepherds her brood along, but the young do not have to feed for their first forty-eight hours.

The turkey is usually thought to be a woodland bird, and certainly the adults are. The poults, however, cannot satisfy their great need for protein in the woodlands. They have to be in grass-lands, where there is an abundance of insects such as grasshoppers and crickets.

Rain is the wild turkey's chief enemy and probably causes greater mortality than any other. During the first ten to fourteen days of their lives, while they are covered only with down, the poults are usually unable to survive a thorough wetting. A wild-turkey population always plummets after a long, cold, rainy spring.

As the hen convoys her flock on their daily rounds, she is constantly on the alert for danger. If a predator is seen approaching,

Both the male and female wild turkey have bare heads; but the male, as shown here, has a larger caruncle—a wartlike appendage—protruding from the middle of his head.

the hen gives the alarm call which causes the young to scatter and secrete themselves under the fallen leaves and underbrush. The hen tries either to drive off a small predator or to decoy a large predator away from the area. Hens with poults have even been known to fly at a man as if to attack him.

By the time the poults are two to three weeks old, their primary wing feathers have developed to the point where the young can escape from most ground enemies by flying up into a tree. Yet they are still brooded on the ground at night by the hen because the rest of their body feathers have not developed sufficiently to provide the needed warmth. When the poults are four to five weeks old, these feathers develop, and the family then takes to roosting in trees at night. After this age, the poults lose all the frailties that plagued their first weeks and become exceedingly hardy. An adult wild turkey seems to be as capable of surviving cold, starvation and other hardships as the deer with which it shares the forest.

FLIGHT: The wild turkey has the short, cupped wings that provide for a high-speed takeoff but are not built for sustained flight. I watched a hen turkey in Okeefenokee Swamp, Georgia, take off from the left side of the road and, by flying on a slight diagonal, clear the tops of the 60-foot slash pines on the right side.

A turkey usually runs a few steps before becoming airborne, but it can rise into the air from a standstill. The wing beats are so strong that the draft created by the wings sends the dry leaves fluttering in all directions. The turkey flaps it wings for a distance of about 300 feet and then glides. If the distance is great, it may flap again to gain momentum before resuming its glide. Half a mile is about the average distance a turkey can fly, although there are records of some birds flying farther. The experts agree that only an exceptional turkey can fly a mile. Many turkeys, while trying to fly across rivers a mile wide, have dropped into the water and swum to the shore.

A turkey in flight has sufficient control of its body to be able to land on the branch of a tree without difficulty.

For so large a bird, the turkey is not only a strong flier but a fast one, easily attaining speeds of 45 to 50 miles per hour. One authenticated record, made with an automobile odometer, clocked a large tom turkey at 55 miles per hour for a distance of $9/10$ mile.

As good a flier as the wild turkey is, it much prefers to escape by running if this is at all possible. A turkey's average running speed is 15 to 18 miles per hour, but there is a record of 30 miles per hour. When a turkey runs, it stretches its neck forward and, if space permits, extends its wings, the volplaning action serving to lift some of its weight off the ground. The adult hen turkeys can neither fly nor run as fast as the adult toms.

MIGRATION: The wild turkey does not migrate in the true sense of the word. It is subject to seasonal shifts, when it changes its range according to the availability of food, snow depth or other environmental factors. Turkeys once moved much greater distances than they do today. In the early days they inhabited almost unbroken stretches of woodland, and such moves were probably forced on them by food conditions. Today the forests have been so broken up that most turkeys have access to many types of habitat within just a few square miles. Today, turkeys that had to travel any distance would subject themselves to all sorts of dangers of human origin.

HABITS: Turkeys are gregarious, traveling in flocks that range in size from strictly family units to large numbers. Early accounts tell of the birds traveling in flocks that numbered into the thousands.

Wild turkeys roost in trees for greater protection and usually select the tallest tree in the area. They normally roost just one bird to a tree so that a flock may be scattered over a considerable area. They are individualistic birds, some nesting regularly in a favorite tree, while others select a new tree each night. The cypress tree is one of their favorites, and wherever possible, they like to roost in trees that are surrounded by water. In areas where this is not possible, they select trees on a steep hillside. Then, if threatened, they can leave the area by simply flying across the valley.

Being an early riser, the turkey is awake before dawn. The tom may gobble from his roost, but if the day is clear, he flies down to feed at first dawn. If the weather is inclement, the turkey may remain on its roost until almost midmorning.

Feeding is done in the early morning and again in the afternoon. Usually by 10 a.m. the turkeys have gone to water and are loafing in the shade or perhaps taking a dust bath, if the weather permits such activities. They start to feed again about 2:30 p.m. and drink once more before going to roost. In the winter the feeding usually goes on intermittently all day because of the scarcity of food.

FOOD: The young turkeys feed on an almost exclusively insect diet during the first part of their life, but their diet changes as they grow older. An adult turkey's diet is about 84 percent vegetable matter and 16 percent animal matter.

The turkey eats beetles, grasshoppers, crickets, ants, wasps, bees, flies, caterpillars, spiders, millipedes, centipedes, snails and crayfish. Its plant food intake is as varied as the terrain and location it inhabits. Acorns, wild grapes, dogwood seeds, greenbrier, blackberry, blueberry, strawberry, crab grass seed, paspalum, ragweed, barberry, goldeneye, hackberry, peavine, brome grass, wheat, oats, buckwheat, corn, clover and ferns are only a few of its favorite foods.

The deer and the wild turkey inhabit the same area and often favor the same food. In most cases as the deer herd increases, the turkey population decreases. Overbrowsing by the deer not only creates competition for food but destroys the underbrush that the turkey needs for concealment.

For several winters I had a wild turkey hen that came into my yard to feed on the corn that I had put out for the birds and gray squirrels. One morning she came in much later than usual, and I watched, and counted, as she picked up 586 kernels of field corn, with no discernible bulge to her crop. As she left the area, she plucked some of the blades of grass that protruded through the melting snow. Often, if she was disturbed while feeding in my yard, she would beat a hasty retreat under a large blue spruce that had branches growing right to the ground. Secure in the knowledge that she wouldn't be seen, she would allow people to pass within 5 or 6 feet of her hiding place.

In the winter one of the best ways to see wild turkeys is to check out every little spring-run brook in the area. Because of the warmer spring water, such brooks do not freeze as readily as surface-water brooks. The turkey therefore has access to water and grit, and quite frequently some of the vegetation is kept warm enough to remain green, thus providing the bird with food.

LIFE SPAN: The average life span of a wild turkey is reckoned to be eight years, but there are accurate records of turkeys having lived to be twelve years old. An old gobbler, killed in the Santee River swamp in South Carolina, was thought to be over fifteen years old. The gobbler was fully mature when first seen, and he eluded the hunters for ten years before being shot.

ENEMIES: The conclusion reached by most biologists is that although the wild turkey is subject to predation by many species, the destruction done to the adult birds by predators is negligible.

The turkey's eggs can be preyed on by crows, skunks, raccoons, opossums, cacomistles, foxes and snakes. The same predators, along with the bobcat, the great horned owl and eagles, can also take the poults. When a turkey is fully grown it is almost impossible for a predator to catch it unless it is old, sick or weakened by lack of food. I know of a gray fox that killed a wild turkey, but this was in midwinter, and the snow was quite deep. Even though the turkey's crop was full of barberry seeds, the bird was quite thin and evidently had not been getting sufficient food.

Cold rains, as already mentioned, are probably the turkey's greatest enemy because of the mortality they cause among the poults. A cold, freezing rain in winter locks food beyond the turkey's reach under layers of ice. Deep snows make foraging for food very difficult, and strong, cold winds will force a turkey to leave an area of sufficient food for an area where it has protection from the elements. It has been found that a turkey can go without food for about a week even in the middle of winter without undue harmful effects.

Parasites, both internal and external, plague the turkey at different stages of its life and at different seasons. Diseases take their toll. Accidents, such as the turkey flying into objects or being run over by automobiles, occur.

TABLE FARE: The succulence of a roasted turkey is legendary. The wild turkey is usually not as fat as a domestic one nor as tender, for it has to work for its living. But it is just as flavorful.

PIGEONS AND DOVES

Order Columbiformes; Family Columbidae

Band-tailed Pigeon

Columba fasciata

About twelve years ago my friend Marge Kimble, who then lived at Millbrook, New Jersey, called me to come and see a bird that she had just found. It had apparently been injured when it had been blown into the side of her house during a terrific rain- and windstorm the previous night.

I had never seen a bird quite like it before, although I recognized it as either a dove or a pigeon. Its most conspicuous mark was a white ring that circled the back half of its neck. On consulting my bird identification books, I discovered that I had just seen my first band-tailed pigeon. It was very surprising to have seen the bird in New Jersey, which is about 2,000 miles from its home range in the southwestern United States. I was also surprised to learn that the bird was called "band-tailed" because the band on its tail was not very conspicuous. Some ornithologists have suggested that this bird be called a ring-necked pigeon, but the suggestion has never been accepted, perhaps because the white marking is really only a half ring. The name white-collared pigeon has also been suggested. The bird is a true tree pigeon and belongs to the same group as the common domestic pigeon and the extinct passenger pigeon.

DESCRIPTION: The adult male band-tailed pigeon is a chunky-looking bird that measures 16 inches in length, has a wingspan of 16 inches and weighs 11 to 12 ounces. It has a yellow eye and the base of its bill is yellow, while the tip is black. The head, throat and breast are purplish brown. A white band at the nape of the neck separates the color of the head from the iridescent green on the back of the neck. The back is a mixture of green and brown, and the rump is a soft grayish blue. The tail starts with a black border and terminates in a wide gray band. The leading half of the wings is grayish blue, whereas the secondaries and primaries are black. The feet, which are used for perching but not for scratching, are small and yellow.

The female is slightly smaller and more subtly colored than the male, but otherwise the sexes are indistinguishable.

DISTRIBUTION: The band-tailed pigeon has two distinct ranges inhabited by two subspecies. The common band-tailed, *C. f. fasciata*, winters in southern coastal California, Arizona, New Mexico, Texas and Old Mexico. Its eastern breeding range is in Arizona, Utah, Colorado and New Mexico. The western breeding range covers coastal California, Oregon and Washington. The western subspecies, *C. f. vioscae*, is found only in California and the

Band-tailed Pigeon

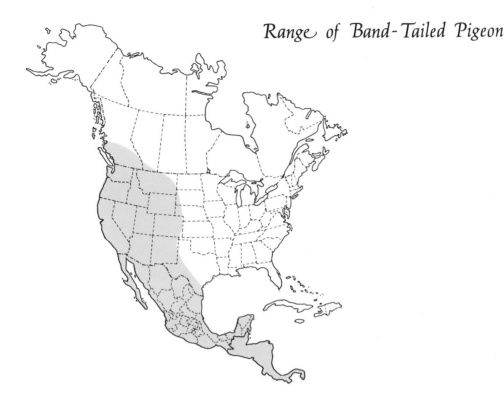

Range of Band-Tailed Pigeon

Baja California area. *Vioscae* is a paler bird than *fasciata,* but this is to be expected as it is an inhabitant of the desert areas.

COMMUNICATION: The calls of the band-tailed pigeon are numerous and frequently heard. Its most vocal time of day is the early morning or late evening, although calling is not restricted to any particular period. The western Indians call the band-tailed pigeon "hubboh," from the *hubboh* or *hop-a-hoh, hop-a-hoh* sound that it makes. Like most doves and pigeons, the bandtail also calls *coo-coo, coo-coo* in a series of eight monotonously toned notes. It also has a *who-who-who-hoo* call much like that of an owl. When the band-tailed pigeons are close together, they keep up a conversational, bubbling cooing like that made by the domestic pigeon.

BREEDING AND NESTING: Some of the band-tailed pigeons are not migratory but stay in the desert regions of southern and Baja California. These birds have been observed nesting in every month of the year except November and December. The birds that migrate to the north nest from April and May on and have only a single brood a year, while those on the southern range have usually two and, on rare occasions, even three broods a year.

The band-tailed pigeon is sociable, and there is little evidence of fighting between the males for the favors of the female. The males are in most cases monogamous, and the birds may remain mated for life. These pigeons are usually paired up by the time they reach their breeding grounds. Their courtship and breeding season are long.

The male band-tailed pigeon sits and calls from the top of one of the tallest trees in the area that the pair has selected for its territory. When he is assured of the female's attention, he flies up in the air in a circle with his wings and tail fanned out as wide as possible. When he lands again in the tree, he makes a long-drawn, wheezing sound.

When cooing at this time, the male stretches his neck out and down and gulps in enough air to inflate his neck to about three times its normal size. Then, in expelling the air, he calls a series of notes. Anyone who has watched the domestic pigeons in a city park will have seen the male do a similar performance as he struts around the female on the ground. The only difference is that the band-tailed pigeon performs this display while sitting in a tree. Copulation also takes place on the limb of a tree.

Nest-building seems to be a chore that the female is not eager to engage in. The male gathers twigs which he brings to the female for the construction of the nest. She may take a week or more to put together one of the most rudimentary, flimsy platforms of twigs imaginable.

The nest may be located in a wide variety of places. Usually, the pigeons prefer to nest in conifer trees, but in some areas they nest exclusively in oaks or alders. The nest may be built in trees from 4 to 160 feet above the ground, or it may be built actually on the ground. Normally it is situated on the twiggy branches of a tree, but sometimes it straddles a heavy limb. The tree may be on a steep mountainside or on the edge of a watercourse. The one common feature of all the nests is their apparent inadequacy to contain the treasured eggs the females deposit there. These pigeons may nest as densely as four pairs to the acre.

EGGS AND YOUNG: The band-tailed pigeon usually lays a single egg, although there are instances where two eggs have been laid. The egg is pure white and slightly glossy. It averages 39 millimeters in length by 27 millimeters in diameter. Both the parents participate in the incubation, which requires from eighteen to twenty days.

When the young squab first hatches, it is ugliness personified. The large nodules on the cere of its beak are most conspicuous. The young pigeon has a very sparse covering of orangy yellow hair-like filaments. The down, when it appears, is white, but this soon gives way to a bluish color when the quills of the feathers begin to protrude.

Both the parents also take care of the young. The baby is fed pigeon's milk, a substance manufactured by glands that are located in the walls of both the parents' crops. This substance appears in the parents' crops about two days before the eggs hatch to assure the young an ample supply of food. To feed, the little one opens its bill, and the parents insert their bills inside and pump the food into its throat.

For the first week the squab is fed only the pigeon's milk. During the second week some of the plant material that the parents are eating is fed along with the milk. At the end of the third week the milk has dried up, and the young is converted to a straight vegetarian diet, usually seeds and fruits.

For the first three weeks of its life, the squab is brooded almost constantly by one of the parents. At the end of this period, when it is almost entirely feathered out, brooding becomes more infrequent and after a month ceases altogether.

FLIGHT: During the third week of its life, the young squab climbs about on the nest and flaps its wings a good deal of the time, and by the time it is a month old it is able to fly.

The band-tailed pigeon is a strong, swift flier, capable of reaching speeds of 45 miles per hour or more. When it takes off, its wings sometimes make a clapping sound and almost always a whistling sound. It reaches top speed in just a few moments and can turn and twist with great agility.

MIGRATION: The band-tailed pigeon does not have a long migration flight. Those birds migrating to British Columbia are on the breeding ground in April and May and stay there as late as October before returning to California. Other birds make a much shorter seasonal shift, when they fly from the lowlands to the higher mountain ranges. And some of the birds don't migrate at all.

HABITS: In migration the birds, especially on their southward flight, often flock up by the thousands. Ordinarily, the band-tailed pigeon is not particularly wary, but once it has been exposed to hunting pressure it no longer allows a close approach. The birds abide, however, by their fatal habit of returning in flocks to their ancestral feeding grounds. In the days of the market hunters, this habit allowed the pigeon to be slaughtered by the hundreds of thousands, until it was close to extinction. It was only a federal law banning the shooting of all band-tailed pigeons from 1914 to 1919 that saved the species. Today, the birds have recovered a goodly portion of their numbers.

The band-tailed pigeon is an early riser and is feeding by daybreak. In the trees the birds clamber about picking at fruits or seeds. When feeding on the ground, they do so with a leapfrog action; the birds in the rear of the flock fly over the rest of the flock to settle in the front. In a few moments, those birds that have dropped to the rear fly forward, and so the action is repeated.

FOOD: The band-tailed pigeon eats very little animal food. Its preference is for the acorns from the various oak trees. It also feeds on the seeds and fruits of the pine, cherry, dogwood, elderberry, mulberry, hackberry and sumac. Of the cultivated grains it eats wheat, oats and barley, as well as feeding on peas, grapes and prunes. The band-tailed pigeon also has a need for salt that it satisfies by drinking ocean or mineral spring water.

LIFE SPAN: The band-tailed pigeon has a life expectancy of from five to six years, but it is unlikely that many reach that age. There are apparently no banding records to substantiate individual longevity.

ENEMIES: The band-tailed pigeon is not subject to heavy predation. Its eggs and young are eaten by squirrels, crows, ravens and jays. The adults are taken at night by owls and during the daytime by goshawks, the Cooper's hawk and falcons.

The bird's habit of concentrating in a small area that contains its favorite food is its greatest mistake. Hunters also concentrate there, and overshooting is common. This excessive shooting, combined with an apparent preponderance of males in the population and the fact that there is usually only one young per year, will continue to threaten this bird's existence.

TABLE FARE: The band-tailed pigeon is usually plump, and the young of the year are considered among the finest game birds for table fare.

White-winged Dove

Zenaida asiatica

The white-winged dove, which is also sometimes referred to as the sonoran pigeon, is an inhabitant of the arid Southwest of the United States. An area receiving 11 inches of rainfall per year or less is considered a true desert, and many areas of Texas, New Mexico and Arizona are classified as either desert or close to it.

Consequently, the best way to see the wildlife of these areas is to watch at whatever springs or water holes there may be there. Every type of wildlife is pulled to these focal points as though to a magnet. I found the white-winged dove along the Rio Grande in Texas and at water holes in Arizona.

DESCRIPTION: The white-winged dove is closely related to the mourning dove. Although it is a slightly heavier bird than its cousin, it appears smaller because of its shorter tail. The adult male white-winged dove is about 12 inches in length, has a wingspan of 19 to 20 inches and weighs about 6 or 7 ounces. The top of the head, nape of the neck and upper back of this bird are a purplish color. The throat, back, lesser wing coverts and middle tail feathers are olive-brown. The wings have two broad white stripes, one on the

White-Winged Dove

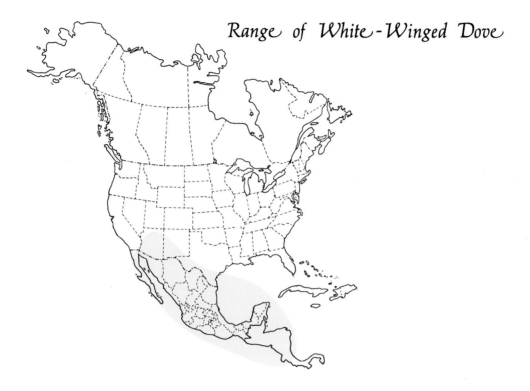

Range of White-Winged Dove

greater wing coverts, the other on the secondary feathers. The secondaries also have a wide black stripe and a white trailing edge. The primary feathers are black, edged with white. The bird's breast, belly, flanks and wing linings are bluish gray. The bill is dark, the feet, legs and eye are red, the pupil black. There is a patch of naked blue skin around the eye.

The female white-winged dove is slightly smaller and duller in color than the male.

DISTRIBUTION: There are two subspecies of the white-winged dove that have two distinct ranges. The eastern form of this dove, known as *Z. a. asiatica,* winters in Old Mexico and has its breeding range in Texas. The western subspecies, *Z. a. mearnsi,* is slightly larger and paler in color than the eastern form. Its wintering range is in Old Mexico, and its breeding range extends up into New Mexico, Arizona and California.

COMMUNICATION: The white-winged dove's most common call is a low, almost owl-like *hhhooo-hoooo-hoo-hooooo.* This call is heard most frequently early in the morning or late in the evening, but there is no daylight hour when it cannot be heard. It varies with each individual and can have one note or several notes. In this species the male is more vocal than the female.

BREEDING AND NESTING: The earliest male white-winged doves usually arrive on their breeding grounds toward the end of March. The females follow about a week later. Males that arrive later in mass flock migrations do so in the company of the females.

These doves use exactly the same nesting spots, and in some cases the same nests, year after year. The male selects his territory and defends it against other males, at the same time trying to attract a female to share it with him by his constant cooing. The extent of the area with suitable nesting sites determines the amount of territory a single male is able to claim as his own. As many as four hundred nests to the acre have been found in the dense thickets of the Lower Rio Grande Valley.

It is the male's cooing and his territory that attract the female; it is his courtship display that convinces her that she has made a good choice. The male flies about 40 feet up into the air then, with set wings, he descends in a large circle with his tail fanned out fully. The contrasting black and white of the wings and tail are thus prominently displayed. The male also displays from a perch by extending his wings and tail fully and then snapping them open and shut as he bends forward toward the female so that she can see his patterning. This display is accompanied by much cooing. Mated birds preen each other's feathers with their bills. When a rival male flies up to intrude on either his territory or his mate, the resident male flies at him to do battle. The males attack each other with jabbing beaks and flailing wings. The resident male fighting on "home" territory is usually the victor and chases the rival away from the area.

Nest-building begins almost at once. At one time the dense mesquite and ebony thickets were the dove's most common nesting sites. Today most of these thickets have been bulldozed away and replaced by citrus farms. Luckily, the white-winged dove has now taken to using the citrus groves as its nesting site. However, it still prefers to nest in thorny trees and bushes, even utilizing the saguaro cactus in some areas. This is because the nests have less chance of being blown out of such sites, and the thorns offer some protection against mammalian predation.

The nest is loosely constructed out of twigs and is usually placed on the large horizontal branches at about 10 feet above the ground.

Its position is normally such as to ensure that it is in shade for as much of the day as possible.

It is the male that selects the territory but the female that chooses the final location for the nest. The male gathers the dead twigs that are used in its construction, but it is the female who does the actual building. The process takes from four to seven days because the birds work for only about two hours each morning.

EGGS AND YOUNG: The white-winged dove's clutch normally contains two eggs. These are glossy and vary in color from almost pure white to creamy buff. They average 31 millimeters in length by 23 millimeters in diameter.

The female usually skips a day between the laying of her eggs but starts to brood the moment the first egg has been laid. The eggs therefore hatch on two different days, which accounts for the difference in the size of the nestlings. The male and female take turns incubating the eggs. The female usually gets on the eggs in the middle of the afternoon and remains on them until about 9 o'clock the following morning. The male then takes over while the female flies off to feed and relax until it is time for her shift again. Incubation requires thirteen to fifteen days.

The white-winged dove is wary and easily flushed from the nest. In its haste to be gone it sometimes knocks an egg or a young bird out of the nest.

When the nestlings hatch, they are covered with a sparse, yellow-white down, through which the blue skin can easily be seen. The large eyes are closed, and the swollen bill does nothing to enhance their appearance. The white-winged dove squab is unique in having an "egg tooth" on both its upper and lower bill, whereas most birds have it on only the upper mandible. This "egg tooth" helps the baby birds to cut through their imprisoning shells prior to hatching.

At the outset, the young squabs are fed pigeon's milk that is pumped into their throats by the parent birds. As the babies grow older, more and more vegetable matter is fed to them along with the milk. Often, both the squabs are fed at the same time, the parent holding their beaks in the corners of its mouth. The young birds are also continuously brooded by one of the parent birds on about the same schedule as was observed during incubation. By the time the squabs are about ten days old, the parents can begin to leave them completely exposed for increasing periods of time.

The young white-winged doves develop very rapidly after the first week, and most of them leave the nest by the time they are fourteen to sixteen days old. However, they usually stay close to it for another couple of days, and even after that they may return for a while to be fed by the parents.

FLIGHT: The white-winged dove is a speedy, direct flier, seldom zigzagging unless pursued or shot at. When the birds take off, their wings make a loud clapping sound. The stiff wing pinions produce a whistling sound at all times. These doves fly at speeds of from 50 to 55 miles per hour.

MIGRATION: The spring migration may extend over a period of from four to six weeks. It usually starts in the latter part of March and continues into May. The distance that the birds cover is not great, so this time lapse depends on the whims of the individual birds. The southward trip is under way from September to November, but most of the birds are out of the United States by October. For many of the birds, on much of the range, there is no migration at all.

HABITS: The white-winged dove ranges widely over exceedingly arid areas and so must often make long flights to secure water. These flights usually take place early in the morning and again at night. During the nesting season, unmixed flocks of males and females drink at different times because either the males or the females are on the nest while their mates are off.

When a drought occurs, the numbers of these doves are greatly diminished through a shortage of both water and food. A really severe drought curtails, or even completely stops, their reproduction.

The dove's dependence on the few available watering places works to its disadvantage. Hunters locate the flight lines that the birds follow from their roosting or feeding areas to the water holes and station themselves accordingly. The birds continue to use exactly the same route no matter how many times they are shot at. They fly at their maximum speed but do not deviate much from their course, just barreling on through the barrage. These habits allow the hunters to take a heavy toll of the birds in a very short span of time.

FOOD: Although the white-winged dove eats a few ants, beetles and insects, plant matter furnishes almost 100 percent of its diet. The birds do some good by consuming quantities of weed seeds, but they also do some harm when they feed on unharvested grain. Their favorite foods are the seeds of doveweed, barley, sunflower, wheat, corn, sorghum, giant cactus, acacia, bristle grass, prickly ash, lycium, desert willow, oak, condalia, prickly poppy, etc.

LIFE SPAN: The white-winged dove has a potential life span of about five years. There is an annual mortality rate of between 30 and 50 percent. The greatest longevity record that I can find was for a bird that was banded with #524-37271 on June 26, 1958, and whose band was recovered on May 19, 1963.

ENEMIES: Drought is this dove's greatest natural enemy. The winter's cold does not harm the birds because they are south on their wintering range. In 1951, however, a heavy frost killed over seven million citrus trees in Texas, almost wiping out the dove's nesting sites in that state. The great-tailed grackle, green jays and tree-climbing snakes such as the bull and indigo do extensive damage by eating both the eggs and the young of these doves. Hawks feed on both the young and the adults, while domestic cats, bobcats, ring-tailed cats, opossums, raccoons and rats take the young from the nest.

TABLE FARE: The white-winged dove is highly esteemed as a table bird.

Mourning Dove

Zenaidura macroura

The arguments as to whether the mourning dove should be classified as a game or song bird continue unabated. This dove has
probably been the subject of more research than any other bird of
questionable status. It is a proven fact that once a bird is relegated
to the status of a non-game species it suffers greatly from a lack of
interest. The preservationists, of course, want to protect all creatures regardless of the results of such protection to the species involved. They point to the passenger pigeon and imply that if such
fantastic numbers of birds could be reduced to extinction, the same
thing could happen again. The analogy is incorrect for several basic
reasons. The passenger pigeon was a colony bird that lived in the
wilderness, and the destruction of the wilderness was probably the
most important factor leading to its demise. The mourning dove,
on the other hand, is a bird of open areas that thrives on its asso-
ciation with man, and a territorial bird that keeps its population
scattered, thus reducing risks to the species as a whole.

The hunters are quick to point out that the extensive research
already done on the dove shows that its natural mortality runs between 50 and 70 percent regardless of hunting. Even with this

mortality rate, its numbers remain fairly constant. The need is for continuing interest and research to highlight any localized problems that may adversely affect the mourning dove population. If the mortality rate increases beyond the norm, hunting pressure should be reduced by curtailing bag limits and shortening the hunting seasons.

DESCRIPTION: The male adult mourning dove is a beautiful, sleek bird that is 12 to 13 inches in length, has a wingspan of 17 to 19 inches and weighs 4 to 5 ounces. The head is small, the black bill slender, the eye brown. The crown of the dove's head is bluish gray, the bare patch around the eye blue, the cheeks are olive-brown, and the throat is buff colored. Its back, rump and center tail feathers are olive-brown and the edges of the outer tail feathers white. The underparts of the bird including the wings are blue-gray. The scapulars are bluish brown, the wing coverts bluish gray and the secondaries and primary feathers dark bluish black. There are black spots on both the scapulars and the wing coverts. The lower sides of the neck are iridescent. The legs and the feet are a dull red.

The female is slightly smaller in size and has a shorter tail and more muted colors than the male.

DISTRIBUTION: The mourning dove is the most widespread of all the wild doves and pigeons. It is the most widespread of any of our native game birds, nesting in all the forty-eight contiguous states, Mexico and all the southern Canadian provinces. It is at

Range of the Mourning Dove

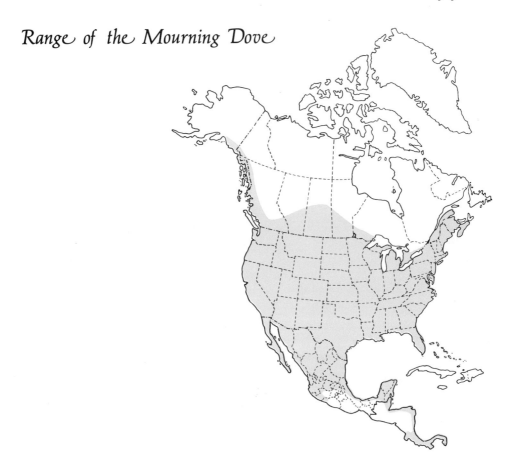

present extending its range and is now thought to nest in all the Canadian provinces and even in the southeastern tip of Alaska. Its wintering range includes most of the United States and extends as far south as Panama. Although it is a hardy bird, extremely cold weather may force it out of our northernmost states.

COMMUNICATION: Both the male and female mourning dove coo, but while the male's cooing is loud and constant, the female's is sporadic and almost inaudible. Over most of his range the male does not coo during the winter months, but as the days lengthen and the urges of spring awaken within him, he fills the air with his soft *cooo, cooo, coooah, coo, coo*. There is a rising inflection on the drawn-out middle note. The call has a plaintive quality that has led to this bird's name, mourning dove. (Turtledove is another nickname given to it.) Cooing is most frequent at dawn, diminishing at midday and increasing again in the evening. Biologists run a cen-

Mourning Dove

sus on the mourning-dove population by counting the number of male doves they hear calling along a given number of miles along specified roads. This count is then projected to the total area of that particular region.

BREEDING AND NESTING: The male mourning dove is monogamous and usually mates for life. The doves are very affectionate, billing and cooing throughout the year but particularly during the breeding season. During this season, the male mourning dove is extremely aggressive. The fights between the males over the females or the division of the available territory are frequent and bloody. Each male tries to maintain as large a breeding territory as possible. These large empires, however, are whittled down as more males migrate into the general area and the original claimant is unable to drive them all away.

When he performs his courtship display, the mourning dove looks like a miniature turkey cock. He struts around with his neck and neck feathers puffed up, his wing tips touching the ground and his tail fanned out. Then, clapping his wings together over his back, he springs into the air and rises to a height of about 100 feet before spiraling downward again on set wings to his mate. Again he struts and again he flies until such time as copulation takes place.

The nest is a haphazard affair constructed by the female. During the early morning hours, the male scours the area for dead twigs and sticks, which he gathers and presents to the female. She constructs a flat platform on the top of a branch near the main trunk or on a widely spaced fork. Occasionally, the mourning dove appropriates the abandoned nest of such birds as robins, bluejays, etc., and uses that as a base for its own nest. Evergreen trees are a preferred site, although many other types of trees and bushes may be utilized. The nest height may vary from 6 inches to 60 feet, and there are numerous records of this dove nesting right on the ground. The bulk of the nest is made of coarse, heavy twigs with finer twigs and rootlets used as a liner. Very little grass appears to be used in the mourning dove's nest. Many of the nests are so poorly constructed that the eggs can be seen through the bottom of the nest. Because of this flimsy construction, storms accompanied by high winds are a frequent cause of nest destruction. If a nest is destroyed, the mourning doves immediately build another one. This dove almost always raises two broods of young a year on the northern portion of its range and from three to as many as five broods in the southern states. When the doves are ready to start their second brood, they usually build an entirely new nest, which may be in the same tree or in a completely new area. When the birds use the original nest for their second brood, they refurbish it with a fresh lining of twigs and sticks.

EGGS AND YOUNG: The mourning dove's clutch normally numbers two eggs, very rarely three and quite exceptionally four. The eggs are pure white and average 28 millimeters in length by 21 millimeters in diameter. Most of the doves start their nesting season in April, but as I write this, on March 19, 1972, I have a mourning dove's nest under observation in the Belvidere, New Jersey, Methodist Church yard where the doves have been brooding for about a week. Records prove that the milder the winter, the sooner the doves begin to nest, and the winter of 1971–72 was an exceptionally mild one.

Both the male and female mourning doves share in the incubation, which takes about fourteen or fifteen days. The male usually broods the eggs from 8 or 9 a.m. until about 4 or 5 p.m., when he is relieved by the female. She then broods the eggs until it is the

Mourning dove, just hatched . . .   *. . . four days old . . .*

male's turn again on the following morning. Quite frequently both the adult birds fly off together at the morning changeover time to drink and perhaps feed a bit, leaving the eggs unguarded. It is at this time that the eggs are most subject to predation.

Just prior to the hatching of the squabs, both the parents begin to produce pigeon's milk in their crops. This development is triggered by a protein called prolactin.

The baby mourning doves are altricial, or completely helpless at hatching time. The parent birds brood them almost constantly at first and in just about the same pattern as they used in incubating the eggs. The cheesy pigeon's milk is pumped by the parent birds directly into the little ones' throats. The squab inserts its beak into the corner of the parent's beak. The parent's head then pumps back and forth, and before long the little one withdraws its beak. Then it is the littermate's turn to feed. Each feeding takes from fifteen seconds to one minute, and occasionally more than one squab feeds at a time. As the young grow older, seeds and some insects are fed to them mixed with the milk. At the end of eight or ten days, the parents' supply of milk has almost stopped, and the young are then fed a straight seed diet.

. . . fourteen days old.

It is an inexplicable fact that the ratio of males to females at the time of hatching is about 160 to 100. A check of hunters' bags in the fall confirms this ratio, and undoubtedly 160 males to 100 females must also be killed by predators.

At hatching time, the young squab is lightly covered with filaments of white down through which the body shows very plainly. The eyes are closed and the beak appears swollen. After three days, the primary feathers begin to protrude through the bluish skin and the eyes start to open. At six days, the eyes are fully open, and the young can climb about in the nest. If disturbed, they hold their wings erect over their backs in a typical defensive position. At the age of nine days, the egg tooth disappears from the upper mandible, and the bird is feathered out enough to fly out of the nest if disturbed. After twelve to fourteen days, the young are capable of flying, but although they voluntarily leave the nest at this time, they stay in the vicinity to be fed by the parents.

As soon as the young are completely on their own, the parents begin to get ready for their next brood. They seem to make no attempt at cleaning the nest, which is befouled with excrement by the time the young leave.

FLIGHT: The mourning dove is capable of flying at speeds of up to 60 miles per hour. When flushed from the ground, it usually shoots into the air with a clapping and whistling of wings, and the white outer tail feathers are clearly visible as the tail is flared out for additional lift. As the dove races off, it swerves and rocks in its flight. Once it has reached top speed, it usually flies arrow-straight unless shot at or pursued, when it employs all sorts of evasive actions. With its tail folded into a long point, the dove is now often confused with some of the smaller hawks. When landing, it usually flutters down almost vertically with its tail bent forward and widely fanned out.

MIGRATION: Many of the doves from Canada winter in the United States, while many of our doves migrate south into Mexico and Central America. The spring migration is under way in March and lasts through April. The fall migration takes place in September and October. Several family groups often join up to form a flock of twenty to twenty-five birds. I have never seen a larger flock than this, although records tell of flocks of five to six hundred. It is exceedingly difficult to tell when the birds are in migration in my state of New Jersey because the doves are here at all seasons of the year. I have had as many as twenty-three doves at my feeders at one time in the winter, and my father has had an even larger number feeding at his station.

HABITS: Unlike most other birds, the dove does not have to fill its beak with water and then tilt its head up to drink. It submerges its bill in the water right up to the nostrils and drinks by suction.

Like most other birds, the dove both dust- and water-bathes. It lies on its side in a hollow of soft dust and shakes the dust through its feathers. The dust clogs the breathing pores of the parasites, causing some of them to drop off and giving the dove much appreciated relief. The water bath is probably taken as much for coolness as for cleanliness.

The mourning dove is exceptionally wary in the fall, becoming more so as the hunting season opens. It is almost impossible to walk within gun range of a mourning dove that has been shot at once or twice already. Usually one group of hunters flushes the birds from one side of a field to send them flying over their companion hunters on the other side. Frequently the birds are pass-shot as they fly into feeding or watering areas. Dogs are seldom used on doves, except as retrievers. Dove-hunting is an extremely sporting occupation because of the bird's wariness, speed in flight and evasive tactics.

As the hunting season passes and the snow begins to fall, the dove loses its wariness and becomes quite tame, coming into farmyards and urban areas to seek food at the feeding stations. It is neither a woodland nor a grassland bird but favors the wooded fringes of open areas.

FOOD: The mourning dove feeds almost 100 percent on plant food, the few insects that it takes being incidental. Its consumption of noxious weed seeds compensates for its forays against farm crops. Its favorite foods are turkey mullein, wheat, bristle grass, corn, pigweed, fiddleneck, doveweed, buckwheat, ragweed, pokeweed, crowfoot grass, cowpeas, crab grass, spurge, knotweed, sunflower seed, star thistle, red maids, mustard, etc.

The dove picks up much of the cultivated grain in its diet after it has been spilled in harvesting or has been missed by the mechanical harvesters used today. In fact, the dove population began to increase noticeably as farmers switched from the slower, more efficient hand-harvesting of grain to more speedy and inefficient mechanical harvesters.

The dove appears to eat land snails for the calcium content of their shells.

LIFE SPAN: The mourning dove has a potential life span of about six or seven years. Although many of the birds are banded, no individual longevity record for them seems to be available.

ENEMIES: The mourning dove can be caught by some of the faster-flying hawks in the daytime and some are taken from their perches by owls at night. However, the dove's swiftness allows it to escape from many of the predators that are able to take lesser birds.

Tree-climbing snakes, squirrels, raccoons, opossums, crows and jays are just some of the predators that regularly destroy the dove's eggs or squabs. House cats are a major enemy because so many of the doves feed at feeders in suburban areas where cats are plentiful. I have often watched adult doves use their threat display against squirrels at my feeders. As the squirrel feeds closer, the dove raises its wings over its back and occasionally snaps them in the squirrel's direction. Each seems to respect rather than fear the other.

A canker disease called trichomoniasis is particularly prevalent among mourning doves. Yellow cankers develop in the dove's mouth and throat and grow until they block those passages, causing death by starvation. Parasites probably cause more discomfort than casualties. Accidents such as collision with telephone wires also take their toll.

TABLE FARE: I have never eaten dove, but it is reputed to be a very rich and delectable food. Only the breast is used, and three or four doves are required per person. The annual harvest of about twenty million birds would seem to support the dove's gastronomic reputation.

Shore Birds

Order Gruiformes and Charadriiformes

Sandhill Crane *(Grus canadensis)*

Virginia Rail *(Rallus limicola)*

Sora Rail *(Porzana carolina)*

Clapper Rail *(Rallus longirostris)*

King Rail *(Rallus elegans)*

Common Gallinule *(Gallinula chloropus)*

Purple Gallinule *(Porphyrula martinica)*

American Coot *(Fulica americana)*

Woodcock *(Philohela minor)*

Common Snipe *(Capella gallinago)*

Introduction

There are one hundred and thirty-two species of rails, coots and gallinules found throughout the world belonging to the order Gruiformes.

Seven members of the Rallidae family found in North America will be discussed here. Most of these birds have solid, somber, subdued plumages, but some are colorfully bizarre. The bill varies from short and stout to long and stout. The necks of these birds are short to long. The body is rounded but laterally compressed. The wings are short and cupped, the tail is short. The legs and toes are long and in some, exceptionally long; the tarsi are bare, the tibia partly bare. The sexes are usually identical except for size.

Most of these birds are solitary, some are gregarious, and most of them are secretive. Many species are crepuscular, others diurnal. Most are marsh dwellers, all swim well, and some are good divers. Most fly poorly, although the majority make long migrations. They communicate with a wide variety of cackles, thumps, boomings and screams.

Some are primarily vegetarians, while others eat mainly animal food. Some inhabit only saltwater marches, others prefer fresh water, most utilize both habitats.

The nest is on the ground, in a bush or more frequently built up on a heap of vegetation made by other creatures or by the birds themselves. Some nest structures float. The young are precocious and are usually cared for by both parents.

Discussion will be confined to only one species of the fourteen members of the worldwide Gruidae family of the Gruiformes order: the sandhill crane.

The members of this family are large, thin birds with exceptionally long legs, necks, bills and wings. Their tails are short. The sexes are almost identical in appearance.

When these birds fly, the strokes are strong but appear labored. They fly very high in migration. The birds are gregarious, except during the breeding season. They indulge in elaborate ritual dances that become even more pronounced during the breeding season. They have very loud, guttural calls. They feed on a wide variety of both plant and animal foods.

The nest is usually a bulky mound either constructed on land or built up out of the water. The young are precocious. Both the incubation and care of the young are done by both parents.

Of the eighty-two members of the Order Charadriiformes found throughout the world, two of the members of the Scolopacidae family that are hunted in North America will be discussed: the snipe and the woodcock.

These birds are somewhat similar in appearance, having mottled black, brown and white plumages and long bills. One has long legs, the other short. Both have fairly long wings, both are strong fliers and migrate long distances. Both sexes are alike.

Both birds frequent wet or marshy areas, feeding mainly on animal matter and to a small degree on vegetation. They have elaborate courtship displays during the breeding season.

The nest is rudimentary, placed on the ground, the females depending upon their camouflage coloration for protection. Both sexes incubate the eggs and care for the young.

Sandhill Crane

Grus canadensis

As we flew along Alaska's west coast from Platinum to Tunu-nak, we passed directly over one of the major waterfowl breeding grounds in the world. For much of the flight, our little craft was only 500 feet above the grassy, water-pocked tundra—low enough for the Piper's drone to flush countless thousands of birds from below. Identifying the birds proved surprisingly difficult, for I had rarely seen top markings from above. A species I soon learned to recognize from this new angle was the sandhill crane. These large, bluish birds are known for their strong flight and their animated courtship rites. In fact, one of my few previous contact with sandhills was in Yellowstone Park, where I photographed a courting couple. The birds in front of my camera never really got warmed up; but even their desultory hops and flaps showed the ease with which they can bounce around when they are ready to mate.

DESCRIPTION: The sandhill crane is such a large bird that it cannot be mistaken for any other. The adult male is about 48 inches in length, has a wingspan of about 80 to 84 inches and weighs about 12 pounds. The bird's overall coloration is slaty blue with a brownish tinge to the wings and back. The adult's most conspicuous field mark is the naked patch of red skin that extends from the bird's bill above the eye and around the crown of the head. The cheeks and throat are white. The bill is about 6 inches long, gray at the base with a dark tip. The legs are grayish black.

The male and female sandhill cranes are identical in plumage and cannot be distinguished when they are seen apart. When the birds are paired up, it is possible to identify the female by her slightly smaller size.

Sandhill Cranes

At a distance, the sandhill crane may be mistaken for a great blue heron, but it should never be mistaken for the rare whooping crane, which is much larger and has a snow-white plumage with black wing tips.

The immature cranes have a brown plumage which they retain until the following spring.

DISTRIBUTION: There are three subspecies of the sandhill crane that occupy three distinct ranges. The northern or lesser sandhill crane is known as *Grus canadensis canadensis*. It winters from California to Texas, and south into Old Mexico. Its breeding range extends from Hudson's Bay west to Alaska and north to the Canadian Arctic islands. This subspecies is slightly smaller than the western crane that has already been described.

The western or greater sandhill crane, *G. c. tabida,* breeds from British Columbia east to Manitoba in Canada and Wisconsin in the United States, south to Colorado, and west to northern California, Oregon and Washington. The range of the western sandhill crane has been greatly reduced in recent years, primarily by the draining of natural marshland. This bird was originally found as far east as Ohio. Its wintering range is the same as that of the northern sandhill.

The Florida sandhill crane, *G. c. floridanus,* does not migrate but remains on the same range throughout the year. This range includes all of Florida, particularly the prairie areas, and extends into the southern part of Georgia.

COMMUNICATION: The sandhill crane's low, trumpet-like calls are frequently heard. Ornithologists have described many variations of its common call, which sounds like *gar-oo-oo-oo.* Each of the variations is supposed to represent a different signal. The call that I have often heard is the *gar-oo-oo-oo* sound, but it has usually been followed by a low-pitched rattling that was much louder than the preliminary part of the call. The adult sandhill crane makes a *purr-r-r* sound when calling the young, who answer back with a long-drawn peep.

BREEDING AND NESTING: Although the sandhill cranes may head north in a large flock, they split up into breeding pairs as soon as they reach their summer range.

The birds perform an elaborate courtship dance, similar to that of the whooping cranes, that may consist of many, several or a single pair of birds. The cranes bow and scrape. They hop, jump and flap about with their wings extended. They leap into the air, aided by a powerful flap of the wings, to a height of 8 or 9 feet. A fertility dance of the Masai of East Africa, in which I participated, is a simulation of the similar courtship dance of the African cranes.

The sandhill crane's nest is a bulky affair, as befits a bird of this size. It is 24 to 48 inches in diameter and has a nest bowl that is from 12 to 18 inches across. The nest is usually built in a wet area, usually on a small natural island or up above the water level like a muskrat house. Although most of the nests are located in open areas, some may be hidden in clumps of vegetation. Both the adults work at gathering the mass of vegetation used in the construction of the nest, although the female probably does the bulk of the actual building. One general requirement for the nesting site is isolation; the cranes do not like to be disturbed.

EGGS AND YOUNG: The eggs of the different subspecies of the sandhill crane vary slightly in size and color. They average about 95 millimeters in length by 61 millimeters in diameter. Their color ranges from dark brown or deep olive to a light olive-buff, with darker spots that are concentrated at the larger end. The eggs are usually quite smooth and strong-shelled. The peak of the egg-laying season falls between April 15 and May 15, the customary two eggs being laid with a two- to three-day interval between them. The bird rarely lays three eggs, although the laying of only one egg is fairly common.

Incubation is done by both parents over a period of twenty-nine to thirty-two days. Sometimes the female starts to brood as soon as the first egg has been laid, so that the young hatch on different days. The female does the bulk of the incubation because she stays on the nest throughout the night, but the male relieves her for various lengths of time throughout the day.

The young cranes take between twelve and forty-eight hours to emerge after they have pipped the first hole through the shell. Although they are precocious and could leave the nest in a matter of hours after their down dries, they usually remain there for one or two days.

After leaving the nest, the young are fed regurgitated food by the parents. In a matter of days they are also seeking food by themselves. When tired, they rest by sitting on their haunches with their head and neck outstretched on the ground.

In the third week the young crane's legs develop at a disproportionate rate, the legs growing longer and the joints much larger. It is also during this period that the primary wing feathers begin to break noticeably through their sheaths. The wing-flapping that the young crane has used since its first week as a form of exercise now increases. As it flaps its wings, the young bird also jumps up into the air. The young are by now digging in the dirt with their bills, searching for the rootlets that will soon become their staple food.

By the beginning of September, the young cranes are large enough to be able to fend for themselves entirely but remain with their parents throughout their first winter.

FLIGHT: At two months of age, the young cranes are able, by jumping and flapping, to lift themselves off the ground. It is about two to three weeks more before they actually become airborne.

The flight of the sandhill crane is strong but seemingly erratic. The downbeat is slow, almost leisurely, but the wings are snapped upward with a quick stroke. In flight, the crane's neck and legs are fully extended. It frequently alternates its flapping flight with a period of gliding. The crane's regular flight speed has been calculated at about 25 miles per hour, but it can fly as fast as 35 miles per hour. Sandhill cranes often spend leisurely hours soaring in the sky on thermals and sometimes fly so high as to disappear from sight.

The smaller crane subspecies fly with a faster wing beat than their larger cousins. The lesser and Florida sandhill cranes beat their wings at a rate that varies between 148 and 187 strokes per minute, while the greater sandhill crane averages 132 to 150 strokes per minute.

Cranes in migration usually fly in V formation and usually at the great height of 1 to 2 miles. Cranes in Asia have been known to fly at elevations that exceeded 14,000 feet. Occasionally the cranes fly in extended lines or in a diagonal or, rarely, in a loose flock.

MIGRATION: The spring migrations usually start toward the end of March. It has been calculated that the distance from the cranes' wintering grounds in Texas and New Mexico to their summer breeding grounds near the Bering Sea is about 3,600 miles. The cranes arrive about May 10 to 15, a flight period of fifty-one to fifty-eight days, with the birds averaging 60 to 70 miles per day.

Often the cranes start north in small flocks that keep joining up with those ahead or behind them so that at times tremendous flocks result. On March 27, 1943, it was estimated that 40,000 sandhill cranes were concentrated on the Platte River in Nebraska.

The sandhill cranes start their southward migration about the middle of September. They do not mass up on their southward journey as they do in the spring migration.

HABITS: The dancing, bowing and jumping about are an activity which the cranes engage in at any time of the year but which, of course, increases during the breeding season. It is a form of greeting, a social activity, a game, an expression of joy of life.

The-cranes often start their day off with a dance. Before it is actually light, they start to call. Some of the birds roost in the trees, some on dry land, others stand all night in water up to their "knees." By the time the sky has lightened enough for the cranes to be visible, dancing will be in progress. By one-half to three-quarters of an hour after dawn, the cranes have left their roosting areas for their feeding grounds. By 3 p.m., they begin to drift back into their roosting areas to loaf about and perhaps engage again in a little social dancing before retiring for the night.

The ability to swim is an asset to a bird that spends so much time around water, and the crane can swim well, although it rarely does so. On the other hand it does not hesitate to use its long, strong legs. It covers long distances in feeding and seems to prefer to walk away from danger rather than fly from it.

Food: The bulk of the sandhill crane's diet is made up of vegetable matter, although it does consume animal material when it is feeding in wet areas. At such times, it eats grasshoppers, beetles, caterpillars, crickets, worms, tadpoles, frogs, fish, lizards, snakes, mice and small rats.

Not a great deal is known about the summer diet of the northern nesting cranes because very little study has been done on them. The Florida sandhill feeds on the roots of the chufa, bulrush, water lily, cow lily and blueberries. All the cranes feed on spilled or ungleaned cultivated grains such as corn, sorghum, wheat, rice and oats whenever they are available.

Life Span: The life span of a wild sandhill crane is about twelve to fifteen years. One sandhill crane in the New York Zoological Park lived to be sixteen years, one month and one day, whereas another in the Washington Zoological Park died at the age of twenty-four years, two months and eighteen days.

Enemies: Because of the crane's fondness for areas that are inaccessible even to many wild creatures, it is not unduly affected by predators. The eggs and or young are preyed upon by crows, ravens, jaegers, hawks, eagles, owls, raccoons, coyotes, foxes and wolves. The adult birds are seldom bothered because of their size.

Table Fare: The Eskimos have always eaten cranes and their eggs whenever they could add them to their diet. Now that the increase in the crane numbers has led to the opening up of a hunting season on the sandhills, white hunters are confirming what the Eskimos have always claimed: sandhill cranes are very good eating.

Virginia Rail

Rallus limicola

Although rail-hunting has long been a popular sport, it was never profitable for the market hunter, and so these birds were not subjected to this kind of pressure. Today, however, the huge rail populations have been severely depleted owing to human encroachment on the birds' habitat. The draining or land-filling of so many of the marshes has dealt the birds a blow from which there can be no recovery.

Our seashores, the fresh- and saltwater marshes and estuaries cannot and should not be looked upon as just so much "waste land." These areas are teeming with the myriad creatures that support the fish life on which both commercial and sport fisheries depend. Admittedly, the rails are a by-product of the marshes, but they are an ideal barometer as to the condition of these areas. When the rails are there, the marshes are healthy, and the food chains are strong. When the rails are forced out by such factors as land-filling, pollution, draining, many food chains are broken, and the marsh, if it is to survive, is in need of rapid and powerful doctoring.

DESCRIPTION: The adult male Virginia rail measures 10½ inches in length, has a wingspan of 14½ inches and weighs about 5 ounces. He is a basically brown bird. His bill is about 1½ inches in length and is a dark reddish brown color. The top of his head is black, the face and cheeks are gray, the eyes a deep red. There is a diagonal white line in front of the eye, and the throat is white. The Virginia's neck and upper breast are a dark cinnamon-brown, the lower breast and the forepart of the belly a lighter red-brown. The back, the top of the tail and the upper wing coverts are reddish brown with heavy black horizontal streakings. The bird's flanks, the rear portion of the belly and the underside of the tail are white with heavy black vertical barrings. The wing primary feathers are dark brown, as are the bird's legs and toes.

The female is identical to the male except that she is slightly smaller in size and lighter in weight. She is also a little paler in color and has a larger white area at the throat.

The immature Virginia rail is dark-colored. Its bill is dark green, the top of its head black, its face dark gray. The throat and upper breast are white. Some white is noticeable on the flanks and the rear part of the belly. The rest of the body is gray-black with horizontal black stripes that give the bird a very somber appearance. Through successive moltings, the young shed this dark plumage and closely resemble the parents by December, although it is another four months before they are identical to the adults.

DISTRIBUTION: The Virginia rail is found throughout all the forty-eight contiguous states and up into the lower regions of Canada. It is one of the best known rails because most of its activities are centered in the United States.

The Virginia rail's breeding range extends from the Atlantic to the Pacific Ocean. It is bounded by a line running from Virginia southwest across to southern California, north to British Columbia and Alberta, down to and around the Great Lakes, north again to encompass Maine and the Canadian Maritime Provinces and south once more to Virginia.

In the winter, the Virginia rail is forced to leave its freshwater marshes because of ice conditions. The bird is then found in the brackish or saltwater marshes of both coasts from British Columbia

Virginia Rail

all the way down to southern Old Mexico in the West, and from New Jersey south along the Atlantic and Gulf coasts and down the full length of Old Mexico in the East.

COMMUNICATION: The Virginia rail is an extremely loquacious bird and makes a great variety of calls. Many of the calls heard in our marshlands that are attributed to frogs, toads and other creatures are actually those made by this rail.

A common call is a sharp, piercing *spee-spee* . . . or *see-see* . . . . The rail often gives a chattering, stuttering, guttural call that sounds *cut-ta, cut-ta, cut-ta*. This call gives the impression that the bird is talking to itself. Some of its calls have been likened to the grunting of a hungry pig. Another high, sharp call comes out as *eh-eh, eh, eh* or *keck-keck, keck-keck*.

During the breeding season, the male Virginia rail utters a soft, melodious *cuckoe, cuckoe* call to the female while he is displaying. To call to her when they are separated by the vegetation, he gives a staccato *kid-ick, kid-ick, kid-ick*. The female answers the male with a lisping cheep, a soft sound like that of a chick.

An assembly or guiding call that the female makes to keep her little family together is *ki, ki, ki* or a slightly longer *kiu, kiu, kiu*. The young respond with a *kee-a, kee-a, kee-a* sound.

BREEDING AND NESTING: The male Virginia rails travel to the breeding grounds about a week to ten days before the females. By the time the females arrive, all the territory has been chosen, divided up and fought over by the males. It is then just a case of the female selecting the male and territory that most appeal to her. Fights sometimes occur between two females that covet the same male or territory.

To impress the female, the male ardently woos her with an elaborate display. Raising his wings up over his body and wildly flicking his tail, he runs around her in a tight circle. Pausing each time he passes in front of his ladylove, he stretches upward to his full height and bows with decorum. Then he resumes his circling. When the female bows back in acknowledgment, the male knows that he has prevailed. She then prostrates herself on the ground and allows the male to mount her. After copulation, the pair of rails often take off and indulge in some aerial acrobatics.

The Virginia rail's nest is usually built in the drier portions of the marsh, although it is sometimes surrounded by water. Some of the nests are built in fairly open areas, while others are hidden in among the vegetation. The nest may be built up from the bottom of the marsh or pond or based on a tussock or hummock of grass.

The nest is made of dried pieces of the local vegetation, cattails being a favorite material. The nest is mounded up so that it is 8 to 10 inches above the water or ground level. It is about 8 inches in diameter and has a bowl 2 to 3 inches deep. In some instances, a ramp is built from the ground or water level to the top of the nest.

EGGS AND YOUNG: Like all rails, the Virginia rail is capable of laying large clutches of eggs, although eight to eleven seem to be an average number. The eggs are 32 millimeters in length by 24 millimeters in diameter. The shells are smooth with practically no gloss and are very light in color. The basic color ranges from off-white to pinkish buff. The spotting of the egg is concentrated on the larger end and rarely spreads over the rest of the shell.

The male helps the female with the incubation of the eggs until the first chick hatches fifteen to eighteen days later. Then, because incubation was started before the clutch was complete, the young hatch out on successive days. Hatching usually takes place at the end of May or the beginning of June.

The Virginia rail chick has jet-black down and a yellowish bill with a wide black band around the middle. As soon as a young rail hatches and its down dries, it leaves the nest to scramble after the male, who then broods and cares for the young while the female completes the incubation.

Both the parent Virginia rails are very solicitous of the young, and both have been recorded as trying to decoy danger away from the chicks. There are also reported attacks on humans who had ventured too close to the young. In one instance, the female rail was observed grabbing a chick in her beak and carrying it into the safety of the dense vegetation. In most cases, the young just scatter in the presence of danger. They swim, dive, climb and run, and within a matter of minutes, the entire brood just vanishes.

The young Virginia rails are particularly agile when it comes to climbing. They can make their way up to the top of cattail stalks. They can also swim well and do some diving and swimming beneath the surface.

FLIGHT: By the end of July, about two months after hatching, the young rails are capable of flying. The Virginia rail has no more taste for flying than the rest of the rails. In the marshland, it runs ahead of impending danger, depending on its speed and stealth to escape detection. When forced to fly, it does so for the shortest possible distance. Even in migration, it flies low. The birds travel in loose flocks at a fairly good speed but seldom at more than 30 to 50 feet above the ground. As almost all its flying is done at night, including its migration flights, this rail frequently collides with objects, particularly power and telephone lines.

MIGRATION: The male Virginia rails usually start for their northern breeding grounds around the first of April. The migration is in full swing by the middle of the month, and most of the rails have selected their territories by early May.

The southward migration in the fall begins about the middle of September, peaks about the first of October and continues until the beginning of November.

HABITS: Like most of the rails, the Virginia rail is nocturnal, the peak of its activities occurring at dusk and again at dawn. It is also at these times that it does most of its calling.

All the rails are fleet of foot, but in a race it would be a tossup between the king rail and the Virginia. The king rail has longer legs, but the Virginia rail is exceedingly fast.

FOOD: Approximately 60 to 70 percent of the Virginia rail's diet is composed of animal matter. The rail probes with its long bill in much the same fashion as the woodcock. It feeds on worms, beetles, snails, slugs, caterpillars, tadpoles, small fish, dragonfly and damselfly nymphs, ants, crickets, grasshoppers and small snakes. These rails have been seen soaking caterpillars in water to soften their bristles. When feeding on crayfish, they shake them violently till the legs are torn off. I watched a Virginia rail pound a frog into submission, a task that took about ten to twelve minutes of wild flailing. The rail would pick up the frog and gulp it with its bill, then it would hold the frog and slam it against the earth. This operation continued long after the frog appeared to be lifeless.

The Virginia rail eats the seeds and other portions of the following plants: wild rice, bulrush, spike rush, sedge, buttonbush, pondweed, cow lily, smartweed, cordgrass and bur reed.

LIFE SPAN: No longevity records are forthcoming for the Virginia rail. It should have a life expectancy of from three to five years.

ENEMIES: Snakes, turtles, alligators, crows, gulls, ravens, hawks, owls, eagles, rats, opossum, skunks, weasels, mink, otter, foxes, coyotes, bobcats and every other meat-eater that is capable of eating the eggs or catching either the young or the adult Virginia rail will do so, given the opportunity. Flooding or drought are problems in some years. Disease, parasites, and accidents take their toll. But these rails are prolific, and if their habitat can be preserved from man's destructiveness, the birds should be able to maintain their present healthy population.

TABLE FARE: The Virginia rail is considered a table delicacy by those who hunt it.

Sora Rail

Porzana carolina

Unlike the proverbial perfect child, the sora rail is often heard but seldom seen. In the freshwater marshes where this, the most common rail, dwells, only the calls of frogs and red-winged blackbirds are more frequently sounded.

Yet, the furtive sora is hard to spot. It spends the daylight hours deep under a protective weed cover, becoming active only at night. Even migratory flights take place under cover of darkness.

In fact, in the early 19th century so few people saw the soras migrate that it was commonly believed this bird passed the winter hibernating beneath the swampland mud.

DESCRIPTION: The adult male sora measures about 9¾ inches in length, has a wingspan of 14½ inches and weighs about 7 ounces. Unlike the Virginia, clapper and king rails, the sora has a short neck and bill. It is "dumpy" in appearance, particularly in the fall, when it is very plump.

Like the clapper rail, the sora is basically gray. It has a short, sturdy, bright yellow beak with a dark tip and bright red eyes. The crown of its head, the front of its face and its throat are a stylish jet-black. The rest of its face and its neck and breast are ashy gray.

The flanks and belly are a darker gray with vertical white barrings. The back and wings of the sora are greenish gray with discontinuous horizontal white barrings. The top of its short, stubby tail is black, while the underside is white. The legs and toes are light greenish yellow. The male and female sora look alike, although the female's black face and throat markings are more subdued, and she is slightly smaller in size and lighter in weight than the male.

The immature sora rail closely resembles the adults, but its markings are more subdued.

DISTRIBUTION: The sora rail is primarily a bird of the freshwater marshes and is commonly found throughout all the forty-eight contiguous states and much of Canada. Its summer range extends from the Atlantic to the Pacific Ocean, north of a rough line drawn from Virginia, through Kansas, to northern California.

Sora Rail

Its winter range extends from roughly the same line south to and including Old Mexico. During the winter, the soras tend more to the coastal saltwater marshes or the freshwater marshes adjacent to the coast.

COMMUNICATION: Heard at a distance, the call of the sora has a very pleasing *er-e* sound that rises on the last syllable. It is repeated almost continuously but not necessarily in a series. Up close, the call is harsher and sounds more like *ka-e*. It issues from the marsh almost without interruption through the hours of darkness.

Another call heard frequently during the breeding season has been described as a "whinny." This call consists of a dozen or more short, whistled notes of exceptional clarity. The first eight or ten notes of the series slide down the scale very rapidly, whereas the last, low notes are all identical in low pitch and more deliberately spaced out. When disturbed, the soras utter a sharp *peek* or *puck* note.

BREEDING AND NESTING: It is known that the sora rails pair up as soon as they reach their breeding grounds, but there is a complete lack of information concerning any breeding display.

The sora rail's nest is usually located in the densest clump of cattails in the area. Although it may be built up on a tussock or on comparatively dry ground, it is much more commonly located in a spot surrounded by water and oozy mud. In such areas, the soras build a mound rising several inches above the water. The nest is made from cattails and also fastened to them. It can float no higher than the length of the material fastening it to the living stalks allows.

The nest is about 6 or 7 inches in diameter and has an inner bowl that is about 4 inches in diameter by 2 inches in depth. Most of the nests appear to have a canopy placed over them, but often this may be merely a result of the natural denseness of the vegetation in which the nest is located. A runway or ramp is usually built up to facilitate entry to the nest.

EGGS AND YOUNG: The sora rail lays a large number of eggs, the average clutch numbering about ten or twelve. As many as eighteen eggs have been found in a single nest, but this is most unusual. The sora often places her eggs in two layers so that she can cover them with her small body. The eggs average 31 millimeters in length by 22 millimeters in diameter and have smooth, glossy shells.

Their basic color is buff, but this varies from cream- to olive-buff. The eggs are dotted with reddish brown spots.

The actual incubation requires fourteen days, but almost twice that time is needed for the whole clutch to hatch. This is because the sora starts to brood its eggs continuously after the first couple of eggs have been laid. If the clutch is a large one, some of the first eggs hatch when the female has just finished laying the last egg.

The male and female share in the incubation, the lion's share of the job falling to the female. It is the male, however, who does most of the brooding and tending of the newly hatched young while the female continues to incubate the rest of the clutch.

The sora rail is a particularly tight-sitting bird while incubating and allows a very close approach before it sneaks off the nest. It is seldom seen leaving the nest although the warmth of the eggs indicates that the nest has just been vacated.

The baby soras are covered with jet-black down. Being precocious, they leave the nest and plunge into the water after the male within hours after hatching. They are equally at home on land or in the water. They can swim, dive, run about on land and climb up, on and over the vegetation that makes their marsh a veritable "jungle-gym."

The young soras remain black until they molt in August, at which time they acquire the plumage that has already been described. By December, they molt again and thereafter closely resemble their parents.

FLIGHT: The sora rail is reluctant to fly when it can escape detection by running away through the vegetation. When flushed, it flaps along, its long legs dangling down. Its labored flight allows it just to clear the tops of the reeds and rushes. After having gone only a short distance, the sora raises its wings up high over its back and swiftly plummets out of sight behind the intervening vegetation.

When the sora rail is making longer flights, it stretches its head and neck forward and lifts its legs out behind the body. At such times its wing strokes are strong and steady. Its strength of flight, when needed, is proved by the many reports of the bird landing on ships 100 miles or more from the nearest land.

While migrating, the sora rails fly in small, tight flocks that may number as many as a hundred birds. They fly fairly close to the ground, but their flight is strong, straight and fairly swift. The flock rises and falls as it flies, according to the terrain or the upward stimulus of some real or imagined danger below.

MIGRATION: Because the sora rails migrate at night, this activity is almost never seen. One day the marsh will be filled with soras and the next day there are none. Warned by instinct of an impending storm or cold front, these little rails just take off for an area that has a more favorable climate.

The spring migration peaks from the middle of April to the first of May. The fall migration gets under way during the first part of October and continues until the end of November. The soras migrate farther than any of the other rails. Those wintering on the Gulf of Mexico but breeding in the Mackenzie Valley in Canada travel at least 2,500 miles one way.

HABITS: The sora rail is not only one of the smallest rails, it is also one of the most elusive and furtive. It is nocturnal in its habits, so that often its presence in the areas where it lives is not even suspected because no one ever sees it. It is only by its constant calling that it betrays its whereabouts.

When feeding undisturbed, the sora walks exceedingly fast, twisting here and there to pick up particles of food. The bird's body appears to be as plump as a butterball, and the tail is carried level or even depressed. When alarmed, the bird seems almost deflated, its tail is raised and flared, and the head and neck are lowered before it takes off on the double.

The sora rail can not only swim on and under the water, it has also been observed crossing small streams by running along the bottom like a water ouzel.

FOOD: The sora rail's diet is exceptionally high in vegetable matter. The small amount of animal matter consists of beetles, aquatic insects, snails, spiders and crustaceans. Its favorite plant foods are the seeds and leaves of sedge, wild rice, bulrush, paspalum, rice, smartweed, cut-grass, spike rush, wild millet, duckweed, algae, cordgrass, panic grass, dock and pondweed. Wild rice is the sora rail's particular favorite. It needs a soft, oozy mud bottom to flourish, and so do the soras. In some areas, for example along the Connecticut River, wild rice, because of its elongated grain, is often called "wild oats." When the wild-rice crop is good, the rail crop is good; if the rice crop is poor, the rails move on to better feeding grounds, much to the hunters' dismay.

LIFE SPAN: The sora rail has a potential life span of three to five years. There seem to be no longevity records for this species.

ENEMIES: The sora rail is subject to whatever predators inhabit its nesting areas. Because of its extensive nesting range, it is preyed on by crows, ravens, jaegers, hawks, owls, eagles, turtles, fish, snakes, raccoons, opossums, foxes, coyotes, otter, mink and weasels. Disease, parasites and accidents further reduce the sora population.

TABLE FARE: Even though the sora rail is the smallest rail that is hunted, it is the most popular one with hunters because it is the most abundant and its flesh is the most succulent.

Clapper Rail

Rallus longirostris

Less than a century ago, the saltwater marshes along the New Jersey coast teemed with clapper rails. Naturalist John James Audubon once calculated that a particular twenty-square-mile marsh harbored a staggering 88,000 clapper nests. In the mid-19th century, a commercial egger could harvest one hundred dozen clapper eggs a day — and as many as twenty eggers could work a single marsh at the same time.

Today, though these shorebirds are surviving nicely, they no longer flock to New Jersey in such profuse numbers. One reason is that their favorite coastal haunts are being fast reduced by developers and land speculators who, to some observers, seem intent on turning the state into a a concrete hyphen between New York and Philadelphia.

DESCRIPTION: The male clapper rail is about the size of a coot, with a length of 16 inches, a wingspan of 21 inches and a weight of about 14 ounces. All the rails have vertically compressed bodies to allow them to pass more easily through the almost impenetrable tangle of reeds and rushes in the marshes where these birds are found.

The male and female clapper rails look alike, although the female is slightly smaller and lighter in weight than the male. This rail is a basically gray bird. This is the overall characteristic that immediately distinguishes it from the brown-colored king rail, which is the bird with which it is most often confused.

The top of the clapper's head is dark gray, and the face and neck are light gray. There is a diagonal white line in front of the eye, and the throat is white. The back, wings and upper surface of the clapper's tail are olive-gray. The breast is light brown, while the flanks and belly are gray with about eighteen to twenty vertical white bars. The underside of the tail is mostly white with a few gray streakings. The legs and toes are long and flesh-colored. The bill is fairly straight, 2½ inches long, yellow with a black tip.

DISTRIBUTION: The clapper rail is an inhabitant of the saltwater marshes, and in that type of habitat it is found from Maine south to Texas in the eastern half of the United States, and scattered along the California coast in the West.

COMMUNICATION: The clapper rail's call is loud and frequently heard. It is usually a series of about eight notes, sounding *cack-cack-cack . . .* or *chack-chack-chack. . . .* To some people, this call sounds like handclapping, which is why this rail is called "clapper."

If the clapper is disturbed or excited, it often gives a coarse, grunting call which is rendered variously as *bruck* or *gruck*. During the breeding season, a *keck* call forms part of its repertoire. The newly hatched chicks cheep exactly like our domestic chicks.

BREEDING AND NESTING: In the south, the peak of the breeding season is the end of March or the beginning of April. Up north, the season reaches its peak about a month later.

Clapper rails are quite common in some areas, and here the competition between the males becomes keen. The males are quick to fight for their chosen territory and for the female. Usually they stab at each other with their long bills, each male trying to grasp the other's head. When one male tires or has been physically abused, he flies up out of the area with the victorious male in pursuit. The chase is not a long one, the winning bird soon returning in triumph to the female.

The male displays before the female by making short runs toward her, then stopping, turning aside and jerking his tail upward to show the light underside. In these sallies toward the female, his head is stretched forward quite low, and his wings are

Clapper Rail

usually about halfway open, if only to give him better balance.

If the female is duly impressed with the male's antics, she lies flat on the ground with her head and neck stretched out in front of her and allows the male to mount her.

The clapper rail's nest is a mass built up from the ground or in a clump of marsh grass to a height of about 12 inches. It is made from pieces of the local marsh vegetation. Most of the nests are built in areas that are subject to the tide and are raised high enough to avoid flooding at high tide. Sometimes the nest is located on higher, dry land. It is usually covered with a canopy of grasses as a means of concealment. Occasionally a ramp is built up to the top of the nest to facilitate the birds' access. The nest has an outside diameter of from 7 to 10 inches, with a fairly deep bowl 5 to 6 inches in diameter. The bowl is lined with much finer pieces of the same material as is used in the construction of the rest of the nest.

EGGS AND YOUNG: An average clapper rail clutch numbers from nine to twelve eggs, but as many as fourteen and as few as six eggs have been found. The eggs average 42 millimeters in length by 30 in diameter. The shell of the egg is smooth and glossy. The basic color varies from a light greenish buff to a light olive-buff. Most of the eggs are covered with many spots and blotches of a darker, richer brown.

In the mid-1800s, the clapper rail was so common in New Jersey that collecting the eggs was a thriving business. No less an expert than Audubon himself tells of collecting seventy-two dozen eggs in a single day.

Incubation of the eggs requires fourteen days and is performed by both the adults.

Once the down of the newly hatched young clapper rails dries, it is a glossy jet-black. As the young grow older, they become mouse-gray and assume the plumage of the adults when they are about eight months old.

The young clappers are precocious and able to run about and swim within hours after hatching. They are soon scrambling after the parent birds through the jungle of reeds that they call home.

The clapper rails raise only one brood a year; late-nesting birds have probably had their first nest destroyed by the spring flooding.

FLIGHT: The clapper rail will not fly from the safety of its marsh unless forced to do so. It prefers to skulk in among the vegetation, where it is far safer than when it is in flight. When forced to fly by a hunter approaching on the incoming tide, the rail jumps into the air with its cupped wings beating strongly and its long legs dangling. As soon as it has cleared the nearest, tallest mass of vegetation, it drops down out of sight and starts to run again.

It is only when the clapper rail is in migration that it flies with strength and speed. On its longer flights its legs are raised up and trail behind the body, reducing air drag and helping the tail to act as a rudder.

MIGRATION: The clapper rail starts north about the end of March, arriving in my home state of New Jersey about the middle of April.

Migrating rails usually fly at night so that they are seldom seen.

However, as soon as they have taken up residence in the marshes again, their resounding calls leave no doubt as to their return.

In New Jersey, the hunting season for rails opens on the first day of September, thus making the rail the earliest legal game bird of the state. The season is set early so that New Jersey hunters get a chance to harvest some of the rails that were raised there before they all take off for the south. The fall migration usually starts about the first of October.

HABITS: The clapper rail is an adequate but not necessarily a strong swimmer. It can swim underwater and sometimes uses this route to escape detection. It sometimes stays below the surface with just its bill protruding and serving as a snorkel.

Once the clappers have established their individual breeding territories in the spring, they very soon lay out a maze of trails through the dense vegetation. When threatened or pursued, they dash up, down and across these countless trails with an ease that speaks of great familiarity, readily eluding most pursuers.

When the clapper calls from the depths of the marshes, its calls have a ventriloquistic property, so that it is all but impossible to pinpoint the bird's location.

The clapper becomes quite aggressive in the defense of its nest, and the birds are frequently seen rising up out of the grass in an attempt to drive off hawks, crows and other predators.

All the rails are subject to cyclic population changes, some of which are understood, while others are not. When the clapper rail population increases, the birds become very pugnacious because their territorial needs are being cramped. When this occurs, the clappers break up each other's nests, and the population takes an immediate drop. This occurred in New Jersey in 1959 and again in 1963. In the long run, this nest destruction is good for the species, as it is only the nests of the weaker birds that are destroyed. The next generation of clappers is therefore parented by the best breeding stock available.

FOOD: The clapper rail's diet is 96 percent animal matter and 4 percent vegetarian. Its favorite foods are shrimp, crayfish, crabs, small mollusks, aquatic beetles and insects, tadpoles and small fish. To obtain some of these foods, the clapper probes in the mud with its long beak.

When feeding on fiddler crabs, the clapper tears off the claw before swallowing the crab. Sometimes it has trouble removing the claw of a really large crab and so seeks help from its mate. With both birds pulling and twisting, the claw is torn off and the crab swallowed. As the prize is indivisible, one may well conjecture whether it goes to the original discoverer or the assistant.

The 4 percent of vegetable matter in the clapper's diet consists of the seeds of the following water plants: pondweed, bogbean, bayberry, widgeon grass, bulrush, smartweed, water milfoil, sedge, spike rush and salt grass.

LIFE SPAN: There are no longevity records available for the clapper rail, but it should have a life span of between three and five years.

ENEMIES: Flooding, caused by a normal high tide being driven in by storm winds, accounts for the greatest destruction of both the adult birds and their nests. Drought, with accompanying fire, also causes damage along the higher reaches of the salt marshes. The clapper rails are caught between the devil and the deep blue sea. If they nest high so that they are safe from flooding, they lay themselves open to fire.

The rails nesting on higher ground also suffer increased predation from raccoons, opossums, skunks, rats, and foxes, which take the eggs and the adults if possible. Snakes, turtles, fish, hawks, owls and eagles also prey on the rails. Disease, parasites and accidents take their toll.

TABLE FARE: The clapper rail is considered very good eating. It should never be skinned because then the savory juices are lost in the cooking process.

King Rail

Rallus elegans

Rail-hunting is declining in favor with many gunners because of the great expenditure of energy required for meager results and the difficulty of hiring a guide or "pusher" and his boat for such hunting.

Rails are hunted in saltwater marshes just before the peak of the incoming tide. The rising water concentrates the rails ahead of the water and also allows a boat to be used in among the marsh grass. A rail boat is a narrow, pirogue-type of craft, pointed in the bow, flat-bottomed and with a slightly turned up stern to lessen friction. The guide stands on a stern platform and pushes the boat through the flooded vegetation with a long pole. The shooter sits on a high stool fastened securely about a quarter of the boat length back from the bow.

In early fall, when the king rails are still in the freshwater marshes, hunters often string out in a row to flush the birds. If the marsh vegetation is short enough to allow them to do so, the hunters drag a fairly heavy rope stretched out between them. This flushing rope allows several men to cover a quite extensive area thoroughly.

King Rail

DESCRIPTION: The king rail is the largest rail found in North America. An adult male measures up to 19 inches in length, has a wingspan of 25 inches and weighs up to 18 ounces. The male and female are identical in appearance, although the female is slightly smaller in size and in weight than the male.

The king rail is a large, basically brown bird. Its bill is about 3 inches in length and is yellowish orange in color with a black tip. The top of the bird's head is dark brown. In front of the eye is a diagonal white stripe, and the throat also is white. The cheeks of this rail are grayish brown, while its neck, breast and the forepart of its belly are light cinnamon-brown. The back, tail and upper wing coverts are light brown, streaked with black, and have a speckled appearance because most of the feathers are edged with white. The primary wing feathers are dark brown, and when the bird is in flight a little white edging to the leading part of the wing is visible. The flanks, belly and underside of the tail are grayish brown, with from sixteen to twenty distinctive white vertical bars.

The immature king rail has a darker back, a lighter belly and no distinctive markings. It keeps this plumage until it is seven to eight

421

months of age, when it molts and acquires a plumage very similar to that of the parents.

DISTRIBUTION: The king rail is an inhabitant of freshwater marshes. It is found in saltwater marshes with the clapper rail only when forced there by the freezing up of its freshwater habitat.

In the summer the king rail can be found from the Gulf coast north to the Canadian border and from the Atlantic Ocean west to the prairie states beyond the Mississippi.

The winter cold reduces the king rail's range so that it is found only along the coastal marshes from New Jersey south to and around Florida to Old Mexico, and up the Mississippi River for perhaps 800 miles. This range shrinks or expands according to the vagaries of the weather.

COMMUNICATION: All rails are noisy birds. This perhaps leads to their undoing because they are all so furtive that if they were not heard, their presence would not be detected.

One of the king rail's most frequent calls is a loud *cluck, cluck,* a call which is easily imitated because it is similar to the sound that one makes to urge on a horse. A variation of this call sounds as *creek, creek.* When the king rail flies, it has a slightly different *cark, clark,* call, and like most of the rails, the king calls almost constantly while in flight.

The baby rails cheep or peep exactly like the young of our domestic chickens.

BREEDING AND NESTING: Little is known about the king rail's displaying prior to breeding. Like all the rails it is so furtive that it is hard to get a glimpse of the bird, let alone observe the various phases of its life.

The nesting habits of the king rail are better known because the nest is more readily visible than the bird. It is occasionally built up from the bottom of the pond, but in most instances, the king rail uses a tussock of grass, a clump of cattails or some other type of vegetation as a base to raise the nest above the shallow water. The nest is made up of pieces of dried marsh vegetation, piled up so that the top of the nest is from 6 to 18 inches above the water level. The king rail's nest is not as subject to flooding as that of the clapper rail, which is exposed to tidal flooding.

Often the nest is roofed over naturally by the plant material growing over it, or else the bird may add extra material over the top for camouflage purposes. The nest is about 8 to 10 inches in diameter at the top and has a bowl 2 to 3 inches deep.

EGGS AND YOUNG: The king rail usually lays between eight and eleven eggs to a clutch, although a larger or smaller number than this may be found. The eggs average 41 millimeters in length by 30 millimeters in diameter. They are pale in color, varying from creamy buff to olive-buff. A few fine spots of a darker brown are sprinkled about on the smooth, slightly glossy surface.

The eggs of the king rail were formerly collected and sold as food because it was claimed that they had a better flavor than domestic chicken eggs.

Both the male and female share in the incubation, which takes about twenty-one days. As the female often starts to brood before her clutch has been completely laid, the chicks hatch at various times. As they hatch, they are cared for by the male, while the female continues to sit on the remaining eggs.

The baby king rail has a glossy, jet-black coat of down and a white bill. The young are precocious and soon follow after the father bird as he leads them about in the swamp in search of food.

There is only one brood per year. Late-nesting birds are likely to be those which have had their first set of eggs destroyed.

FLIGHT: Somewhere between their fifth and sixth weeks, the young learn to fly.

The king rail flies better and more often than most of the other rails. When it feels that it can no longer escape by running and hiding, it jumps into the air and with wildly beating, cupped wings, rises up over the vegetation. If the flight is a short one, the rail's legs and feet are allowed to dangle beneath the body. On longer flights, the bird stretches out its bill, head and neck as far as they can go and extends its legs straight out behind.

This rail usually flies low, rather slowly and in a straight line. Only in migration does it fly higher and in a flock.

MIGRATION: The distances that the king rail travels in migration prove that the bird is a stronger flier than it appears to be. Some of its flights entail traveling almost 1,000 miles.

Most of the spring migrations are under way about the first to the middle of April. As the king rail is a lover of warm weather, it may delay its migration if it is a late spring or if a sudden cold front moves down.

The king rails' fall migration starts about the first of September and peaks about the middle of the month. Here again, early cold weather pushes the birds south sooner and farther than they might ordinarily choose to go. All the king rails' migrations are done at night.

HABITS: Like all rails, the king depends on its legs and its skulking ability to escape detection or danger. Although it can swim, it does not take to water as readily as its cousins, and it seldom dives beneath the surface.

Being larger than the other rails, it has longer legs and can run much faster from danger. It can also climb well, which it frequently does in the larger types of marsh vegetation. Flying is only a last resort.

FOOD: The bulk of the king rail's diet is made up of animal matter. No dietary percentages are available. Insects, beetles, grasshoppers, aquatic bugs and dragonfly and damselfly nymphs are this rail's favorite foods. It also eats spiders, snails, crayfish, slugs, leeches, tadpoles and small fish.

It eats the seeds, tubers and some grassy parts of the following plants: arrowhead, smartweed, pondweed, arrow arum, bur reed, common ragweed, bristle grass, wheat, oats, rice, bulrush, naiad, widgeon grass, bayberry and spike rush.

LIFE SPAN: No longevity records have been kept for the king rail. Its life expectancy is probably three to five years.

ENEMIES: The freshwater marshes that the king rail inhabits are much more subject to drought than the coastal saltwater marshes. Drought conditions, with attending fires, are the most destructive force. Crows, hawks, owls, eagles, snakes, turtles, alligators, raccoons, opossums, foxes, skunks, dogs, bobcats, otter, mink and weasels are all predators equipped and more than willing to prey on the king rail's eggs, its young or the adults. Disease, parasites and accidents cause further mortalities.

TABLE FARE: The king rail is highly esteemed as a table bird by the sportsman.

Common Gallinule

Gallinula chloropus

The heat-producing ability of a bird's body is exceedingly efficient. Most birds have a normal body temperature of 108°–109°. When the air temperature drops, their heart rate increases, forcing the blood through the body at a greater rate, as it picks up internal heat and carries it to the extremities to compensate for external heat loss. Its body metabolism, or ability to convert food into energy, is more than able to keep the bird warm provided it has sufficient fuel in the form of food. A bird does not migrate south in the winter because of the cold, but because of a food shortage caused by the cold.

Although I am well aware of this basic law of avian biology, I was still surprised to see a common gallinule walking along the edge of an ice-ringed pond near my home in northwestern New Jersey. Snow covered the ground and the wind rattled the dead cattail stalks. Ignoring the wintry blast, the gallinule walked along the edge of the ice, pecking at food particles in the water. Its large feet, adapted to give it support on floating vegetation, did little to give it a grip on ice.

DESCRIPTION: The adult common gallinule is a small, chicken-like bird that measures 14¾ inches in length, has a wingspan of

425

Common Gallinules

23 inches and weighs up to 14 ounces. Its most conspicuous field marks are the base of its bill and its frontal shield, both of which are a brilliant red. The eye also is red. This gallinule's head, neck, breast, belly and flanks are a deep, slaty blue. Its back and wings are dark brown, and its short, stubby tail is black on top and white underneath. When the bird is walking or swimming about, a distinctive white line can be seen running down each of its sides from the base of the neck to the tail. The legs and feet are a light, bright greenish yellow. The toes are extra long to allow this bird to distribute its body weight over the greatest area possible.

The immature gallinule has the same dark back and wings as the adult, but it has a white frontal shield and also a light brown neck, breast and flanks, with the brown tapering to a whitish belly. This immature plumage is kept until December, when the molting of the young is almost completed and they closely resemble the adults.

DISTRIBUTION: The common gallinule is a widespread bird, being found in summer throughout the eastern two-thirds of the United States, from Florida north into Ontario, and from the Atlantic Ocean to the prairie states west of the Mississippi River, wherever suitable marshlands can be found. There are also resident common gallinules along California's Pacific coast and southern California and Arizona.

In the winter the gallinule is found along the coast of North and South Carolina, Georgia, the whole of Florida and along the Gulf coast of Alabama, Mississippi, Louisiana and Texas.

COMMUNICATION: The gallinule is very vociferous and is heard much more frequently than it is seen. Secreted in the dense vegetation of the swamps and marshes, the gallinules are aware of an intruder's presence long before he is of theirs. The first indication of their whereabouts is a loud *chuck* sound. This is the gallinules' call of inquiry; they know where the intruder is but perhaps not what he is.

All the gallinules' calls are loud and coarse and cover a wide repertoire of *cluck*s, *kruck*s, *klock*s and similar sounds. During the breeding season the male calls *ticket, ticket, ticket* in a series of six to eight calls. The female with young makes a purring sound similar to that of a brooding domestic hen.

The hours just after dawn and just before sunset are the hours of peak vocalization. During the middle of the day the calls are sporadic, if heard at all, and unlike its cousins, the rails, the gallinule seldom calls at night.

BREEDING AND NESTING: Courtship begins as soon as the gallinules have settled on their individual territory. While the female feigns disinterest, the male swims toward her with his head lowered and his wings partly spread. He approaches from different angles, but when he is within a foot of her, he suddenly turns completely around and swims away with his little tail fanned out so that she can see the white underside.

If the mated pair is apart, they keep in touch with each other through an almost constant calling.

The Florida gallinule's nest is made up of pieces of cattail, flag and whatever other water plants are growing in the vicinity. The nest is based on a tussock or any other object that rises above the water level. If no suitable base can be found, the gallinules do not hesitate to build one up from the bottom of the pond. Frequently these nests will float if the water level rises. The nest may be secreted among vegetation or be built right out in the open. One universal requirement seems to be that the water be at least 12 inches deep all around the nest.

The gallinules have an inexplicable habit of building multiple nests, yet using only one. This is all the stranger because most of their nests are raised at least 12 inches above the water and involve considerable labor. The birds also build an inclined runway so that they are able to get up into the nest without flying.

EGGS AND YOUNG: The common gallinule normally lays a clutch of ten to twelve eggs. Some clutches are smaller, while others have been found with as many as sixteen or seventeen eggs. The eggs average 44 millimeters in length by 31 millimeters in diameter. The shells are smooth in texture, and the base color may vary from cinnamon- to olive-buff. The shell is speckled with small dots of a darker brown.

Unlike most birds, the gallinules begin incubation as soon as the first egg has been laid. The incubation is shared by both sexes and requires twenty-one days per egg. As the eggs are laid on consecutive days, the chicks hatch on consecutive days. Usually it is the female who finishes the incubation while the male takes care of the chicks as they hatch.

The young gallinules are precocious and are able to leave the nest in a matter of hours after their down has dried.

The chicks are covered with a hairy, black down, except for a light spot under the chin. Although their toes are not lobed or webbed, they can swim well. A sharp, thumb-like spur that develops on the leading edge of the wing is used by the chicks in clambering about among the reeds and rushes. The young are cared for until they are about one month of age, by which time they have developed sufficiently to look after themselves.

In the southern part of the gallinule's range, the female may raise two broods a year. Over the rest of the range, one brood a year is the rule.

FLIGHT: Long before the young are able to fly, they run about on the plants and vegetation, their wings outstretched or wildly flapping, the water splattering in all directions. As the wing primaries develop, the birds soon become airborne, but they always have to run to gain momentum before they can rise into the air. Even when they have the ability to fly, they are reluctant to do so, much preferring to run away from danger and to seek sanctuary in the sedges. When flying from place to place, the gallinule flies low and often circuitously because it follows the contours of the water rather than flying directly overland.

Only in migration does the gallinule fly as if it were not afraid to do so. The birds do not fly in large flocks but in a rather loose formation at an elevation of about 1,000 feet. Their flight at such times is direct and fairly swift.

MIGRATION: The spring migration north usually starts about the middle of April, peaks around the first of May and then tapers off. The gallinule does not have a great distance to cover, hence its late start and leisurely trip. As already mentioned, the birds are hardy, usually remaining on their northern breeding grounds long after most of the ducks and other water birds have departed south. Usually it is only with the October freeze-up that the gallinules start on their fall migration.

HABITS: The common gallinule is a nervous bird, quick and jerky in its actions, and seemingly in perpetual motion. It is very skittish in temperament, but at the same time secretive and elusive.

The gallinule swims well and often. Although most of its food is picked up on land or snatched from the surface of the water, it can dive beneath the surface to feed. Sometimes when it feels threatened, it dives beneath the water and surfaces again with only its head above the water, hidden from sight by the vegetation.

The gallinule leads a rather solitary existence, spending the bulk of its time alone. Even paired birds do not spend a great deal of time in each other's company.

FOOD: Ninety-six percent of the common gallinule's diet is made up of vegetable matter. Leafy water plants, grasses and rootlets form 90 percent of this, the other 6 percent consisting of plant seeds. Insects and snails make up the balance of the bird's fare. Actually, very little is known about the food habits of this species.

LIFE SPAN: The life span of a common gallinule is probably from three to five years. There appear to be no records of longevity for this bird.

ENEMIES: Although the common gallinule is exposed to a wide range of predators, the species is prolific and is holding its own numerically. The greatest threat to it, of course, comes from the draining of swamps and land-filling of marshes. Habitat destruction means eventual complete destruction of any species.

Of the natural predators, fish preying on the young birds probably rank number one. Crows, snakes and raccoons eat the eggs. Raccoons, otter, mink, hawks, eagles, owls and alligators eat the young and the adults when they can catch them.

TABLE FARE: I have never eaten a gallinule, but its flesh is said to be palatable.

Purple Gallinule

Porphyrula martinica

I was trying to photograph egrets in Everglades National Park when I saw my first purple gallinule. As I came around the corner of a marshy area a small, chicken-like bird strode daintily across the tops of the floating vegetation and disappeared into the high grass beyond. I remained motionless, and in a few minutes the bird reappeared. So intent was it on the insects that it was snapping up that it did not see me, although I remained in plain sight. It was certainly one of the most gaudy birds I had ever seen, a living rainbow as colorful as any bird the tropics could boast of.

DESCRIPTION: The tip of the purple gallinule's beak is yellow, the base of its beak and its eye are bright red, its frontal shield is pure white. The head, throat and breast are, as its name suggests, deep purple. The back of the bird's neck, and its flanks and belly are a light, bright blue-purple. It has a green back, greenish brown wings, a darker brown top of the tail and pure white underparts. Its legs and feet are a bright greenish yellow. An adult purple gallinule is about 15 inches in length, has a wingspan of approximately 24 inches and weighs about 14 ounces.

Purple Gallinule

The immature purple gallinule has a brown bill and frontal shield. Its throat is whitish, its face, cheeks and breast are buff colored, and the crown of the head, the back of the neck and back are a darker brown. The young purple gallinule lacks the white side line of the young common gallinule. Its flanks are buff, grading to white on the belly. Although the young birds do not achieve their full adult plumage until the following spring, they closely resemble the adults by December.

DISTRIBUTION: The purple gallinule has a restricted range. It is by no means as widespread or as common as its cousin, the common gallinule.

On its summer breeding range, the purple gallinule is found from the Mississippi River north as far as Tennessee, east to North Carolina, down to the tip of Florida and west again to Texas. In the winter, it is found in the Gulf portion of Louisiana, Mississippi and Alabama and throughout Florida.

COMMUNICATION: Like its cousin the common gallinule, the purple gallinule announces its presence to the world with a variety of loud *chuck*s, clucks and gurgles. The marsh areas that it inhabits often sport such rank vegetation that the bird remains unseen.

When the purple gallinule flies, which it does as seldom as possible, it makes a cackling *keck, keck, keck* sound. The bird that I first saw was making a guttural *puck* sound as if it were talking to itself.

BREEDING AND NESTING: April ushers in the breeding season for the purple gallinule. Certainly no female ever had a more resplendently attired male to pay her court. And yet she does not seem to be unduly impressed. In fact, often while the male is swimming about in the open water displaying his gorgeous colors, the female remains hidden in the vegetation along the shoreline.

Instead of swimming with his body on an even keel, the male bends forward, partially submerging his breast, an action which elevates the rear portion of his body so that the white underside of his tail may more easily be seen. The white of the tail seems, inexplicably, to be a greater stimulant to the female than the gorgeous red, green or purple of the other parts of the male's body.

The purple gallinule usually builds a floating nest and shows a preference for a plant called wampee. This plant grows in water 1 to 2 feet deep and has long, erect, spearhead-like leaves. The gallinule builds its nest out of wampee leaves and stalks and then fastens the floating mass to living wampee plants. Unlike so much swamp vegetation, this plant does not grow in masses, but with a distance of at least a foot between each plant. Thus, the nests of the purple gallinule are easily seen and are therefore probably extra vulnerable to predation by crows. The purple gallinule builds multiple nests, starting a number of them and then using only one. This habit may stem from indecision on the part of the female or from an attempt to confuse predators as to the location of the nest actually being used.

Occasionally the nest is flooded if an exceptionally high tide comes in. The nest floats as high as the vegetation to which it is fastened allows. When it can float no higher, it may be inundated and the eggs ruined.

EGGS AND YOUNG: The purple gallinule's clutch usually consists of six to eight eggs, with some clutches falling slightly above or below that norm. The eggs average 39 millimeters in length and 28 millimeters in diameter. The eggs are very attractive, their pale pinkish-brown base color being spattered with fine dots of contrasting reddish brown. The shells are smooth and strong.

Both the male and female share in the task of incubation, which takes about twenty-one days. Occasionally both the birds are off the nest for a short time, and it is at such moments that crow predation is most apt to occur.

The newly hatched young are covered with a shiny, black down with which the little yellow bill contrasts sharply. Within hours after hatching, the young can clamber out of the nest and swim about. In climbing, they use their wings as well as their feet. Although they lack the claws on the wing of the South American hoatzin, their wings are a most useful appendage for climbing.

The young are carefully tended by the parents until they are about a month old. During the last two weeks of this period the primary feathers develop, and the young learn to fly.

FLIGHT: The purple gallinule does not fly unless it is forced to. It prefers to seek sanctuary among the reeds and rushes of the marshland. If flushed, it runs along the surface of the water, strenuously flapping its wings, and then finally becomes airborne. When in the air, it does not streamline its body by lifting its feet. With legs dangling, it flutters over the top of the nearest vegetation, only to plop down again a few yards farther on as though exhausted by the exertion. But now it is hidden from sight, and further flight is not really needed.

Only when migrating does the purple gallinule fly with a strong wing beat and at a height of approximately 1,000 feet.

MIGRATION: All birds are subject to erratic flights, so that they may show up on rare bird lists in very farflung places. The purple gallinule has been recorded in Quebec and Ontario, Canada, and Arizona, but these are not the places to look for it. Sightings in such places are most unusual and result from the birds being blown ahead of a hurricane or storm.

Under normal conditions the purple gallinules seldom have to travel more than about 600 to 800 miles, and most of them migrate much shorter distances. Usually they travel in a series of very short hops from one marsh to the next, slowly working their way north as the season advances.

HABITS: The gallinule's usual mode of locomotion is to walk from place to place. Its apparent dislike for flying has already been described. The bird swims well even though its feet are neither lobed nor webbed. It can swim either on the surface or underwater. Some feeding is done by diving, although this is not the general practice.

When walking about the gallinule looks like a small chicken, its head bobbing back and forth at each step. This motion is to keep the body weight over a central fulcrum so that the bird does not lose its balance. While swimming, the gallinule moves its head forward with each forward stroke of the feet.

FOOD: The purple gallinule's diet contains a much higher percentage of animal matter than that of the common gallinule. According to the season, animal matter ranges as high as 65 percent in the spring, 29 percent in summer, 17 percent in the fall and about 6 percent in winter. Mollusks, spiders, caterpillars, aquatic bugs and beetles, flies and the nymphs of dragonflies and damselflies are the foods most commonly eaten, although an occasional small fish or tadpole is also taken.

The purple gallinule is very commonly found in the huge rice fields of the southeastern states. Here the bird is considered a pest because it not only eats the fallen grain but also pulls down the ripening grain and eats it. In addition to rice, it eats windmill grass, paspalum, duckweed, wild millet, signal grass, spike rush, sawgrass, Bermuda grass, panic grass, widgeon grass, giant cutgrass and water lily.

LIFE SPAN: No longevity records are available for the purple gallinule. Its potential life span can be estimated as ranging from three to five years.

ENEMIES: Crows and snakes probably take the greatest toll by eating the purple gallinule eggs. Fish and turtles undoubtedly take many young gallinules while they are still small enough to eat and incapable of flying away. Raccoons, otter, mink, skunks, alligators, hawks, owls and eagles all prey on the gallinule in various stages and at various times. Disease, parasites and accidents take their toll.

TABLE FARE: The purple gallinule is not as highly esteemed as a table bird as the common gallinule, probably because of the higher incidence of animal matter in its diet, but it is nonetheless avidly hunted and eaten.

American Coot

Fulica americana

A friend of mine, Helen Ward Gall, feeds a fantastic number of ducks, geese and swans at her home at North Point on Pine Lake. She is the only person that I know who has made pets of American coots, which she feeds by the dozens each day. She somehow discovered that alfalfa hay could be used as a substitute for the water plants that the coots ordinarily feed on.

Each morning the coots leave the open water of the lake and march up the bank and across the lawn to feed on her patio. It is a most unusual occurrence just to see coots walking about on dry land. They are awkward walkers because of their large, lobed toes that look like oversized clown shoes.

The coots don't care for the heavier alfalfa stalks; they are primarily interested in the leaves, which they strip off very methodically. After feeding, most of the birds march back to the lake, but some remain behind to doze in the sunshine, protected from the wind by the house.

DESCRIPTION: The American coot is one of the easiest of all birds to identify. It is the only bird in the United States that has a

American Coot

white bill and frontal shield. There is a small dark ring near the tip of the bill. The coot's head, neck, and breast are black. The rest of the body and the wings are dark gray or slate-blue. The outer under tail coverts are white, as are the edges of the wing secondaries. The coot is a small, chicken-like bird that has the chicken's habit of jerking its head back and forth with each step or paddling stroke. It has a total length of 16 inches, a wingspan of 28 inches and weighs about 22 ounces. It has long, greenish legs and long, lobed toes. The latter are designed to allow the bird to walk on the vegetation that is floating on top of the water. The lobes also provide a large surface area and therefore efficient propulsion when the bird is swimming.

DISTRIBUTION: The coot is plentiful throughout the United States. Its breeding range extends from British Columbia east to Quebec, south to Texas, west to California and north again to British Columbia. Few of the coots nest east of the Mississippi River.

The coot's wintering range is decided by the weather. They are hardy birds, and many of them stay as far north as the climate and icing conditions permit. Although some migrate to the southern United States and down into Mexico and Central America, both these areas also have large, year-round resident coot populations.

COMMUNICATION: Coots are very noisy birds and are often heard long before they are seen. This is particularly true if the birds are walking among the tall reeds and grasses that grow in the areas they inhabit. Their *cuck, cuck, cuck, cuck* call is probably the one most frequently heard. They also make a higher pitched *squack* call that is quite duck-like, as well as a low-pitched, hoarse, guttural call. Yet another call, often heard at night, is *coo, coo, coo, coo.*

BREEDING AND NESTING: The American coot is a most pugnacious bird during the breeding season. The birds are often paired by the time they reach the breeding grounds. The nesting area is selected by the male, who then patrols the chosen piece of shoreline, engaging any rival coot in battle. He also attempts to drive away whatever grebes or ducks happen to come by.

When the coots fight, they charge at each other, swimming as hard as they can, their necks held low and extended in front of them. Both males jab at each other with their sharp, stout bills, each trying to grab the other's head. When the battle is actually joined the coots, holding fast to each other with their bills, lie sideways on the water and bring their feet into play. Each tries to rake the other with his long, sharp claws. Sometimes the coots lock their feet together in a tight hold and fight again with their bills. Usually one male finally admits defeat and is driven from the area, although on occasions one male kills the other.

To display for the female, the male extends his head and neck out over the water and swims slowly toward the female. When he gets close to her, he turns around and, with his wings and tail elevated, swims slowly away from her again. By so doing, he presents to her his very white rump patch, which is a sexual stimulant. If she has accepted him, she follows after him. The female and male then engage in mutual preening, using their bills to caress each other's feathers. The female then assumes a prone position on the water, and copulation takes place.

The coot's nest is usually a floating construction built of whatever material is at hand, such as various rushes, weeds and water plants. The nest is well hidden from sight among, and fastened to, the tall marsh plants of the region. It may be from 12 to 18 inches in diameter and mounded up as much as 7 or 8 inches above the water level. If the nests were not fastened to plant stalks, they would undoubtedly float away. The lining of the nest is made of fine plant material, to which no down is added.

EGGS AND YOUNG: The coot's clutch may contain from six to ten eggs, eight being the number most commonly found. The eggs are a buff color, heavily spotted with dark brown. In size they average 49 millimeters in length by 33 millimeters in diameter.

Incubation takes twenty-one or twenty-two days, and the task is shared by the male and female. When the female is on the nest, the male stands guard and tries to drive off or divert anything that approaches.

The coot, like some of the grebes, starts to incubate the eggs before the entire clutch is laid, so that the young hatch at different times. Then, while one parent, usually the female, continues to incubate the remaining eggs, the other cares for the young that have already hatched. These young leave the nest as they hatch, and the male shepherds them about as they feed and broods them when they need warmth.

The young coot is black with the exception of its head, throat and bill, which vary in color from light orange to bright red.

The young grow very fast, but the body and wings do not grow as fast as the feet and legs. This is to be expected because the adult coot depends on its legs and feet to swim away from danger rather than on its wings to fly away.

FLIGHT: It is at least sixty days before the young coots are able to fly. Coots are in the habit of flapping their wings, mainly to help buoy up their body, as they "spatter" over the surface of the water. They run on the water for long distances and then dive beneath the surface; they do almost anything to avoid having to fly.

When the coots do take to the air, they have a strong wing beat and fly well. The neck and head are extended forward, and their feet trail out behind. Because the tail is so short, it is ineffective as a rudder, and the coots use their feet for steering. I have never seen coots fly higher than about 5 or 6 feet above the water, but during migration they fly at a considerable altitude.

MIGRATION: Coots habitually mass in large flocks on their wintering grounds and also migrate in large flocks. Their northward migration gets under way about the first of March, and the birds are usually on their breeding grounds by the last part of April. The fall migration starts about the first of October and continues until the end of November. Many of the birds go south only when forced to do so by the freezing up of the northern lakes and sloughs.

HABITS: Except during the breeding season, the coot is a sociable bird and mixes well with the wild ducks. It is often referred to as "the clown of the pond" because of its constant calling and general activity. The birds are usually skittering over the water, diving for food or just swimming about. They are strong swimmers and expert divers, usually going underwater with a loud plop.

As winter progresses, the coot concentrations increase in size until the water in some areas is blackened with them.

Coots are not wary birds nor really very sporting birds because of their reluctance to fly. Most of the coots that are shot are bagged while they are on the water.

FOOD: The coot feeds primarily on vegetation, most of which it gathers on the surface of the water. It can dive for its food and often steals it from another coot or from diving ducks that surface with fronds of food trailing from their beaks.

Some of its favorite foods are naiad, pondweed, bulrush, wild rice, duckweed, widgeon grass, musk grass, algae, coontail, waterweed, wild celery and spike rush. It also eats some animal matter such as aquatic beetles and bugs, small fish, tadpoles, snails and worms.

LIFE SPAN: The coot probably has a potential life span of about seven or eight years, but there appear to be no band records of longevity for this bird.

ENEMIES: The coot is plagued by the same enemies as the ducks because it lives in the same habitat and under the same conditions. Raccoons, mink, otter, turtles, hawks, owls, and eagles are among its many wild enemies. Hawks and eagles hunt the coots by swooping down on them, forcing them to dive underwater. The aerial predators then fly over the submerged bird and force it under again when it surfaces. This tactic is continued until the coot is exhausted and has to come up for air, when it is snatched from the water and quickly dispatched.

TABLE FARE: Although the coot is hunted, it is not considered desirable as food by most sportsmen.

Woodcock

Philohela minor

Like the birds they pursue, woodcock hunters are a breed apart. A good friend of mine, who shall remain nameless, is a prime example. In autumn it is almost impossible to get in contact with him because he is up in New Hampshire, Vermont, Maine or over the border in New Brunswick hunting woodcock. This fellow was part owner of a large chemical plant that was about to merge with an even larger chemical company. After much negotiation, all was in readiness for the papers to be signed and the deal consummated. But my friend suddenly announced that he couldn't possibly be there on the appointed day, or even any time that week. When pressed for an answer he admitted that he would be up in New Brunswick during that period hunting woodcock. All that the incredulous banker who headed the group could say was, "What the hell is a woodcock?"

DESCRIPTION: The woodcock is one of the most ridiculous looking birds imaginable. Its large, protruding eyes are set farther back on its head than those of any other bird. Thus placed, they can watch for danger while the woodcock is feeding. The woodcock's bill is 2½ to 3 inches in length and has a flexible tip. This

Woodcock

long bill is used for probing in soft earth for earthworms, which make up the bulk of the bird's diet. The woodcock is a chunky-bodied bird, the male weighing up to 6 ounces and the female up to 8 ounces. Checking over the measurements of a bird I took last fall, I found that it had a 19-inch wingspan and was 11 inches in length from bill tip to tail tip. The wings are broad and strongly cupped. The basic coloring of the woodcock is a buffy brown, the breast and belly being almost unmarked, while the back is heavily splotched with brown, black and white.

DISTRIBUTION: The woodcock is a bird of the eastern half of the United States. Its western range covers the states bordering the west bank of the Mississippi River. It breeds from southern Manitoba to New Brunswick, Canada, south to New Jersey, and west to Missouri. The bird winters in the Gulf states. Its general range is not shrinking, although its localized habitat is being destroyed by constantly expanding urban development.

COMMUNICATION: The woodcock is usually a very silent bird. Authorities differ as to the source of the twittering sound that it makes as it flushes. Some claim that the sound is made vocally, others believe that it is made by the beating wings, but there is no conclusive proof for either theory. The woodcock also makes a sort of chirping vocal sound when flushed. However, its most distinctive sounds are made during the courtship display while the bird is on its "singing" ground.

BREEDING AND NESTING: By the first or second week in April the woodcock is in its nesting areas. Each evening the male performs for the female. Those I have watched usually started their performance punctually at 7:10 p.m. and kept it up for almost half an hour. The singing ground is always a clearing about 25 feet square, in the middle of the woods, on an old wood road, or along the edge of woods.

The male suddenly flies into the center of the clearing, to stand there most solemnly with his bill resting on his chest. Suddenly he springs into the air and begins a spiraling ascent until he is 200 to 300 feet above the earth. The twittering sound can easily be heard as the bird climbs skyward. Then the woodcock peaks and makes a musical calling as he flutters down to the earth to land within a short distance of where he had taken off. On the ground he makes a "peenting" call that sounds like a buzzy, raspy

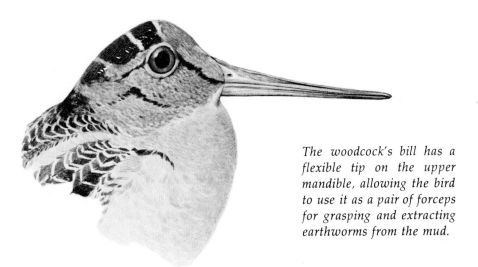

The woodcock's bill has a flexible tip on the upper mandible, allowing the bird to use it as a pair of forceps for grasping and extracting earthworms from the mud.

"Bronx cheer." Each flight lasts about one minute, and the bird makes a flight about once every five minutes.

At some time during this display the female usually sneaks out into the clearing, where copulation takes place at once. As quietly and quickly as she came, the female retires to her nearby nest, and the male continues the rest of his performance.

The woodcock's nest is a mere depression in the leaves. It may be situated in the drier portion of a swamp or in an alder or birch thicket, but it is almost always in close proximity to water. The nest may be near a concealing clump of grass or else right out in the open. Concealment is not really important because the female's protective coloration is so perfect that it is almost impossible to see her on her nest.

A brooding female woodcock is fearless and will even allow herself to be stroked as she sits on her eggs. There are records of a female woodcock, her nest and some of the surrounding earth being dug up, placed in a box and carried to a studio. Here pictures were taken, and everything was returned to its original location —all this without the female leaving the nest.

On the occasions when I have flushed a female woodcock from her nest, she never remained off for more than ten to twelve minutes. She fed a little or flew off for a drink and then returned to her duties.

EGGS AND YOUNG: Four eggs would seem to be the rule for a woodcock's clutch. The eggs are well pointed to prevent their rolling and are always placed with the pointed tip in the center of the nest. The eggs, like the female, are masterpieces of camouflage. The base color is a buffy brown with a splashing of reddish brown blotches over the large end of the egg. The eggs average 45 millimeters in length by 32 millimeters in diameter. Both the male and female share in the incubation, which takes about three weeks.

The young woodcock are precocious and leave the nest as soon as their down dries off. Even with their down fluffed out they are only about the size of a golf ball and like their parents, they have a camouflage pattern. I found four baby woodcock only a few hours old that had moved several feet from their nest. When the mother flew off, the chicks played dead. Even though I touched them lightly with a twig, they lay upside down and motionless. After taking a few photos I went to get a friend who had never seen baby woodcock, but when we came back ten minutes later the babies were not to be found. Either they were hiding a short distance away or else the parent woodcock had carried them off. Adult woodcock carry their young between their legs or in their beaks. They have even been known to move their eggs by carrying them in their beaks when their nest had been consistently disturbed.

FLIGHT: Although baby woodcock are precocious, their wing primaries develop more slowly than those of the ruffed grouse chicks, and it is probably a week or more before they can flutter off the ground.

Adult woodcock fly more slowly than adult ruffed grouse. They could have been the prototype for our new vertical takeoff airplanes. Both the grouse and the woodcock frequent the same type of dense alder and birch thickets, but while the grouse zooms off horizontally, the woodcock is more apt to "tower" vertically. After clearing the tree tops, it flies horizontally. A grouse usually flies out of sight when flushed, whereas the woodcock flies only 200 to 300 feet before alighting and can be flushed again and again. The woodcock often flies with its tail fanned out and pointing downward. This action is similar to that of the foils on an airplane's wing and definitely slows the bird's flight.

MIGRATION: The woodcock migrates at night and singly, but in good years there is an almost continuous stream of the birds. It usually arrives in New Jersey in the latter part of February on its journey north. The fall migration starts in the latter part of

September and hits its peak in the middle of October. One day the coverts are bare, and the next day and thereafter until freeze-up, the woodcock are there. During migration the bird's flight is much swifter than it is under normal conditions. In its faster flight, the woodcock flies with its bill pointing toward the ground.

HABITS: The woodcock not only migrates at night, it prefers to carry out almost all its activities under cover of darkness. Twilight and first dawn are its moments of peak activity. During the daytime the woodcock may frequent higher, drier woodlands or fields, but it begins to feed as the light fades.

FOOD: The woodcock's long beak is used as a probe to extract worms from beneath the soil. This habit has earned it the localized name of bog sucker. It is not known how the woodcock detects worms. Maybe it uses a trial and error method, or perhaps it hears the earthworm burrowing as the robin does. While earthworms make up the bulk of its diet, it also feeds on ants, grubs and insect larvae.

LIFE SPAN: The woodcock has a potential life span of about five years, but a bird that survives two years can be considered fortunate.

SIGN: The common sign of woodcock is the very conspicuous "whitewash" splashing of its excrement. These splashes are usually 2 inches or more in diameter, and their profusion proves that there is no such thing as a constipated woodcock.

In feeding, the woodcock punches its bill into the ground, and twenty or more of these borings are often to be found in 1 square foot of soft soil. The bore holes are not round because the bird's bill is not round. The mark left by the ridge on top of the beak is clearly visible. Along the side of brooks the woodcock often feeds in areas that would seem to be too wet for earthworms.

ENEMIES: Like many of the ground-nesting birds, the woodcock is subject to the predation of skunks, weasels, raccoons, opossums, foxes, bobcats, lynxes, house cats and dogs, snakes, wood hawks and owls. The woodcock's greatest enemy is frost. When the freeze-up occurs in the north, it merely determines the time of the autumn migration. The damage to the species is done when the freeze-up occurs in the south ahead of the migration, and today many snowstorms hit first in the south and work their way north. When snow blankets the land, the woodcock is hard put to it to find food, and widespread starvation may occur.

TABLE FARE: Although the woodcock is a small bird, its flesh is considered a delicacy. The flight birds in autumn are fat. In the autumn of 1970, this fat was the cause of great concern. In some sections of Canada the birds had picked up abnormally high amounts of DDT which had been sprayed on the forests. The DDT was concentrated in the fat, so that the birds were considered safe to eat if every vestige of fat was removed. With the banning of DDT on an ever increasing scale, that problem should not arise again.

Common Snipe

Capella gallinago

About a quarter of a mile below my home is a little pond where the water is never more than 18 inches deep yet never quite dries up in the summer. Tall, thick sedges line the lower banks, with stands of alder and birches higher up. In the fall, usually at least one common snipe can be found in this spot.

No longer are great flights of snipe to be seen, no longer is the "winnowing" of their wings heard above the sound of the wind. Accounts of such large concentrations are still common, however, in the records of the late 1800s and early 1900s. James J. Pringle, in 1899, wrote of his shooting experiences with snipe in Louisiana. From 1867 to 1897, he shot a grand total of 78,602 common snipe. On his best single day, December 11, 1877, he shot 366 snipe in six hours. The winter of 1874–75, when he took 6,615 snipe, was his best season. Pringle often said that the snipe was such a migrant that a snipe missed was a snipe he would never get another shot at, so he killed every one he saw.

Other men helped in the slaughter but did not keep such accurate records. It was such constant hunting pressure that pushed the snipe down the road toward extinction. Fortunately, the com-

Common Snipe

mon snipe is no longer in any such danger, although it will probably never regain its former numbers.

DESCRIPTION: The common snipe's most prominent identification feature is its bill, which is about 3 inches in length. The upper mandible is flexible, the forward third bending upward so that food can be grasped as though in a pair of forceps. The bill is flesh-colored except for its dark, bulbous-looking tip.

The adult male common snipe is 11¾ inches long, has a wingspan of 20 inches and weighs about 5 ounces. The basic color of the bird's upper body is light brown, buff and black overlaid with white streaks and stripes. The stripes start at the base of the bill and extend over the crown and face to the tail. The throat, breast, belly and flanks are white. The breast has many rows of dark spots, while the flanks have dark bars. The upper tail is a bright rusty red with a black stripe and a white edge. The red shows when the bird flies. The legs and feet are a greenish color.

The female is only slightly smaller than the male and is identical in color.

DISTRIBUTION: The common snipe, which was formerly known as the Wilson's snipe, is found throughout North America. Its numbers, as already mentioned, have been greatly reduced, but the bird is still common over most of its range. Its wintering range lies roughly below a line drawn from the state of Virginia across to California and runs south as far as South America. Its breeding range extends roughly north of the same line, including Alaska and most of Canada, except for the Arctic regions north of Hudson's Bay.

COMMUNICATION: Today, April 14, 1972, as I trudged out into a swamp to photograph a Canada goose on her nest, I flushed three common snipe. As the birds flew off, they all made a very raspy, buzzy *scaipe* or *scape* call. This is probably the best known call of the common snipe because it is made by both sexes at all times of the year, whenever they are flushed. The call seems to be automatically given every time the snipe flies.

Much has been written about the winnowing sound of the common snipe's wings and the sound made by the bird's flight during its courtship display, but these are not vocal sounds. The snipe does, however, make many vocal sounds.

When the bird is disturbed, it has the habit—typical of the shore birds, particularly the yellowlegs—of sitting on the very top of a tree or bush and uttering an alarmed *kep, kep, kep, kep, kep*. It keeps up this call for long periods of time.

During the breeding season, the common snipe has several calls that can be described as *wheat, wheat, wheat, wheat* and *whuck, whuck, whuck, whuck*. The first call is a loud, clear whistle, while the other is much lower toned. These calls are given in either a four- or five-note series. Another call is given while the bird is flying low over the ground, each note seeming to be wrenched from its body. This call sounds either *yack, yack, yack, yack* or *yuck, yuck, yuck, yuck*, and the bird's body and wings twitch with each call.

A call that seems to be used by only the female is a stuttering *okee, okee, okee*, in response to the male's "wind song."

BREEDING AND NESTING: To attract and display for the female, the male common snipe flies up to a height of about 500 feet and then describes a large circle with a series of swoops and climbs. The bird slowly flaps its wings as it flies, then partially closes them and plummets into a dive. The widely fanned tail feathers vibrate as the air rushes through them, producing a whirring, winnowing sound. As the bird climbs back up to its original elevation, the wings produce pulsing *who, who, who, who, who* notes. At this time the male often gives out the vocal love calls already described.

Then the bird dives toward the earth like a plane out of control. At the last moment, it rights itself and, with wings reaching high over its back, appears to alight, although its feet do not touch the ground. It flies up into the air again and again appears to land, giving the impression of a ballet leap. It is now that the female's *okee* call is most often heard, probably signifying her approval.

The common snipe prefers a wetter, more swampy breeding area than the woodcock. Its nest is usually built in a tangle of grass and is not easy to locate. The clump or tussock of grass is often completely surrounded by deep water, so that the nest is protected from many predators. The snipe frequently adds grass above the nest to roof it over and provide extra camouflage. The bowl of the nest is about 4 inches across and is well constructed of interwoven local grasses.

EGGS AND YOUNG: Like most of the shore birds, the common snipe normally lays a clutch containing four eggs. These average 38 millimeters in length by 28 millimeters in diameter. Their pyriform shape prevents them from rolling, the narrow tips being pointed in to the center of the nest. The eggs are usually an olivaceous buff color, heavily spotted and blotched with dark brown.

The incubation of the eggs requires eighteen to twenty days and is done by both the adults.

The young, when they first hatch, are as blotched and spotted as their eggshells had been, a patterning that provides excellent camouflage. The female snipe is a most devoted mother and does her best to decoy danger away from her young. Like a mother killdeer, the mother snipe lies on her side, usually on the underwing, and flops around as if she had been mortally wounded. Her act is so convincing that one has to look at her, even knowing it is just a trick. And in the twinkling that that look requires, the young snipe secrete themselves under the vegetation. Both the adults care for the young, but the male usually leaves the decoy trick to the female while he calls from a treetop.

The young feed on anything small that is shiny or mobile. Bright objects, because of their resemblance to shiny beetle shells, naturally attract all precocious chicks.

FLIGHT: The chicks' primary wing feathers develop rapidly, and within eight days the young birds can make short flights of a few feet to a number of yards. After two weeks, they are capable of strong flight.

The common snipe has the long, strong, sharply-tapering wings that are typical of long-distance fliers. When flushed, the bird has a very twisting, erratic flight, zigzagging from side to side, rising high, then dropping down to skim the earth, only to rise again. If the snipe is unhurried, it flaps its wings casually in flight. When it is frightened, its wing beats are steady and it can reach speeds of 45 miles per hour and sometimes more. One of the reasons why the common snipe ranks so high as a game bird is its elusive flight.

In migration the snip travel in small flocks at 500 to 600 feet above the ground. At other times, they fly just high enough to clear the tips of the vegetation in the area.

MIGRATION: The common snipe travels many thousands of miles in migration each year. The exact distance depends upon where it spends the winter and where it nests in the summer. If it winters in South America and nests in Alaska, the round trip entails a flight of 12,000 to 15,000 miles per year.

The spring migration is usually under way by the first of March, although it is usually April before the snipe pass through my home state of New Jersey in any numbers. Most of them are on their breeding grounds in the north by the middle of May and depart from these grounds in September.

HABITS: The common snipe swims well and can dive, although it rarely does so. There are several records of mortally wounded snipe diving underwater, grasping a piece of submerged vegetation in their beak to serve as an anchor, and then dying there.

The common snipe is rather hard to flush. It allows a very close approach before it takes to the air because it instinctively knows that its coloration protects it from being detected. As the bird is essentially a loner, even if other snipe are in the immediate vicinity, it flushes alone and not as part of a covey, Even when a number of snip are flushed simultaneously, they usually fly off in different directions. If the area is fairly open, the snipe may elect to run rather than fly from approaching danger. When traveling from one area to another, the snipe usually flies at night.

The snipe's long bill is used to probe in the soft mud of marshes, swamps and coastal areas. It feeds in wetter areas than the woodcock but exactly like this bird, plunging its bill into the earth up to its eyes. The snipe is a very active feeder, thrusting its bill into the ground an average of about six times per minute. Usually the holes are about 2 inches apart, so that by the time the bird has worked on an area for a few minutes, it looks as though it had been peppered with a scatter-gun. It is difficult to establish whether the bird uses a suction method to feed or whether it swallows its food as the bill rises for another thrust.

FOOD: Eighty percent of the common snipe's diet is made up of animal matter. Its main foods are earthworms, snails, fly larvae, aquatic beetles, dragonfly nymphs, crustaceans, grasshoppers, locusts and mosquito larvae. Its most common plant foods are the seeds of smartweed, bulrush, panic grass, bur reed, bristle grass, ragweed and pondweed.

LIFE SPAN: The common snipe should have a potential life span of about four years, but no longevity records for the species are forthcoming.

ENEMIES: Only the faster hawks and falcons can catch a common snipe because of the bird's erratic flight. Raccoons, crows and ravens take the eggs, while northern gulls and jaegers are among the predators that take the chicks. Predation, however, is not a controlling factor as far as the common snipe's population is concerned.

TABLE FARE: The common snipe is considered an excellent food, but because of the bird's small size it takes a large number of them to make a meal.

Nuisance Birds

Order
Passeriformes
and
Strigiformes

Common Crow (*Corvus brachyrhynchos*)

Starling (*Sturnus vulgaris*)

Black-billed Magpie (*Pica pica*)

Great Horned Owl (*Bubo virginianus*)

Introduction

Three birds in this section — the crow, magpie, and starling —
belong to the largest order of birds, the Passeriformes. The crow
and magpie are two members of the Corvidae family that are
native to North America. The starling was imported into North
America from the Old World. It is one of the one hundred and
three members of the Sturnidae family.

The great horned owl is one of the one hundred and
twenty-three members of the Strigidae family found throughout
the world in the Strigiformes order of birds.

Common Crow

Corvus brachyrhynchos

Henry Ward Beecher once said, "If men were birds, few would be smart enough to be crows." The crow is the most intelligent bird in North America, as anyone who has ever tried to hunt it will agree. The conflict between man and crows goes back to the days of the American colonists, and its outcome can only be called a draw.

The conflict stems from the crow's opportunism, which has enabled it to survive over almost all its original range despite the pressures of civilization. The crow is not an unmitigated villain, however. It is true that in the spring it pulls up grain sprouting in the farmer's field and eats birds' eggs, nestlings and baby animals. Studies have shown that it is responsible for at least 4½ percent of the nest depredation suffered by ruffed grouse in the forest and by blue-winged teal on the prairies. In New Jersey, the crow, through its nest destruction, is definitely a limiting factor to the mallard duck's nesting success. However, the crow also plays an important role as a scavenger and consumes vast tonnages of insects.

DESCRIPTION: There are three species of crows, the common crow being the largest with a total length of 19 to 20 inches, a wingspan of up to 38 inches, a bill length of 2½ inches and a weight of up to 20 ounces. The fish crow is rather smaller, measuring about 16 inches in length, with a wingspan of 35 inches and a weight of about 1 pound. The northwestern crow is slightly smaller and thinner than the fish crow. The crow's iridescent black plumage is a well-known feature. Albinism is a rather common occurrence in crows, and of course such white birds are very conspicuous among their black counterparts.

DISTRIBUTION: The common crow is found across most of North America, and its range extends almost up to the Arctic. Although it is restricted by the lack of trees in the prairie and arid areas of our country, it resides in every one of the forty-eight contiguous states. Its range overlaps with that of the fish crow, which is found along the eastern coastal regions of the United States from Massachusetts south to Texas and up the lower Mississippi Valley. The common crow also overlaps the range of the northwestern crow along the west coast from Washington north to the Yukon. Along Alaska's south coast the northwestern crow is the only species found.

COMMUNICATION: The cawing of a crow is probably the most distinctive and widely known bird call in North America. There is a wide range in the inflections of the call and in the number or sequence of the calls in each series. The northwestern crow has the lowest pitched and hoarsest call of the three species. The fish crow's range is somewhat higher, and its call is often confused with that of the young common crow. Probably the best known call is the single, sharp, short "caw" that is used as an alarm signal.

The crow is also an imitator and has a wide repertoire of non-crow sounds. Its Asiatic relative, the Indian hill myna bird, is famed throughout the world for its ability to imitate human speech. The crow can also be taught to talk, and without the barbaric practice of slitting its tongue.

BREEDING AND NESTING: Crows apparently mate for only one season, although they have been known to return to the same nest three seasons in succession. The flocks begin to break up in mid-March, and fights between rival males are common at this time. Taking advantage of the capricious March winds, the male crow does elaborate, erratic courtship flights in an effort to impress the female. He also takes up a position near the female, perhaps on the same tree limb, puffs out his feathers, lowers his wings and tail and while bowing to her, makes a rattling sound in his throat. If the female accepts his advances, copulation takes place then and there, and nest-building is then started.

Although the female does the bulk of the work, both sexes gather material for the nest. Where evergreen trees are common they are the preferred nest sites, but in other areas deciduous trees, particularly oaks, are used. Although there are exceptions, most of the nests are high above the ground. While rearing its young the crow makes as little noise as possible so as not to call attention to itself or to its nest.

The nest is a bulky affair and appears crudely made on the outside. It is about 22 inches across and 9 inches deep, the actual basin being about 12 inches in diameter by 4 inches deep. Twigs and sticks comprise the bulk of the material, but almost anything else may be used, too. The inside of the nest is always neatly and softly lined with shredded bark, usually cedar or grapevine. In my area, every nest I have seen had large quantities of deer hair in the lining.

EGGS AND YOUNG: Within a matter of days after the nest is completed, the female starts to lay the four to six eggs that make up the clutch. The eggs average about 32 millimeters in length by something over 25 millimeters in diameter. They are usually a bluish or olive green with heavy brown markings or gray spots and splotches. Both parents participate in the incubation of the eggs, a chore that requires eighteen days.

When the young first hatch, their pink skin color is clearly seen because of the lack of body covering. Their eyes open after about five days, and they take on a bluish-gray cast as the tips of their feathers begin to protrude through the skin. At ten days of age the young start to clamor loudly for food, and their vociferousness may cause the nest to be raided by some enemy. They cannot fly at one month but are capable of hopping about and often climb out of the nest to sit on the branches nearby. At this stage they are clothed in the somber black garb of the adults, although traces of their natal down are still visible.

FLIGHT: At five weeks of age the young crow, who has been testing out its wings by fluttering them rapidly while holding onto the nest, is ready to embark on its first aerial adventure. This period is one of great excitement for all mother birds and can only be likened to the coming-out party of our human debutantes.

The crow is a strong flier and does very little soaring unless it is particularly windy or there are exceptional thermals rising. Its average flight speed is 20 to 30 miles per hour, but when eluding a charge of number 7½ shot, it can zoom out at about 60 miles per hour.

MIGRATION: Contrary to popular opinion, the crow is a migratory bird. For some crows in some areas the distance traveled may be short. The longest migration flight is that recorded for a crow shot at Meadow Lake, Saskatchewan, that was 1,480 miles from its winter home in Oklahoma, where it had been banded.

HABITS: In the winter crows gather together in large roosts, the one at Fort Cobb, Oklahoma, being the largest in the world, with over two million individuals. The crows assemble in nearby fields in the late afternoon. Then just as darkness is descending, the entire flock lifts into the air and makes its way into the roost for the night. Just two weeks ago I watched about 20,000 crows mill about in the sky before the leaders lined out for the roost that is about 15 miles from my home.

The crow is well known for its ability to detect danger. A man carrying a gun will cause every crow in the area to vacate it immediately. By using a system of guards, the rest of the crows can feed and feel secure. Nothing that moves can escape detection by these guards, and at the first note of alarm, the crows depart. The one chink in their armor is their gregariousness. This liking for the company of their own kind means that they can be decoyed into gun range with the judicious use of a crow call.

Crows also love to mob an enemy in an attempt to drive it out of their area. This habit allows owls, live, stuffed or artificial, to be used as decoys. A combination of owl and crow decoys and the proper use of a crow call is almost sure to attract whatever crows are in the area.

Curiosity is a sign of intelligence, and the crow is extremely curious. It is also highly attracted to anything that is very shiny and often picks up and hoards such things as bits of tinfoil, pieces of glass, bottle caps, etc. Pet crows are notorious for their pilfering.

FOOD: A crow will consume anything edible that it can find, gather or subdue. The U.S. Biological Survey identified 650 different items that crows had eaten. They have been known to kill prey as large as newborn lambs. Kalmbach reported that 28 percent of a crow's year-round diet consists of animal matter, the other 72 percent being vegetable matter. Given a choice, the crow would eat more animal matter, but at certain times of the year it is difficult to obtain. Part of the 28 percent of animal matter is carrion, but over two-thirds of it—19 percent of the crow's total diet—consists of insects, most of them injurious. Thus the crow is, in most instances, beneficial to man. Beetles, grasshoppers, crickets, caterpillars, moths, flies, ants, spiders, crayfish, mollusks, fish, reptiles, amphibians, birds, eggs, mammals, carrion, corn, grains, fruit and berries are all grist for its mill.

LIFE SPAN: In the wild the crow is thought to live four to seven years. Pet crows have been known to live over twenty years.

SIGN: Although sign is normally taken to be something visible, the cawing of crows will call attention to them and their activities much more often than anything else. When there is snow on the ground, the pellets of indigestible material that the crow has regurgitated are often seen. These pellets are usually about 1 to 1½ inches in length and often have a pinkish color that leaves a stain on the snow. Many seeds and pits of vegetable matter are also ejected. The whitewash splatterings of excrement are clearly visible under the old, dead trees that the crows favor as perches while doing guard duty.

ENEMIES: Crows constantly harass owls in an attempt to drive them so far out of the area that they will not prey on the crows at night. These constant attacks have a nuisance value but seldom achieve their goal. The great horned owl is undoubtedly the crow's main predator. Some of the other larger owls and hawks also feed on crows. Most of the four-footed predators are unable to catch a crow, but those that can climb, such as the raccoon and the opossum, eat the crow's eggs and young. The tree-climbing blacksnakes also prey on the eggs and young. Lice, mites and parasites are as common with crows, both externally and internally, as they are with all types of wildlife.

TABLE FARE: The unfavorable connotation of the phrase "to eat crow" sums up the general opinion about the crow as table fare. Young crows' breasts are sometimes eaten, but presumably old crow deserves its reputation for toughness! At many of the organized crow shoots, the featured item on the menu for the supper that follows is crow. The breast meat of the crow is almost as dark as its feathers.

Starling

Sturnus vulgaris

Despite the unfortunate results of the introduction of the English house sparrow, the starling, a native of Europe, was introduced to North America in 1872, 1875, 1877 and 1889. All these importations failed. Finally, in 1890 Eugene Schieffelin of New York released sixty starlings in New York's Central Park, following this up the next year with the release of forty more pairs. This he did because he thought that the United States should have every bird mentioned in William Shakespeare's plays, and in *Henry the Fifth,* Shakespeare mentions the starling.

The starling may have been a slow starter, but it is certainly a strong finisher. It is estimated that there may now be as many as one hundred million starlings in North America, making them perhaps the most populous bird on the continent. Several years ago, at a symposium held in Ohio, a study was made to determine the damage done by blackbirds, i.e., the starling, the grackle and the red-winged blackbird. On a world-wide basis it was calculated that these species were consuming fifteen million tons of grain per year, enough to feed a nation of ninety million people for one year. The starling is unprotected everywhere in the United States, and if ever a bird needed control it is this one.

DESCRIPTION: The male and female starling are indistinguishable in appearance. They have a total length of about 7½–8½ inches, a wingspan of up to 15½ inches and a body weight of 3½ ounces. The long, sharp bill is dark in autumn, turning bright yellow in the breeding season. The plumage in the breeding season is a glossy, iridescent black with highlights of purple and green. In the winter the bird's color is more subdued but heavily spangled with "darts" of white.

DISTRIBUTION: Following its inauspicious start, the starling's takeover of the continent has dwarfed the accomplishment of even the house sparrow. It is found from coast to coast, its range extending from Mexico in the south up to and including Alaska.

COMMUNICATION: The starling is no songbird, its call being a harsh, raspy, whistling chirp. It can, however, make pleasant sounds when imitating some other bird's song. It is quite a mimic and can imitate any sound in the range of 1,200 to 8,250 vibrations per minute, be it that of a rusty hinge or an eager boy's whistling at a girl.

Starling

BREEDING AND NESTING: From January on, starlings begin their courtship. At such times the male's whistled calls become more frequent, strident and insistent. They evidently get through to the female because the pairs start splitting away from the wintering flocks. The paired starlings investigate every nook, cranny and hole in the area. The nest is a bulky affair composed mainly of grasses and always set in some protective hollow. The starlings' nesting habits conflict with those of our more desirable species such as the blue bird, tree swallow, flicker, downy and hairy woodpecker, etc. All these birds have to give way before the determined onslaught and constant harassment of the starlings. And if a single pair of starlings cannot achieve their encroachment objective, they enlist the help of all their relatives. Starlings that have become established utilize the same nest site throughout the season and year after year. Throughout the United States the starling raises two, if not three, broods per year.

EGGS AND YOUNG: The eggs are usually laid at the rate of one a day until the clutch of four to six has been completed. The eggs are about 25 millimeters long and not quite as wide. They are either pale blue or whitish in color, with a glossy cast. The incubation takes about twelve days and is performed by both sexes.

The young are fed and cared for by both parents, who are constantly tracking back and forth, bringing food to cram into the gaping mouths. No attention seems to be paid to nest sanitation, and the entire nest cavity is soon befouled with excrement.

After they are ten days old the young starlings are so eager to feed that they climb up to the cavity opening and sit there waiting for their parents. In another ten days they are large enough to fly and leave the nest.

FLIGHT: The starling is a strong flier, capable of reaching speeds of up to 50 miles per hour. The silhouette of its body and sharply tapered wings resembles that of the sleek World War II fighter plane, the British Spitfire. This silhouette is particularly noticeable when the starling makes its customary long gliding approach before landing.

MIGRATION: The starling does not migrate north and south as do so many of our birds. Its migrations cover a short distance, perhaps only a few miles, and are motivated by the search for communal sleeping shelter in the winter. It may also temporarily shift its home range to be near a larger food supply when snow has blanketed most of its area. A garbage dump, a farmer's feed lot, any constant source of food invariably becomes the focal point for every starling in the vicinity.

HABITS: After their usurpation of our native birds' nesting sites, their communal roosting habits are the main cause for complaint against starlings. In the winter the starlings often gather in flocks numbering thousands of individuals. These birds feed in the countryside throughout the day and then usually repair to the city for the night. If they stay in the rural areas they often seek out dense conifers in which to spend the night. However, the temperature in most of our large cities is higher than that of the surrounding countryside owing to the heat and air pollution generated chiefly by industry and automobiles. Moreover, the starlings can keep warm by snuggling up next to chimneys or outdoor electric light fixtures, or simply by crowding together inside structural steel edifices, on ledges and copings, or under eaves.

Not only is the noise of such starling concentrations ceaseless but the showers of excrement soon make such chosen places both unsightly and unsanitary. The most ingenious schemes have been thought up to disperse the starlings. Some of them have involved the use of decoys and even live owls and falcons, firecrackers and all types of noisemakers, sticky repellents and sharp edgings for the ledges, and recordings of the squalling of a frightened starling. Congress has had to spend $29,500 to install electrical shocking devices along the ledges, cornices and copings of the United States Supreme Court Building in Washington, D.C., in order to prevent an estimated 35,000 starlings from roosting there.

When a jetliner crashed upon takeoff a few years ago, killing sixty-two persons, it was found that the cause was a flock of starlings that had been sucked into the huge jet engines. Concentrated efforts to rid all airports of their starling populations resulted in almost all trees, bushes and high grasses being cut down. Some airports now employ trained falconers and their birds to disperse not only the starlings but all other birds that may be in the area.

FOOD: Its enormous food consumption is yet another cause for objection to the starling. It is an opportunist that will eat almost anything, and its size allows it to force out more desirable birds for whom food has been put out. This is just small-scale pilfering, however, compared to what large flocks can do.

In Iowa, a farmer was feeding second-grade potatoes to his beef cattle to fatten them for market. It was a large feed-lot operation, and the starlings arrived daily in clouds. The farmer figured that they were consuming at least 20 tons of potatoes per day.

I have several friends who own and run shooting preserves and raise thousands of pheasants and mallard ducks every year in wire pens outside. The mesh of the wire is large enough to allow wet snow to pass through — and unfortunately also large enough to admit starlings, which then feed in the pens. There are times when the success of the entire operation hinges on the successful control of the number of starlings.

A redeeming feature of the starling is that 60 percent of its diet consists of animal matter, such as caterpillars, beetles, grasshoppers, millipedes, crickets, etc. The balance is made up of such vegetable matter as grains, berries and fruit. Starlings are also efficient scavengers.

LIFE SPAN: Apparently not much banding of starlings has been done because there would seem to be only one record of a bird that lived to be six years old. Myna birds, however, which are a close relative of the starling, often live ten to fifteen years in captivity.

ENEMIES: Wood hawks such as the Cooper's and the sharp-shinned, and sometimes the sparrow hawk take starlings in the rural areas. Peregrine falcons are now almost extinct on the eastern seaboard, but a few years ago this falcon often nested in cities such as New York and fed on both the pigeons and the starlings there. Tree-climbing snakes feed on the eggs, the young and any adults they can catch.

TABLE FARE: The four and twenty blackbirds that were baked in a pie and set before the king may have been starlings. Starlings have always been plentiful and have long been one of the prime ingredients in European pot pies.

Black-billed Magpie

Pica pica

In the western regions of our continent, which the magpie favors as home, the wind blows almost constantly. The magpie is built like a weathervane and reacts to the wind in the same fashion by turning its streamlined body into the wind. Otherwise a strong wind blowing against its tail would almost throw it off balance.

The magpie is found not only in North America but also in Europe and Asia. In Africa I saw a very close relative to the magpie, a bird called the piapiac.

Folklore and old wives' tales concerning the magpie prove that the bird is well known wherever it is found. Its large size, conspicuous markings and noisy chatter advertise its presence. And some of its bad habits result in its classification as a nuisance bird.

The bird's name has an interesting derivation. Magpie is a bastardization of the bird's Old English name of Magot Pie, which in turn was the Anglicized version of the French Margot Pie. The Margot in this name is derived from the French girl's name Marguerite, thus comparing the bird's noisy chattering with the prattle of a very talkative woman. The Pie is abbreviated from the Latin *pica,* meaning black and white.

Black-billed Magpie

DESCRIPTION: The black-billed magpie is one of the larger small birds. It has a total length of about 20 inches, of which 10 to 11 inches are just tail. Its wings are short and cupped, with a span of about 18 to 20 inches. It weighs between 5 and 6 ounces. The male and female are identical.

The magpie is considered a black and white bird, but its black feathers, particularly those of the tail, are so iridescent that they usually appear green. The bird's bill, feet, head, breast and most of its back are jet black. The wing coverts and the tail are the green-black already mentioned. The scapulars and the belly are white. The wing's secondary feathers are bluish and the primary feathers white with black edgings and tips. The magpie is a strikingly handsome bird.

DISTRIBUTION: The black-billed magpie is a bird of the western mountains with a range extending from Colorado and Nevada north up into Alaska. I have photographed this magpie in Mount McKinley National Park, on Kodiak Island, Alaska, in Yellowstone National Park, Wyoming and in Rocky Mountain National Park in Colorado.

The bird is not a strong long-distance flier and so does not usually venture far from heavy cover. It is ever alert and at the first sign of danger seeks sanctuary in a dense piñon or lodgepole pine stand. Such stands must be adjacent to open land where the magpies can feed. These two conditions determine where the birds are found in the mountains. They usually frequent brushy edges of streams in such areas.

COMMUNICATION: The most commonly heard sound of the black-billed magpie is a harsh, strident, high-pitched *cack, cack, cack*. The bird also makes an indescribable gabbling sound that comes tumbling out mixed with an occasional whistle. This not unpleasant sound gives the impression that the magpie is chuckling to itself.

BREEDING AND NESTING: Very little is actually known about the magpie's breeding habits. The birds are very wary and and secret themselves in dense cover at the first sign of danger. Magpies are seen traveling in pairs throughout the year so in all probability they mate for life. In the spring two or three magpies, presumably male, may be seen chasing after another single magpie in what can be interpreted as a courtship display. This chase probably entails an older bird replacing a lost mate or the preceding year's young birds being absorbed into the current year's breeding population.

Although not much is known about the magpie's breeding habits, it cannot conceal its nesting habits. The magpie probably makes a larger nest, compared to its own size, than any other bird in the country. The nest on, the average, is about the size of a bushel basket, although some have been found that were 4 feet high. Such a large nest is the result of the birds building on top of the original nest in succeeding years.

The nest is made up of fairly heavy sticks and is roofed over—a rare feature among the nests made by birds of this country. Inside the nest is a heavy mud lining which in turn is lined with fine grasses, rootlets and some feathers. There are usually two openings into the nest. Many of the sticks used in the roof of the nest are thorny, perhaps because the spikes help to hold the branches in place.

Although this in no way forms part of the magpie's plan, many other birds, and occasionally small animals, utilize old magpie nests for shelters of their own. Robins, blackbirds, English sparrows, bluebirds, warblers, sparrow hawks, horned owls, long-eared owls, screech owls, mourning doves, sharp-shinned hawks and even a gadwall duck have all been recorded as using the magpie's nest for shelter or for nesting purposes of their own.

Magpies nest in colonies, and a dozen nests may be scattered through a quarter mile of streamside copse. The nests are usually located between 15 and 25 feet from the ground, about 20 feet being the most common height.

Frequently magpie nests are located near the nests of such predators as the eagle, osprey or the larger hawks. The magpies then feed upon scraps of food that are dropped from the larger nest or that they can pilfer directly from it.

EGGS AND YOUNG: The standard magpie clutch seems to comprise seven eggs; it may contain more, but seldom less. The eggs are gray-green, heavily blotched with dark brown. They average 32 millimeters in length by 22 millimeters in diameter.

The incubation seems to be performed solely by the female, but this is hard to prove because it is almost impossible to tell the sexes apart. Whichever the incubator may be, it takes eighteen days for the young to hatch.

The newly hatched young are naked with just vestigial traces of down. Their skin is a pinkish color because of the blood vessels beneath its surface. It gradually turns yellow and then gray as the tips of the first feathers begin to protrude. Within three weeks the young birds are almost fully feathered and a couple of days later are capable of flying. The young magpies are very active, and even before they can fly they climb all over the nest.

FLIGHT: When a young magpie first tries to fly, its greatest problem is controlling its tail. Even the adults seem to have that trouble on a windy day, when their tail is certainly an unwieldy appendage.

The magpie usually flies fairly close to the earth. The harder the wind blows, the lower it flies, barely skimming the tops of the bushes. Its flights are seldom of any length and are always a purely functional means of locomotion.

MIGRATION: The magpie's migration is merely a seasonal shift brought about by changing climate and food conditions. In the southern part of the magpie's range there is practically no seasonal movement, while up in Alaska the bird abandons its summer range in or near the mountains to go to the coast for the winter.

HABITS: The magpie, like jays and crows, is an opportunist. The birds regularly patrol the highways to feed upon any wildlife that has been killed by automobiles. They often follow coyotes, wolves and foxes in the hope of being able to scavenge some scraps from these predators' kills. The body of any large dead animal is a magnet that will attract magpies from all directions.

Magpies occasionally fight with one another, but they are sociable birds. In the winter they often concentrate in rather large numbers to roost in the manner of crows.

FOOD: The magpie is unpopular largely because of its habit of picking insects from many of the wild herbivores. The birds often clamber over mule deer, elk and bighorn sheep, feeding off the blood-gorged ticks. I have photos of their African counterpart, the piapiac, doing similar grooming on the cape buffalo. This practice is common with many birds in Africa, and I have often wondered why more species did not engage in it in North America. No harm is done when the magpies pick the ticks from domestic livestock or wild herbivores, but if these animals have an open wound, the magpies keep picking at it and aggravating it. What started out as beneficial symbiosis may later cause irreparable damage to the livestock and has put the magpie on a par with the predators.

Around the campgrounds of our western parks, the magpie makes an interesting visitor, but it can also be a nuisance because no form of food that it can carry off is safe from its depredations.

The magpie is well known for its raiding of other birds' nests to obtain either the eggs or the young. Its destruction of mouse nests and their contents, however, is less commonly known.

The magpie comsumes vast numbers of insects such as grasshoppers, caterpillars and flies. It also eats wild fruits, berries, some nuts, and occasionally cultivated grains. Its diet is determined by what is available in any particular area at any particular time.

LIFE SPAN: There appear to be no longevity records for the magpie nor even an estimated life span. However, the corvids, such as the crow, have a potential life span of about five to six years and there is no reason why the magpie's span should be any less.

ENEMIES: The magpie shares a kill or carrion with many predators and would therefore seem to be exposed to danger from such predators as coyotes, mountain lions and foxes. On occasion, these predators may kill a magpie, but their usual reaction to the bird is one of indifference. Some of the hawks and owls kill a magpie for food if the opportunity presents itself.

Great Horned Owl

Bubo virginianus

The appellation "tiger of the air" is a fitting one for the great horned owl because it is one of our most aggressive and efficient predators. Many people think of it as a predator because it feeds upon pheasants, grouse and rabbits, forgetting the fact that it feeds also on rats, mice, crows and other undesirable forms of life. A predator was once defined as any creature that took a game bird or animal that man wanted to take for himself. Such an improper definition is often the basis for our thinking and actions toward those creatures that dare to compete with us, the supreme predators.

DESCRIPTION: The great horned owl, the largest owl in the United States, is surpassed in size only by the great gray owl of the Canadian north. The female is larger and heavier than the male and may measure up to 25 inches in length, weigh up to 3 pounds and have a wingspread of 48 inches or more.

The most conspicuous feature is the feathered tufts that can be erected on either side of the top of the head. These are the so-called "horns" from which this owl derives its name.

The great horned owl is endowed with exceptionally keen hearing in the higher registers. Its ears, which are behind and below its eyes, are hidden by its feathered facial discs. The bird is easily identified by its feathered ear tufts and large body.

The large yellow eyes are set in the front of the owl's head, giving it binocular vision. The eyes appear even larger than they actually are because of the flattened, feathered facial discs around them. To see an object on either side of its body, the owl must turn its head. When an object moves behind it, the bird cannot rotate its head completely around as is commonly thought. But it can swivel its head to the front and then around to the other side so rapidly that the movement may not be visible.

The owl's ears are completely hidden by the feathers. This covering, though, does not impair its sense of hearing because it has been proved that owls can catch their prey in total darkness when their eyes are of no help. A fleshy rim in front of the great horned owl's ear may serve to "cup" sound into the ear opening.

The great horned owl has a hearing frequency range of from 300–8,000 cycles per minute. This allows it to hear the squeak of a mouse but not the muffled drumming of the ruffed grouse.

A bird capable of living in an extremely cold climate, this owl has soft, dense feathers right down to its talons. Its basic color ranges widely from a very pale gray to a deep buff. The pattern is

Great Horned Owl

complemented with a black barring. The breast, belly and underside of the wings and tail are lighter in color than the back, head and wing and tail top. Both sexes sport a white bib patch, but the male's patch appears to be larger than that of the female and may provide an external clue to the sex of the bird.

DISTRIBUTION: There are ten subspecies of the great horned owl whose combined ranges completely cover North America, except for the treeless Arctic regions.

COMMUNICATION: The great horned owl is the common "hoot" owl that is so commonly heard in rural areas. The usual call, which resembles that of a mourning dove, is a low-pitched, single note repeated five times in the pattern *whoo-whoo, whoo-whoo, whoo.* The male calls louder, more deeply and more frequently. The female, when she does call, has a shorter, softer note. The birds are also supposed to make a chuckling sound, but this is rarely heard. An angry adult may hiss and snap its bill.

BREEDING AND NESTING: The calling of the great horned owl is most commonly heard in January and February. This owl is the first bird to nest each year over most of its range. The birds pair for life, and many maintain a permanent resident territory. This saves a great deal of time when the breeding season commences because the birds know their own territory intimately and settle upon a nesting site early. Often they nest in the same site for years. I know of one pair that used the same hollow sycamore for at least four years. The great horned owl frequently utilizes the abandoned nest of a crow or red-tailed hawk. Most of the nests are situated at quite a height above the ground.

EGGS AND YOUNG: The great horned owl usually lays its eggs in the latter part of February or the first part of March. A clutch comprises two to four eggs, although it is rare to see more than two young to a nest. The eggs are oval in shape and off-white in color and have a rough exterior. They are about 50 millimeters in length and slightly less in diameter. Unlike most birds, which complete their clutch before beginning incubation, the great horned owl starts incubation as soon as the first egg is laid. As the eggs may be laid one week apart, the young also hatch one week apart. This accounts for the differences so often noted in the development of the young.

Incubation is done primarily by the female with the male

helping out occasionally. About thirty-five days are required for the first egg to hatch, but the female must continue to brood whatever eggs are still unhatched. The burden of feeding the female and the young thus falls on the male. In some cases the male is so zealous in this task that he literally overwhelms both the female and the nest with his food offerings. As much as 18 pounds of food has been found in a single nest.

The young have voracious appetites and grow quite rapidly. Their eyes open after nine days, but they are still brooded almost continually until they are about three weeks old. At this stage they are almost half-grown. The young remain in the nest for at least another three weeks.

FLIGHT: The young owls are capable of fluttering about when they are four to five weeks old. They often fall from the nest or are knocked out accidentally at this time by their litter mates. They are unable to fly back to the nest, but the parents continue to care for them and feed them on the ground. Young owls do not engage in the wing-flapping exercises that are so common among young hawks. At eight to ten weeks of age they are capable of sustained flight but are still cared for by the parents. It is because of this long period of adolescence that the great horned owls start their broods so early in the season.

The great horned owl's wing primaries are soft. This enables the owl to fly almost silently but at a slower pace than the hard-winged hawks. For flying under cover of darkness, silence is of greater benefit than speed.

MIGRATION: The great horned owl is not thought of as a migratory bird as most of the owls occupy their regular range all of their lives. When they do migrate, it is not because of the cold but because of a shortage of food. The owls living farthest north are the ones most likely to migrate because they are most dependent upon the lemmings, voles and various hares for food. Any decline in the population of these animals creates a food shortage that forces the owls to migrate.

HABITS: Evergreen trees are the preferred roosting spots of the great horned owl because they offer good concealment and protection from the wind. The owl usually sits close to the trunk of the tree so as to be as inconspicuous as possible. If not disturbed, it usually awakens about sunset and may start to hunt at once, especially in the winter. Most activity stops shortly after dawn.

The owl usually flies to the area in which it is going to hunt and then perches until it has spotted its prey.

Its prey includes anything that moves that it is capable of over-powering. It will even attack a porcupine and may be able to kill it before it can erect its quills. Great horned owls have been known to perish, however, because of porcupine quills. The skunk is one of this owl's favorite foods. The owl has a poor sense of smell so the skunk's spray has little effect upon it. Moreover its nictitating membrane, or third eyelid, protects the owl's eyes against the acid in the spray and so renders the skunk almost powerless. I have never encountered a great horned owl that did not smell of skunk.

Any prey that is small enough to be carried the owl takes back to its perch to eat. Small prey is swallowed whole, and the indigestible material is regurgitated in a pellet that is usually about 2 inches in length and 1 inch in diameter. Larger prey, of course, is eaten on the ground.

When the great horned owl preys on pheasant, it always eats the head, neck, crop and part of the backbone, leaving all the meat of the breast and legs to go to waste. Except under an extreme shortage of food, the owl will not return to such a carcass, preferring to kill again when hungry.

On several occasions, in Canada, I have seen these owls plunge after fish exactly like an osprey. This never occurred in still, deep water but usually in the shallow riffles above a rapid. The fish taken were usually northern pike, and records show that the owls frequently take catfish, suckers and eels.

The great horned owl can turn its outside toe either to the front or to the rear. It usually walks with two toes pointing forward and two toes to the rear. Thus when it lands in the snow it imprints its signature with a large letter X.

Food: As already mentioned in the preceding section, the horned owl eats porcupine, skunk, pheasant and various types of fish. Its diet also includes mice, voles, shrews, squirrels, rabbits, hares, grouse, quail, crows, songbirds, poultry and small predators such as the weasel and mink.

Life Span: Owls are long-lived birds and in the wild probably reach an age of fifteen to twenty years. The record for longevity goes to a captive bird that lived to be sixty-eight.

Enemies: Man is the horned owl's chief enemy, not the hunter but the man who sets pole traps for owls and hawks. In many states the use of these traps is illegal because they are indiscriminate, killing or at least maiming any bird that lands on them. For all its scholarly mien, the owl is not a "wise" bird and seemingly never learns that such spots as the pole trap are dangerous.

The crow is probably the owl's main natural enemy. It attacks the eggs and the young owls if they are left unattended. However, this seldom happens unless the adult owl is disturbed by a human. Raccoons may prey on the eggs and young, but this is not a common occurrence.

The owl sometimes attacks some creature that is too large to overcome and may be killed in the ensuing fight. In most instances the bird's large size, tremendous talons, sharp beak and natural fierceness are a match for any assailant.

TABLE FARE: Owls, despite their apparent size, are, when stripped of their fluffy feathers, little more than sinew and bone. People living in the far north have been known to eat this owl in times of starvation. However, the phrase "as tough as a biled owl" is evidently grounded on fact, and almost no one is tempted to try this bird.

Photo Credits

LEONARD LEE RUE III, *pages 13, 37, 43, 44, 59, 89, 115, 125, 143, 156, 184, 276, 284, 303, 349, 350, 359, 384, 396, 467.*

FROM NATIONAL AUDUBON SOCIETY

A. W. AMBLER, *pages 20, 48, 189, 311, 439.*

G. RONALD AUSTING, *pages, 402, 452.*

ALFRED M. BAILEY, *pages 109, 199, 263.*

ALLAN D. CRUICKSHANK, *pages 97, 103, 138, 139.*

JACK DERMID, *page 426.*

HARRY ENGELS, *pages 163, 254.*

HUGH M. HALLIDAY, *pages 409, 421.*

ERIC HOSKING, *page 77.*

PAUL JOHNSGUARD, *page 196.*

VERNA JOHNSTON, *page 297.*

H. C. KYLLINGSTAD, *pages 26, 192.*

KARL H. MASLOWSKI, *pages 160, 179, 222.*

NEAL F. MISHLER, *pages 245, 338.*

DAVID MOHRHARDT, *page 71.*

CHARLIE OTT, *pages 173, 229, 270.*

JAMES P. PERDUE, *page 19.*

O. S. PETTINGILL, JR., *page 416.*

LEONARD LEE RUE, III, *page 184.*

GORDON S. SMITH, *page 73.*

ALVIN E. STAFFAN, *page 64.*

MARY M. TREMAINE, *page 262.*

JOE VAN WORMER, *page 334.*

Index